Globalizing Europe

NEW HORIZONS IN INTERNATIONAL BUSINESS

General Editor: Peter J. Buckley
Centre for International Business,
University of Leeds (CIBUL), UK

The New Horizons in International Business series has established itself as the world's leading forum for the presentation of new ideas in international business research. It offers pre-eminent contributions in the areas of multinational enterprise – including foreign direct investment, business strategy and corporate alliances, global competitive strategies, and entrepreneurship. In short, this series constitutes essential reading for academics, business strategists and policy makers alike.

Titles in the series include:

Globalizing America
The USA in World Integration
Edited by Thomas L. Brewer and Gavin Boyd

Information Technology in Multinational Enterprises
Edited by Edward Mozley Roche and Michael James Blaine

A Yen for Real Estate
Japanese Real Estate Investment Abroad – From Boom to Bust
Roger Simon Farrell

Corporate Governance and Globalization
Long Range Planning Issues
Edited by Stephen S. Cohen and Gavin Boyd

The European Union and Globalisation
Towards Global Democratic Governance
Edited by Brigid Gavin

Globalization and the Small Open Economy
Edited by Daniel Van Den Bulcke and Alain Verbeke

Entrepreneurship and the Internationalisation of Asian Firms
An Institutional Perspective
Henry Wai-chung Yeung

The World Trade Organization in the New Global Economy
Trade and Investment Issues in the Millennium Round
Edited by Alan M. Rugman and Gavin Boyd

Japanese Subsidiaries in the New Global Economy
Edited by Paul W. Beamish, Andrew Delios and Shige Makino

Globalizing Europe
Deepening Integration, Alliance Capitalism and Structural Statecraft
Edited by Thomas L. Brewer, Paul A. Brenton and Gavin Boyd

China and its Regions
Economic Growth and Reform in Chinese Provinces
Edited by Mary-Françoise Renard

Emerging Issues in International Business Research
Edited by Masaaki Kotabe and Preet S. Aulakh

Globalizing Europe

Deepening Integration, Alliance Capitalism
and Structural Statecraft

Edited by

Thomas L. Brewer

*Editor, Journal of International Business Studies, and Professor,
Business Faculty, Georgetown University, Washington, DC*

Paul A. Brenton

*Senior Research Fellow, Centre for European Policy Studies,
Brussels*

Gavin Boyd

*Honorary Professor, Political Science Department, Rutgers
University, Newark, New Jersey, USA, and Adjunct Professor,
Management Faculty, Saint Mary's University, Halifax, Canada*

NEW HORIZONS IN INTERNATIONAL BUSINESS

Edward Elgar

Cheltenham, UK • Northampton, MA, USA

79340 2

Published by
Edward Elgar Publishing Limited
Glensanda House
Montpellier Parade
Cheltenham
Glos GL50 1UA
UK

Edward Elgar Publishing, Inc.
136 West Street
Suite 202
Northampton
Massachusetts 01060
USA

A catalogue record for this book is available from the British Library

Library of Congress Cataloguing in Publication Data
Globalizing Europe : deepening integration, alliance capitalism, and structural statecraft / edited by Thomas L. Brewer, Paul A. Brenton, Gavin Boyd.
    p.   cm. – New horizons in international business
    Includes index.
    1. European Union countries—Economic integration. 2. European Union countries—Economic policy. 3. Globalization. I. Brewer, Thomas L., 1941– II. Brenton, Paul. III. Boyd, Gavin. IV. Series.

HC241 .G57 2002
337.1'4—dc21
                                                                2001040966

ISBN 1 84064 641 1
Printed and bound in Great Britain by MPG Books Ltd, Bodmin, Cornwall

Contents

List of figures

List of tables

List of contributors

Ray Barrell is on the staff of the National Institute of Economic and Social Research, London, UK

Gavin Boyd is an Honorary Professor of Political Science at Rutgers University, Newark, New Jersey, USA, and an Adjunct Professor in Management at Saint Mary's University, Halifax, Canada

Paul A. Brenton is a Senior Research Fellow at the Centre for European Policy Studies, Brussels, Belgium

Thomas L. Brewer is a Professor in the Business Faculty at Georgetown University, Washington, DC, and Editor of the *Journal of International Business Studies*

Jordi Canals is a Professor at IESE, University of Navarra, Barcelona, Spain

John H. Dunning is Emeritus Professor of International Business at the University of Reading, UK, and Rutgers University, USA

Christian Eigen-Zucchi is a Professor in the Economics Department, George Mason University, Fairfax, Virginia, USA

William R. Emmons is on the research staff at the Federal Reserve Bank of St Louis, Missouri, USA

Pier Carlo Padoan is a Professor of Economics at the University of Rome, Italy

Nigel Pain is on the staff of the National Institute of Economic and Social Research, London, UK

Frank A. Schmid is on the research staff at the Federal Reserve Bank of St Louis, Missouri, USA

Brian Scott-Quinn has the ISMA Chair in Investment Banking at the University of Reading, UK

Duane Swank is a Professor of Political Science at Marquette University, Milwaukee, Wisconsin, USA

Paul Taylor is a Professor in the Department of International Relations at the London School of Economics and Political Science, UK

Willem Thorbecke is a Professor of Economics at George Mason University, Fairfax, Virginia, USA

Preface

This volume examines the involvement of the European Union at the policy and structural levels in the deepening integration which results as trade and transnational production link economic systems across the world, and especially between Europe and the USA. Asymmetries in the Atlantic policy and structural interdependencies, due to problems of collective management in the Union and its slower growth, as well as to very different policy dynamics and stronger structural competitiveness in the USA, are well-recognized challenges for decision-makers on each side. Imperatives for effective engagement with fundamentals in the relationship are becoming more urgent as the Union enlarges, with the admission of East European countries, and as its Monetary Union becomes established: the Union clearly has to initiate a highly constructive foreign economic policy, with the cooperation of its firms. Meanwhile the USA has to cope with difficult issues in its interdependencies, the most urgent being its very large trade deficits.

Contributors to the volume accordingly give much attention to problems in Atlantic relations, but also refer to the European Union's economic and political links with Japan, although these have become less important, for the present, because of that country's severe recession. In long-term planning provision will have to be made for more active cooperation with a resurgent Japan. Meanwhile, as other contributions to the volume indicate, the Union will have to assume a more substantial role in multilateral negotiations on global trade liberalization, and in the shaping of institutions for stability in the international financial system.

A theme implicit in the volume's treatment of the Union's external problems is that they may receive inadequate attention because of all the complexities in the Europeanization of policy processes in member states, which tend to make Union level decision processes inward-looking and indecisive. There are multiple policy-learning problems, and for the resolution of these there is a need for sound contributions to the work of European policy communities.

Work for this volume has been sponsored by the Center for Global Change and Governance at Rutgers University, Newark, New Jersey. We are very grateful for the support and hospitality of the center, and we wish to express our gratitude in particular to the Director, Richard Langhorne, whose participation in our discussions was very welcome.

Thomas L. Brewer
Paul A. Brenton
Gavin Boyd

Introduction

Thomas L. Brewer

The terms 'globalizing' and 'globalization' seem to be appearing in book titles with an exponentially increasing frequency. Such popularity is no doubt due in part to the pervasiveness and the complexity of the processes of change that the terms reflect. Even if one adopts a narrowly economic notion of the concept of globalization, it can reasonably be interpreted to have several dimensions, as well as multiple causes and consequences. If one expands the domain of analysis to include processes of political and/or cultural change, then the analytic scope of course becomes enormous

The studies in this book generally represent a middle ground in terms of the diversity of the dimensions – economic, political and cultural – that they cover. Yet, there is a decidedly combined economic-political emphasis in the studies, taken as a collection. Political factors as causes of economic conditions, and political conditions as consequences of economic processes – and of course government economic policies as well – are typically included among the central concerns, In that sense, this is a collection of studies of political economy. However, not all of the studies are of macro-economic or macro-political topics, some are principally firm or industry studies. This is thus in part a collection of studies of business strategy as well as government policy, In addition to the firm, industry and country levels of analysis, there is of course the regional level of analysis that focuses on EU institutions and policies. Indeed, the unifying theme of all of the studies is the focus on the extent and forms of globalization of the EU (either as a unit or as a set of 15 member countries).

Among the methodological issues about research on globalization, therefore, are those concerning the level of analysis (or unit of analysis). In business management studies, it is possible to study globalization processes at the level of managerial functions (strategy, finance, marketing, and so on) or at the level of other organizational units. Indeed, many firms are marked by globalized strategies in the sense that basic decisions about market entry or production facilities in one country, for instance, are dependent on parallel decisions about business presence in countries all over the world. Financial operations, meanwhile, may be globalized in the sense that decisions about funds sourcing and international transfers in all countries are made through a centralized treasury unit in the headquarters of the parent corporation in the home country of a global corporation. The extent to which such trends are apparent in EU-based firms, relative to firms based in other countries, is of course an empirical issue. At the macro level of the national economies of the EU, there is an issue about convergence – that is the increasing similarity of macroeconomic conditions such as inflation rates that is central to the process of monetary unification. It is of course such regional integration issues within the EU and their relationship to broader globalization trends in the world and the EU's external relations that create special interest in the topic of globalization as regards the EU. These and other issues are addressed in the chapters of this volume.

Two aspects of globalization processes that are of special interest within Europe, as well as between Europe and the rest of the world, concern convergence and governance. Much of the research and popular commentary on globalization processes have focused on the increasing diversity and quantity of international transactions. Within the EU, there has also been much attention devoted to issues of convergence, especially the convergence of economic conditions among the EU members' economies in the context of the monetary unification process and the adoption of a single currency. Thus, formalized convergence criteria were developed to establish thresholds for membership in the euro zone. An interest in indicators of convergence is thus reflected in the chapters of the present volume. More encompassing analyses of convergence issues in the broader context of globalization could address similar issues about economic convergence between the EU and the US, for instance, and issues about cultural and political convergence within the EU and between the EU and other regions of the world. There remain, for example, many issues within the EU where there are strong northern (especially Scandinavian) versus southern (especially Mediterranean) lines of conflict. This is so for many environmental issues and for issues concerning transparency in governmental policy-making. Cultural diversity is an enduring feature within the EU – and it has continuing economic and political significance.

At the same time, even though there continues to be some shift of governance functions to the regional EU-level institutions, there are also pressures to maintain national and sub-national functional responsibilities within the member countries, These pressures led, for instance, to the formalization of the principle of 'subsidiarity' in the Maastricht treaty. And it is a principle with economic as well as legal significance. It means, for instance, that on 'new' issues on the agenda at the World Trade Organization – issues such as intellectual property and investment – power is shared between EU institutions and national governments, whereas the EU institutions continue to have exclusive responsibility for the traditional GATT issues of trade in goods.

The continued importance within the EU of cultural differences and of national and sub-national governmental functions, despite the increasing

concentration of some functions and the increasing scope of EU-level regulations, suggest that many common notions about globalization between the EU
and the rest of the world are quite exaggerated. Though some processes of globalization may have transformed Europe's economic relations with the rest of
the world in important ways, it is also true that culturally and governmentally,
countries remain very much embedded in the traditional nation-state system.

On these and other matters, the individual chapter authors can not only speak
for themselves quite effectively; they can of course present their ideas and information in a more compelling way than brief editorial summaries. I therefore
invite you, without further ado, to explore the diverse and provocative chapters
that follow.

1. The European Union in the global economy at the Millennium

Paul Taylor

The question which is addressed in this chapter is that of how relations between the member states of the European Union, and between the European Union as a whole and the outside world, were affected in the early twenty-first century by the forces of globalization. This is a central theme of the whole book, and various answers are given in succeeding chapters, But in this chapter particular attention is given to the problems of the social democratic, welfare-orientated countries in the Union, led by France, Germany and Italy. What compromise did they have to make with the so-called Anglo-American model of low tax, lower welfare spending and regulatory reform, of which the UK was the prime example in Europe, in order to cope with the economic forces of globalization? The conclusion reached is that adaptation was necessary but this did not mean the triumph of the Anglo-American model. Indeed the necessity of the opposition between the two had been much exaggerated. In consequence the general applicability of the neo-liberal approach to international political economy could also be questioned.[1]

Firstly, the context of the problem is identified in an introduction. Secondly, the economic and political differences between the member states in the Union are discussed. There were political disagreements between the social democratic states and the others about the integration process and the powers and potential of the institutions. This section concludes with a report of the stage reached in this process as reflected in the allocation of responsibilities between the main central Brussels institutions, and between them and national governments. Thirdly, a range of scenarios concerning the future development of the Union is proposed. Aspects of these are then examined in greater detail. These themes all touch on the changing structure of the Union and its relations with the global economy.

THE EUROPEAN UNION IN THE GLOBAL POLITICAL ECONOMY

In the international political economy the European Union assumed greater significance in the late 1990s because of the prospect of a further massive enlargement, its establishment of a Monetary Union, and its increased growth potential, which had become more important in global trade, investment and finance while the Japanese economy recovered, with difficulty, from its financial crisis of 1997–99. The continuing attraction of prospective entrants indicated how the opportunities of the Union's market drew outside states toward participation in its system of collectively managed economic integration. The Monetary Union among 11 of its members greatly facilitated intra-zonal commerce and constituted a major new entity in the international monetary system, resulting in unprecedented Atlantic monetary interdependence. Meanwhile the weakened role of Japan in the world economy made management of all Atlantic interdependencies much more important for each side, and for the international community.

Structurally, the evolution of the European Union and its production, trade and investment links with the rest of the world was being shaped by the operations of vast numbers of national and international firms. Their activities caused the Single Market of their region to become more integrated, and established a stable environment in which they could make long-term plans with relative security. The Single Market Programme, announced by the Single European Act of 1985, had led to great strides in freeing up the market in goods and services, but it was clear that more was needed in that area and that of employment.[2] Many firms retained their national identities, but there were increasing cross-border mergers and acquisitions. Linkages between the economics of the Union members meanwhile were extending outside the region, especially in Atlantic patterns of cross-investment and trade. Outside enterprises, mainly American, were also very active, through mergers, acquisitions and organizational growth. Altogether there was a very extensive pattern of complex deepening integration.

Interpenetrating policy environments set the political context in which the European and other corporate activities were changing and linking national economic systems of production and marketing. Corporate associations, connected with political parties, represented their interests and views to member governments and to Union institutions, notably the European Commission. These associations, however, mostly remained distinctly national, and the possibilities for aggregating their interests transnationally were therefore limited. The political parties to which they related moreover also remained distinctly national, further limiting the possibilities for transnational interest aggregation. Moreover, many of the corporate associations functioned in well-established political networks, linked informally with their national administrations. There was collaboration across borders, to represent interests to Union-level decision-makers, but the national governments sought to build strong ties with the leading corporate associations in their own economies: there was structural policy competition to enhance gains from commerce in the Single Market.

Macromanagement processes, at the national and Union levels, responded to differing challenges in the dynamics of competitive and cooperative policy processes. Regional market integration promised higher growth, with more productive corporate specializations driven by competitive pressures, but with market failures as well as efficiencies, including the acquisition and possible abuse of dominant positions. The mixes of market failures and efficiencies that could be considered regional had been elements of a larger mix in the Union's trade and investment links with the rest of the world – the globalization process. For Europe, as for the USA, home market changes associated with that larger process had costs as well as benefits. Related changes in patterns of interest representation had exerted pressures at policy levels: there had been challenges to improve overall economic management by governments, while policy-makers, however, had been influenced by streams of neo-liberal economic advice stressing the efficiencies of market forces and, therefore, the need to allow them wide scope.

The macromanagement problem that had been given most attention was that described by Rodrik, in work focusing on the USA.[3] The benefits of globalization were diffused across borders but the costs of globalization (insecurity and loss of employment) were borne disproportionately by workers, who were not mobile, while corporations, with the advantages of mobility, appeared able to reduce tax exposure. The globalization process appeared to threaten the ability of governments to pursue national social purposes such as maintaining full employment. Hence public support tended to shift more to political parties which were nominally aligned with worker interests, though the new parties of the left were unlike earlier socialist parties in that they all realized it was necessary to work with capital rather than against it. This was true equally of New Labour in Britain, of the Social Democrats in Germany and of Lionel Jospin's Socialists in France, though New Labour was much more prepared than the others to carry through welfare reform programmes which seemed to be a mere continuation of the previous Conservative government's policy of cutting back. In power, all parties had to cope with the problem that it was hard to find the tax revenue to satisfy expectations in pensions and health provision, and had incentives to resort to investment bidding, to encourage favourable location decisions by international firms.

In Europe increased levels of unemployment, which were fairly evenly distributed among the member states of the Union – despite the view promoted in the UK[4] – tended to give credibility to a scenario in which stronger assertions of worker interests, tipping political balances, had effects on tax policies which added to the incentives of firms to move operations to lower-cost locations. In

1999 unemployment levels were at around 10 per cent across the Union, declining modestly to 9.6 per cent in 2000.[5] The costs of globalization (including those of regional market integration) could thus increase, tending to tip political balances further. Whether this prognosis was accurate is the main subject of this chapter, but whatever the conclusion there were clear imperatives for policy learning about such matters as how to get more flexible labour policies and fewer supply-side bottlenecks, Understanding of these imperatives and the development of appropriate responses in the public interest, however, could be obscured by subjective preferences associated with political strategies in competitive contexts. Because of the political diversity of the European Union, assessments of the overall pattern had be highly judgemental, but concerned scholars had to relate earnestly to the needs of policy-makers and corporate managements for advice: implicit in much of the research literature was the desirability of working toward broadly cooperative solutions.

There were indeed differences between the character of the investment flows into and out of the European Union. The main outflow destination, and inflow source, was of course the USA, where the investment was essentially attracted by the growth of the US economy and the expansion generated primarily by positive factors within the US. European investment there could be described as passive. US investment into the EU was, however, more active, seeking a stronger political role, and being an important consideration in government policies with regard to economic performance. There were structural difficulties in Europe in areas such as labour policy, research and development, and transport and communication systems with which European governments had to deal, and because of which they were open to pressure and exploitation by multinational enterprises. The latter's apparent mobility, together with a pretty cohesive political agenda, constantly challenged the instinctive European preference for effective and more comprehensive welfare systems. Europe's structural problems also led governments to try to offset their disadvantages with a greater range of supports for industry and a greater anxiety about the further freeing of trade in key economic sectors before successful structural initiatives had taken effect.

Potentials for broadly cooperative solutions had to be discerned with understanding of the problems of advanced political development in the Union members. These related especially to institutional capacities for functional responses to assertions of interests and preferences. The most vital institutional capacities were those for knowledge-intensive consensus formation oriented toward the common good, especially the provision of the 'public good' of systemic development – the orderly coordination of specializations for interdependent growth.

DIVERSITY IN EUROPEAN POLITICAL ECONOMIES

Economic Diversity

The arguments in this chapter reflect the heterogeneity of the member states of the Union. There were social democratic states, there were states which felt they had to compromise with the Anglo-American model of light regulation and low levels of taxation, particularly for companies, in response to globalization; and there were differences between the levels of economic performance of states, the extent to which their structures had been reformed, and indeed where they stood in the business cycle. The most Anglo-American of all was the United Kingdom, and what follows assumes a broad distinction between

Table 1.1   EU Gross Domestic Product per capita, 1999

	Using current PPPs		Using current
	$	OECD =100	exchange rates $
Austria	24600	110	20700
Belgium	24300	109	24200
Denmark	26300	118	32600
Finland	22800	102	24900
France	21900	98	23600
Germany	23600	106	25700
Greece	14800	66	11800
Ireland	25200	113	24200
Italy	21800	98	20100
Luxembourg	39300	176	43100
Netherlands	25100	112	25000
Portugal	16500	74	11100
Spain	18100	81	15000
Sweden	23000	103	27000
UK	22300	100	23900
EU 15	22000	99	22400
Eurozone	22100	99	22100
US	33900	152	33900

Note: Purchasing Power Parities (PPPs) are the rate of currency conversion which eliminates the differences in price levels between countries. They are used to compare the volume of GDP in different countries. PPPs are obtained by evaluating the costs of a basket of goods and services between countries for all components of GDP; PPPs are given in national currency units per US dollar.

Sources: *Main Economic Indicators*, OECD, Paris, April 2000; National Accounts Division, STD.

the Anglo-American states and the social democratic core. This was of course an oversimplification, though the greater complexity of the reality did not affect the validity of the arguments. There were a number of states that had started on reform of their welfare and regulatory systems, in the direction of the Anglo-American model, which could easily halt that process and move back to an unambiguous commitment to social democracy. The diversity of state political-economic models was revealed in OECD economic indicators from which the tables below were derived. Four groups of states may be distinguished.

The first group included Germany, France and Italy, which might be regarded as the core social democratic states. They had a high per capita income (Table 1.1), and a pattern of taxation which took significantly more than the others in the form of social security payments from business, which formed a significant proportion of the total tax take (see Table 1.2). These were also economies that were relatively slow-growing, and in need of the lower interest rates made possible by the moderate recent level of wage settlements and, with the exception of oil, falling commodity prices.[6] OECD figures in 1997 also showed that higher than mean benefits could be obtained for total GDP in these states from deregulation at 4.9 per cent for Germany (Table 1.3).

The second type was also high on the ranking of per capita GDP, but had a different taxation pattern, tending to put less stress on the social security payments from business, and more on taxation on goods and services and income tax. It included Denmark, Austria and Ireland, with the lightest social burden placed directly on business, and Finland, Sweden, Luxembourg, Holland and Belgium, which had a somewhat larger burden (Table 1.2). The indications were also that these states would gain rather less from regulatary reform than those in the first group: the evidence for Holland was that a gain of 3.5 per cent was likely, the same as for the United Kingdom which had already allegedly undertaken significant reform (Table 1.3). The states in this group were generally those that had begun to reform their welfare systems, in the sense that there had been a degree of deregulation and some lessening of welfare expenditure. But this was politically difficult and these states remained potentially members of the first group. They were reluctant welfare reformers, with a significant support among the electorates and political elites for social democracy.

A third group included those states which were the lowest-ranking in the Union in terms of per capita GDP. These were also the states which were growing most rapidly. It included, in ascending order of per capita GDP, Greece, Portugal and Spain (Table 1.1). Spain and Portugal had rather low levels of taxation for both corporate income tax and for employer's social security payments. Spain had a higher level of employers' social security contributions, but a low level of corporate income tax.

Fourth was the state that was allegedly closest to the Anglo-American model, the United Kingdom. This was a state which the OECD argued was likely to

Table 1.2 Taxation in EU countries, 1997

	Total tax receipts % of GDP	Tax structure as % of total tax receipts						Highest rates of income tax	
		Personal income tax	Corporate income tax	Social Security contributions Employees	Social Security contributions Employers	Taxes on goods and services	Other taxes	Personal income tax	Corporate income tax
Austria	44.3	22.1	4.7	14.2	16.8	28.2	14.0	50.0	34.0
Belgium	46.0	31.0	7.5	9.5	19.5	26.7	5.8	61.0	40.2
Denmark	48.5	52.4	5.2	2.5	0.7	33.0	6.2	58.7	34.0
Finland	46.5	33.3	8.1	4.3	19.9	30.9	3.5	57.5	28.0
France	45.1	14.0	5.8	12.2	25.2	27.8	15.0	54.0	41.7
Germany	37.2	23.9	4.0	18.1	20.9	27.7	5.4	55.9	58.2
Greece	33.7	13.2	6.4	17.2	14.3	41.0	7.9	*	*
Ireland	32.8	31.4	10.0	3.9	8.2	39.7	6.8	48.0	32.0
Italy	44.4	25.3	9.5	6.6	23.5	25.9	9.2	46.0	37.0
Luxembourg	46.5	20.4	18.5	10.6	11.5	27.0	12.0	46.6	39.6
Netherlands	41.9	15.6	10.5	26.5	6.2	28.0	13.2	60.0	35.0
Portugal	34.2	17.7	10.9	9.6	14.6	42.0	5.2	40.0	37.4
Spain	33.7	21.9	7.8	5.6	24.6	28.9	11.2	56.0	35.8
Sweden	51.9	35.0	6.1	5.0	23.8	22.3	7.8	59.6	28.0
UK	35.4	24.8	12.1	7.5	9.6	35.0	11.0	40.0	31.0
USA	29.7	39.0	9.4	10.4	12.5	16.7	12.0	46.6	39.5
EU average	41.5	25.5	8.5	15.9	15.9	30.9	9.0	49.7	36.3

Note: * Not available.

Source: Revenue Statistics, 1965–1998, OECD, Paris, 1999.

7

Table 1.3   Estimated effects of regulatory reform: summary (percentage change relative to baseline)

	United States	Japan	Germany	France	United Kingdom	Netherlands	Spain	Sweden
Par val effects[a]								
Labour productivity	0.5	2.6	3.5	2.3	2.0	1.3	3.1	1.7
Capital productivity	0.5	4.3	1.3	3.3	1.4	2.9	3.1	1.3
Total factor productivity	0.5	3.0	2.8	2.7	1.8	1.8	3.1	1.5
Business sector								
employment	0.0	-1.0	-0.4	-0.4	-0.5	0.6	-0.7	-0.6
Wages	0.0	0.0	-0.1	0.0	0.0	-0.2	-0.1	0.0
GDP price level	-0.3	-2.1	-1.3	-1.4	-1.2	n.a.	n.a.	n.a.
Economy-wide effects[b]								
GDP	0.9	5.6	4.9	4.8	3.5	3.5	5.6	3.1
Unemployment	0.0	0.0	0.0	0.0	0.0	0.0	0.0	0.0
Employment	0.1	0.0	0.0	0.0	0.0	0.0	0.0	0.0
Real wages	0.8	3.4	4.1	3.9	2.5	2.8	4.2	2.1

Notes:
[a] These effects are based on an aggregation of estimated sector-specific effects. They cover the business sector only.
[b] These effects include long-term and dynamic interactions in the economy as a whole and are based on simulations with a simplified macroeconomic model. The simulations for the Netherlands, Spain and Sweden are preliminary but the estimates nevertheless include some dynamic effects, and thus go beyond those reported in the individual Country Notes tables. For Spain the estimates are based on 1990 cost structures, and subsequent reforms may have affected them to some degree.

Source: Tables 3.1 and 4.1 for G7 countries, other countries from Country Notes, OECD, 7 Nov. 1997.

benefit in terms of GDP relatively little from further regulatory reform: an increase of 3.5 per cent was anticipated, no more than the next lowest, which was Holland. The UK was also the smallest gainer in terms of GDP price level, at −1.2 per cent (Table 1.3). The UK was also a low-cost country for business in terms of employers' social security contributions (Table 1.2). In 1999 it was among the middle-ranking states in terms of per capita GDP (defined in terms of purchasing parity prices), at tenth in the EU league table, grouped at the bottom end of the middle-rankers, which included France, Germany, Sweden and Italy (Table 1.1). In terms of the level of taxation defined as a percentage of GDP, the UK was among the lowest payers, at 35.4 per cent. The only countries which paid marginally less in these terms were Portugal, Spain and Greece (Table 1.1).

Member states of the EU could also be differentiated in 2000 in terms of their style of government and their trend with regard to social welfare provision. Changes in these areas were broadly in line with the groups. On style of government in 2000 the range moved from unchanging corporatism in Austria to the rejection of corporatism and reliance on the market in the UK.[7] A number of other states had shown some movement away from corporatism (Table 1.4). Those which had moved furthest included Sweden and the Netherlands, but Germany, Italy and Spain had a modified corporatist position. Germany had tried to reduce the role of the major social partners, particularly in the late Kohl period, and Italy and Spain had adopted a system whereby bargains were struck – pacts – between the social partners, unions, management and government, on specific social economic questions. The broad conclusion is obvious from Table 1.4: corporatism had retained a clear presence in the member states of the EU, but there had been some retreat in most members, with Austria remaining unchanged, and the UK entirely opposed. France remained unique in having retained a system which gave pride of place to the state and central government. The trend of social welfare provision broadly reflected the trends in governance (See Table 1.5). By 2000 Austria had made few welfare system retrenchments. The level of retrenchment was greater in Sweden and the Netherlands, where there had been an increased role for the private sector. In Germany and France there had been small retrenchments. But all systems except Ireland and the UK were described as generous. The conclusion on welfare provision was therefore broadly in line with that on governance. It was being somewhat reduced overall, with an increased private contribution, but with the exception of Ireland and the UK, the systems remained generous. The social democratic model remained strong though it was in modest retreat.

Among the deductions which could be made from this evidence is that the pattern of direct investment flows, according to the OECD figures, appeared not to be correlated with total levels of taxation or with forms of taxation like

Table 1.4 Form of governance in selected countries

	1960s–70s	1980s	Most recent	Trend
Austria	Centralised, strong corporatist	Centralised, strong corporatist	Centralised, strong corporatist	Relatively unchanging
Sweden	Centralised. strong corporatist	Centralised, strong corporatist	Intermediate corporatist	Decline of corporatism, extension of markets
Netherlands	Strong corporatist	Intermediate corporatist	Intermediate corporatist	Move to supply-side corporatism and market
Germany	Intermediate corporatist	Intermediate corporatist	Weak corporatist	Decline of corporatism/consensus
UK	Weak corporatist	Market oriented	Market oriented	Rejection of corporatism
France	Statist	Statist	Statist	Relatively unchanging
Italy	Weak corporatist	Weak corporatist	Experimenting with pacts	Experimenting with pacts
Spain	Authoritarian corporatist	Experimenting with pacts		Experimenting with pacts
Ireland	Market oriented	Experimenting with pacts		Intermediate corporatist
USA	Market oriented	Market oriented	Market oriented	Unchanged

Note: 'Centralised' means that a high score was given by the OECD for the prevailing wage bargaining level/degree of coordination of collective bargaining.

Source: Bernard Casey and Michael Gold (2000), *Social Partnership and Economic Performance*, Cheltenham, UK: Edward Elgar, p. 14.

income tax and indirect taxation (Table 1.6). There was greater correlation with total company taxation, and particularly with employer's social security contributions. In 1998 the only countries which had a positive position on direct investment flows defined as a percentage of GDP were Austria, Denmark and – though the OECD lacked the relevant figures at the time of writing – probably Ireland. Denmark and Austria both had higher levels of total taxation in EU terms, with Ireland towards the lower end of the range. Denmark (figures not given here, but compare with Sweden) and Austria had generous social protection systems. All the rest, including the United Kingdom, had a negative position. Close to balance, though still in deficit, were Sweden, Belgium and Luxembourg. The UK's negative balance, with inward flows at 55 per cent of outward flows, was at the lower end of a group which formed the majority of member states with the corresponding figure at around 60 per cent. The figures were somewhat confused by the increase in inward investment into the UK after the setting up of the currency system. It seemed, though, that the inward movement was either concentrated in the so-called 'dot.com' sector, that is, internet businesses, or was a consequence of decisions made before Euroland's establishment. In any case, movement out greatly exceeded movement in.

This evidence suggested that the doubts cast on the viability of the social democratic states in the context of the debate about the euro in 2000, and of globalization, were exaggerated. Investment movements into, and out of, European states were more closely correlated with something much more basic and much simpler, namely the level of specific taxes on companies, like company income tax and employer's social security contributions, rather than with the overall level of taxation and the level of spending on welfare. It was impossible to demonstrate, on this evidence, that high overall taxation, and generous public welfare provision, made states less attractive to international capital. Denmark had a clear significant net inflow of direct investment with income tax at 52.4 per cent, and there appeared to be no correlation there between the balance of direct investment and the other economic indicators. The balance of inward and outward flows, and of positions, was not greatly different between states with a range of total tax takes and levels of welfare provision. France had a balance of flows of investment which was about the same as that of the UK, and the positions on investment showed that the French had not much less capital investment abroad than the British, yet had a much more generous level of social provision. Two countries had a significant excess outflow of investment funds compared with the others, namely Germany and Italy, but with regard to the balance of total sums abroad and at home they were not that different from the UK in 1997. These two cases would appear to support the contention that high levels of social spending discouraged

Table 1.5 Principal features of social protection in selected EU countries

Country	Past	Current	Trend
Austria CC	Proportional insurance-based Generous	Proportional insurance-based Generous	Minor retrenchments
Sweden SDU	Proportional insurance-based Redistributive underpin Generous	Proportional insurance-based Redistributive underpin Generous	Retrenchments
Netherlands CC/SDU	Proportional insurance-based Generous	Proportional insurance-based Redistributive underpin Generous Private complements	Retrenchments Increased importance placed on private complements
UK LR	Redistributive (flat rate) Ungenerous (need for means-tested supplements for many receiving only basic payments) Substantial private complements	Redistributive (flat rate) Ungenerous (need for means-tested supplements for many receiving only basic payments) Substantial private complements	Substantial retrenchments Increased importance placed on private complements
Germany CC	Proportional insurance-based Generous	Proportional insurance-based Generous	Small retrenchments
France CC	Proportional insurance-based Generous	Proportional insurance-based Generous Extension of means-tested backups	Small retrenchments of insurance system, extension of means-tested backups
Italy CC/LatR	Insurance-based Generous Limited unemployment benefit except in case of redundancy Reliance on family support as well as means-tested benefits as backup	Insurance-based Generous Limited unemployment benefit except in case of redundancy Reliance on family support as well as means-tested benefits as backup	Retrenchments

Spain CC/LatR	Proportional insurance-based Reliance on family support as well as means-tested benefits as backup Transition from pre-democratic/authoritarian corporatist structure	Proportional insurance-based Reliance on family support as well as means-tested benefits as backup	Construction of structures appropriate to democratic, industrialised society Adjustments including minor retrenchments
Ireland LR	Redistributive (flat rate) Ungenerous Limited private complements Construction of structures appropriate to industrialised society	Redistributive (flat rate) Ungenerous Limited private complements	Increased importance placed on private complements
USA LR	Proportional insurance-based Reasonably generous redistributive underpin Substantial private complements No universal health insurance Limited means-tested assistance	Proportional insurance-based Reasonably generous redistributive underpin Substantial private complements No universal health insurance Limited means-tested assistance	Retrenchments of means-tested assistance

Note: CC Conservative-Corporatist; SDU = Social Democratic-Universalist; LR = Liberal-Residual (based upon Epsing-Anderson, 1990, typology); LatR = Latin Rim (based on Ferrara, 1996, typology).

Source: Bernard Casey and Michael Gold (2000), *Social Partnership and Economic Performance: The Case of Europe*, Cheltenham, UK: Edward Elgar, p. 16.

Globalizing Europe

investment and encouraged flows abroad, but overall the pattern was much more mixed. Indeed the case of Germany could be a special one in that the flows of investment to Eastern Europe, the primary direction of German investment flows, was as much a reassertion of traditional links as a reflection of economic pressures. The varied experience of the EU states indicated that the idea of social democracy had to be detached from the broader agenda of structural and supply-side reform, which might proceed a long way without any necessary threat to welfare.

Table 1.6   Direct investment in the EU

| | Flows 1998 $ million | | | | | Positions 1997 $ million | | |
	a. inwards	%GDP	b. outwards	%GDP	a/b%	a. inward	b. outward	a/b%
Austria	6494	2.79	671	1.42	967.8	17510	57212	30.61
Belg.Lux.	20887	8.34	23111	9.23	90.73	*	*	*
Denmark	6452	3.69	3868	2.21	166.8	*	*	*
Finland	12141	9.73	18643	14.9	65.12	9530	20297	46.95
France	28033	1.96	40578	2.83	69.08	141136	189681	74.40
Germany	19888	0.93	86641	4.06	22.95	185980	280779	66.23
Greece	3709	3.08	*	*		*	*	*
Ireland	2236	2.69	*	*		*	*	*
Italy	1212	0.10	15591	0.66	7.77	81082	81082	64.87
Netherlands	22491	5.96	35942	9.52	62.57	127434	209594	60.80
Portugal	1773	1.67	2923	2.76	60.65	18555	5933	312.74
Spain	8680	1.57	15427	2.79	56.26	100684	47606	211.49
Sweden	18900	8.33	21231	9.36	89.02	41767	75283	55.47
UK	63545	4.68	114947	8.47	55.27	259595	371119	69.94
USA	188960	2.30	121644	1.48	155.3	693207	865531	

Note: *Figures not available.

Source: *International Direct Investment Statistics Yearbook, 1999*, OECD, Paris, 2000.

The concept of the Anglo-American model was questionable with regard to a number of its prescriptions about low public welfare provision, low taxation and deregulation. Even the United States fitted this bill somewhat awkwardly. Total tax level there in 1997 was well below that of any European state, but levels of tax on companies were higher than in a number of EU states (Table 1.2). All this fitted the general conclusion, developed below, that the main explanation of the weakness of the euro was the mismatching of European and US business cycles. Whether or not European states had a greater or lesser degree of welfare provision – whether or not they were social democracies – was not clearly the key issue.

Political Diversity

The principles of difference

The European Community had developed by the 1970s into a unique inter-national organization, which combined two features which had usually been seen as mutually contradictory: a high degree of common management together with a system of states which retained their sovereignty. The reconciliation of these two features was achieved by the splitting of the idea of competence and the idea of ultimate responsibility. Governments learned that their sovereignty could survive, albeit altered, even if they extended competences over key areas like currency to a central set of institutions – those in Brussels – as long as they remained ultimately responsible. If things went wrong they retained the legal and constitutional right to take back the competences they had extended, and in any case they were accountable to their domestic constituencies for the protection of their interests in the common framework.

The cautious governments, such as Britain, were under pressure to extend competences to the centre, but had to have the confidence that they retained ultimate responsibility. This was a trick which had largely been learned by the original six member states. It involved being reconciled to the possibilities of sovereignty for small or middle-sized states in the modern world, understand-ing how circumstances had changed, so that an absolutist view of sovereignty was no longer sustainable, and being careful to protect the reserve powers inherent in the national constitutions on which the legality of the whole Community legal system rested. Sometimes the language used by leaders of the more ambitious countries, such as Germany, alarmed the British. For instance in May 2000 the German Foreign Minister, Joshka Fischer, said that a federal outcome should be sought. A reading of the text, reported in Britain as a plan for a European super-state led by Germany[8] revealed a more modest appeal for a clearer division of responsibilities between the centre and the states, and an assertion, yet again, of the primary role of the nation states.

But in Britain many failed to make the distinction between competences and powers, and many in government and the media, who came to be called the Eurosceptics, could not get beyond the view that granting a competence to Brussels was the same thing as abdicating ultimate responsibility and sover-eignty. This view was a key part of the primitive sentimental nationalism that was a feature of Prime Minister Thatcher's ideology, but in the context of the later debate about membership of the single currency system, it was a per-spective that became more common.

The argument can be illustrated by a comparison of two types of states. The first type would include small states where hardly any task could be done in-dependently. National autonomy has little foundation in the capacity to do significant tasks separately – even defence, foreign policy and the control of the currency. Autonomy does, however, find justification in the right to withdraw from arrangements at the regional level, and in the right to participate in the discussions about their formation. This is precisely the situation of Luxembourg, or a prospective independent Scotland, in the early twenty-first century, and explains why the Scottish Nationalist Party, like all the minority nationalist parties in Europe, are in favour of the European Union. They had come to think that they could have national independence and be a sovereign state because they had the right to participate in international negotiations in pursuit of their own interest, in this case in the European Union, and had the legal right to withdraw from the Union or from particular acts of Community legislation.

On the other hand are those who regard the autonomy of states as involving doing nothing in common with other states, and therefore no competences could be extended to international organizations. The latter is, of course, a delusion: no modern states are in this situation in the early twenty-first century, though some, usually the bigger ones, could do more by themselves without needing to work with others. Some states, such as the candidate states in Eastern Europe, are as yet unsure and untried with regard to their preparedness to extend competences to the central institutions. Most states are, however, in fact more like Luxembourg. The main problem is one of perception: the delusion of the possibility of autonomy in the sense of having the power to act independently over all significant areas. This delusion is a part of the false consciousness of the Eurosceptic trend in cautious states like Britain in the years leading up to the early twenty-first century: they thought it was the norm to do things independently of the other states in international society – there are even MPs in Britain who believe that the House of Commons controls the value of the pound sterling. These same people also mistakenly believe that if they were out of Europe this difficulty would go away. In fact it would remain, and the capacity to have a greater impact by working through the regional group would be lost. Being in the European Union involves a greater range of shared competences, but it also gives a share of a greater capacity to exercise a collective influence on outside states. Being outside means a smaller range of shared competences, but a lessened capacity for the individual state to exercise such influence.

The reconciliation of a high degree of shared management in the EU with the retention of sovereignty also depends on a range of characteristics of the Union's decision-making. The whole system rests on a treaty, the Treaty of Rome, which was legitimized through national constitutions. It is the latter and not the former which gives legitimacy to the Union. It follows that states could withdraw if they wished. It also follows that as long as they follow their own constitutional procedures – that is, that they act legally according to the terms of their own system, they could individually and separately reject Community legislation.

The chances are, however, that this would not happen because the member states share economic and political interests in staying together – even the

British remained convinced in early 2000 that they were better in than out. It is also unlikely to happen because the way in which legislation was made in the main EU institutions rests on the principle of consensus. In many areas there was by the turn of the Millennium the formal possibility of qualified majority voting. But the reality is that no states could or would be regularly outvoted on matters about which they care deeply. All participants understood that it was better to avoid breaking the consensus: to do so would be dangerous. Whenever majority voting was used it was in effect with the consent of the dissenting states in each case, which were conceding that they were prepared to be outvoted, and was most often used on more technical questions in support of a policy that had been agreed earlier, on the basis of unanimity. The new major initiatives were always determined in meetings of the heads of states and governments, called the European Council, on the basis of unanimity.

The correct image of the Union's institutions is that they are not something outside of or apart from the states, an outside actor which could threaten or impose on states. Even the Commission, the Union's executive body, has a representative quality despite its formal task of administering the Union's rules – acting as guardian of the treaty – and proposing European policies. In doing this, members of the Commission are strictly forbidden from seeking or receiving instructions from their national governments. Nevertheless states are always anxious to get their people into key positions where they felt their interest could best be served, as when Lord Cockfield became the commissioner responsible for the Single Market Programme in the early 1980s. The Eurosceptics in Britain and elsewhere wilfully misunderstood the situation – they talked of the Commission as if, to quote Charles de Gaulle, it was 'a foreign bureaucracy' with opposing interests. The fact is that all the Commission's actions have been in pursuit of policies which the states had approved. If they did not like those policies they had no one but themselves, or earlier governments in their state, to blame. But usually the statements of the Eurosceptics revealed ignorance about the tight linkages between the national and collective systems. In Britain in the last quarter of the twentieth century, a press dominated by deracinated individuals such as Rupert Murdoch were all too willing to promote anti-European views, and if the cause was best served by misinformation, then so be it.[9]

By the mid-1980s the terms of the diplomatic relationship between the British and the other cautious states, and the more ambitious core states in the European Community, led by France and Germany, had turned against the former group. This has remained the case till the time of writing in the early months of the twenty-first century. The nature of the problem could be summed up as follows: initiatives to extend integration, such as those pushed by the French and the Germans after the mid-1980s, posed the threat of the emergence of a powerful political actor on the Continent which could potentially dominate the reluctant integrators. There was a kind of diplomatic trap: either the British, and the other non-core states, had to stay with the negotiations on the new proposals to deepen integration, and make whatever concessions that had to be made to stay in the convoy, or they could withdraw and risk being isolated. This was in effect a replay of the diplomacy of the late 1950s when the Conservative government in Britain had decided that the proposal to set up the European Economic Community was not for them, and in any case would probably not work. It did work, however, despite the British-led creation, strongly opposed by the USA, of the rival European Free Trade Area. They, therefore, had to seek admission later on less favourable terms than those they could probably have obtained earlier. After the 1980s, up to 2000, the British government, a Conservative one until 1997, and then New Labour, was determined to avoid making this mistake again.

The divisions about integration: the historical pattern
Beginning in the mid-1980s, the pace of integration between the member states of the European Community once more accelerated.[10] There were a number of reasons for this, in particular pressures from the business community to increase market integration to allow a stronger response to economic penetration from Asia, and the integrative ambitions of Chancellor Kohl of Germany, President Mitterand of France, and the able President of the European Commission, Jacques Delors. The main events included: the settlement in 1984 of the British complaint about what they judged were excessive budgetary contributions to Europe, a problem which had led to quarrels between Prime Minister Thatcher and, in particular, President Mitterrand; the initiation of a campaign to strengthen the European institutions, especially the European Parliament, which led it to adopt a Draft Treaty on European Union on 14th February 1984; and the agreement of the Single European Act at Luxembourg in December 1985, which included a plan to create a 'Europe without frontiers', in particular to establish a Single European Market by 1992.

There came a point in the mid-1980s at which President Mitterrand realized that expressions of support for a higher level of integration, such as had been proposed by the European Union Treaty, were a very good strategy for putting pressure upon the British to accept a compromise in the settlement of their budgetary grievance. Helmut Kohl's government in West Germany, partly in response to the French and partly on its own initiative, acted in ways which gave credence to this strategy. The key to further integration was getting the British to move, and the perception of the need to do this, particularly by the French, was itself a crucial factor in placing high on the agenda of the Community items which involved extending the scope of integration and strengthening the central institutions. Prime Minister Thatcher's speech at Bruges of 20 September 1988, in which she scorned the idea of European unification, was no evidence to the contrary:[11] indeed it indicated that the weight of the pressures towards greater unity was being felt.

One problem for the British was that by early 1985 the various items on the agenda of integration, the completion of the Common Market, the strengthening of the machinery for political cooperation, and the rather ambitious proposals for institutional reform, had been refined and increasingly firmly linked together in a single package. The British had tried to prevent this: they only wanted the Single Market. In the discussions of the Ad Hoc Committee for Institutional Affairs, which in effect was the preparatory meeting for the intergovernmental conference on reform of the second half of 1985, the pattern was set. It established a 'convergence of priorities' in the particular sense that the need for a 'homogeneous internal economic area', the 'promotion of common values of civilisation' and the 'search for an external identity' was spelled out, and made conditional upon the achievement of 'efficient and democratic institutions', meaning 'a strengthened Commission', the extension of the powers of the European Parliament and the reform of the Court of Justice.[12] A method for obtaining these goals was recommended in the report: it was held that a 'conference of the representatives of the governments of the member states should be convened in the near future to negotiate a draft European Union Treaty'. President Mitterrand indicated his approval for this general line by appointing a known Euro-enthusiast, Maurice Faure, as the French member of the committee. In other words, it proposed an explicit and detailed programme for action leading to a new treaty. The best that the British representative, Mr Rifkind, could do in the face of this enthusiasm was to enter a number of reservations which were noted in footnotes.

The underlying dynamics of the negotiations leading up to the conclusion of the Single European Act, which initiated the Single Market, were now clearly visible. On the one hand were a group of states, including in particular the French, Italians, Dutch, Belgians, Luxemburgers and Germans, which inclined to support a more ambitious set of changes for the European institutions. The French government did not need to lead this faction at all stages and, indeed, it was the Italians who in practice in 1985–86 often carried the Euro-banner. The British headed a group of doubters – themselves, the Greeks and the Danes – which was necessarily and invariably on the defensive in the negotiations, particularly with regard to the institutional questions. They were placed in the position of having to make specific concessions in order to avoid incurring non-specific and longer-term costs and of having to fight a rearguard battle to prevent more 'federalist' alterations in the structure of the Community of which they did not approve. Thanks to the Mitterrand strategy, success in this depended paradoxically upon making concessions on precisely those questions, whilst at the same time struggling to make them as small as possible.

This pattern of diplomacy has prevailed through to the time of writing. The reasons for the convening of the major intergovernmental conference at Maastricht on 9, 10 and 11 December 1991, which led to the next set of integrative amendments of the Treaty of Rome, were strongly reminiscent of those which explained the meeting at Luxembourg which negotiated the Single European Act. The main project in this case was, of course, monetary union. President Mitterand again called for a constitutional conference – to be held no later than the autumn of 1990 – and strongly supported the proposal for economic and monetary union 'as the lynchpin of European political integration', the centre of 'a real Union – that is European Political Union'.[13] At the Strasbourg conference of 8–9 December 1989 decisions were taken to call an intergovernmental conference to open if possible in December 1990.[14] On this occasion the British were outvoted by 11 votes to 1. This conference took place shortly after the fall of the Berlin Wall, and the idea of German unification was also strongly supported. Thatcher was ignored and subdued. She said, 'there is no other European forum where we would rather be'. Mitterand gallantly replied: 'we are pleased to have you among us'. Still the guest rather than the family member.

The most important new item on the agenda was monetary union, which was to be achieved in three stages, subject to states meeting a set of five convergence criteria. The British Conservative government, now led by John Major, was implacably opposed to this and the United Kingdom obtained an opt-out from the third phase of this process; even if it met the criteria, it was still up to the British Parliament to opt in. But the governments, including the British, accepted an obligation to work for economic convergence. 'Economic policies are a matter of common concern' (Maastricht Treaty, Article 104). Accordingly the Council was now given the power to address recommendations if states adopted disruptive behaviour. Adjustments to promote convergence could be required of states other than those which had opted out. The British also vigorously opposed proposals to harmonize social policy, and opted out of the so-called Social Chapter.

In 2000 this pattern of diplomacy continued. The lead as regards the further strengthening of the powers of the central institutions, and adding more competences to the centre, remained with the core Continental social democratic states, usually with the support of the second group of states, excluding Denmark. But now the more ambitious states were increasingly pressing for a more flexible Europe, which they interpreted as meaning the right of the more ambitious states to go ahead of the others. In the Treaty of Amsterdam of 1997 a step was taken towards this in articles which permitted a majority of members to go ahead, using the institutions of Title One – the European Economic Community – on certain stated conditions, on the basis of qualified majority voting. A state which objected on the grounds of a major, and stated, interest could require that the decision be transferred to a meeting of the heads of state and government where it would be subject to unanimity. There seemed to be ample opportunity for the more cautious states to prevent the emergence of a vanguard, but the inclusion of such arrangements in the treaty even in this form reflected an increasing impatience of the core states with the rest.[15] They also retained the option of action outside the Treaty of Rome, by agreeing among themselves a separate treaty which the dissenting states could not veto. This had been threatened on a number of occasions since the early 1980s.

This was a step too far for the British Eurosceptics; – they wanted everyone to proceed at a slower pace. But as in earlier years, the more ambitious could push the British by reminding them of the late 1950s – if they were permitted to become more integrated, Britain was at risk of becoming a peripheral part of Europe. The irony was again visible that Britain could only slow the others down by agreeing to some of their proposals. And frankly the British government was frightened by the possibility of being placed in the slow lane of a multi-speed Europe. In a speech in Warsaw on 4 October 2000 British Prime Minister Blair showed this was still the case. He supported the weakening of the Commission by transferring some of its powers to a committee of national ministers, and was cautious about the Franco-German proposal for a two-speed Europe.[16] The same pressures generally applied to the cautious states as in previous years. As will be seen below, however, the more ambitious were less prepared to put up with the obduracy of the cautious members.

Institutional competences in the year 2000

Where had all this led the institutions by 2000? The question of the distribution of responsibility and competence among the various institutions in the European Union then reached was a very important one for multinational enterprises seeking presence in the 15 member states. It was a key variable in explaining the areas where the Union was vulnerable to pressures from the outside, to the forces of globalization as reflected in the power of multinationals. A secondary issue was that an understanding that distribution was also important in deciding where a multinational should focus its attention if it wished to exercise influence on the policy-making process. The answers to these questions were not straightforward and there were surprising differences between policy areas. Enquiry had to be made with regard to each specific policy area. Because of the complexity, in this section only general arrangements and guiding principles can be discussed.[17] The broad principles in 2000 were as follows.

In a first area of activity the Community had competence under the Treaty of Rome as amended by a series of further treaties agreed by the member states, in particular the Single European Act (1985), the Maastricht Treaty (1991) and the Treaty of Amsterdam (1997). In this area implementing legislation conferred responsibility on the Commission and member state governments to execute the specific policy goals which had been agreed. Both member states and the Commission acted within a common legal framework – the law of the Community – which provided a guarantee that they could not interpret the policies to suit their own interests. Illustrations of areas where the Commission had primary responsibility included the protection of the Common Market, which forbade any form of discrimination against the goods of other member states, judgements about the conformity of proposed mergers of companies with the rules of the Community, and the common commercial policy, namely trade agreements with non-members, The Commission also determined whether national supports for their companies – special grants and the like – were acceptable.

National governments acted under Community law when responsibility had been delegated to them to maintain community standards. For instance they ensured that goods conformed with agreed specifications – very important under Article 100 of the Single European Act, which was designed to complete the Single Market. They were also charged with maintaining such common policies as those on the transport of goods, and environmental and consumer protection. Under Community law they also ensured that agreed practices were followed with regard to workers. Certain rules on pension arrangements were subject to Community law, as were aspects of policy on the equality of men and women in the workplace, and the rights of workers and their dependants from other EU states. The point should be stressed that action in these areas was subject to the law of the Community and that this had precedence over national law: it should be assumed that states had little or no discretion in this context. In consequence the EU was relatively impervious to pressures from multinational companies in this area, apart from the question of how far the rules were carefully and properly applied. But transgressions, including the ignoring of deadlines, exposed the perpetrator to legal sanctions.

The issue of competence – of 'who is responsible?' – also arose, and was of crucial importance in the process of making new Community legislation. Most of the attention of governments with regard to EU work focused on this process, and it consumed massive amounts of the time and energy of national and Community officials. Twice a year, on the occasion of meetings of the European Council – which were essentially EU summit meetings – attempts were made to agree new agendas for policy and legislation by the prime ministers and presidents of the member states, together with their top officials and senior advisors. But the process was a continuous and intense one affecting every aspect of the work of national officials and causing them to be in consultation with officials in other national capitals and in Brussels each and every day of their working lives. The consultation was intense enough to justify describing the bureaucracy of the member states of the European Union as a multi-centred unitary system rather than as a series of discrete national ones. This was a characteristic which outsiders often found difficult to comprehend as it meant there was no clear single authority where claims could be addressed or influence exercised.

By 2000 the process of policy agreement generally involved three primary entities at the level of the Union. Firstly, the Commission formulated proposals after widespread consultation. Secondly, the Council of Ministers and its subordinate committees considered the proposal and adopted a position. And thirdly, the European Parliament considered the proposal and either approved it, put forward amendments or applied a veto. By the year 2000 the safest general working assumption would be that decisions in the Council of Ministers could formally be taken by qualified majority vote, but that consensus was in practice the norm, and that the Parliament, through the procedure laid down in Article 189(b) of the Treaty of Rome, as modified by the Maastricht and Amsterdam treaties, could apply a veto. The measure could only be approved on the basis of co-decision-making – that is, both the European Parliament and the Council of Ministers had to accept it. If they could not agree there were conciliation procedures.

Enough has been said in the preceding paragraph to indicate that these arrangements made it hard for external actors, like multinational companies, to fix on a single point of influence and to be sure that any alliances they formed could have an effect. The possibility of qualified majority voting in the Council of Ministers meant that everything depended on negotiation between the member governments which inevitably was unpredictable, with concessions being won and lost during negotiations which took place behind closed doors. It was impossible for a government to be held to a commitment made to entities outside this process. The further problem arose that in much legislation, the Parliament had won by 2000 at least the ability to stop something from happening, though still lacked the power to initiate legislation. But even marshalling a negative coalition among the disparate members of such a large body was likely to prove impossible for lobbyists. The conclusion therefore had to be that there were a reasonable range of pressure points where influence could be exercised, and evidence and interests fed into the process of making legislation, but no way of telling how effective these operations would be. The system had a set of inner dynamics which were very hard for outsiders to fix, or even identify, with any degree of accuracy. That was not to deny that a large number of multinational enterprises made the effort and were often members of European lobbies with headquarters in Brussels. The rapid increase in these since the mid-1980s was a measure of the problem: no lobby could rely on the promises of national governments, and the second-best was an enduring presence in as much of the system as possible.

A third area of competence and responsibility remained in the hands of national governments in 2000 and it was in this area that multinational companies were most likely to be able to exercise leverage on their own account. At every stage in the development of the Union there had been a frontier of integration, and an area of the economic arrangements of the states which had not yet fallen within the area of competence of the Treaty of Rome. In 2000, after the start of the third phase of the process of setting up the single currency, attention was focused on areas functionally adjacent to the monetary policy for states, now controlled collectively for the 11 members of the euro zone by the European Bank (essentially a committee of central bankers). These were, in particular, taxation and government spending, which seemed to be next on the list for inclusion in the integrated area, but which some states, especially Britain, Denmark, Greece and, this time, Spain, were determined to keep under national control. Beyond that frontier there was, of course, a very large terrain of unintegrated sectors. In addition to tax and spending policies these included fiscal policy, the whole of the area of criminal justice, and others too numerous to mention here.

The fact that some areas were now within the competence of the Union and other areas were outside it allowed companies a particular kind of leverage. The Common Market, and its supporting arrangements, coexisted with an unintegrated area which included taxation and spending. The implications of this are discussed below. The governments in the single currency system in 2000 were to maintain a government debt of 60 per cent or less of GDP, and a deficit of no more than 3 per cent of GDP. But although some governments in Euroland faced difficult choices in keeping to these limits, they were still left with considerable discretion as to the extent of taxation and spending.[18] Incentives to companies to locate new investment in a territory included a range of benefits, such as tax incentives, green field sites and weak unionization. Governments, therefore, sought to retain control of these so that they could compete with each other for the benefit of capital investment. After the introduction of the Monetary Union in January 1999 one persistent theme in the discussion was the costs and benefits of being in Euroland, that is the territory of all states apart from Britain, Denmark, Greece and Sweden. On the whole the evidence seemed to suggest that capital regarded being a member of the Monetary System as a plus, and companies outside it threatened to move out of non-members into that territory.[19]

The general point remained that companies were free to chose their location in the Union, that countries used their competence in the unintegrated sector to attract inward investment, and that the advantages of the integrated sector, especially the Common Market, were available to companies wherever they located in the Union. It followed, of course, that countries were anxious to protect their ability to manipulate the costs of production to attract capital in the absence of other resources, and it was therefore the poorer states that could be expected to resist integration if that reduced this ability. Hence countries like Britain led the way in opposing proposals put forward by the core countries, such as Germany, to bring taxation into the integrated sector, and to have common social policies favouring higher levels of worker protection and higher levels of welfare.

The logic of the arrangements for managing relations with the outside world in some ways mirrored the logic of the internal arrangements. In areas where the Community had competence and where that competence had in fact been exercised by the Commission, it was the latter which acted for the Union in its negotiations with outside members. It was, therefore, the Commission which acted for the Community in trade negotiations, and which was the representative of the Community in the major international institutions dealing with commodity arrangements and the like. This was entirely logical as it would have been hard to defend the Common Market if each state was free to negotiate its own deals with outsiders. There were procedures and committees for reconciling the positions of states and the Commission during negotiations with non-members.

In areas of external relations which included both Community and national competences, which were not clearly under the Treaty of Rome, both states and the Commission shared in the negotiations. This area included such questions as negotiations on North–South preferential trade and aid arrangements, like the various Lomé, and APC Agreements with developing countries. In a third area, which included areas of traditional foreign policy and defence, it was the separate states that retained responsibility, though by 2000 various arrangements had been agreed through which the states consulted with each other and sought to coordinate their positions. The Union had acquired many of the characteristics of a state in this area in that national Foreign Offices had developed habits of close consultations. But there was no certainty of a common foreign policy, there was no common army, and there remained the range of national representations in foreign capitals.

But this brief description should not conceal the point that the states had a strong preference for acting together on foreign policy questions and reacted against any attempts by outsiders, even the USA, to join the club. There had been a steady strengthening of the habit of consultation since it began in the early 1970s, and increasing coordination on defence policy.[20] In November 2000 those described by Prime Minister Blair as anti-Europeans complained bitterly about British participation in a European multinational rapid response force. Mrs Thatcher came out of retirement to describe it as a 'monumental folly'. Through successive enlargements this process has continued. There were some who wonder whether that will still be the case after the next enlargement, which could add as many as seven new members from Central and Eastern Europe.

SCENARIOS OF FUTURE DEVELOPMENT

What conclusions may be drawn in 2000 from this account of the evolution of the European Union? One view, though this was not supported by Eurosceptics, was that state and Community could have a positive relationship with each other.[21] The positive states did not see their sovereignty as threatened. This was not surprising. States such as Spain, Portugal, Greece and Germany had joined the Community in order to rediscover themselves as states, indeed in order to consolidate their national arrangements. There was a sufficient identity with the common values to allow this to be recognized as a possibility by anyone who was not actually in the grip of Europhobia. The history of the Community reflected the idea of Europe as a unity in diversity. But the European Union level had also acquired its own integrity and a degree of self-containment. It was not just a matter of providing a mechanism to help the state, though this was a limitation on which successive British governments tried to insist.

There are three scenarios about the future of the European Union. All three assume that there would be enlargement to include most of the states of Central Europe, stopping short of Russia. All three also involve a response to globalization, interpreted as the process of liberalizing the international movement of capital and goods.

The first scenario accepts the dilution of the existing arrangements of the EU by granting derogations and exceptions to all members in the enlarged community, which implies the immersion of the whole in the global economy, and the triumph throughout of the Anglo-American model of economic management. This would mean the further liberalization of trade, and low levels of government intervention and spending on welfare throughout. The neo-liberal agenda would triumph. This is very much the agenda of the British Eurosceptics, since it removes the challenge of supra-nationalism to which they have strongly objected. It would also fit with the social and political agendas of the sceptics – who have tended to be Thatcherite in the UK – with regard to internal policy, since very low tariffs, adopted within the framework of multilateral free trade negotiations, would mean that the costs of adaptation were more likely to be placed on labour, whilst the advantages of free trade would accrue to companies and richer individuals.

The second scenario, however, is the successful adjustment of the Union's arrangements to accommodate all members in a higher level of integration, comparable with that which existed at the Millennium. This would involve the careful working out of transitional arrangements with new members, on the assumption that their accommodation was possible, and the least possible dilution of existing cooperative arrangements. The institutions would also be adjusted so as to protect the powers of the centre and to find a generally acceptable compromise between national independence and supra-nationalism. There would be a measure of adjustment of welfare spending, but the principle of state responsibility for individual welfare would be acknowledged throughout the Union. In this way the Union would continue much as before, but with a considerably increased membership, and a lowering of ambitions for future integration, combined with a measure of compromise with the forces of globalization. This would be a kind of half-way house between the first and third scenarios.[22]

The third scenario is the most challenging both with regard to the continuing liberalization of global economic arrangements and with regard to non-core states' participation in the core activities of the Union. In this model there would be differentiation between the core states of the existing Union and the peripheral states, which would include Britain and the newly admitted states from Central Europe.

The basis of the differentiation would be, first, the preference of the core states for protecting their higher levels of integration and making continuing progress towards a confederal union with a formal settlement of powers between the centre and the member states, as was proposed (mentioned above) by German Foreign Minister Joschka Fischer on 12 May 2000 in a lecture at the Humboldt University in Berlin. President Chirac of France echoed this proposal in a speech in Dresden on 3 October 2000. He called for Germany and France to lead a core of countries towards deeper integration within an enlarged European Union.[23] In the Treaty of Amsterdam this theme was reflected in the notion of flexibility, intended to allow states that wished to go ahead of the others the right to do so – if all agreed to this. But flexibility, as already pointed out, has become a contested concept in the sense that the more cautious states, and those sceptical about integration, are fearful about the prospect of a more integrated core.

The second basis of differentiation would be the wish of the core states to protect their ability to pursue a social purpose in the face of perceived difficulties in the way of this resulting from globalization and the implied triumph of the Anglo-American model. They would be anxious to protect their social democratic approach – sometimes described as Alliance Capitalism – in the face of the pressures to reduce the costs of labour and welfare support resulting from more open economies. This is not surprising: the core states have consistently pushed for a more advanced social agenda than the British would accept, and are convinced that there could not be a successful integrated market without further development of social welfare measures. Labour has to benefit as much as capital. The strength of the commitment of the cores states to this position is usually not fully taken on board by those outside the core, even New Labour in Britain. This is not to suggest that there is root and branch opposition to any reform of labour and welfare arrangements, but rather that it is a question of appropriate adjustment.[24] Unlike with doctrinaire neo-liberalism, there could be a compromise between welfare and competitiveness.

The core states could move ahead by signing a separate treaty among themselves, or by exploiting the new flexibility arrangements of the Amsterdam Treaty. The former strategy had been proposed by the leading core states on several occasions in the 1980s and 1990s in the face of the reluctance of the cautious states, led by the British, to accept stronger powers for the central institutions. They would also move towards a greater degree of harmonization of welfare in the core and maintain higher levels of spending on welfare: they would need to calculate carefully the level of costs which they could impose on capital without driving it out of the Union. But, as pointed out above, it was logically necessary that a higher welfare zone should have tariff protection. (The point should be noted that there were good theoretical reasons for predicting increasing pressures towards social and geographical redistribution as a result of the consolidation of the Single Market and the Monetary Union, since both encouraged European mergers of firms and the closing of less efficient branches in order to maximize the advantages of greater specialization.)

The third basis of the differentiation would be the strengthening of the perception of insuperable practical difficulties in the way of adjusting the existing arrangements of the Union to include the Central European states, in particular difficulties which would lead to greatly increased demands on the European budget and the implication of higher contributions by the richer member states. The attempt to accommodate the new states to higher levels of integration would fail in this scenario. In this context the core states would be inclined to place Britain in the outer group, and would lose their reluctance to go ahead without the British. The outer group would remain members of the Common Market, but would be excluded from more integrative arrangements.[25]

The problems of Britain as a spoiler and scavenger in the Union would reach a threshold at which demotion to the second rank of membership would be preferred by the core states to making adjustments to keep Britain fully in the convoy. Indeed the emergence of the new problem candidate states would make it easier to limit British involvement since they could then be placed in the large company of states with problem credentials. The core states would be much more prepared than Britain to resist opening up to the global economic pressures, because of their implications for the responsibilities of governments, and this could mean maintaining protective measures of various kinds. The calculation would be that such a market would be large enough, and successful enough, to persuade mobile capital to pay the required price of access. The calculation of this would always be a difficult question: it would become a major item on the agenda of economic management in the core countries, a new form of optimum tariff. The close scrutiny of OECD economic and social indicators in the late 1990s, ventured above, did not provide any hard evidence of the vulnerability of the social democratic model in the European Union, despite the claims of the British. With regard to the wide range of indicators the social democratic states were either performing better than the British, or were doing as well.

The importance of this third scenario derives from its proposing of reasons both for resisting the pressures of globalization, and for greater integration of a core ahead of the peripheral states. These derive from economic, political and ideological factors, and in the light of these Britain and the core states would be likely to be divided. But it is a challenge to the inevitability of globalization, previously intimated very rarely. It raises an important question: how would such a differentiation affect the economic organization of the Union and its relations with the world economy? In the next section aspects of this relationship are explored. Arguments which support the view that the social democratic states could succeed are explored. A case is argued that will be reconsidered at various points later in this book.

The Social Democratic States and the Globalizing Economies

The location of capital

The question arises of how the *acquis communitaire*, in particular the Common Market, could survive in such a system. At this point the account is less concerned with historical analysis and more with the logic of the situation. The calculation of costs and benefits concerning the location of capital in the European Union must take account of the different arguments about the core compared with the periphery. This is a two-stage calculation, the first being the calculation of the advantage of being inside the Common External Tariff (CET), and the second about where to locate within the EU. If the core states were to succeed in defending their higher level of welfare spending within the Common Market, against peripheral or Anglo-American member states with cheaper welfare costs, there must be additional benefits for capital in the core compared with the periphery. The benefit of access to the Common Market would be equally available in both locations, since both would be within the CET. The conclusions were likely to vary with the sector, but for most manufacturers the core was likely to possess benefits, such as the proximity of suppliers of components and support infrastructure, and a more prosperous local market, as well as greater specific and general skills of workers, and a range of attractions for managers and their families. As already argued, peripheries would have the advantage of a cheaper and more flexible workforce, weaker unions, green field sites and lower welfare costs, but these advantages would have to be set against a deficiency in the assets normally found in the core.

In these circumstances three areas of policy disagreement between the core states and the peripheral states in the European Union suggested themselves: about taxation, about the level of protection and its implications for globalization, and about the new social democracy. On taxation the disagreement about levels of social spending would be bound to lead to short-term differences of interest which would be hard to reconcile. The states with a higher social wage would recognize the short-term competitive disadvantage of that and prefer to have a generally agreed scale of taxation at a level necessary to achieve higher social standards throughout the Union. They would seek to equalize taxation costs upwards. The Anglo-American states in contrast would seek to protect their competitive advantage in this regard and resist attempts to harmonize taxation upward: indeed they would prefer no harmonization at all as the higher social spending of the core could be seen as a benefit for themselves. This was exactly the position of the British in 2000. On protection, the social democratic states had an interest in maintaining around the Union, probably through the Common External Tariff, a level which offset the competitive advantages of lower-cost producers in third countries. The interest would be to induce inward investment by making the costs of supplying the European market from outside exceed the costs of establishment inside the Union. The assumption would be that there could be an optimum level of protection to support the social democratic agenda within the Union, but which minimized the risk of tariff wars, or mercantilist strategies. This strategy could however only work on the basis of the European market, and hence it required integration. No individual state in Europe could present an attractive enough market to persuade multi-national enterprises to pay the entrance fee demanded.

But the kind of social democracy was also key in this argument. The assumption of the right-wing advocates of flexible labour was that it should be easy to hire and fire, meaning low employment protection, little attempt to build a communality of interest between labour and management through co-determination arrangements, workers councils and the like – which were a feature of German labour relations, low levels of unionization, and low levels of pension provision. This last was key in welfare provision and is discussed separately below. But there was an alternative model which involved a recon-ciliation of traditional social democracy with the needs of global capital.

In contrast, a high social wage could be devoted to developing effective arrangements for a more flexible labourforce, by providing retraining, support for relocation, and a guaranteed trans-employment income, by the action of the state.[26] The social wage would reflect the change in the structure of employment, being used to support enhanced flexibility, with economic success being a primary target of policy, but nested firmly in policies for maintaining civilized standards for employees. The aim would be to protect the right to employment, but to recognize that the concept of employment had to be detached from the right to stay in a particular job. Indeed the aim would be to generate a labour-force that was unlike that of previous generations in that, while traditionally flexibility was greater for the least skilled, now it would be greater for those with the highest levels of technical training. It should be stressed, however, that such employment strategies, which would seem ideally suited to the new capitalism, were social democratic rather than Anglo-American. They required higher, rather than lower, levels of social policy spending.

The arguments were also the context in which the weakness of the strategy of relying on cheap labour and low associated costs in anything but the short term were revealed. Three problems arose. Firstly, in the Anglo-American model a low level of labour protection was a fair-weather asset in that it was only of benefit as an attraction to mobile capital in a period of economic expansion. In economic decline the areas of cheap labour were the first to suffer because it was cheaper, and easier, for companies to fire labour there than in areas where the worker had more protection. The history of the links between the Rover car company and the German car manufacturer BMW in the UK illustrated this point very well in 2000: facing the need to restructure production BMW determined to abandon Rover and British workers partly because it was cheaper than reducing its German workforce. This indicates that in a period of decline having a low social wage was likely to make things worse rather than better for the less successful economies in that it facilitated the building up of larger pools of unemployed with all the economic, social and political burdens this implied. It was also much riskier from the point of view of political stability.

Secondly, as a low social wage usually meant inadequacy in training and other support for re-employment and resettlement, it was also likely to lead to a further deskilling of labour and a further reduction of the attractiveness of that area to mobile capital. In this situation cheap labour was part of a strategy for further economic decline rather than recovery, unless there were powerful countervailing economic and social pressures – compulsion – of a kind not usually found in liberal Western democracies. Thirdly was the problem that the lesson that cheap labour was an asset, was not capable of being generalized or universalized, and was therefore revealed as profoundly flawed as a global concept. Capital that relied on universal cheap labour was capital that was strangling its own market. Even when production benefited from cheap labour, in the mass market sectors – which remained crucial – there had to be somewhere a pool of well-rewarded high-spending labour to provide their market. The cheaper the labour in an enclosed market the smaller the market for a wide range of goods: this was a lesson that was well known to economists such as Hobson, and was a key factor in his critique of imperialism.

These arguments obviously had implications for the institutional development of the European Union which were in flat opposition to those developed hitherto by Eurosceptics with regard to the Social Charter in Maastricht, Amsterdam and later. The traditional argument rested on the conviction in the Anglo-American states that a greater degree of social spending, and a degree of obligation to that in the common institutions, was likely to be a handicap with regard to their capacity to attract capital and their level of economic performance. In contrast, this argument suggested that a higher level of social spending could be part of a strategy for maintaining a greater range of benefits which were attractive to mobile global capital, provided that, as argued above, the costs of such programmes were not placed too directly and obviously on companies. Such policies would mean that the wise economic move would be to opt in, and to have a higher degree of common decision-making on welfare questions, and for the less successful economies to work for welfare policies that were well funded but rethought to suit modern employment needs. In this welfare provision the central theme would be having arrangements which guaranteed a continuing supply of flexible and highly-trained labour, which must involve governments' collective responsibility – the public sector – as it was difficult to see how individual companies could remain immune to the temptations to freeload. Capital-friendly welfare provision was not a difficult concept, but it did need at least medium-term thinking about the convergence of the interests of labour and capital in the context of a well-developed market.

The arguments above did not need quantification. They were sufficient as they stood to suggest that the social democracies in the Union had at their disposal policies which could increase the advantage for capital of establishing within them, to a level which exceeded the advantages of establishment in the low-welfare-spending countries. The arguments also suggested that public action at the level of the European Union would be useful, but not essential, in that it would reduce the chances of irrational action by the low-welfare countries in a competition for capital which they could not win in anything but the short term, The appropriate level of welfare spending could be agreed and legitimized through the Union and, as with all stable regimes, fair play refereed and cheating identified. There were also important implications for multinational corporations. The argument suggested that the commitment to social democracy on the part of developed market states, as in the European Union, was likely to generate costs which they could not avoid. Costs and benefits could be manipulated so that they preferred to stay within rather than to exit from the Union. The idea that capital would inevitably flee from welfare provision, as was claimed by neo-liberals, was challenged.

The movement of investment funds

The movement of investment funds was thought to be the primary reason for the decline of the euro against the dollar in 2000. The explanation for this, commentators alleged, was that investment managers judged that the US economy would grow faster than that of Europe because the latter was over-regulated and the level of government spending on welfare was excessive. Frequently the main reason for this excessive spending was said to be the high level of pensions brought about by the population structure – too many old people – and too few tax-payers, who were being called upon to shoulder an increasing burden of taxation (discussed below). Business was also said to be subject to too many rules and regulations concerning a wide range of matters from environmental to health and safety standards. The solution, therefore, was to cut back on pension provision, to stop being what was described as 'tax and spend' economies, to reduce the level of taxation and to deregulate the economies. This was essentially a neo-liberal logic and it often clothed arguments about social welfare with a prejudicial terminology. Higher levels of taxation were described as 'tax and spend', employment protection was seen as 'excessive regulation', and the reduction of pension payments, and welfare payments generally, was seen as 'reform'. Welfare provision was also often categorized by neo-liberal moral crusaders as an instrument for the creation of a dependency sub-culture of work-shy frauds.[27] Bonoli et al. demolish this argument, and make it look like the shallow dogma it is, simply by referring to the current research. The remedy was for the guilty governments to stop these unhappy practices, and thereby persuade investors to move their money back into Europe.

In September 2000 the economic advisor to the International Monetary Fund, Michael Mussa, recommended an international rescue operation for the euro by collective intervention in the money market. The IMF Director supported this on the following day. The point had come, he alleged, at which the weakness of the euro was in danger of becoming a threat to the stability of the international economy. In the following days the central banks of the main global economies did in fact intervene in the market to buy euros in an attempt to halt the currency's decline against the dollar, and at the time of writing there is evidence to suggest that this has achieved some short-term success. But according to many commentators the pressures to reform the 'bad' economies was now overwhelming.[28]

In the view of the present writer the neo-liberal explanation of the weakness of the euro in 2000 was relevant but insufficient. The major cause was almost certainly to do with a mismatch of the business cycles in the United States and Europe, and abandoning social democracy could only have a modest short-term positive impact on this underlying difficulty. A key aspect of this was the timing of reductions in budgetary deficits. The US had entered the recession of the early 1990s with a low deficit, which permitted more expansionist policies, while the Europeans had a higher level of deficit which they were then required to reduce according to the convergence criteria applicable to monetary union. They therefore had to follow tighter monetary and fiscal policies through the 1990s.[29] As Sarah Hogg put it 'the Euro's launch coincided not merely with cyclical strength in the US economy but with serious re-rating of its economic potential. Euroland actually managed a quite respectable 3.8% growth over the past year (to mid summer 2000) but the supposedly exhausted US economy managed a stunning 6%'.[30] But it was hardly surprising that funds were sucked in from Europe when US interest rates were almost twice those in Europe (on

21 September at 9.5 per cent (Prime) and 5.5 per cent (ECB O/N Marginal, respectively), and when US companies were growing much faster, in part because of the self-fulfilling prophecy generated by the inflow of capital. Arguably the introduction of the euro should have been timed to coincide with the business cycles, not only of the members, but also of the main rival economies, but that would have been impossible and was excluded from the discussion. The managers of funds were also bound to be rather cautious with regard to the new multinational currency – this was an arrangement which had never been tried before – and the dice were therefore loaded in favour of US investment from the outset.

If these factors – the business cycle and the fear of the unknown – were important and arguably dominant, the abandonment of the marks of a civilized society, a well-founded welfare system, for dubious short-term benefit would seem a price not worth paying. Indeed the price only seemed right in the context of an ideology which made social as well as economic claims, namely, neo-liberalism. This is not to say that intervention in the money markets, as recommended by the IMF, could not be helpful, but only if such intervention was timed to coincide with a turning in the tide of the business cycle. By late 2000 the assumption that the US economy had discovered the secret of eternal youth, in defiance of all the arguments about the inevitability of a downwards turn in the business cycle, was looking increasingly suspect. There were warnings of the falling away of profit margins, and the selling of industrial shares in the US stock markets.[31] Both the Dow Jones and NASDAQ had entered a period of decline. The US trade deficit was also causing concern as it soared to a new peak of $389 billion in July 2000.

IMF action could nudge in the right direction and give positive psychological signals, but without the crucial background of a change in views about the future of the US economy this would achieve nothing but the depletion of central bank reserves. The question was whether this point had been reached; at the time of writing this question cannot be answered. But the point emerged very strongly that the lack of harmony in the business cycles of the US and European economies at the launch of the euro was a crucial variable in explaining the euro's subsequent difficulties, and it was probably the most important one. In retrospect it was highly likely that funds would be drawn to the US, and that this would set in train a self-fulfilling prophecy of euro decline and dollar ascendancy. But this was caused more by judgements about the US economy than about the failures of the core social democratic states of Euroland.

It was also likely that the rules of the structure of the international economic system would prevail. Given the mismatch of the business cycles the correction of this situation would have to wait until there was a downturn in the US economy. But a further point lies behind these observations. The difficulties of the euro may have been an indication that there is a major structural problem in the international monetary system in the early years of the twenty-first century, that has arisen from the reduction of the number of players in the system and the absence of any dominant player. In the new system there are at most three main players – the dollar, the yen and the euro – and, in a world of floating exchange rates, no fixed yardstick of monetary value. In this situation the chances of an uncontrolled oscillation in the value of currencies was a real possibility. The money was likely to flow one way or another, and was likely to flow in great volume and at great speed. It was hard to see what stabilizing measures could prove effective, given the nature of the system and the way it tended to amplify the problem as manifest in the volume and speed of movement.[32]

In this situation the question could be put as to whether the move to the euro had itself created a context in which it would be hard for it to defend itself. Unless deliberate measures were taken, the danger was that business cycles in different economic areas would become increasingly disharmonious, as the movement of funds to the better-performing economy would act as an amplifier of its success. The problem of the euro was revealed as an aspect of a major structural problem in the international monetary system, and an increased tendency to disequilibrium, rather than of any modest overspending by European governments.

The further point could also be made that the neo-liberal argument could be reversed: if social democracy was the cause of Europe's failure then Europeans had the right to argue that the US should have more of it. The fact was that globalization also meant that Europeans had an interest in the proper resourcing of the US welfare system. The development of an increasing cosmopolitanism, in which there was a mutual responsibility for maintaining standards, meant they had the right to say so. Why should they accept the demolition of their social democracy as a consequence of low social standards and cheap energy in the US? In the US in 2000, 44 million people had no medical insurance and therefore had inadequate medical support.[33] Similarly much of US labour had little or no unemployment protection. This was no doubt a plus for American capital in the short term, but it amounted to a penalty for European business. In September 2000, a time of fuel strikes in a number of European states as a result of high levels of energy taxation, it also became clear that everyone was paying a price for the low cost of US energy: in effect Europeans were paying for a global energy strategy on behalf of the Americans.[34]

The conclusion had to be that in 2000 the US was the happy beneficiary of a neo-liberal orthodoxy which made it appear that maintaining civilized welfare standards was suspect, and that low standards were beneficial. The economic playing field could, however, be made level by equalizing upwards as well as downwards. There was a strong argument for doing this if this meant a more effective reconciliation of the principles of a civilized society and the long-term needs of industry.

Policy response to pension costs

Excessive pension payments to the elderly in social democracies were often a central concern of those seeking reform of welfare systems. As pointed out above, the problem arose, it was alleged, because of long-term changes in the age structure of populations: the number of elderly pensioners was increasing and the number of tax-payers, the main providers of funding, was declining. This was a problem in most of the developed world, and affected both the social democratic states and the USA. In the US it has been calculated that, if payments continue at the present level, current surpluses in the Social Security Fund would have to be tapped after 2015 and they would be exhausted by 2037. There would then only be two workers to support each beneficiary, as opposed to 3.4 in 2000.[35] The question of the future financing of the fund was brought up in the 2000 presidential election with the Republican and Democratic candidates both accepting the need for an increased role for the private sector. Their main difference was that the Democrat wanted to maintain matching federal government funding. In Germany the issue was also a particularly important one because of the generous level of pension provision and, as mentioned, reducing this expenditure was regularly identified by neo-liberals as the main plank of the required 'reform' of the German welfare system. The fact that Germany and the US had the same problem would, however, cast doubts on the view that in the former it was a special problem.

The privatization of pension provision was the preferred policy option in the discussion. There was little reference to alternatives, though privatization was itself not without serious problems in the way of implementation and operation. Not least was the question of social justice, and the implication that the obligation of the state to its citizens, after a lifetime of work, could be evaded. The irritation was fuelled in Britain by the allegation that the government had on a number of occasions, after the introduction of the National Insurance system, taken money out of funds hypothecated for pensions, in order to boost the short-term tax take; they promised that provision would be made up as required out of future general taxation, but then faced the awkward problem that the money they had promised was not available. The future problem was in part a consequence of past government risk-taking.

There were however other options. The obvious course was to focus on the root problem: would it be possible to increase the supply of workers and through that hold the necessary ratio of worker to pensioner? One way of doing this would involve having more flexible retirement arrangements, with those who wished to continue in work being allowed, indeed encouraged, to do so, and thus increase the worker stock. This policy proposal looked more sensible when the need, discussed above, to have a high level of worker training to produce a more flexible workforce for the new industrial age was recalled.

Why throw away such investment in labour by encouraging, even insisting on, early retirement?

The British authority on pensions, Frank Field, argued that many retirees had sufficient savings and entitlements to finance the early years of retirement themselves and only required full pension provision when these resources began to run out, which in Britain was at around 70 years old.[36] Given the increase in life expectancy it indeed seemed odd to stay with the expectation that retirement would normally take place at 65 or earlier, and that there should be a general guarantee of a pension at that date. Why not have a later date of retirement, and entitlement to a non-means tested pension, with those unable to work until then supported out of unemployment protection resources? Individuals who wished to retire earlier could do so, though the level of their pension would be lower.

One response could be that older workers had to give way to create jobs, and careers, for younger ones. But this then became a problem of the overall size of the economy, or of working hours, not of retirement: a larger economy and more civilised working hours – and years – would create the necessary number of tax-payers. In the Union there was, however, a need to standardize these arrangements and to accept a common, sensible retirement age. In some countries, such as Italy, the retirement age had been brought down to 55 in flat defiance of demographic trends. This could not be sustained. But the underlying problem was not as profound as neo-liberals claimed. The problem of the cost of pensions was in reality a problem of adjustment to the new realities of demography and/or of economic growth, rather than of an inherent economic impasse. The fact that there were more elderly need not be either a problem for particular countries or a general drag on economic development, And it was hard to see how the total charge to an economy could be reduced by moving its cost from the state to the private sector, assuming that the aim of reform was not to reduce the total level of pension provision.

Beneath the pro-privatization argument there was frequently another assumption which derived from neo-liberalism: that the private sector was necessarily more efficient than the public one. Anyone who has dealt with a large US health insurance company knows that this is not the case. But if the level of pension was to be maintained, payment would have to be made from the national product at the same rate, be it out of the wages of those in employment, company taxation or general taxation. Private provision would not be without public costs since a greater degree of reliance on the individual's private pension plans would also have the effect of driving wage and salary bills upwards, which in turn would create inflationary pressures. It might of course be politically easier for governments to do this as the cost would only appear in the medium and long term. But any form of provision had to be paid for, and any level of welfare could be supported by the individual if salaries were high enough.

CONCLUDING REMARKS

By the first year of the new Millennium there was the real prospect of a change
of tactics by the more ambitious states in the European Union. The problem
was that the old dynamics were likely to be less successful in a European Union
which was in prospect of being increased to 25 or 30 members, including most
of eastern Central Europe as well as Turkey and island states such as Malta and
Cyprus. This prospect of enlargement made it seem much less likely that the
integration process could continue in its present form as the new states were
simply so diverse and numerous. The stark alternatives as perceived by
increasing numbers of social democrats were either succumbing to the pressures
of globalization – which were driven by the ideology of neo-liberalism and a
partially concealed agenda for protecting American hegemony – or of pursuing
policies of relative enclosure.

There was in consequence a slow realization by the Germans, French and
Italians – the lead Continental core states – that they may have to work out a
new strategy, to which they would not need the agreement, however reluctantly
given, of the British. Hitherto, they could believe in keeping the convoy together
because the British, Danes and Greeks could be pushed to keep up in spite of
themselves. There were no specific problems of a technical, policy-related kind
in the way of this. The difficulty was more to do with will. But in the new
Europe there were real technical problems in keeping the convoy together, so
it was tempting to find a strategy which allowed them to opt out, for real reasons,
and those which simply lacked the will could be left with them. The route of
flexibility was one way in which they could achieve this, but at the time of
writing that concept is still highly contested and the sceptics are unlikely to
accept a more advanced core.[37]

This chapter has also argued, however, that the core states could also protect
their social democracy against the forces of globalization in the European Union.
They could compete against the lower-cost states within, though there are
optimal taxation and tariff strategies. There is no evidence to suggest that the
problem with the euro was to do with the costs of social democracy, though
adaptation was necessary, as the primary cause appeared to be the mismatch of
the business cycles in the US and in Europe. There was evidence to suggest
that the total level of company taxation played a role in company decisions to
invest, but even countries with lower levels of overall taxation had net outflows
of investment funding, and countries with high levels of overall taxation had
significant net inflows. The main indicators of high levels of welfare spending
had little correlation with low levels of direct investment funding. There was
no reason on grounds of competition for investment for social democracies to
adopt low social wage strategies, though they would be well advised to adopt
policies which combined civilized employment strategies with training for flex-

ibility in the workplace. All this added up to support, in circumstances and in logic, for the core states adopting more advanced integration in the EU without abandoning their social democracy. That they would seek higher levels of integration, regardless of the wishes of the British and the other cautious states, seemed highly likely. But it was also probable that they would link this with the defence of their social democracy, thereby acting as a pole of attraction for the more hesitant states, and confounding the neo-liberal forces of globalization. Such a strategy for the core states would not only push integration forward, but would put pressure on the reluctant states, including the Anglo-Americans, to maintain the necessary level of welfare spending.

One key element of the new strategy had been contemplated before, and used as a threat to keep Britain in line. That was to proceed by negotiating a new treaty between the more ambitious states, rather than seeking amendments of the Treaty of Rome. The reluctant states could not veto such a treaty, precisely because it was negotiated according to the principles of international law, between sovereign states. The amendment process of the Treaty of Rome allowed a veto by a dissenting state, which could now be avoided.

The British are approaching a period of historic choice if the third scenario is realized. The problems of their hesitations would become increasingly apparent. Now they would either have to place themselves fully with the ambitious states, or resign themselves to a period of continuing and possibly accelerating decline in a semi-detached relationship with Europe. It remains to be seen what the response of New Labour in Britain to this would be. For all the optimism of the early period of New Labour there was a gradual sinking into an apparent Euro-pessimism. It was not until the time of writing in late November 2000 that the first signs of a more proactive pro-European policy have begun to emerge. Prime Minister Blair vigorously attacked the anti-Europeans for their dishonesty and publicly rebuked Mrs Thatcher. He seemed to have decided that the anti-Europeans now had to be tackled head on. The alternative was marginalization and decline.

What of the future of the European Union in the Atlantic and global context? This has to be a matter of judgement. The two major variables in the equation in 2000 were the future of the US economy and of the euro. On both those counts the advantage seemed to be marginally with the European Union. The rules of business cycles suggested that the growth in the US economy would slow down sooner rather than later. In 2000 there were already indications of increasing difficulties with the US stock market, and this was happening even in the so-called high-tech stocks. At the same time the US negative balance of trade was becoming a greater problem. The relatively greater propensity of the US public to invest in the stock market, as compared with Europe,[38] would suggest that this would lead to a falling away of consumer demand and a move into recession. For the European Union, however, the position was on balance more positive. The question was whether sufficient adjustments in the structure of the European economy could be made to support a period of economic take-off, but there was an increasing determination to tackle these problems.

The Europeans were continuing to increase their proportion of trade between themselves. Trade with the rest of the world had declined steadily since the 1960s: they were becoming more interdependent, and less dependent on external markets for economic growth.[39] At the same time the arrangements for managing the euro were steadily improving, and in any case there were advantages as well as costs in the decline in its value.[40] In 2000 the jury is still out among economists about whether its fall was a problem for Europe. The case pressed by the IMF and the US authorities was that it was a problem for the international system – this did not mean a balance of short-term costs for the Union. Europe was becoming less vulnerable, though not insensitive, to turbulence in the international monetary and trading systems. The one exception to this was the supply of oil.

Somewhat surprisingly, therefore, the social democratic states of Europe could find that the cards they hold become stronger in the future and that their apparent vulnerability in the very early twenty-first century is a product of short-term adverse factors, rather than any underlying problem with the way they have dealt with the global economy. This does not mean, however, that they need not proactively pursue policies conducive to the development of a form of social democracy that is indeed capital-friendly. They have had to resist efforts and trends which diluted the core of the Union, both because if they failed, they could be obliterated by the social and economic forces of neo-liberalism, and because of the need to strengthen their institutional and policy coherence. In particular they have needed to develop a capacity to resist the aggressive stance which often characterized American policy.[41] This aggression and insouciance about the rest of the world is most likely to be countered by a swing of the economic and political pendulum towards Europe. This would bring two major advantages: it would protect social democracy in Europe – a key value in itself, and it would make the Americans more likely to contemplate stronger multilateral arrangements in building stronger monetary and trading global structures. But on the other hand, if the new Republican regime in the US became more quaintly isolationist it was important that Europe should be capable of taking charge of its own destiny.

But it was necessary to find appropriate compromises with the need for economic efficiency and the need to protect a civilized society. Trade was not for its own sake – it was for people. The EU's significance in the international political economy has been discussed in the economics literature mainly with reference to concerns about the effects of regionalism on world trade. Regional trade arrangements remove commerce between members from WTO disciplines, cause diverse combinations of trade diversion as well as creation, and alter the pattern of multilateral interactions. General trade liberalization, it is argued, would benefit all countries. If a group of states forms a large internal market, however, the economies of scale and scope for their firms, under a system of common governance, may enable them to achieve higher (although probably unequal) growth – higher than might have been possible if multilateral trade liberalization had been promoted mainly on terms favoured by the USA. In the absence of the EU, moreover, the acceleration of concentration trends in the world economy that is now visible would be dominated even more by US international firms, advantaged by strengths in their home market.

The EU can thus be seen to have enhanced the growth prospects of its members and established a degree of balance in the hierarchical pattern of structural interdependencies in the world economy. There have been inefficiencies, perpetuating a lag in structural competitiveness, but the costs of globalization have been less than they would have been otherwise, and the union's vulnerability to a financial crisis in the USA, due to its high level of speculative asset appreciation, is less than it would have been for the individual members if the Union had not been formed.

The EU's progress in deepening integration, despite current problems, has resulted in a capacity to assist the development of Third World regional integration systems. European aid and advice could support ventures in collectively self-reliant industrialization by such systems. If such systems are not formed, the pattern of structural interdependencies in the world economy will tend to become more hierarchical, and current international concentration trends will probably become more pronounced.

NOTES

1. For a critique of neo-liberalism see Robert Went (2000), *Globalization: Neoliberal Challenge, Radical Response*, London and Sterling, VA: Pluto Press and the International Institute for Research and Education.
2. Tsoukalis, Loukas (1997), *The New European Economy Revisited*, Oxford: Oxford University Press, 114–32, and see Dani Rodrik in Richard E. Baldwin, Daniel Cohen, Andre Sapir and Anthony Venables (eds) (1999), *Market Integration, Regionalism and the New Global Economy*, Cambridge: Cambridge University Press, Ch. 5.
3. See Rani Rodrik (1997), *Has Globalization Gone too Far?* Washington, DC: Institute for International Economics.
4. In 1999, according to OECD, unemployment in the UK stood at 6.3 per cent, while that in Germany stood at 9.3 per cent. But this gap ignored the fact that in the UK 23 per cent of jobs were part time, and previous Conservative governments had changed the statistical base to exclude all those workers who were not eligible for unemployment benefits, while in Germany the statistical base had not been 'massaged'.
5. Commission of the European Communities, *1999 Annual Economic Report: The EU Economy at the Arrival of the Euro: Promoting Growth, Employment and Stability*, Brussels, January, COM (1999) 7 final. For comparative material on the EU and the US see Kurt W. Rothschild, 'Europe and the USA: comparing what with what?' *Kyklos*, 53 (3), 2000, 249–64.

6. Beattie, A., 'The deflationary ogre smiles', *Financial Times*, 9 April 1999.
7. The argument here relies heavily on evidence in Bernard Casey and Michael Gould (2000), *Social Partnership and Economic Performance: The Case for Europe*, Cheltenham: Edward Elgar, pp. 15–21. See also *Cambridge Journal of Economics* 24 (6), November 2000, Special Issue on Social Justice and Economic Efficiency.
8. *The Times*, 14 May 2000.
9. British Prime Minister Tony Blair was moved to an energetic criticism of the way the British press reported European issues in November 2000.
10. See Paul Taylor (1992), *International Organization in the Modern World*, London: Pinter Publishers, especially Ch. 3.
11. *The Times*, 21 September 1988.
12. Ad Hoc Committee for Institutional Affairs, *Report to the European Council*, Brussels, 29–30 March 1985, SN/1187/85.
13. *Guardian*, 26 October 1989.
14. *Observer*, 10 December 1989.
15. Neunreither, Karlheinz and Antje Wiener (eds) (2000), *European Integration after Amsterdam: Institutional Dynamics and Prospects for Democracy*, Oxford: Oxford University Press, esp. chs by Alexander Stubb, Helen Wallace, Peter Leslie and Ulrich Sedelmeier.
16. Reported in the *Independent*, 5 October 2000.
17. For a good introductory account of EU institutions see Desmond Dinan (1999), *Ever Closer Union? An Introduction to the European Community*, London: Macmillan, rev. edn.
18. Grimwade, Nigel (1999), 'Developments in the economies of the EU', *Journal of Common Market Studies, Annual Review 1998/1999*, ed. Geoffrey Edwards and Georg Wiessala, Oxford: Blackwell Publishers, pp. 136–7.
19. A number of multinational manufacturers, such as Nissan and Toyota, did this in 2000.
20. *Independent*, 23 November 2000.
21. Taylor, Paul (1996), *The European Union in the 1990s*, Oxford: Oxford University Press.
22. See arguments of Sedelmeier in Neunreither and Wiener, op. cit., pp. 218–37.
23. *Financial Times*, 4 October 2000.
24. See the excellent critique of the neo-liberal assault on the welfare state in Giuliano Bonoli, Vic George and Peter Taylor-Gooby (2000), *European Welfare Futures: towards a Theory of Retrenchment*, Chapter 3, Polity Press.
25. The objections to enlargement are in *The European Union in the 1990s*, op. cit., ch. 3.
26. See Bonoli, George and Taylor-Gooby, op. cit., pp. 50–71.
27. A leading example is C. Murray (1984), *Losing Ground*, New York: Basic Books and *The Emerging British Underclass* (1990), London: Institute of Economic Affairs.
28. Hamish McRae, *Independent*, 21 September 2000.
29. Nigel Grimwade, op. cit., p. 138.
30. *The Independent*, 25 September 2000.
31. *The Independent*, 21 September 2000.
32. A picture of a global financial system that after the 1994 Mexican crisis, was increasingly out of control is effectively painted by Went, op. cit.
33. *Consumer Reports*, 65 (9), September 2000, 42–53.
34. A further illustration of US obduracy on fuel and linked environmental issues was their stance at the Environmental Conference at the Hague in December 2000. The European Union nego-tiators were united in resisting US arguments on tradeable environmental quotas and the setting up of alternative strategies to cutting fossil fuel consumption by using new afforestation.
35. *Consumer Reports*, October 2000, 65 (10), 62–4.
36. Interviewed, BBC News, 'The World at One', 28 September 2000.
37. See Julie Smith, 'Destination Unknown', *The World Today*, 56 (10), October 2000, 20–22.
38. Grimwade, op. cit.
39. Tsoukalis, op. cit., pp. 225–33.
40. Binin Smaghi, Lorenzo and Claudio Casini (2000), 'Monetary and Fiscal Cooperation in EMU, *Journal of Common market Studies*, 38 (3), September, 375–92, and articles in symposium on EMU in same.
41. Tsoukalis, op. cit., p. 234.

2.   Globalizing Europe: the overall picture

John H. Dunning

The purpose of this chapter is to document and explain a key aspect of the internationalization of the Western European economy in general, and those of individual European countries in particular, in the closing years of the twentieth century. That aspect is the extent, growth and pattern of the outward foreign direct investment (FDI) by European firms. We accept, of course, that FDI is only one measure of a firm's or country's cross-border economic involvement, but given the limited statistical data available, it is perhaps the best guide to the intensity or depth of that involvement.

In our discussion of this issue, we will make use of two statistical indices – at both a country (or regional) and a firm level. The first is a transnationality index (TNI). At a country or regional level, this index, TNI(c) or TNI(r), is defined as the proportion of the outbound FDI stock of firms from a particular country or region to that country's or region's domestic product (GDP); and the latter, as the (average) proportion of a firm's global assets, sales and employment accounted for by its foreign affiliates, TNI(f). The second index – the globalization index (GI) is defined as that part of TNI(c) or TNI(r), or of TNI(f), accounted for by the foreign activities of firms outside the countries or region in which their head offices are located. The difference between this index GI(c) or (r), TNI(c) or (r) and TNI(f) represents the (European) regionalization indices, R(c) and R(r), and R(f).

The chapter proceeds in the following way. First, it sets our analysis of the extent and form of the internationalization of European firms in a wider context, by briefly describing the overall trend towards the increased globalization of the world economy over the past 20 years. It then presents an encapsulated historical profile of the cross-border activities of European firms. The next section describes, and attempts to explain, the changes in the TNIs and GIs both for Western Europe, or the European Community (EU) as a whole,[1] and for individual European countries, during the 1990s; and also the sectoral composition of extra-European FDI. The following section then turns to examine one of critical components of outbound European FDI in the 1990s, namely cross-border mergers and acquisitions (M&As); and it does so in the light of attempts by European firms to improve their global competitiveness by accessing

additional strategic assets outside their national boundaries. A final section of
the chapter summarizes its main conclusions.

THE GLOBAL PICTURE

Globalization continues apace. In the closing years of the twentieth century,
all forms of cross-border economic transactions reached new heights; and none
more so than those recorded by the world's leading multinational enterprises
(MNEs). According to data published in October 2000 by UNCTAD,[2] in 1998
and 1999 annual outward foreign direct investment (FDI) flows rose 33.1 per
cent – a faster per annum rate of growth than that attained over the whole of the
previous decade. Some 72.2 per cent of this new investment was directed to
developed countries, compared with 63 per cent over the previous seven years.
     For some years now, FDI has been the fastest-expanding form of international
business activity. In 1999, for example, the sales of the foreign affiliates of the
world's MNEs were twice the value of the global exports of goods and non-
factor services. At the same time, more than one-half of these exports were
accounted for by the foreign affiliates of MNEs. Throughout the 1990s, the rate
of increase of production financed by FDI has consistently outpaced that of
cross border trade by a factor of three to four.
     However, perhaps the most dramatic growth of cross-border transactions in
recent years has been that of mergers and acquisitions (M&As). Since 1990, the
annual value of international M&A purchases has risen from $151 billion to
$720 billion in 1999, and in the first half of 2000, it was 80 per cent higher than
in the corresponding period of the previous year (UNCTAD, 2000). While the
great majority of these cross-border M&As were between developed countries,
the share of global purchases involving firms located in developing countries
has steadily risen from 10.4 per cent in the first half of the 1990s to 13.4 per
cent between 1996 and 1999.
     Though no direct comparison between FDI flows and cross-border M&As
can be made,[3] there is no question that in the case of many countries, the former
now account for the larger and increasing proportion of trans-border direct
capital flows. In 1998 and 1999, UNCTAD estimated the figure, on average,
to be between 75 per cent and 80 per cent; and in the case of some developing
countries, nearer 90 per cent. Together with non-equity cross-border strategic
alliances, which number several thousand each year, and the dramatic growth
of all forms of international communications, particularly the Internet, these
data are perhaps the best indication we have of the deepening integration of the
world economy – which is occurring both at a regional and global level.
     As a result of these trends, which predominantly reflect a series of dramatic
technological advancements, the liberalization of international markets and the

Table 2.1 Stock of outward foreign direct investment by home regions 1980–99 ($ billion)

	1980			1990			1995			1998			1999		
	Value	%	% of GDP	Value	%	% of GDP	Value	%	% of GDP	Value	%	% of GDP	Value	%	% of GDP
Developed regions of which:	506.2	96.8	6.4	1634.1	95.2	9.8	2601.1	90.8	11.7	3649.5	89.8	16.4	4277.0	89.9	18.5
Western Europe	234.7	44.9	6.5	866.5	50.5	12.2	1468.4	51.2	16.5	2135.3	52.5	24.3	2574.9	56.2	20.0
North America	244.0	46.6	8.2	515.4	30.0	8.4	817.1	28.5	10.7	1141.5	28.1	12.5	1309.8	27.5	
Other*	27.5	5.3	2.1	252.2	14.7	7.3	315.6	11.0	5.6	372.7	9.2	8.5	392.3	8.6	7.7
Developing regions of which:	16.3	3.1	0.9	81.9	4.8	2.6	258.3	9.0	4.9	403.9	4.9	6.7	468.7	9.8	7.6
Africa	1.0	0.2	0.4	12.2	0.7	4.5	14.5	0.5	5.4	16.3	0.4	4.8	17.0	0.4	4.6
Latin America and the Caribbean	9.0	1.7	1.3	20.4	1.2	1.9	48.2	1.7	2.4	77.4	1.9	3.3	104.6	2.2	5.3
Asia	6.3	1.2	0.7	48.9	2.8	2.8	194.2	6.8	6.1	308.4	7.6	9.0	345.2	7.3	9.2
Central and Eastern Europe	nsa	nsa	nsa	0.4	0.0	0.0	5.3	0.2	0.8	11.9	0.3	1.7	13.6	0.3	1.9
World	523.2	100.0	5.4	1716.4	100.0	8.6	2870.6	100.0	10.2	4065.8	100.0	14.1	4579.3	100.0	15.8

Note: *Including Japan.

Source: Derived from UNCTAD (2000).

Table 2.2 Stock of inward foreign direct investment by host regions 1980–99 ($ billion)

	1980 Value	%	% of GDP	1990 Value	%	% of GDP	1995 Value	%	% of GDP	1998 Value	%	% of GDP	1999 Value	%	% of GDP
Developed regions	374.0	75.4	4.7	1380.8	78.4	8.3	1967.5	71.7	8.8	2690.1	67.0	12.1	3230.8	67.7	14.0
of which:															
European Union	200.7	40.4	5.5	770.4	48.7	10.9	1127.3	41.1	12.7	1546.0	38.5	17.6	1757.2	36.8	20.0
North America	137.2	27.7	4.6	507.8	28.8	8.3	658.7	24.0	8.7	955.0	23.8	10.5	1253.6	26.3	13.4
Other	36.1	7.3	2.7	102.6	5.8	3.0	181.5	6.6	3.1	189.2	4.7	4.3	220.0	4.6	4.3
Developing regions	121.2	24.4	5.4	377.4	21.4	10.5	739.5	27.0	13.4	1241.0	30.9	20.0	1438.5	30.1	22.2
of which:															
Africa	19.2	3.9	6.0	20.9	1.2	12.4	30.8	1.1	19.9	35.3	0.9	21.1	38.2	0.8	23.8
Latin America and the Caribbean	44.1	8.9	5.7	118.3	6.7	10.5	204.9	7.5	11.9	404.6	10.1	19.5	485.6	10.8	23.3
Asia	56.6	11.4	4.9	211.6	12.0	10.2	462.0	16.8	13.6	741.3	18.5	20.2	846.7	17.7	22.2
Central and Eastern Europe	neg	neg	0.0	3.0	0.2	1.5	36.4	1.3	5.2	84.2	2.1	12.1	102.7	2.2	13.7
World	495.2	100.0	4.9	1761.2	100.0	8.6	2743.4	100.0	9.6	4015.3	100.0	13.7	4772.0	100.0	15.7

Note: neg = negligible.

Source: As for Table 2.1.

emergence of new global players, the degree to which both firms and countries are becoming locked into global economic networks is fast increasing. More firm specific data compiled by UNCTAD and Erasmus University reveal, in 1998, the extent of multinationality or transnationality of the 100 largest MNEs: their TNI(f) was 54.0 per cent; and that of the 51 largest European MNEs was 64.3 per cent. Hardly less impressive was the corresponding TNI(f) for the 50 largest MNEs from developing countries of 36.5 per cent. Yet even these figures underestimate the global spread of international production, as they exclude the activities of firms which arise as a result of a plethora of cross-border research and development, production and marketing inter-firm agreements which, if included in the TNI(f) of the leading MNEs, would increase it by upwards of 5 per cent.

Some of the relevant statistics on the growth and geography of FDI stocks are set out in Tables 2.1 and 2.2. Table 2.1 clearly shows that, over the 1990s, there has been some shift in the relative importance of the world's leading foreign direct investors. The US, while retaining its position as the leading source country of MNEs, has shed some of its earlier pre-eminence to the Western European economies, while the 1990s saw a dramatic fall in the relative significance of Japanese outbound FDI (from 10.7 per cent in 1990 to 6.7 per cent in 1999).[4]

The geographical distribution of inbound FDI also changed in the latter half of the 1990s. Table 2.2 sets out some details which reveal that there has been a gradual shift of MNE activity towards developing and transitional economies. Inward FDI grew especially rapidly in virtually all Asian economies, especially in China, prior to the financial crisis in 1996–97; and since then, in South Korea and Hong Kong. However, the most rapid growth of inbound FDI in 1998 and 1999 occurred in Latin America and the Caribbean countries.[5] This area accounted for 42.4 per cent of all new FDI in developing countries in these years, compared with 26.9 per cent between 1990 and 1997.

THE EUROPEAN DIMENSION

From the Perspective of European Countries

Europe has long since been the world's leading global investing and trading region. From the Middle Ages to the late eighteenth century, merchants from all parts of Europe, Italian banking houses, British and Dutch trading companies, and British, French, Portuguese and Spanish colonizing ventures spread their business activities across the then known globe. Sometimes, such as with the Hanseatic League in the fourteenth century, these activities chiefly took the form of cross-border trade and investment within Europe. In other cases, the search for precious metals, spices and other natural resources prompted the establishment and expansion of large trading and colonizing companies, whose territorial horizons extended to North America and Asia. Such enterprises, the forerunners of the modern global corporation, were frequently state sponsored and financed, and were geared towards the mercantalist ambitions of their home governments.

During these years, the metropolitan hub of international business fluctuated between Antwerp, Florence, Amsterdam and London, but by the end of the eighteenth century, London had established itself as the premier European commercial and financial city, while, of the great trading and colonizing companies of the earlier centuries only the British East India Company and the Hudson's Bay Company remained (Jones, 1996). However, notwithstanding the global reach of these companies, most European trade and investment continued to be intra-regional, and conducted by small or relatively small family enterprises. The strong movement towards extra-European transnationalization did not occur until the following century (Wilkens, 1986).

In the nineteenth century, the Industrial Revolution, which originated in Europe, spread outwards to embrace most of the then developed world. But for the greater part of this period and, indeed, right up to the First World War, Europe remained the world's leading producer and trader of manufactured goods, and its pre-eminent exporter of capital. However, of the European powers, only the UK began to emerge as a truly global player, with its extra-European trade and investment considerably exceeding that of its intra-European equivalent.

Reliable data on the outward FDI of most European countries have only recently become available. However, drawing on a variety of sources[6] it has been estimated that the outward FDI stake of European firms in 1914 accounted for 82 per cent of the world's FDI stake, then valued at $14.5 billion. An even more tentative assessment suggests that the average transnational index (TNI) of European countries (TNI(r)) was between 1 per cent and 2 per cent; with the TNC(c) for the UK being the highest at 2.5 per cent. At that same time, the globalization index (GI) worked out at around 40 per cent for Continental European countries, and 70 per cent for the UK.

The First World War and its aftermath saw a considerable retrenchment in European outbound FDI, while at the same time American MNEs, particularly in the newer industrial sectors, began to widen their territorial horizons. By 1938, Europe's share of the stock of global outward FDI had fallen to around two-thirds. However, the percentage of that stock accounted for by extra European FDI (that is, the GI(r)) had risen to around 90 per cent.

The Second World War saw a further curtailment of the outward FDI of European firms, but it was not long after hostilities ended that Europe began to resume its role as a major international direct investor. However, it had to share this responsibility with the US which until the early 1970s accounted for more than one-half of the world's stock of outward FDI. At the same time, because of the growing attractions of the US domestic market and the opportunities offered by European economic integration, the proportion of extra-European FDI began to shrink. By 1985, the average TNI of Western European countries (TNI(r)), had risen to 10.7 per cent (from about 6 per cent in 1967). However, notwithstanding this increase, the GI(r) of European firms fell from its pre-war peak of 90 per cent to 71.5 per cent in 1985. But the real trend towards European regionalization occurred later in the 1980s and early 1990s, with the removal of most intra-European non-tariff trade and investment barriers, as required by the European Internal Market programme. As a result, although the European TNI(r) rose to 12.2 per cent by 1990, the GI(r) fell to 38 per cent and to 20 per cent in 1992.[7] Since that date, and most noticeably since 1995, both the TNI(r) and the GI(r) have risen, the former to 24.3 per cent and the latter to 46.7 per cent by 1999.

Table 2.3   Outward FDI stock TNI(r) and GI(r) for EU (15) countries, 1984–99

	FDI stock (ECU billion)	TNI(r) %	GI(r) %	Developed countries %	Developing countries %	Central and Eastern Europe %
1984	21.5	n.a.	80.9	n.a.	n.a.	n.a.
1985	21.3	10.3	70.9	n.a.	n.a.	n.a.
1990	65.5	11.7	31.3	n.a.	n.a.	n.a.
1992	67.1	n.a.	26.6	16.2	7.2	3.2
1993	64.4	n.a.	37.6	24.2	8.4	5.0
1994	74.7	n.a.	32.7	16.0	12.9	3.8
1995	99.2	15.4	46.0	31.2	9.6	5.6
1996	110.4	17.9	43.4	23.2	15.2	5.0
1997	162.4	18.6	55.7	29.4	20.5	5.8
1998	325.9	22.9	60.9	45.7	12.3	2.9
1999	556.3	n.a.	46.9	35.1	9.4	2.2

Notes:
TNI(r) = EC stock as % of EC GDP.
GI(r) = Extra EC FDI stock as % of all EC FDI stock.
n.a. = not available.

Sources: UNCTAD (2000); EUROSTAT (2000).

Table 2.4   *TNI(c) and GI(c) for selected West European countries, 1990–98*

	1990 (%)				1995 (%)				1998 (%)			
	A	B	C	D	A	B	C	D	A	B[a]	C[a]	D[a]
France	9.2	33.6	75.3	25.3	12.0	39.1	56.7	43.4	15.9	46.3	58.6	38.0
Germany	9.2	40.0	78.5	20.5	11.1	38.0	65.7	25.4	17.3	43.1	72.3	17.2
Italy	5.2	31.6	38.9	61.1	10.0	28.7	40.8	56.7	14.1	30.9	35.3	63.2
Netherlands	38.4	47.7	68.3	31.6	45.4	43.5	65.1	32.6	68.9	47.1	64.6	30.6
Norway	9.4	25.0	80.8	19.2	15.4	25.7	64.6	34.2	22.6	22.8	70.6	24.4
Portugal	0.7	16.5	41.8	58.2	3.5	49.6	12.9	87.1	8.6	29.6	12.2	84.7[b]
Spain	3.2	38.0	34.6	64.8	6.3	59.2	19.4	80.0	12.5	66.0	13.5	85.7[b]
Sweden	21.5	39.4	71.1	28.8	31.6	29.4	46.9	53.1	41.3	32.0	69.7	24.0
Switzerland	28.9	50.1	56.5	43.5	46.3	50.1	62.1	35.4	69.1	53.2	56.2	41.1
UK	23.4	71.3	74.2	25.7	27.4	61.7	69.4	29.9	35.9	57.5	68.3	28.3

Key:
A = % of outward FDI stock to GDP (TNI(c)).
B = % of extra West European FDI stock to total West European FDI stock (GI(c)).
C = % of extra West European FDI stock directed to other developed countries.
D = % of extra West European FDI stock directed to developing countries.

Notes:
[a] Mostly 1997 figures apart from Spain, Portugal and the UK.
[b] In the case of Portugal and Spain FDI outflows for 1989–91 were used to calculate the 1990 figure, 1994–96 flows to calculate the 1995 figure and 1990–98 flows to calculate the 1998 figure.

Source: OECD (1999).

Table 2.3 sets out some further details. *Inter alia*, the data that show the very substantial increases in the share of EU (15) FDI directed to the US and Japan, and also a recovery of investment in some developing countries, most noticeably in the Latin American region, which between 1997 and 1999 attracted 65 per cent of all extra Triad FDI.[8] The corresponding percentage for the preceding five years was 43.8 per cent.

Table 2.4 presents the TNIs and GIs for each of the leading European countries. It shows the value of both indices to be highly country-specific. Thus in 1994, the TNI(c) was highest in the case of the UK, Spain, the Netherlands and Sweden, and the lowest in the case of Spain, Portugal and Italy. The GI(c) was most pronounced in the case of Spain, the UK and Switzerland, and least pronounced in the case of Norway, Italy, Sweden and Germany. Over the period 1970–97, the TNI(c) rose markedly in all European countries. The GI(c) however, only showed noticeable increases in the cases of France, Spain and Portugal; and it actually fell in five of the ten European countries, and substantially so in the US. The table also illustrates some convergence in both the TNI(c) and GI(c) of the countries identified.[9]

At this point, it may be instructive to compare the changing geographical pattern of European FDI with that of US and Japanese FDI. Taking the NAFTA countries to be part of the UK region, and ASEAN countries to be part of the Japanese region, we see that the GI(c) of US MNEs (taken as a whole) rose from 82 per cent in 1980 to 90 per cent in 1995, and then dropped to 87 per cent in 1998 (OECD). The corresponding share of US FDI located in Latin America in these same years rose from 14.2 per cent to 16.4 per cent and then to 17.4 per cent. No doubt the increased FDI propensity to invest in Latin America reflected the consequences of the NAFTA agreement, and the partial retrenchment of US FDI in East Asia. Over the same period, the Japanese GI(c) also rose from a (surprisingly high) figure of 75 per cent in 1989–91 to 89 per cent in the mid-1990s, and 88 per cent in 1996–8 (OECD 1999).

From the Perspective of European Firms

So much for region- and country-level data. What about those with respect to individual European MNEs? To what extent have they increased the transnationality of their activities over the last decade or more, and how far (if at all) have they widened the geography of these activities?

Table 2.5 sets out some details of the 51 largest European MNE's contained in the list of the 100 largest MNEs published by UNCTAD in October 2000. As indicated earlier the TNI at a firm level is the equivalent of the FDI propensity, that is, TNI(c) at a country level. In 1998, the average TNI(f) of European firms was 64.3 per cent compared with the average for US MNEs of 41.6 per cent and for Japanese MNEs of 38.7 per cent. The corresponding TNI(f)s for 1990 were 60.9 per cent, 38.5 per cent and 35.5 per cent.

Table 2.5   The leading European multinational enterprises and their transnationality (TNI(f)) and globalization (GI(f)) indices

Rankings in top MNEs)	Corporations	Country	Sector	Foreign Assets ($ billion)	TNI(f)	GI(f
3	Royal Dutch/Shell Group	Netherlands/UK	Petroleum	67.1	58.0	58.5
8	BP Amoco	UK	Petroleum	40.5	74.9	63.2
9	Daimler Chrysler	Germany	Autos	36.7	50.4	54.4
10	Nestlé SA	Switzerland	Food/Beverages	35.6	94.2	60.8
11	Volkswagen Group	Germany	Autos	n.a.	53.8	35.8
12	Unilever	Netherlands/UK	Food/Beverages	32.9	90.1	56.0
13	Suez Lyonnaise des Eaux	France	Diversified	n.a.	45.6	n.a.
15	ABB	Switzerland	Electrical Equipment	n.a.	89.1	40.9
17	Diageo PL	UK	Beverages	22.9	76.7	n.a.
19	Siemens AG	Germany	Electronics	n.a.	59.3	27.1
21	Renault SA	France	Autos	23.6	61.8	11.2
23	BMW AG	Germany	Chemicals	21.4	59.9	24.0
26	Bayer AG	Germany	Chemicals	21.4	62.8	40.0
27	Roche Holding SA	Switzerland	Pharmaceuticals	21.2	78.7	62.5[a]
28	Hoechst AG	Germany	Chemicals	21.2	71.6	42.7[a]
29	Elf Acquitaine	France	Petroleum	n.a.	51.6	29.6
30	Viag AG	Germany	Diversified	n.a.	55.3	19.0
31	Rhone-Poulenc SA	France	Pharmaceuticals	n.a.	69.1	42.0
32	Total fina SA	France	Petroleum	n.a.	69.0	42.3
33	Philips Electronics	Netherlands	Electronics	19.0	77.8	55.0
35	Cable and Wireless	UK	Telecommunications	17.7	67.5	70.2[a]
38	ENI Group	Italy	Petroleum	n.a.	34.1	13.9
40	BASF AG	Germany	Chemicals	n.a.	57.9	26.1
42	Alcatel	France	Electronics	16.7	59.1	20.5
43	Peugeot	France	Autos	15.9	44.2	5.1
50	Fiat Spa	Italy	Autos	14.2	32.1	20.6
52	Telefonica	Spain	Telecommunications	13.8	29.9	n.a.
53	Vivendi	France	Diversified/Utility	n.a.	31.5	8.0

54	Rio Tinto	UK	Mining	12.4	80.4	n.a.
60	Robert Bosch GmbH	Germany	Auto parts	n.a.	56.3	28.0
62	Holderbank Fianciere Glatus	Switzerland	Construction Materials	11.6	90.5	n.a.
63	Stora Enso Ows	Finland	Paper	11.5	72.8	n.a.
64	Michelin	France	Rubber Tyres	n.a.	76.0	n.a.
65	VEBA Group	Germany	Diversified	n.a.	28.2	16.7
66	RWE Group	Germany	Utility	10.8	22.1	9.3
67	Glaxo Wellcome	UK	Pharmaceuticals	10.8	75.5	n.a
69	British American Tobacco	UK	Food/tobacco	10.5	91.0	48.9[a]
71	Smith Kline Beecham	UK	Pharmaceuticals	10.4	82.3	59.4
72	Danone Groupe SA	France	Food/Beverages	10.3	64.6	30.1
73	Carrefour SA	France	Retailing	10.3	55.9	27.3
75	Compart Spa	Italy	Food	10.2	63.4	n.a.
77	Alzo Nobel NV	Netherlands	Chemicals	10.1	76.8	30.1[a]
79	Montedison Spa	Italy	Chemicals	n.a.	63.1	n.a.
80	Ericsson LM	Sweden	Electronics	9.6	60.4	29.1
82	Electrolux AB	Sweden	Electrical Equipment	n.a.	92.7	45.2
83	Volvo AB	Sweden	Autos	n.a.	57.4	32.8
84	Royal Ahold NV	Netherlands	Retailing	n.a.	62.9	65.0
86	L'Air Liquide Group	France	Chemicals	n.a.	77.0	n.a.
87	Mannesman AG	Germany	Telecommunciations	n.a.	44.4	n.a.
96	Imperial Chemical Industries	UK	Chemicals	7.2	60.2	52.8
98	SCA	Sweden	Paper	7.0	80.8	n.a.
	Average for all firms			7.0	64.3	37.0[b]

Notes:

Both TNI(f) and GI(f) are calculated as an average of three percentages (or of one or two of these if the three are not available) viz foreign assets to total assets, foreign sales to total sales, and foreign employment to total employment.

[a] 1997 data.

[b] Unweighted average.

n.a. = not available.

Source: Derived from UNCTAD (2000), van Tulder, van der Berghe and Miller (2000). I am also most grateful to Professor van Tulder and his colleagues at Erasmus University for providing me with data so that I could compile Column 7 of this table.

Table 2.6 shows that the TNI(f) varies considerably by European country of origin. It is highest in the case of Switzerland, the Netherlands and the UK, and lowest in the case of Spain and Italy. Data on individual MNEs show the highest TNI(f) in 1998 was recorded by Nestlé (94.2 per cent) followed by that of Electrolux AB (92.7 per cent), British American Tobacco (91 per cent) and Unilever (90.1 per cent). All but two of the top ten most transnational MNEs were of European origin.

Table 2.6   Average TNI(f) and GI(f) for leading MNEs from selected European countries, 1990 and 1998

	TNI(f)		GI(f)	% share of foreign assets of top 100 MNEs	
	1990	1998	1998	1990	1998
France	50.9	58.8	24.0	10.4	10.5
Germany	44.4	57.4	29.3	8.9	12.6
Italy	38.7	48.2	17.3	3.5	2.7
Netherlands	68.5	73.1	52.9[1]	8.9	7.2
Norway	58.1	–	–	0.4	–
Spain	–	29.9	n.a.	3.5	2.7
Sweden	71.7	72.8	35.7	–	1.9
Switzerland	84.3	88.1	54.7	7.5	5.1
UK	68.5	75.7	58.9	16.8	12.3
All West European countries	60.9	64.3	37.0	53.4	48.7
US	38.5	41.6	n.a.	31.5	32.9
Japan	35.5	38.7	n.a.	12.0	14.5
All countries	51.1	54.0	n.a.	100.0	100.0

Note: n.a. = not available.
1. Erasmus University (2001). Specially compiled data on GI(f).

Source: UNCTAD (2000), Erasmus University (2001) (specially compiled data on GI(f)).

What next of the globalization indices (CGI) of European firms? The final column of Table 2.5 gives some estimates of the GI(f) of some 38 European MNEs. The percentages are derived from information provided by Erasmus University[10] on the non-European sales, assets and employment of the MNEs. The GI(f) represents an average of these data, expressed as a percentage of the MNEs worldwide sales, assets and employment for 1998 (or occasionally 1997 where data for 1997 are unavailable).[11]

The table shows that around an (unweighted) average of 37 per cent, the GI(f) of European MNEs ranges from 8 per cent to 70.2 per cent. In 12 of the 38 firms, the GI(f) exceeded 50 per cent indicating that their cross-border activities were more globalized than regionalized, but in more than two-thirds of MNEs, the majority of their activities were intra-European, The GI(f) ratios seem to vary considerably both between the country of origin and industrial sector. The UK, Swiss and Dutch (or Anglo-Dutch) firms with GI(f)s of 58.9 per cent, 54.7 per cent and 52.9 per cent were the most globalized, and Italian and French firms with GI(f)s of 17.3 per cent and 24.0 per cent were the most regionalized. The pharmaceutical, and food, drink and tobacco MNEs recorded the highest GI(f)s (of 54.6 per cent and 49.0 per cent), while the auto companies, with a GI(f) of 26.8 per cent appeared to be the least globalized.

THE CHANGING MODE OF EUROPEAN GLOBALIZATION

As mentioned earlier in this chapter, M&As have become the most important modality of new FDI in the last two decades. This section explores this phenomenon and the reasons for it.

The contemporary cross-border M&A boom began in earnest in the mid-1980s. It lost pace in the early 1990s with the slow-down in world economic growth, but then gathered a new momentum for the rest of the decade. By 1999, cross-border M&A purchases had reached a new peak of $720 billion, and in that year were valued at 90 per cent of FDI flows and 2.5 per cent of the world's GDP. The corresponding figures for 1990 were $151 billion, 72 per cent and 0.8 per cent.

Western Europe was the source of 72.1 per cent of all global cross-border mergers in 1998–99 compared with 54.1 per cent of the world's outward FDI stock. The corresponding figures for 1990–91 were 58.4 per cent and 50.5 per cent. These data, then, suggest that over the 1990s, not only were European firms internationalizing their activities to a greater extent than their counterparts from most other countries (Japan and some less developed countries are exceptions); but that this expansion occurred mainly through M&As.

At the same time, as Table 2.7 shows, the vast majority of M&As take place among developed nations. In 1999, these countries accounted for 94.1 per cent of all cross-border purchases: the corresponding figure for Western European firms was 91.7 per cent. These percentages can be compared with their share of world outward FDI stock of 54.1 per cent, flows directed to developed countries of 73.5 per cent, and that of EC (15) countries so directed of 84.8 per cent (EUROSTAT 2000).

Table 2.7   Cross-border M&A purchases by firms from EU (15) countries, 1987–99

	1 World $ billion	2 Intra-Europe %	3 Other developed countries %	4 Developing countries %	5 Central and Eastern Europe %	6 Extra-Europe (total)*%
1987	32.6	24.7	74.1	1.2	neg.	75.3
1988	40.1	34.2	63.1	2.7	neg.	65.8
1989	71.4	41.0	55.5	3.5	neg.	59.0
1990	86.5	52.0	37.0	11.2	neg.	48.0
1991	39.7	53.1	40.8	4.2	1.9	46.9
1992	44.4	71.6	19.8	3.6	5.0	28.4
1993	40.5	63.3	30.8	4.4	1.5	36.7
1994	83.9	60.6	32.7	5.6	1.1	39.4
1995	81.4	45.1	43.9	5.0	6.0	54.9
1996	96.7	33.4	55.5	9.5	1.6	66.6
1997	142.1	54.0	33.0	11.0	2.0	46.0
1998	284.4	32.1	55.4	11.2	1.3	67.9
1999	497.7	51.2	40.6	6.4	1.8	48.8

Note: *To GI(r) in respect of M&A purchases.

Source: Data provided by Thomson Financial Securities Company, and UNCTAD (2000).

The situation with respect to developing countries, and the Latin America region in particular, is very different. In 1999, the ratio between the foreign purchases of developing country firms and inflows of FDI into developing countries was 0.32 per cent, compared with 0.18 per cent in 1989. The corresponding figures for Latin America as a host were 0.41 per cent and 0.26 per cent. In the case of EU investors, the figures suggest that between 1992[12] and 1999 the value of M&A purchases both of developing country and Latin American firms rose three times faster than that of European FDI in those countries.

The reasons for the increase in cross-border M&As are well known.[13] They are, firstly, the imperatives of technological development, and the ever-increasing costs of innovatory activities, which have compelled firms to more fully exploit the economies of scope and scale, and of product and process innovation. Increasingly, firms now invest overseas to augment their global resources and capabilities, and one of the speediest ways to do this is by M&As. Secondly, M&As have been facilitated by the liberalization of markets, by the privatization of large state-owned enterprises, the removal or reduction of restrictions on inbound FDI, and on the acquisition of domestic firms by foreign MNEs.

These twin forces have increased inter-firm competition to such an extent that it is only by pursuing a strategy of inter-firm alliances and M&As that many firms can (or perceive that they can) adequately meet the challenges of the global economy. Understandably, since the greater part of technological innovation in the 1990s has been centred in the industrialized nations,[14] most of the asset-acquiring M&As have taken place within the Triad. At the same time, the renaissance of the market economy and privatization of many state-owned sectors in developing countries has induced a wave of acquisitions as a means of exploiting a home-based competitive advantage and of entering relatively unfamiliar markets.

Table 2.8   Value of cross-border M&As of privatized firms by country of sale, 1987–99

Country	$ billion	% of total	% of all M&A sales
Developed countries	89.1	40.2	3.6
of which:			
Australia	24.3	10.9	25.6
Germany	9.0	4.1	7.5
Belgium	8.3	3.7	16.0
Sweden	8.3	3.7	7.7
France	5.9	2.7	4.5
UK	4.5	2.0	1.0
Developing countries	104.7	47.2	31.9
Latin America	84.1	37.9	40.0
of which:			
Brazil	31.9	14.4	52.0
Argentina	26.4	11.9	52.1
Venezuela	5.4	2.4	58.7
Peru	5.1	2.3	70.8
Mexico	4.6	2.1	22.5
Others	20.6	9.3	17.4
Central and	27.9	12.5	78.5
Eastern Europe			
of which:			
Poland	8.3	3.7	81.7
Kazakhstan	4.6	2.1	76.7
Hungary	4.3	1.9	66.2
Total	221.7	100.0	7.8

Source: Derived from UNCTAD (2000), Table A.IV.21, p. 262.

The large expansion of M&A purchases by developed country firms, in the 1990s, particularly in Central and Eastern Europe and Latin America, was essentially to acquire the assets of indigenous state-owned firms at competitive (or

Table 2.9 Top privatization deals of $1 billion or more involving European firms as acquirers, 1992–99

Rank	Privatized firm	Year	Value of Acquisition $ billion	Country	Acquiring firm	Acquiring country
1	YPF SA	1999	13.2	Argentina	Repsol SA	Spain
2	TELESP (Telebras)	1998	5.0	Brazil	Investor Group	Spain
3	Telesp Celular Participacoes	1998	3.1	Brazil	Investor Group	Portugal
4	Nobel Industries Sweden AB	1994	3.0	Sweden	Akzo NV	Netherlands
5	Telekom Austria	1998	2.4	Austria	Telecom Italia SpA	Italy
6	Entel Peru SA, Cia Peruana	1994	2.0	Peru	Investor Group	Spain
7	YDF SA	1999	2.0	Argentina	Repsol SA	Spain
8	Telecentro Sul (Telebras)	1998	1.8	Brazil	Investor Group	Italy
9	Cia de Electricade do E Stado	1997	1.6	Brazil	Investor Group	Spain
10	SPT Telecom	1995	1.5	Czech Republic	Telsource consortium	Netherlands and Switzerland
11	Condensa	1997	1.2	Columbia	Investor Group	Spain
12	Telesudente (Telebras)	1998	1.2	Brazil	Investor Group	Spain
13	Santa Fe Exploration	1996	1.2	UK	Saga Petroleum AS	Norway
14	Retevision	1997	1.2	Spain	Investor Group	Italy
15	FSM	1992	1.1	Poland	Fiat Auto SpA	Italy
16	Ceskoslovenska Obehodni Banka	1999	1.1	Czech Republic	KBC Bancassurance Holding NV	Belgium
17	Bank Polskakasa Opieki SA	1999	1.1	Poland	Investor Group	Italy
18	ASLK–CGER Insurance	1993	1.1	Belgium	Fortis International NV	Netherlands
19	Cellulose du Pin – Paper and Pkg	1994	1.0	France	Jefferson Smurfit Group PLC	Ireland
20	Cia Riograndense de Telecom	1998	1.0	Brazil	Investor Group	Spain

Source: Derived from UNCTAD (2000), Table IV.8, p. 134.

below competitive) prices. In the main, these purchases have been concentrated in capital-intensive manufacturing, information-intensive service, and in infra-structural sectors such as telecommunications, utilities and energy. However, the recent wave of acquisitions of already privately owned firms in the Republic of Korea[15] was prompted, firstly by the need of these firms to obtain finance and knowledge capital to reconfigure their organizational structures, and upgrade their technological capabilities, so they could better meet the needs of the global market place; and secondly by the desire and the ability of foreign investors to take advantage of the low price of assets, which itself was a reflection of the financial crisis and economic vicissitudes of the mid-1990s.

What now of privatization schemes? Table 2.8 reveals that, overall, only 7.8 per cent of all cross-border M&A purchases were targeted towards state-owned enterprises. However, in Central and Eastern Europe and some developing countries, such schemes wore responsible for the majority of the purchase of domestic assets by foreign firms. The Latin American region, in fact, accounted for 37.9 per cent of all privatizing M&As, and 80.2 per cent of those in developing countries. Over the period 1987–89, Brazil and Argentina alone attracted 69.4 per cent of all foreign purchases of Latin American state-owned enterprises.

What of the European share of these privatization schemes? Table 2.9 identifies 21 cross-border acquisitions, worth $1 billion or more, of state-owned firms by European MNEs between 1992 and 1999. These amounted to $46.8 billion or 44.5 per cent value of all privatization deals valued at $1 billion or more. Of 21 purchases, ten, worth $17.7 billion, were intra-European and the balance, valued at $29.1 billion, were extra- European. Thus, the GI(f) of privatization-related M&As for European firms worked out at 62.2 per cent, a considerably higher figure than the GI(f) of the 38 European MNEs identified in Table 2.5, and of all cross-border M&As set out in Table 2.7.

CONCLUSIONS

This chapter has shown that, although European countries and firms have above average TNIs – and these have continued to increase over the last decade – the greater part of their FDI-related activities continues to be within Europe.

However, at a region and country level, the data suggests that the GI(r) and GI(c) peaked in the early 1990s; and in the latter half of the decade European firms were investing more outside their home regions than within it.

Both the TNI and GIs are country and industry specific. MNEs from the UK and the smaller European countries generally record higher than average TNIs and GIs, and those from the larger continental European countries lower than average TNIs and GIs. At the same time, it is firms from these latter countries, for example Prance, Germany and Italy, which have increased their TNIs the most during the 1990s.

NOTES

1. Which of these geographical coverages of Europe is chosen largely depends on the statistical data available.
2. *World Investment Report, 2000: Cross-border Mergers and Acquisitions and Development*, New York and Geneva: UN.
3. This is primarily because M&As may be financed by means other than by FDI.
4. In fact, most of this fall occurred between 1990 and 1996.
5. Most noticeably that of Argentina, Brazil, Chile, Colombia, Mexico, Peru and Venezuela which increased their share of the world's stock of inward FDI from 8.5 per cent in 1997 to 12.8 per cent in 1999.
6. These are summarized in Dunning (1993) and Jones (1996).
7. Since 1992, data on the GI(r) of European firms refers to those from the 15 member countries who are currently members of the EU.
8. The Triad is made up of the EU, the US and Japan.
9. Thus the standard deviation (SD) of TNI(c) in 1990 was around an arithmetic mean (AM) of 14.9, and in 1998 it was 18.2 (around an AM of 30.6). The corresponding SDs and AMs for GI(c) were 14.3 (39.3) and 13.0 (42.9).
10. I am especially indebted to Professor Rob van Tulder and his colleagues for providing me with these data. The Scope Project of the Faculty of Business Studies at Erasmus University, Rotterdam is a major investigation into the internationalization strategies of the world's largest enterprises (for further details see van Tulder, van den Berghe and Muller (2001).
11. Sometimes only one of the three percentages ware available; sometimes only two; but In 17 cases, these were available.
12. Data before this date are not available.
13. These are set out in detail in UNCTAD (2000)
14. Where, according to OECD data, more than 90 per cent of the world's R&D is undertaken.
15. Over four-fifths of new FDI in Korea in 1998 and 1999 took the form of M&As (UN 2000).

REFERENCES

Caves, R. (1996), *Multinational Enterprises and Economic Analysis*, Cambridge: Cambridge University Press.

Dunning, J.H. (1993), *Multinational Enterprises and the Global Economy*, Wokingham, UK: Addison Wesley.

Eurostat (2000), *European Union Direct Investment Analytical Aspect*, 1998/9, Brussels: European Commission.

Jones, G. (1996), *The Evolution of International Business*, London and New York: Routledge.

OECD (1999), *International and Direct Investment Statistics Year Book, 1999*, Paris: OECD.

UNCTAD (2000), *World Investment Report: Cross-Border Mergers and Acquisitions and Development*, New York and Geneva: UN.

van Tulder, R., D. van den Berghe and A. Muller (2001), *Erasmus S(Coreboard) of CoreCompanies: The World's 200 Largest Firms and Internationalization*, Rotterdam: Rotterdam School of Management/Erasmus University.

Wilkins, M. (1986), 'The history of European multinationals: a new look', *Journal of European Economic History*, 15 (3), 483–510.

3. Specialization matters, and so does technological accumulation: the case of Europe

Pier Carlo Padoan[*]

The EU has launched a new strategy (eEurope) to exploit the benefits of Information and Communications technology so as to spur its rate of growth and increase employment prospects. The stimulus is the exceptional performance of the US economy during the 1990s in terms of employment and growth.

This is not new. In the mid-1980s a fashionable term was 'Eurosclerosis' to describe more or less the same problem, that of a Europe lagging behind a dynamic US economy pushed up by what was then known as 'Reganomics'. The EU response strategy materialized in what then became 'Europe 1992', the Single Market. The underlying idea was simple: to exploit the benefits, in terms of higher efficiency and scale economies, of deeper integration. Microeconomic reforms would lead to better macroeconomic results: higher growth and employment.

The launching of the Single Market project in 1985 coincided with a period in which economic theory was exploring the notion of endogenous growth, according to which, once a stimulus is given to an economy output will keep on growing rather than eventually settle down to a stationary state level, as traditional growth theory would predict. The engine for endogenous growth lies on the exploitation of externalities in the market. Such externalities may derive from several sources, one of which is expanding market size. As one firm invests to increase its capital stock and hence production, the size of the market increases, thus stimulating further investment. In a nutshell, this is the logic of endogenous growth applied to the Single Market initiative.

Another source of externalities is accumulation of knowledge, both in terms of R&D investment and/or in terms of human capital accumulation. To the extent that knowledge is transferable (it is, at least partially, a public good) an innovation introduced by one firm increases the aggregate stock of knowledge for the whole economy and hence the aggregate boost to growth. A similar point can be made about human capital, assuming that this too increases the aggregate growth potential. Again in a nutshell, this would be the endogenous growth implication of having an EU-wide 'innovation space'.

The two effects are, at least to some extent, cumulative. A fully completed Single Market and a truly integrated EU-wide innovation space would permanently increase the rate of growth of the Union. The gap with the US would finally be closed (to say the least).

Aggregate endogenous growth theory is a useful benchmark. It gives a rough idea of what could be obtained when the Single Market will be fully completed and if an EU innovation space is in place, supporting a vigorous effort in innovation and human capital accumulation. To measure the distance between the benchmark and reality a number of steps backward must be made, however. One of which is recognizing that innovation activities and their effects on economic performance are, to a large extent, still a national affair and for two main reasons: differences in specialization and differences in national systems of innovation.

National systems of innovation are based on the institutional networks linking the private sector, public bodies and research institutions in ways that strongly reflect the historical evolution of national strategies. They shape the efficiency of technological processes, their modification and their contribution to growth. While there is no obvious 'optimal design' for national systems of innovation, some national experiences are clearly better than others in terms of innovation success and economic performance. The key policy issue in this respect is how to move from a set, or even a network, of national innovation systems towards an EU-level innovation system.

The role of specialization structures can be described as follows. Specialization matters for the purpose of producing innovations and translating them in factors of economic performance. An economy that is specialized, say, in traditional products, will exhibit a much lower propensity to innovate and to apply innovation to production processes than an economy specialized in electronics. This has implications for the growth potential of the economy if we believe that knowledge accumulation is the main source of growth. In the above case, when hit by the same technology shock, the second economy will grow faster than the first one. In addition, the growth gap will probably widen given the cumulative nature of knowledge accumulation.

If we take into consideration national differences, then the overall impact of a technology shock – such as ICT – on the EU economy may well be both lower and unevenly distributed as not all national systems will be able to exploit in full the benefits of innovation. In other words, we cannot retain the assumption of aggregate growth theory that all countries share the same technology and the same factor endowment.

In theory this problem could be solved to the extent that knowledge diffusion is complete; that is, if innovation is produced (or rather introduced) in the more advanced countries the less advanced ones will be able to exploit new knowledge through innovation diffusion. This is where the Single Market element comes in to interact positively with the innovation factor. It is the full operation of the Single Market that provides the most relevant boost to innovation diffusion. Innovation needs diffusion vehicles to spread over the economic space, the most relevant of which are capital, trade in goods and services, skills and intangible assets (such as patents). So the 'four freedoms' of movement brought about by the Single Market will produce not just the efficiency gains associated with a larger scale but also the gains from technological advancement.

This leads to a first implication: the completion of the Single Market is a major prerequisite for the success of a knowledge-based economy.

There is, however, another element to be considered. As the 'new economic geography' has proved in theory, and evidence is showing in practice, a larger, more integrated market and a higher-factor mobility (especially capital mobility) lead to agglomeration effects, that is, concentration of industry (especially high-tech industry) in some core regions. Increasing specialization follows and the differences in growth rates between countries and regions might increase.

This is not necessarily the case, however, as many (not all) peripheral regions are able to catch up with the richer ones precisely because they are able to attract new technology from abroad through direct investment, trade and, in some cases, human capital.

The rest of this chapter provides some evidence to the general conjecture set out above, firstly offering a description of sectoral specialization in Europe, then looking at the different degrees of flexibility and adaptability of national specialization models. The following section uses a sectoral dynamic growth model to provide examples of the role of sectoral specialization on performance. The chapter then looks at the role of technological integration in Europe.

SECTORAL ASPECTS OF INDUSTRIAL EMPLOYMENT AND TRADE SPECIALIZATION IN EUROPE[1]

A first effect of different specialization patterns can be seen on employment performance. The moderate rates of growth and rising unemployment in Europe are clearly in contrast with recent trends in the US. On the whole, the US unemployment rate fell three percentage points from 1992 to 1998, to a low of 4.5 per cent, while in the EU it has fluctuated around 10 per cent. The difference is even more relevant in the manufacturing sector; from 1985 to 1997 industrial employment fell by 1.1 per cent per year in the EU, for an overall decline of 13 per cent, while the annual rate of contraction was only 0.2 per cent in the US and was nearly zero in Japan, until 1997.[2] Two aspects are evident: first, industry in general tends to expel labour even when the growth rate is sustained, as in the case of the US; second, employment dynamics in European industry have been particularly negative in the 1990s.

A number of interpretations of these facts have been suggested. Technology and social organization have been invoked[3] to explain the long-term decline of manufacturing employment, and of its recent acceleration. The assumedly negative effect of expanding world trade on employment and wages in the industrial countries has also been widely discussed.[4] Even though they consider several aspects of the evolution in the industrial countries, these interpretations are not fully satisfactory. For example, in the US, where the so-called 'information revolution' started earlier, and has been more widespread, than in Europe, the contraction of industrial employment since 1970 has been smaller. This begs for an explanation of the negative performance of Western Europe; one hypothesis is that the consequences of international integration in Europe have been absorbed through changes in employment levels, while in the US the adjustment has operated through wage changes.[5] An alternative explanation is that the excessive fiscal burden on labour in Europe has led to a more capital intensive restructuring of European industry.[6] Even though these interpretations are partially supported by the data, they do not offer a full explanation for the decline of industrial employment in Europe. A different interpretation can build on the characteristics and sectoral dynamics of the models of specialization.[7]

The sectoral dynamics of industrial employment are differentiated in both Europe and the US (Tables 3.1 and 3.2). While the number of employed has grown in some sectors in absolute terms or with respect to the industrial average, in others the relative and absolute decrease of employment has been even larger. In general, the relative growth of employment has been greater, or the decrease smaller, in part of the chemical sector, food, electrical and non-electrical machinery (which includes consumer electronics and computers), professional instruments and plastic products. The largest decrease has occurred in textiles and clothing, and leather and footwear, in petrochemicals and in steel, and in beverages, tobacco and in glass and rubber products.

These trends can be ascribed to a number of factors. On the one hand, the dynamics of world demand and of trade volumes have differed across sectors, and affected sectoral employment; on the other hand, the evolution of the international division of labour may have produced different impacts on employment associated with the specific features of national specialization models. Finally, the restructuring processes have impacted on industrial sectors with different intensity, inducing changes in labour intensity – and in value added per worker – with respect to industry as a whole.

Table 3.1   Sectoral employment in eight European countries, 1980–94
(Austria, Finland, Germany, Netherlands, Portugal, Spain, Sweden,
United Kingdom)

		% change	
Isic code	Sector	total	annual average
356	Plastic products	18.81	1.25
342	Printing & publishing	3.70	0.25
352	Other chemicals	−2.30	−0.15
385	Professional goods	−5.89	−0.39
332	Furnitures & fixtures	−8.93	−0.60
311.2	Food	−10.33	−0.69
381	Metal products	−15.65	−1.04
383	Electrical machinery	−17.34	−1.16
341	Paper & products	−18.85	−1.26
382	Non-electrical machinery	−20.19	−1.35
331	Wood products	−22.81	−1.52
3000	Total manufacturing	−23.50	−1.57
361	Pottery, china, etc.	−24.23	−1.62
384	Transport equipment	−24.67	−1.64
372	Non-ferrous metals	−26.42	−1.76
369	Non-metallic products	−26.46	−1.76
362	Glass & products	−28.87	−1.92
351	Industrial chemicals	−29.68	−1.98
353	Petroleum refineries	−37.73	−2.52
355	Rubber products	−48.76	−3.25
322	Wearing apparel	−51.26	−3.42
313	Beverages	−52.21	−3.48
354	Petroleum & coal products	−71.06	−4.74
324	Footwear	−73.21	−4.88
321	Textiles	−74.16	−4.94
323	Leather & products	−75.51	−5.03
371	Iron & steel	−86.40	−5.76
314	Tobacco	−108.39	−7.23

The interaction among the three aspects (composition of national industrial
product, world demand dynamics and labour intensity) may explain the unsatisfactory European performance.

With some elaboration on medium- to long-term data, it is possible to
quantify these components. The dynamics of world demand are frequently
associated with traditional (or mature) sectors with low growth rates of demand,

Table 3.2   *Sectoral employment in the United States, 1980–94*

		% change	
Isic code	Sector	total	annual average
356	Plastic products	59.25	3.95
342	Printing & publishing	26.32	1.75
332	Furnitures & fixtures	11.71	0.78
331	Wood products	8.62	0.57
311.2	Food	4.28	0.29
352	Other chemicals	2.14	0.14
341	Paper & products	0.73	0.05
321	Textiles	–4.78	–0.32
383	Electrical machinery	–7.92	–0.53
384	Transport equipment	–7.97	–0.53
3000	Total manufacturing	–8.62	–0.57
361	Pottery, China, etc.	–10.98	–0.73
355	Rubber products	–12.35	–0.82
354	Petroleum & coal products	–12.91	–0.86
381	Metal products	–13.14	–0.88
372	Non-ferrous metals	–13.74	–0.92
385	Professional goods	–16.39	–1.09
369	Non-metallic products	–16.99	–1.13
382	Non-electrical machinery	–21.58	–1.44
351	Industrial chemicals	–24.21	–1.61
362	Glass & products	–25.70	–1.71
322	Wearing apparel	–29.67	–1.98
313	Beverages	–30.74	–2.05
353	Petroleum refineries	–31.70	–2.11
314	Tobacco	–37.31	–2.49
323	Leather & products	–46.95	–3.13
371	Iron & steel	–48.86	–3.26
324	Footwear	–62.00	4.13

and innovative segments (often those with a high value added) with high growth rates.[8] Nevertheless, several studies offer a more complex picture.[9] Over the long-term time-horizon some medium to high added value sectors have shown percentage growth rates lower than the industrial average; this is the case of the petrochemical and steel segments, construction materials, and food and beverages. On the other hand, trade volumes have grown at a sustained pace in 'traditional' segments such as furniture, footwear and clothing, in addition –

as is to be expected – to chemistry (including pharmaceutics), machinery (including computers, consumer electronics and telecommunications) and vehicles (see Table 3.3). Thus, the equation 'traditional equals static' is not always confirmed.

Table 3.3   OECD countries: ratio of growth rate of international trade by sector to total manufacturing

Isic code	Sector	1994–80	1994–70
3000	Total manufacturing	1.00	1.00
31	Food. beverages & tobacco	0.72	0.63
311.2	Food	0.69	0.59
313	Beverages	0.81	0.72
314	Tobacco	1.07	2.46
32	Textiles, apparel & leather	1.04	0.85
321	Textiles	0.75	0.65
322	Wearing apparel	1.56	1.10
323	Leather & products	1.06	1.04
324	Footwear	1.17	1.14
33	Wood products & furniture	0.95	0.95
331	Wood products	0.75	0.71
332	Furnitures & fixtures	1.42	1.94
34	Paper, paper products & printing	0.82	0.70
341	Paper & products	0.79	0.67
342	Printing & publishing	0.98	0.85
35	Chemical products	0.70	1.18
351	Industrial chemicals	0.82	1.12
352	Other chemicals	1.65	1.98
3522	Drugs & medicines	2.13	1.77
3529	Chemicals products	1.42	2.13
353	Petroleum refineries	–0.11	0.63
354	Petroleum & coal products	0.18	0.51
355	Rubber products	1.02	1.12
356	Plastic products	1.64	1.80
36	Non-metallic mineral products	0.78	0.87
361	Pottery, china etc.	0.69	0.71
362	Glass & products	0.99	0.94
369	Non-metallic products	0.74	0.92
37	Basic metal industries	0.27	0.40
371	Iron & steel	0.32	0.41
372	Non-ferrous metals	0.21	0.39

Table 3.3   continued

Isic code	Sector	1994–80	1994–70
38	Fabricated metal products	1.38	1.26
381	Metal products	0.78	1.03
382	Non-electrical machinery	1.36	1.09
3825	Office & computing machinery	3.85	2.75
3829	Machinery & equipment	0.85	0.78
383	Electrical machinery	1.95	1.79
3832	Radio, TV & communic. equip.	2.25	1.96
3839	Electrical apparatus	1.59	1.58
384	Transport equipment	1.27	1.19
3841	Shipbuilding & repairing	0.52	0.28
3842	Railboard vehicles	1.52	1.51
3843	Motor vehicles	1.36	1.31
3844	Motorcycles & bicycles	0.51	0.70
3845	Aircraft	1.21	1.44
3849	Transport equipment	0.81	0.83
385	Professional goods	1.39	1.46
39	Other manufacturing	0.88	1.36

One explanation for this paradox is that the dynamics of international trade leads to transfer segments (or whole lines) of production to non-OECD countries as a response to the competitive pressures from emerging economies. Hence, trade expansion reflects the growth of net imports of the OECD area (for instance, in the shoe and clothing sectors). The ability of European and US producers to compete in markets where the technological or dimensional barriers to entry are low is often based on restructuring to preserve profit margins through the reduction of labour intensity.[10] This process has occurred in traditional sectors, where the pressure of the newly industrialized countries is felt more strongly[11] but also in some of the advanced sectors (such as semiconductors or PCs, where some emerging Asian economies gained considerable competitive advantage over the 1980s and 1990s).[12] As for the EU, several studies have shown that the internal market has intensified competition and 'vertical' specialization in the European industrial systems leading to higher added value and skilled labour intensive products even in traditional sectors.[13] A check on the intensity of the restructuring processes implemented in the 1980s and the first half of the 1990s is obtained from an analysis of value added per worker at constant prices in manufacturing. Sectors with higher value added per worker with respect to the industrial average show increased intensity of physical or human capital, or of R&D, and *ceteris paribus*, a decline in the intensity of unskilled labour.

The above considerations call for a more careful sector classification between high and low demand growth. Several studies classify industrial sectors on the basis of parameters such as market concentration, the share of the factors of production in value added, returns to scale, intensity of R&D, and the number of patents.[14] According to these studies some sectors with high R&D and skilled-labour intensity are associated with high rates of growth of world demand (computers, telecommunications, other chemicals and some segments of the transport equipment). Capital-intensive sectors include skilled labour-intensive ones (food, motor vehicles) and unskilled labour-intensive ones (textiles, steel, glass, rubber and plastics). Finally, labour-intensive sectors include high-skilled labour-intensive ones (machinery, professional instruments, electrical equipment) and unskilled labour-intensive ones (clothing, furniture, leather, some metal products).[15] In the high-tech and high added value sectors, Europe generally displays a low 'quality' of production specialization, that is, ability of generating value added and of rewarding factors of production with high returns (Table 3.4). While the US and Japan are specialized, respectively, in computers and telecommunications equipment,[16] both are also specialized in vehicles (together with Germany and Spain); some EU countries are specialized in chemicals (including Germany, France, the UK and the Netherlands) and in industrial machinery (Germany, France, Italy, the UK, Sweden and the Netherlands). Europe's limited presence in the high-tech sectors is generally ascribed to a modest intensity of R&D in many European countries, (excluding Scandinavia, as well as non-EU Switzerland), as measured both by low input levels of R&D and low output levels of patents.[17] There is, however, another relevant aspect that concerns the dynamics of labour productivity (that is, value added per worker). In fact, a rise in value added per worker, *ceteris paribus*, coincides with a drop in average labour intensity which could depend on the nature of the restructuring processes. These processes can develop in two directions: a virtuous one of upgrading and increase of skilled labour intensity, and a vicious one, of downsizing and reduction of the labour-force. A comparative analysis shows that the two aspects are both present and that these trends are common to both Europe and the US.[18]

Sectors that show a sustained trade dynamics and a decline of the unit value added are those in which one expects a better employment performance than the manufacturing average. This is the case in the plastics and furniture segments but also for motor vehicles (in the US) and non-electric machinery (in Europe), while in the case of footwear the trade dynamics are pulled by the imports of the OECD countries and thus do not, on average, lead to higher employment in the industrial countries (Tables 3.1 and 3.2). The case of sectors which show weak trade dynamics and rising unit value added is symmetrical. This is the case of steel, industrial chemistry and, at least in Europe – to which the value added data refer – in textiles. The two intermediate cases are equally interesting.

Table 3.4 Comparative sectoral specialization in 12 OECD countries, 1970–93 (S indicates specialization)

Isic code	Sector	United States	Japan	Germany	France	United Kingdom	Italy	Spain	Portugal	Sweden	Netherlands	Denmark	Finland
356	Plastic products						S	S				S	S
332	Furnitures & fixtures						S	S				S	S
352	Other chemicals	S		S	S	S	S	S			S	S	S
342	Printing & publishing	S		S	S	S	S	S			S	S	S
311.2	Food	S		S			S	S			S		
361	Pottery, china etc.	S	S	S		S	S		S				
385	Professional goods	S	S	S		S	S						
384	Transport equipment	S	S	S			S	S					
381	Metal products		S	S	S			S					
383	Electrical machinery	S	S	S	S	S	S						
382	Non-electrical machinery	S		S	S	S	S			S			
362	Glass & products	S					S		S		S		
351	Industrial chemicals	S				S			S	S			
341	Paper & products	S							S	S			S
331	Wood products					S			S				S
353	Petroleum refineries								S		S		
324	Footwear						S	S	S				
372	Non-ferrous metals						S						S
369	Non-metallic products			S			S	S	S		S	S	
354	Petroleum & coal products					S			S				
313	Beverages				S		S	S	S				
355	Rubber products		S		S		S		S				
322	Wearing apparel						S	S	S				
323	Leather & products						S		S				
321	Textiles				S					S			
371	Iron & steel			S	S	S	S	S		S	S		
314	Tobacco	S				S						S	

71

On the whole, sectors with strong demand dynamics, where one also observes rising value added, show excellent employment performance (with the exception of professional instruments in the US); this is the case of industries with high intensity of R&D and skilled labour, in which the effect of expanding demand prevails over the reduction of labour intensity. There is less homogeneity in the group of industries where international trade growth is below average while relative value added per worker is shrinking. This group includes resource-intensive sectors with strong economies of scale such as oil and coal, affected by a deep and widespread decline of employment, but also sectors in which increasing labour intensity produces positive employment growth (for example, publishing and wood products).

The above classification raises two issues: firstly, up to what point do the restructuring processes require the relocation of highly labour-intensive segments and downsizing?; secondly, what is the relative weight of individual sectors in the national specialization models? By combining the data in Table 3.4 (sectors of national specialization) with the data illustrated in Table 3.5 (changes in industrial employment in the main countries), we note that the international division of labour for a given macroeconomic profile explains: (1) the greater resilience of industrial employment in the US compared to the EU as a whole (larger presence of dynamic sectors of the high-tech group; and of capital-intensive industries where stagnant or modestly shrinking 'apparent' labour productivity is observed, such as, for example, the food sector); (2) in the European context, industrial employment resilience in some countries.

Table 3.5   Changes in total manufacturing employment in OECD countries, 1980–94

Finland	−33.45
United Kingdom	−28.28
Sweden	−25.25
France	−24.83
Belgium	−23.96
Italy	−23.17
Austria	−19.97
Spain	−16.69
Netherlands	−13.26
Germany	−12.66
Portugal	−11.07
United States	−8.62
Denmark	−2.57
Japan	9.72

For instance, Denmark, which contained the employment decline after 1980 (Table 3.6), is specialized in segments of high demand-growth (furniture, plastics) or where labour intensity has deepened (food, publishing). This is also partly the case of the Netherlands (specialized in food, chemicals and machinery) and of Germany (chemicals, vehicles and machinery).[19] The picture is more complex for France, Finland, Sweden or the UK, where specialization in some segments in which employment creation has been satisfactory (other chemical products, publishing, machinery) is offset by other sectors where employment has been declining markedly (beverages, tobacco, steel); the overall result has been a significant lay-off of workers from 1980 to 1994. The Mediterranean countries show, on the one hand, a decline of sectors with declining employment (textiles), and increasing specialization in food and vehicle sectors, which has allowed Spain to limit the loss of employment in industry. This has not been the case in Italy, whose specialization in sectors such as furniture, plastics and machinery has not been sufficient to offset the constant dwindling of the traditional lines of textiles and clothing, and leather and footwear. Above all, what bears on the Italian experience is the gradual despecialization in industries where world demand has been buoyant, such as office machines (computers) and motor vehicles. The second aspect, which regards Portugal, is connected with its entry into the European Union in the mid-1980s; this economy has exploited the favourable cost differentials and deepened its specialization in labour-intensive sectors (with positive employment balances in footwear and clothing and contained losses in beverages). This has allowed Portugal to attain better employment dynamics than the European average from 1980 to 1994 (Table 3.5).

As I have argued, the national specialization model is relevant for industrial employment as world demand trends and labour intensity vary across sectors. In the following section, I analyse the changes that have taken place in the specialization models.

MOBILITY AND FLEXIBILITY: ADAPTATION OF THE SPECIALIZATION MODELS

This section discusses the capacity for change or, alternatively, of passive adaptation, in European industry. I consider the process of industrial (de)specialization as measured by indicators of revealed comparative advantage (Table 3.4), and also discuss synthetic indices of overall mobility and flexibility.

In our terminology, 'mobility' means reshaping the 'hierarchy' of comparative advantages of a national economy by reducing specialization in some segments and acquiring it in others. 'Flexibility' measures the change in the

Globalizing Europe

value of specialization indices; this does not necessarily imply substituting sectors of specialization but rather gradually transforming one's structure of comparative advantages.[20] A joint evaluation of the two indices offers an appraisal of the overall change that has taken place in specialization models in Europe since 1980.

Table 3.6   Index of mobility of export structure in OECD countries, 1980–94

United States	53.80
Finland	53.70
Canada	50.80
Portugal	49.90
Denmark	48.00
United Kingdom	48.70
Germany	47.50
Spain	46.40
Netherlands	43.80
France	43.20
Austria	41.00
Belgium	35.10
Sweden	33.30
Italy	22.00
Japan	16.20

Tables 3.6 and 3.7 show, respectively, the indices of mobility and flexibility of the main OECD economies, calculated for the period 1980–94 on the basis of the Balassa indices of comparative advantage for sectoral exports (see note to Table 3.4). It emerges clearly that, for example, the North American countries have considerably modified the hierarchy of their comparative advantage over the 1980–94 period, while countries that have joined the EU over the same period (Portugal, Denmark, Finland and Spain) have reoriented their specialization model. Specifically, adaptation of the specialization model has been remarkable in the Iberian countries, even though the changes have taken different directions. Germany, France and the UK display comparable values of indices of mobility and – with the exception of France – of flexibility. Italy ranks low in terms of both indicators, exhibiting a notable immobility of the specialization model.[21]

In general, comparative advantages in the high value added and demand-dynamic sectors (high-tech sectors with large economies of scale) tend to reinforce themselves; countries which had an established specialization in the early 1970s have preserved them, with few exceptions (for instance, the despecialization of Italy and Sweden in computers and office machinery, and of France in motor vehicles; the gradual specialization of Spain in vehicles). This relative stability in the high value added segments is not surprising if we consider the role of dynamic increasing returns, economies of scale and oligopolistic markets, which produce high entry barriers for new competitors.

Table 3.7   Index of flexibility of export structure in OECD countries, 1980–94

Portugal	10.20
Spain	8.00
United Kingdom	7.80
United States	7.80
Germany	7.70
Austria	6.90
Belgium	4.30
Japan	3.60
Netherlands	3.10
Finland	3.10
Canada	2.60
France	2.40
Sweden	1.70
Denmark	1.60
Italy	1.50

Conversely, the transformation of the international division of labour has been more intense in the 'mature' segments with high capital and energy intensity (petrochemicals and steel) and in the 'traditional' sectors. In the former case, specific events have played a role (the discovery of the North Sea oil fields has substantially strengthened the British position in the refining segment, and that of the Netherlands in the segments of petroleum derivatives and coal). In traditional sectors, we observe a widespread tendency to despecialization. Specifically, the UK loses positions in textiles and leather, Germany in furniture and ceramics, France in the leather and footwear, and textile and clothing lines, and Spain in textiles and clothing, footwear, and beverages. Two European countries have moved in the opposite direction: Portugal, by substantially strengthening its specialization in traditional sectors (clothing, footwear, ceramics) and Italy, by maintaining its comparative advantage in leather and footwear, textiles and clothing, and furniture.

The stability or transformation of national industrial structures is closely connected to the direction towards which they evolve. At least three models can be singled out in Europe: first countries that hold positions of comparative advantage in dynamic, high added value sectors (Denmark, the Netherlands and Germany) and have transformed their industrial structure by downsizing the weight of the traditional segments. While these economies have suffered losses of employment these have been contained through a process of moderate reshaping of the hierarchy of comparative advantages (Table 3.6).

A second group includes countries that have modified the sectoral structure more radically: the UK, Finland, Spain and Portugal. The former two have seen a significant contraction of industrial employment, especially in resource-intensive sectors (petroleum, paper mills) and in the case of the UK, an intense tertiarization of the economy. The Iberian countries, on the other hand, have modified their production structures in opposite directions: Spain has downsized several traditional sectors while specialization in high economies of scale segments has increased; Portugal has deepened its comparative advantage in labour-intensive segments. Both Iberian experiences have taken advantage of the one-off effect of joining the EU and have been rewarding in terms of employment.

France and, above all, Italy are the countries where the industrial structure has changed the least. Nevertheless, while the French economy has lost its comparative advantage in the traditional sectors (but also in motor vehicles), it has preserved its comparative advantage in segments – of both dynamic (other chemicals) and 'mature' (steel) type – with large economies of scale. Conversely, Italy has maintained its specialization in a number of traditional sectors. As noted above, employment performance is unsatisfactory in many specialized sectors of these two economies, regardless of whether they are 'mature' and highly capital intensive, or traditional (the main exceptions are other chemicals in France, and furniture and plastic products in Italy). The gradual decline of industries facing sustained international demand, such as vehicles and office equipment, has contributed to falling industrial employment in these two countries.

Finally, the sectoral dynamics of industry and the national models of specialization do have an impact on labour market performance. Econometric estimates[22] confirm the greater sensitivity of employment and industrial wages to international competition in sectors where the country shows a comparative disadvantage, while in sectors in which the country enjoys a strong or moderate comparative advantage the ability to resist international competitive pressure is stronger. In most cases, employment and wage elasticities are larger (a fall of import prices, indicating higher competitive pressure, has a greater depressing impact on wages and/or employment) in the sectors in which the country has no comparative advantage. This result is not surprising and indeed it is consistent with the definition of the sector of specialization as that sector where competitive advantages are sustained over time – and have been firmly established.

SPECIALIZATION AND GROWTH: RESULTS OF A MORE FORMALIZED ANALYSIS[23]

The evidence discussed above suggests a relationship between trade and industrial specialization and economic performance in terms both of employment and growth. In this section I report results developed from the estimation of a model that links trade specialization and knowledge accumulation. The model is also used to perform some simulation exercises.

Theoretical and empirical research on the relationship between trade and knowledge accumulation suggests at least two causal links: one stresses the role of knowledge accumulation in determining trade performance and competitiveness,[24] the other looks at the role of trade in enhancing knowledge accumulation through imports.[25] The model discussed here captures both elements in a unified perspective. The approach followed is 'sectoral' in the sense that it considers an economy where more than one good is produced. As discussed in the previous section two reasons can be suggested in favour of such a choice. The first (Pasinetti 1981) stresses the role of growth in different sectors in affecting aggregate performance, because, *inter alia*, different rates of change of sectoral demand will lead to growth through structural change. The second stems from the opportunity of adopting a sectoral perspective in the investigation of the relationship between knowledge accumulation (and diffusion), dynamic comparative advantages and trade (and growth) performance. This second point is also not new. Grossman and Helpman (1989, 1990) and Romer (1990) consider an economy with three sectors (R&D activity, intermediate goods, consumer goods) to study the role of knowledge accumulation and diffusion through the introduction of intermediate goods in the production of final goods. More generally, the role of intermediate goods in the knowledge diffusion process is well recognized in the literature on new growth theory.[26] Other more institutionally-oriented approaches[27] stress the role of knowledge spillovers between sectors and the consequences on trade and growth of the performance (and relative weight) of knowledge-producing sectors.

In the model I follow Pavitt's (1984) taxonomy to group manufacturing goods into four macrosectors. In this taxonomy[28] manufacturing sectors are grouped according to the position each sector holds in the process of knowledge accumulation and diffusion, as well as on the role of knowledge and of other factors in determining performance. The main features of the model (see Appendix) are the following: export shares in the four macrosectors depend on both price and non-price (relative technology accumulation) factors; technology accumulation is endogenous and it depends on innovation efforts, sectoral specialization and technology absorption from abroad. The four macrosectors are given below.

Traditional Goods

Innovative activity in this sector is limited yet necessary to allow absorption of innovations from other sectors. Process innovation leads to productivity gains and 'price competition' is crucial. Typical sectors include clothing and footwear.[29]

Scale-Intensive Goods

Innovative activity in this sector is relevant especially in process and organizational innovations. Innovation diffusion from other sectors is obtained largely through acquisition of intermediate goods. Competitiveness derives from the exploitation of scale economies. Sectors include transport equipment, consumer electronics and household appliances.

Specialized Suppliers

Innovative activity relates to both process and product innovation and is often the result of consumer–producer interaction leading to special 'customer relationships' with other sectors. Competitiveness derives from 'quality', mainly understood as the capacity to adapt to the users' needs in terms of both performance and prompt delivery. Sectors include machine tools and scientific instruments.

Science-Based

Innovation activity through substantial R&D investment is the main characteristic of these sectors whose competitiveness derives essentially from product innovation success. R&D performed in these industries typically leads to knowledge spillovers to other sectors which tend to be stronger the closer is the user–producer relationship. In this respect science-based firms acquire knowledge from other sectors as well as disseminating it. This relationship is usually strong with specialized supplier's firms. Sectors include aerospace industries, computers and telecommunications.

Parameter estimates have been obtained for Germany, France, Italy, the UK and Japan.[30] Results show different importance of price and non-price effects in determining national performance as well as different models of technological accumulation, and may be summarized as follows.

Germany

The relative price elasticities in the traditional and scale-intensive sectors were constrained to take on the same value, which is smaller than one, while the price elasticity in the specialized suppliers sector was constrained to take on the value of one. Technology elasticities in the specialized suppliers and science-based sectors were also constrained to take on the same value, which turns out to be smaller with respect to other cases. These results are partly consistent with the distribution of RCA in Germany which shows a strong advantage in specialized suppliers.

Estimates of parameters in the knowledge accumulation equation show a moderate elasticity of patenting with respect to R&D expenditure, but also an important domestic spillover effect, a moderate role of the stock of foreign knowledge[31] but a more relevant role of high-tech imports in enhancing domestic knowledge accumulation; this last point is confirmed by the relatively high elasticity of the high-tech import share to the high-tech export share.

France

This is the only case where the three knowledge elasticities are not significantly different, and so they were constrained to take on the same value, which is also one, the highest knowledge elasticity obtained. This result suggests a high degree of integration among the knowledge-sensitive sectors. The relatively strong domestic spillover effect is also consistent with a high degree of integration among knowledge-sensitive sectors. On the contrary, estimation results suggest a slow process of domestic knowledge accumulation. Contrary to the case of Germany, the elasticity to domestic R&D accumulation is low, while the influence of the world stock of knowledge is much more important with imports of high-tech goods playing a somewhat more limited role; this is also confirmed by a relatively low value of the elasticity of high-tech imports to high-tech exports. In sum, the non-trade channels of international knowledge diffusion seem to play a relevant role in the case of France.

Italy

As in the previous two cases the price elasticities in the traditional and scale-intensive sectors were constrained to take on the same value, which is also the highest among the five country cases: the price elasticity in the specialized supplier sector was constrained to zero while the estimate of knowledge elasticity in the same sector turned out to be very high, consistently with Italy's strong specialization in this macrosector. The weak specialization in scale-intensive products seems to account for the low knowledge elasticity. Note that Italy is the only country case where the knowledge elasticities turned out to be significantly different (and low), suggesting a weak integration among the knowledge-sensitive sectors.

The knowledge accumulation equation shows a high elasticity to domestic R&D, a limited domestic spillover effect (again a sign of low integration among

knowledge-sensitive sectors) a modest effect of international diffusion limited
to high-tech imports and no effect of the world stock of knowledge. To some
extent Italy's model of knowledge accumulation appears to be closer to the
German than to the French (and the UK's, see below) case.[32]

United Kingdom

The knowledge elasticities in scale-intensive and science-based sectors turned
out not to be significantly different and were constrained to take on the same
value which is also quite high consistently with the country's specialization.
The knowledge elasticity in the scale-intensive sector is also relatively high,
but significantly smaller. Contrary to the other European cases, price elasticities turned out to be all significantly different from one another.

The process of knowledge accumulation stands out as being quite different
from the other European cases as well as from Japan's. It appears to be the fastest
of the four European cases, highly sensitive to domestic R&D and with a very
strong domestic spillover effect. It also seems to benefit more strongly from
international diffusion, both through high-tech imports and through the effects
of the foreign stock of knowledge. In sum, the UK model of knowledge accumulation seems to be efficient and highly integrated in the international economy,
also as a consequence of the strong presence of foreign multinationals.[33]

The model just discussed was used to explore the links between growth performance, technology accumulation and changes in trade specialization through
simulation exercises. The five simulation exercises presented here will be
discussed separately, looking at the behaviour of output, export market shares
and the stock of domestic knowledge (T). Figures 3.1–3.5 report differences in
output levels from the base run. Table 3.8 presents percentage changes with
respect to the base run in export market shares and in the level of T at the end
of the simulation run (20 periods = years). Overall, simulations confirm the
relevance of differences in both trade specialization and in domestic knowledge
accumulation processes in affecting growth, and highlight the relationship
between growth performance and changes in the structure of trade specialization, as well as the relationship between trade, growth performance and
knowledge accumulation.

Simulation 1. No Trade Spillovers in Knowledge Accumulation

One of the vehicles of international knowledge diffusion considered in the
model is the amount of high-tech imports. The elimination of knowledge
diffusion through imports produces a depressing effect on output; however,
significant country differences emerge according to the role of technology
imports in domestic knowledge formation. France and the UK present the most

substantial ones with Japan taking an intermediate position. France and the UK also suffer the largest relative loss in domestic knowledge accumulation and in export market shares (see Table 3.8). In general, differences in market share behaviour reflect differences in knowledge elasticities as well as the different values of the sectoral adjustment speeds.

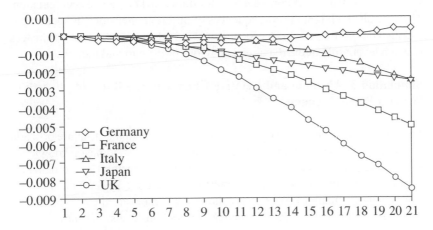

Figure 3.1   Output, no international spillovers, case 1

Simulation 2. No International Spillovers in Knowledge Accumulation

In this exercise the second source of knowledge spillover, acting directly through the stock of foreign knowledge T_w (a proxy of non-trade vehicles of knowledge

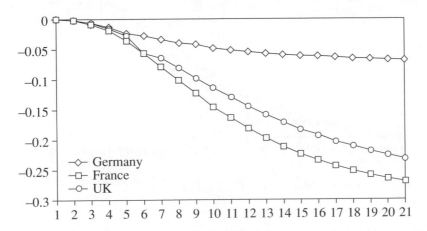

Figure 3.2   Output, no international spillovers, case 2

diffusion such as patents, FDIs, and so on) is eliminated in addition to the first one. Output losses are reported in Figure 3.3 where the results for Germany on the one hand and for France and the UK on the other look quite different.[34] Table 3.2 also shows that differences in aggregate performance are reflected in differences in sectoral performance and in the change of the specialization structure as well as in the consequences for domestic knowledge accumulation. These results highlight the consequences of different intensities in 'technological integration' for growth. As documented in Padoan (1998) these differences play a relevant role in the dynamic behaviour of the national models.

Simulation 3. Absolute and Relative Change in the Rates of Growth of Sectoral World Demand[*]

This simulation explores the consequences of a change in the structure of world demand. Results show that market shares and the level of domestic knowledge are not affected by changes in the rates of growth of sectoral world demands (that is, both export market shares and the level of T take on their base-run values in the simulation). We observe, however, some consequences for output behaviour. All countries display increases in output levels, but they do so to different degrees, reflecting their relative specialization. If the rates of growth of sectoral world demand increase, the rate of growth of aggregate export share

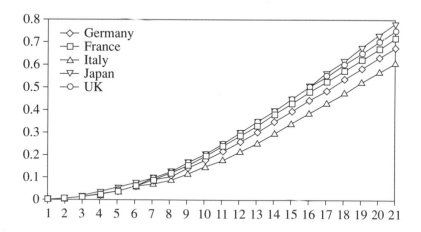

Figure 3.3   Output, change in world demand

---

[*] Traditional no change, scale intensive = science based +33%, specialized suppliers +50% (investment boom).

and, *ceteris paribus*, the rate of growth of output will increase proportionally to the initial trade specialization structure. Accordingly, the ranking of the output gains in the national cases in descending order is as follows: Japan, the United Kingdom, France, Germany and Italy.

Simulation 4. Doubling of the Rate of Growth of Domestic R&D (Same for all Countries)

All countries benefit in terms of output but, again, with significant differences – see Figure 3.4 – with Japan gaining the most and Germany and Italy the least. This is only partially the result of Japan's high elasticity of domestic knowledge accumulation to domestic R&D. Italy, for example, has a comparable elasticity, resulting in a similar increase in the stock of domestic knowledge, but relatively lower knowledge elasticities in knowledge-sensitive sectors as well as a weaker specialization in these sectors. This generates a lower rate of growth of the aggregate export share. In addition, contrary to (for example) the case of the UK, which exhibits an even higher increase in the value of *T* and presents even higher knowledge elasticities, the growth in high-tech export shares does not stimulate as large an increase in high-tech imports – which depress growth. Finally, in this case too, differences in output per-formances generate differences in the trade specialization structures, since this exercise, as the others above, modifies the difference between the growth rates of foreign and domestic knowledge and the rates of growth of sectoral export market shares.

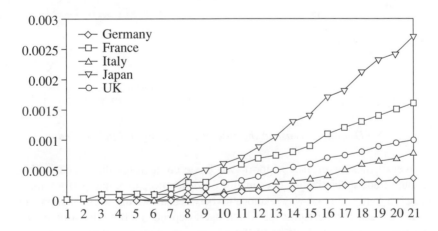

Figure 3.4   Output, increase in the rate of growth of R&D

Simulation 5. Doubling the Rate of Growth of the Stock of Foreign Knowledge

This final simulation allows us to appreciate the combined results of the two opposing effects of foreign knowledge on domestic performance: the depressing effect of increased technological competition and the enhancing effect of knowledge diffusion. As shown in Figure 3.5 the net effect on output is negative in all cases but, once again, with significant national differences. The UK experiences the highest absolute loss, followed by Japan. The important difference between these two cases, however, is that the UK also witnesses the highest absolute increase in the stock of domestic knowledge – see Table 3.8 – while the net change in the case of Japan is zero. Obviously this is the consequence of the different role that the foreign stock of knowledge plays in knowledge diffusion. Changes in market shares – see Table 3.8 – occur in all sectors but are more marked in those where knowledge elasticities are higher.

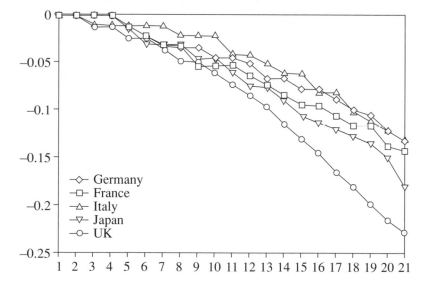

Figure 3.5   Output, increase in the rate of growth of foreign knowledge

Overall these exercises support two basic conjectures discussed in this chapter: trade specialization does matter for differences in output performance; there is a significant two-way relationship between knowledge accumulation and trade (and growth) performance which itself depends on both the structure of specialization and the features of the national innovation systems in an open economy. This latter aspect, however, needs to be further scrutinized by looking at the relationship between knowledge diffusion and international integration.

Table 3.8 Percentage changes in market shares and in technology

	Simulation 1				
	Germany	France	Italy	Japan	UK
Sc. int.	–0.8	–5.6	–1.9	–2.9	–7.7
Spec. sup.	–0.7	–5.2	–1.9	–2.7	–8
Sc. based	–0.6	–5.3	–4.8	–3.24	–10.5
Technology	–5.7	–6.25	–5.38	–4.9	–10.95
	Simulation 2				
	Germany	France	Italy	Japan	UK
Sc. int.	–10.04	–27.9	–	–	–17.3
Spec. sup.	–7.62	–27.7	–	–	–17.3
Sc. based	–7.62	–27.9	–	–	–26.8
Technology	–10.88	–32.7	–	–	–25.7
	Simulation 4				
	Germany	France	Italy	Japan	UK
Sc. int.	0.5	1.8	0.56	3.7	0.9
Spec. sup.	0.45	1.4	0.65	2.7	1.4
Sc. based	0.36	1.9	0.19	3.52	1.4
Technology	5.4	2.05	5.47	5.6	7.7
	Simulation 5				
	Germany	France	Italy	Japan	UK
Sc. int.	–1.7	–1.5	–0.8	–1.8	–1.7
Spec. sup.	–1.8	–1.2	–0.9	–1.1	–1.8
Sc. based	–1.6	–1.5	–2.7	–1.4	–2.4

TECHNOLOGICAL INTEGRATION IN EUROPE[35]

In this section we provide some tests of the hypothesis that national patterns of technological accumulation and diffusion are influenced by the absorption of foreign knowledge through a regional, as opposed to a global, pattern. This is a relevant issue for the European economy which has widely relied on its internal integration as a source of growth. Is the regional dimension of technology accumulation relevant and worth considering? The literature offers few, yet interesting, suggestions. Grossman and Helpman (1991) show that the geographical concentration of knowledge spillovers may be important in affecting long-run comparative advantage and specialization. If spillovers are geographically concentrated, some countries can 'lock in' their specialization pattern through cumulative processes that deepen specialization given an initial technological lead. Grossman and Helpman (1991) find this to hold theoretically considering national as opposed to global spillovers; however, if spillovers are less than global, these results may hold for geographically limited areas such as regions. Hence specific regions can deepen their specialization and acquire a technological lead.

Breschi and Malerba (1996) study the implications of geographical proximity on the transmission of knowledge according to the characteristics of the knowledge base, itself linked to sector specific characteristics: 'The more the knowledge base is tacit, complex, and part of a larger system ... the more likely geographical proximity plays a relevant role in facilitating the transmission of knowledge ... The more the relevant knowledge base is codifiable, codified, simple and independent ... the more likely spatial proximity does not play a relevant role in permitting the transfer of relevant knowledge' (p. 15).

In order to do this in Padoan (1999) I re-estimate the model with a new version of the knowledge accumulation equation, which takes into account different geographical sources of international knowledge spillovers (see Appendix).

The hypothesis of regional effects in knowledge diffusion has been tested by disaggregating the share of world imports of high-tech goods and the foreign stock of knowledge in two components, a 'regional' component, and a 'non-regional' component. Regional variables are European[36] for the four European cases, and US variables for Japan. Non-regional variables are: non-European and non-US variables respectively. We assume the presence of 'strong' regional effects when only regional foreign knowledge affects significantly domestic knowledge accumulation. A 'weak' regional effect is assumed when both regional and non-regional foreign knowledge affects domestic knowledge accumulation, but the former exerts a stronger effect.

Germany is the only case that shows strong regional effects. The same is true when high-tech imports are included in place of the stock of knowledge. This result is confirmed when only European variables are included. The case where only non-European variables are included presents mostly non-significant variables. Estimates with only one foreign variable suggest that high-tech imports, rather than the foreign stock of knowledge, capture the foreign spillover effect.

France exhibits weak regional effects. The opposite holds, however, when imports of high-tech goods are considered. While both variables are significant, non-European high-tech imports show a significantly larger parameter with respect to the European high-tech imports. Regional effects, therefore, seem to depend on the vehicle of knowledge diffusion. The European stock of knowledge and the non-European high-tech imports show the best results in terms of parameter values and goodness of fit.

The case of Italy should be classified as one showing weak regional effects, nevertheless such effects appear stronger than the case of France. The strong relevance of high-tech imports as vehicles of knowledge diffusion is confirmed. This reinforces the impression that the regional effect of knowledge diffusion works mainly through imports rather than through other vehicles.

The case of the UK presents rather weak regional effects and confirms that the role of foreign knowledge is much more relevant than that of high-tech imports in knowledge diffusion. The UK is the only country case where all foreign variables, when included individually in the equation, are significant. This confirms that the pattern of foreign knowledge diffusion for the UK economy is both global (that is, not strictly regional) and associated with different vehicles.

Finally, Japan exhibits 'regional' effects in technology diffusion in its linkages with the United States. However, these are limited to the role of high-tech imports as the stocks of foreign knowledge, both US and non-US, are never significant. This is confirmed by the cases including only one foreign variable.

In conclusion, all countries show some regional effects of technology diffusion, although only Germany shows what we have defined as a strong regional effect. It is interesting to note that, in the cases of France and the UK, regional effects are working through the foreign (European) stock of knowledge and not through high-tech imports. Results for Germany and Italy, however, suggest that imports of high-tech goods, rather than, or in addition to, other vehicles of knowledge diffusion, reveal a regional pattern. The case of Japan also supports the role of trade as a vehicle of knowledge diffusion. Our evidence suggests that regional trade linkages represent only partially a factor of technological regionalism. On the other hand, our results also support the view that vehicles of knowledge diffusion other than trade are relevant in regional linkages.

I then consider sectoral aspects of technological diffusion in order to test whether technological specialization and diffusion is sector specific and whether the results obtained at the aggregate level hide a sectoral dimension. To this purpose in Padoan (1999) I estimate a simple model which links trade and production specialization to technological specialization.

The descriptive continuous time model is based on the following elements: (1) we know from 'New Trade Theory' (see for example Venables, 1995; Krugman and Venables, 1996) that as barriers and other impediments to trade decrease, production (and trade) specialization deepens, especially in sectors that exhibit increasing returns; (2) trade and production specialization interact with technological specialization, leading to cumulative effects and 'lock in' phenomena (Lucas, 1988); (3) specialization patterns, both in technology and in production and trade, tend to change slowly over time. This is especially true of Europe (Cantwell, 1989; Amendola, Guerrieri and Padoan, 1992); (4) large countries are less specialized than small countries, both in production and in technology (Dollar and Wolff, 1993; Archibugi and Pianta, 1994); (5) the extent of technology diffusion varies greatly across sectors (Dollar and Wolff, 1993; Breschi and Malerba, 1996); (6) as discussed above, technological accumulation is the result of both domestic and foreign efforts, hence one should detect a correlation between domestic and foreign technological specialization.

The model has been estimated for six sectors – aerospace, chemical products (excluding drugs), electrical and electronics, mechanical equipment, motor vehicles and textiles – characterized by different features and degrees of technological intensity and innovation activity and by a different knowledge base. The sectors chosen differ substantially with respect to market structure and the presence of technological barriers (Archibugi and Pianta, 1992; Breschi and Malerba, 1996). Aerospace, chemicals and electrical and electronics present high barriers to entry in technological investment but also global knowledge boundaries; motor vehicles feature few innovators that are also geographically concentrated with local knowledge boundaries; mechanical equipment presents strong cumulative features in technological accumulation, but also many innovators geographically concentrated with local knowledge boundaries; finally, textiles present high pervasiveness in technological accumulation and diffusion as the many innovators are geographically dispersed with no specific knowledge spatial boundaries. *A priori* one should expect stronger regional and cumulative effects in motor vehicles and mechanical equipment, and less so in the other sectors. Results of the estimation of model are as follows.

Textiles

In three European cases, Germany, France and Italy, domestic technological specialization is highly correlated to US rather than to European technological specialization. With the exception of the UK, European technological specialization does not seem to exert any significant effect. The case of Japan suggests a strong effect of US technological specialization on domestic technological specialization. In general, results seem to confirm the pervasive nature of technology in this sector.

Motor Vehicles

Results for the four European countries suggest a strong influence of European technological specialization on domestic technological specialization. This supports the assumption of few innovators that are also geographically concentrated with local knowledge boundaries. Estimates confirm the presence of a cumulative interaction between production and innovation activities. Geographical concentration also appears in the case of Japan where foreign (US) technological specialization does not significantly affect domestic technological specialization.

Electrical and Electronics

Regional (European) technological specialization influences domestic technological specialization in the cases of Germany, France and the UK. In the latter two cases estimates confirm the presence of a cumulative interaction between production and innovation activities. In the case of the UK, however, US technological specialization apparently exerts a stronger effect, suggesting global rather than local knowledge boundaries. Finally, no effect of foreign specialization can be found in the cases of Japan and Italy.

Chemicals

As expected, the chemical industry does not show any significant effect of regional technological specialization on domestic technological specialization. The case of Germany shows that domestic technological specialization is strongly related to US technological specialization. In this case estimation results confirm the presence of a cumulative interaction between production and innovation activities.

Mechanical Equipment

The US specialization index influences domestic technological specialization in Germany, France and the UK as well as in Japan. European specialization is also important in the case of Germany. In several cases strong cumulative interaction with technological specialization is present.

Aerospace

US specialization produces a significant influence on domestic specialization in the cases of France and Germany; however, European specialization is important in the case of Germany. The estimates for Italy improve dramatically when the European, rather than US, specialization index is included.

In general, estimates support the view that regional effects on technological specialization are sector specific, that is, some sectors show some regional patterns while these are totally absent in others. Within sectors country patterns

Globalizing Europe

are also different and they confirm some of the country results discussed above. However the *a priori* expectations about the behaviour of specific sectors are only partially confirmed.

Our estimates both at the country and at the sectoral level yield mixed results that are summarized in Table 3.9.

Table 3.9   Regional technological integration: summary of results

	Germany	France	Italy	UK	Japan
Country effect	XX	X	X	X	XX
Textiles				X	XX
Motor vehicles	XX	XX	XX	XX	
Aerospace	X		XX		
Chemicals					
Electrical/electronics	XX	XX		X	
Mech. Equip.	X				XX

Note: X = weak regional effect, XX = strong regional effect

Germany, and to a lesser extent Italy, show stronger regional effects both at the country and at the sectoral levels. France and the United Kingdom show weak regional effects at the country level and stronger effects at the sectoral level in the case of motor vehicles, which appears to be the most highly region-alized sector, followed by the electrical and electronic machinery. Interestingly, these two sectors also show a relatively strong interaction between production and technology specialization. As sectoral estimates show, cumulative effects are particularly relevant in chemicals, aerospace and mechanical equipment, where regional effects are weak or totally absent. Finally, Japan shows relevant regional links with the US. One point to be stressed is that country effects differ somewhat according to the variable that is used to capture the presence of regional technology patterns, that is such patterns may be associated with stocks of knowledge and much less so when high-tech imports are considered (as in the cases of France, the UK and Japan).

These results point to the fact that regional trade agreements do not necess-arily lead to regional knowledge spillover patterns, at least indirectly. Regional patterns, however, may be present through vehicles of knowledge diffusion other than trade. These conclusions are also partially confirmed by sectoral estimates, that show that regional patterns of knowledge diffusion are highly sector-specific as the knowledge base varies greatly across sectors. National differences in the role of vehicles of diffusion found in the country estimates possibly reflect sectoral rather than national features, as well as different degrees of internationalization of the national economies. These results could also partially explain the puzzle that countries belonging to the same regional agreement (the EU) show different degrees of technology regionalism.

CONCLUSIONS

We may summarize our results as follows. Trade and industry specialization matter for employment and growth performance. EU countries have different specialization patterns which also exhibit different degrees of mobility and flexibility. Theoretical, empirical and simulation analysis confirm the relationship between trade specialization, knowledge accumulation and growth. National economies with different specialization patterns and different systems of knowledge accumulation diffusion react differently in terms of output performance to the same external shocks which also produce changes in trade specialization patterns (sectoral export shares). There is a two-way relationship between knowledge accumulation and trade performance. The former influences positively the latter, however deeper trade integration enhances domestic knowledge accumulation. Knowledge diffusion has both a regional and a global dimension, but also a sectoral dimension. We find support therefore to the conjecture presented in the introduction that Europe is well in the position to exploit the virtuous interaction of the completion of the Single Market and the enhanced technological accumulation associated with the new innovation wave. A simple yet demanding policy implication follows. To fill its competitiveness gap Europe must further progress in the completion of the Single Market and support the process of technology accumulation and diffusion towards the establishment of a fully integrated European system of innovation.

APPENDIX

In this appendix we report the model discussed in the section 'Specialization and growth'. All equations are expressed as adjustment equations where each endogenous variable X adjusts with a coefficient α,[37] to its partial equilibrium value X^*. D is the derivative with respect to time and γs are the constant terms, and log is the natural logarithm. We start by discussing the sectoral export share equations. The size of adjustment speeds is also an indicator of sectoral competitiveness as it is determined, *inter alia*, by the 'capacity to deliver', hence higher values of α signal higher competitiveness. In principle the export shares of all four groups should be a function of both price and technology factors, however in order to minimize the number of parameters some simplifying assumptions were made. Let us now discuss each equation in more detail.

$$D \log S_A = \alpha_2(\log S_A{}^* - \log S_A) \tag{1}$$
$$\log S_A{}^* = \log\gamma_1 - \beta_1 \log P$$

Equation (1) states that the export share of traditional goods S_A adjusts to its partial equilibrium value $S_A{}^*$ which varies inversely with the real effective exchange rate P, that is, we assume that relative technology does not directly affect international competitiveness in this sector.[38]

$$D \log S_B = \alpha_3(\log S_B{}^* - \log S_B) \tag{2}$$
$$\log S_B{}^* = \log\gamma_2 - \beta_2 \log P + \beta_3 \log(T/T_W)$$

$$D \log S_C = \alpha_4(\log S_C{}^* - \log S_C) \tag{3}$$
$$\log S_C{}^* = \log\gamma_3 - \beta_4 \log P + \beta_5 \log(T/T_W)$$

$$D \log S_D = \alpha_5(\log S_D{}^* - \log S_D) \tag{4}$$
$$\log S_D{}^* = \log\gamma_4 + \beta_6 \log(T/T_W)$$

Equations (2)–(4) describe the adjustment of the export market share in the three other sectors to their respective partial equilibrium values. We assume that partial equilibrium values of the export shares for the scale-intensive (B) and specialized suppliers (C) sectors are a function of both the real effective exchange rate and of the relative (domestic over world) stock of knowledge T/T_W, while the science-based sector's share (D) is a function of relative knowledge alone.[39] *A priori*, sectoral price and relative knowledge elasticities are assumed to be different. Empirical estimation results (see above) show that this is not always the case.

$$D \log T = \alpha_6 (\log T^* - \log T) + \beta_9 \log T_W + \beta_{10} \log S_{MH} \quad (5)$$
$$\log T^* = \log \gamma_5 + \beta_7 \log F + \beta_8 \log S_D$$

Equation (5) describes the process of knowledge accumulation in the economy, where the output of the knowledge production process is represented by patents. While the role of relative knowledge in affecting trade performance may vary across sectors, knowledge accumulation is country-specific, that is, the ability of a country to accumulate knowledge depends on specific national features involving institutional as well as economic aspects.[40] This formulation is not fully satisfactory when one chooses to adopt a sectoral perspective. A more extended modelling strategy would require to introduce sector-specific, as well as country-specific, knowledge accumulation processes and study their interaction.[41]

More specifically the idea behind Equation (5) is the following. The accumulation of the stock of domestic knowledge T is basically determined by a domestic effort, that is, the partial equilibrium level of T is a function of domestic variables, the exogenous domestic stock of R&D expenditure, F, and the 'size ' of the science-based sector in the economy, proxied by its export market share S_D.[42] The rationale for F is that R&D represents the most important input in the knowledge production process. The rationale for the second variable is that, according to Pavitt's taxonomy, the science-based sector generates an externality in the domestic knowledge production process.[43]

The two foreign variables entering Equation (5), the exogenous stock of foreign knowledge T_W, and the endogenous share of high-tech imports S_{MH},[44] do not affect the partial equilibrium level of T; rather one can think of Equation (5) as being a linear approximation of a non-linear form where the adjustment speed α_6 is a function of foreign knowledge variables, that is, $\alpha_6 = \phi (T_W, S_{MH})$. Such a formulation implies that the absorption of foreign knowledge, the intensity of which may be thought of being a function of what Abramovitz calls 'social capability'[45] (captured by parameters β_9 and β_{10}), increases the speed of the process of domestic knowledge accumulation. The reason why two different foreign knowledge variables are included is that the channels of international knowledge diffusion are several (indeed more than two). The literature on knowledge diffusion and trade[46] stresses the role of imports as vehicles of diffusion, however other channels (such as foreign direct investment, R&D cooperation, joint ventures and human capital transfers) may be just as relevant, especially for developed countries.[47] The stock of foreign knowledge, T_W, can be thought of as a proxy of sources of knowledge diffusion other than imports.[48]

$$D \log S_X = D \log S_A (S_A/S_X)(W_A/W) + \lambda_A (S_A/S_X) (W_A/W) + D \log S_B$$
$$(S_B/S_X) (W_B/W) + \lambda_B (S_B/S_X) (W_B/W) + D \log S_C (S_C/S_X) (W_C/W) + \lambda_C (S_C/S_X)$$
$$(W_C/W) + D \log S_D(S_D/S_X) (W_D/W) + \lambda_D(S_D/S_X) (W_D/W) - D \log W \quad (6)$$

Equation (6) defines the rate of change of the aggregate export share S_X.

$$D \log S_{ML} = \alpha_7(\log S_{ML}^* - \log S_{ML}) \tag{7}$$
$$\log S_{ML}^* = \log \gamma_6 + \beta_{11}\log P$$

$$D \log S_{MH} = \alpha_8(\log S_{MH}^* - \log S_{MH}) \tag{8}$$
$$\log S_{MH}^* = \log \gamma_7 + \beta_{12}\log P - \beta_{13}\log T/T_W + \beta_{14}\log S_{XH}$$

Equations (7)–(9) define the rate of change of import shares where $\lambda_i i$ indicates the exogenous rate of growth of demand of sector i. In order to minimize the size of the model, we do not present the four-sector disaggregation for imports as well. Rather, we consider the distinction between traditional and high-tech imports, where 'traditional' includes the same foods defined in sector A above and 'high-tech' includes the remaining three. Accordingly, S_{ML}^* is a function of the real effective exchange rate alone while S_{MH}^* is a function of both the real effective exchange rate and of the relative stock of knowledge. In addition, we assume that the high-tech import share is positively related to the high-tech export share S_{XH} defined below (Equation (10)). Equation (8) captures the fact that foreign high-tech goods are both substitutes of (to the extent that imports compete in the domestic market against similar domestic goods) and complements to (to the extent that they enter as intermediate goods) domestic high-tech goods.[49] These two conflicting roles played by imports in influencing domestic growth are often neglected in the literature, which stresses the role of imports as vehicles of technology.[50]

$$D \log S_M = D \log S_{ML} (S_{ML}/S_M) + D \log S_{MH} (S_{MH}/S_M) \tag{9}$$

$$S_{XH} = S_B(W_B/W_H) + S_C(W_C/W_H) + SD(W_D/W_H) \tag{10}$$

Equation (9) defines the proportional rate of change of the aggregate import share S_M, and equation (10) defines the level of the high-tech export share.

$$D \log Y = \alpha_1(\log Y^* - \log Y) \tag{11}$$
$$\log Y^* = \log W + \log P_X + \log S_X - \log P_M - \log S_M$$

Finally, Equation (11) defines the rate of growth of output, $D \log Y$, which is obtained by assuming trade account equilibrium.[51] We follow Fagerberg (1988) by defining first the level of output implicit in current account equilibrium $P_X X = P_M M$, where P_X and P_M are the export and the import price respectively, both in domestic currency, and X and M are the export and import quantities. Dividing and multiplying by the level of world demand W, and of domestic output Y, respectively the two sides of the identity above, and defining $S_X = X/W$ the share of domestic exports and $S_M = M/Y$ the share of imports over output, after rearranging, the level of output consistent with current account equilibrium (the 'equilibrium output') is:

$$Y^* = WP_X S_X / P_M S_M$$

Taking logs we obtain $\log Y^*$ in Equation (11). The equation assumes that the rate of growth of output is the result of an adjustment mechanism (controlled by policy) which tends to maintain current account equilibrium, and hence $Y^* = Y$, thus ruling out the possibility of indefinite net debt accumulation. The adjustment parameter α_1 captures the intensity of the balance of payments constraint as lower values imply a slower adjustment towards the equilibrium output level and hence the possibility of running current disequilibria for longer periods.

To consider the distinction between regional and extra regional sources of knowledge diffusion, Equation (5) was modified as follows:

$$D \log T = \alpha_6 (\log T^* - \log T) + \sigma_1 \log T_{F1} + \sigma_2 \log T_{F2}$$
$$+ \sigma_3 \log S_{MH1} + \sigma_4 \log S_{MH2} \qquad (5a)$$
$$\log T^* = \log \gamma_5 + \sigma_5 \log F + \sigma_6 \log S_D$$

Equation (5a) differs from Equation (5) only with respect to the variables representing the foreign knowledge spillovers. The four foreign variables entering Equation (5a) are the stocks of foreign knowledge T_{F1}, TF_2 and the shares of high-tech imports S_{MH1}, S_{MH2} (1 = regional, 2 = extra-regional).

NOTES

*   University of Rome, 'La Sapienza', College of Europe, Bruges.
1.   This paragraph draws on Padoan (2000), Ch. 7.
2.   Source: European Commission (1998).
3.   See Rifkin (1995).
4.   For a review, see IMF (1997).
5.   On this point, see Neven and Wyplosz (1996).
6.   See F. Daveri and G. Tabellini (1997).
7.   See, for instance, European Commission (1998), Padoan (2000), Ch. 7.
8.   See again, European Commission (1998).
9.   See CER–Svimez (1998).
10. We refer to the intensity of non-specialized labour, while the intensity of skilled labour may increase after restructuring.
11. See, for example, D. Audet (1996).
12. See Lall (1998), Ernst and Guerrieri (1997).
13. Fontagnè, Freudenberg and Péridy (1998), De Nardis and Traù (1998).

14. See Davies and Lyons (1996). A comparison of the sectoral dimension of R&D in Europe and in the US is presented in Eaton, Gutierrez and Kortum (1998).
15. Neven and Wyplosz (1996) suggest a similar classification.
16. These areas are identified as subsectors, respectively, of Non-electric equipment (ISIC 3825) and Electric equipment (ISIC 3832), which do not appear separately in Table 3.4.
17. J. Eaton et al. (1998), op. cit.
18. With regard to Europe, see Neven and Wyplosz (1996), and Padoan (2000). Regarding the US, see *The Economist*, 'The strange life of low tech America', 17 October 1998.
19. Data for Germany do not include the eastern Länder.
20. An analytical definition of the indicators of mobility and flexibility presented in this chapter, as well as a discussion of their merits and limits, is in Padoan (2000), Ch. 7, Appendix.
21. See also Guerrieri and Manzocchi (1996). Similar conclusions are found in studies that utilize data for industrial production rather than for exports; see, for example, De Nardis and Malgarini (1998).
22. See Padoan (2000), Ch. 7, Tables 7.11–7.14.
23. This section draws on Padoan (1998) and (1999).
24. Theoretical contributions include Grossman and Helpman (1989, 1990), Romer (1990), Verspagen (1993). Empirical contributions include Fagerberg (1988), Amable and Verspagen (1995), Amendola, Guerrieri and Padoan (1992), Magnier and Toujas-Bernate (1994), Greenhalgh (1990), Greenhalgh, Taylor and Wilson (1994).
25. Theoretical contributions include Ben David and Loewy (1995), empirical analyses include Coe and Helpman (1993), Coe, Helpman and Hoffmeister (1994), Keffer (1995). Padoan (1999) offers a brief survey.
26. A survey is offered in Fagerberg (1994). Ben David and Loewy (1995) develop a model of trade and growth where aggregate results depend on structural characteristics. While the model shows that openness enhances growth thanks to knowledge diffusion through trade it remains unclear where, in a n-country world, knowledge is produced in the first place.
27. See Pavitt (1984), Dosi, Pavitt and Soete (1990), Bell and Pavitt (1995).
28. Pavitt's taxonomy considers more than four sectors. Other sectors in addition to the ones introduced in the model, are 'food and agriculture' (resource-intensive), energy-intensive, information-intensive (finance and retailing). For a recent reassessment and for the implications for development policies see Bell and Pavitt (1995).
29. A complete classification of sectors used in this chapter is available on request from the author.
30. See Padoan (1998).
31. In the case of Germany the stock of foreign knowledge excludes patents granted to US and Japanese firms (i.e. it includes only patents granted to European firms in the US). Different definitions of the variable T_W were tried in estimation for all national cases but with the exception of Germany the best results were obtained with the 'world' stock of patents.
32. Amendola, Guerrieri and Padoan (1992) find that Italy's technological specialization structure is not related to her trade specialization structure.
33. See Perez (1995).
34. This simulation was not carried out for Italy and Japan as β_9 was set to zero in estimation in these two countries' cases.
35. This paragraph draws on Padoan (1999).
36. Each time defined so as to exclude the country under investigation. This also implies that the high-tech import share is split between a 'regional' and an 'extra-regional' component.
37. In continuous time the reciprocal of the speed of adjustment $1/\alpha$ is the mean time lag. That is, the time necessary for about 63 per cent of the discrepancy between the actual and the partial equilibrium value to be eliminated. See Gandolfo (1981).
38. This is consistent with results obtained by Verspagen (1993) and by Amable and Verspagen (1995).
39. Both Verspagen (1993) and Amable and Verspagen (1995) find empirical support to this assumption.
40. This aspect is discussed in the literature on 'national system of innovations'. See for example Nelson (1993).

41. This would require to consider for example both sector-specific and country-specific R&D efforts, the latter possibly limited to pre-competitive research investment, as well as sector-specific patent counts. The size and empirical tractability of the model would obviously be modified.

42. Actually, the size of the science-based sector should be proxied by the share of domestic production in the sector or, alternatively, by the share of science-based exports in total domestic exports, rather than by S_D. Model parsimony in the first case and irrelevant differences in estimation in the second case suggested the use of S_D, allowing to gain something in analytical and empirical handling.

43. Equation (5) represents the accumulation of what may be defined 'tangible' knowledge, thus omitting that significant part of knowledge accumulation and diffusion that is intangible and tacit. See Dosi Pavitt and Soete (1990). While we are quite aware of this omission we would argue that at least part of the accumulation and transmission of tacit knowledge may be captured in the form of the adjustment equations where the adjustment coefficients are (also) a function of such components.

44. As Keller (1996) suggests not all imports are vehicles of technology diffusion but only imports of intermediate goods. In the context of Pavitt's taxonomy this role is played by the aggregate we have defined as high-tech imports.

45. See Abramovitz (1986) and Ben-David and Loewy (1995).

46. See Coe and Helpman (1994), Coe, Helpman and Hoffmeister (1994), Keller (1995) and the survey in Padoan (1999).

47. For the case of developing countries see Freeman and Hagedoorn (1994). For the role of foreign direct investment in technology diffusion see Lichtenberg and van Pottelsberghe de la Potterie (1996).

48. Of course alternative specifications of the channels of diffusion of foreign technology are possible. One possibility is to build a composite variable linking imports to the stock of foreign knowledge. I thank one referee for pointing this out.

49. In principle, the aggregate export share S_X rather than the high-tech export share S_{XH} should have been considered as high-tech imports enter as intermediates in traditional goods as well. The specification presented reflects some of the empirical findings discussed below. It could also be argued that the component associated with β_{14} is redundant as domestic firms will choose between domestic and foreign intermediate goods, included in S_{MH}, according to their quality as proxied by the relative stock of knowledge. While this is correct in principle the sectoral aggregation chosen here is such that both complements and substitute goods are included in the same macrosector. Empirical results below support this assumption.

50. Note that parameters β_{10}, β_{14} play two different roles in the model. The first captures the intensity of spillover of high-tech imports on domestic knowledge accumulation. The second captures the intensity of high-tech import contents in domestic exports.

51. In its present formulation the model considers only trade in manufactures as aggregated according to Pavitt's taxonomy, hence the rate of growth of output defined here is not obtained under the assumption of full current account equilibrium. This is only an apparent limitation. Nothing prevents the extension to the other components of the current account.

REFERENCES

Abramovitz, M.A. (1986), 'Catching Up, forging ahead and falling behind', *Journal of Economic History*, 46, 385–406.

Amable, B. and B. Verspagen (1995), 'The role of technology in market shares dynamics', *Applied Economics*, 27, 197–204.

Amendola, G., P. Guerrieri and P.C. Padoan (1992), 'International patterns of technological accumulation and trade', *Journal of International and Comparative Economics*, 1, 173–97.

Archibugi, D. and J. Michie (1995), 'The globalisation of technology: a new taxonomy', *Cambridge Journal of Economics*, 19, 121–40.

Archibugi D. and M. Pianta (1992), *The Technological Specialization of Advanced Countries*, Dordrecht, Kluwer.

Audet, D. (1996), 'Globalisation in the clothing industry', in OECD, *Globalisation of Industry*, Paris.

Bell, M. and K. Pavitt (1995), 'The Development of technological capabilities', in I. ul Haque et al., *Trade, Technology and International Competitiveness*, Washington: Economic Development Institute of The World Bank.

Ben-David, D. and M. Loewy (1995), *Free Trade and Long-Run Growth*, CEPR working paper 1183.

Breschi, S. and F. Malerba (1996), 'Sectoral innovation systems', in C. Edquist (ed.), *Systems of Innovation: Theory and Evidence*, Oxford: Oxford University Press.

Cantwell, J. (1989), *Technological Accumulation and Multinational Corporations*, Oxford: Basil Blackwell.

Cer-Svimez (1998), *Rapporto sull'industria e sulle politiche di industrializzazione nel Mezzogiorno*, Bologna: il Mulino.

Coe, D. and E. Helpman (1993), *International R&D Spillovers*, NBER working paper 4444.

Coe, D., E. Helpman and A. Hoffmeister (1994), *North–South R&D Spillovers*, IMF working paper 94/144.

Daveri, F. and G. Tabellini (1997), 'Unemployment, growth and taxation in industrial countries', *CEPR Discussion Paper n. 1615*.

Davies, S. and B. Lyons (1996), *Industrial Organisation in the European Union*, Oxford: Oxford University Press.

De Nardis, S. and M. Malgarini (1998), *Cambiamento, stabilità, rafforzamento. I vantaggi comparati dei paesi europei nell'era della globalizzazione*, Centro Studi Confindustria.

De Nardis, S. and F. Traù (1998), 'Specializzazione settoriale e qualità dei prodotti: misure della pressione competitiva sull'industria Italiana', *CSC working paper n.17*, Confindustria, October.

Dollar, D. and E. Wolff (1993), *Competitiveness, Convergence and International Specialization*, Cambridge, MA: MIT Press.

Dosi, G., K. Pavitt and L. Soete (1990), *The Economics of Technological Change and International Trade*, Brighton: Wheatsheaf.

D. Ernst and P. Guerrieri (1997), 'International production networks and changing trade patterns in East Asia: the case of the electronics industry', *DRUID working paper n.9717*, Copenhagen.

Eaton J., E. Gutierrez and S. Kortum (1998), 'European technology policy', *Economic Policy*, 27, 405–58.

European Commission (1998), *European Competitiveness in the Triad*, European Economy, Supplement A n.7, July 1998.

Fagerberg, J. (1988), 'International competitiveness', *Economic Journal*, 98, 355–74.

Fagerberg, J. (1994), 'Technology and international differences in growth rates', *Journal of Economic Literature*, 32, 1147–75.

Fagerberg, J. (1996), 'Technology and competitiveness', *Oxford Review of Economic Policy*, 12(3).

Fontagnè, L., M. Freudenberg and N. Péridy (1998), 'Intra-industry trade and the Single Market: quality matters', *CEPR Discussion Paper n. 1959*.

Freeman, C. and J. Hagedoorn (1994), 'Catching up or falling behind: patterns in international inter-firm technology partnering', *World Development*, 22, 771–80.

Gandolfo, G. (1981), *Qualitative Analysis and Econometric Estimation of Continuous Time Dynamic Models*, Amsterdam: North Holland.

Greenhalgh, C. (1990), 'Innovation and trade performance in the UK', *Economic Journal*, 100, 105–18.

Greenhalgh, C., P. Taylor and R. Wilson (1994), 'Innovation and export volumes and prices: a disaggregated study', *Oxford Economic Papers*, 46, 102–34.

Grossman, G.M. and E. Helpman (1989) *Growth and Welfare in a Small Open Economy*, NBER w. p. 2970.

Grossman, G.M. and E. Helpman (1990), 'Comparative advantage and long run growth', *American Economic Review*, 80, 796–815.

Grossman, G.M. and E. Helpman (1991), *Innovation and Growth in the Global Economy*, Cambridge, MA: MIT Press.

Guerrieri, P. and S. Manzocchi (1996), 'Patterns of trade and foreign direct investment in European manufacturing: convergence or polarisation?', *Rivista Italiana degli Economisti*, 2(1),

IMF (1997) *Globalization: Opportunities and Challenges*, World Economic Outlook, May 1997, Washington, DC.

Keller, W. (1995), *International R&D Spillovers and Intersectoral Trade Flows: Do They Match?*, mimeo, Yale University.

Keller, W. (1996), *Are International R&D Spillovers Trade-related? Analyzing Spillovers among Randomly Matched Trade Partners*, mimeo, University of Wisconsin-Madison.

Krugman, P. and A.J. Venables (1996), 'Integration, specialization and adjustment', *European Economic Review*, 40(3–5), 959–67.

Lall, S. (1998), 'Exports of manufactures by developing countries: emerging patterns of trade and location', *Oxford Review of Economic Policy*, 14(2).

Lichtenberg, F. and R. van Pottelsberghe de la Potterie (1996), *International R&D Spillovers: A Closer Examination*, NBER w. p. 5763.

Magnier, A. and J. Toujias–Bernate (1994), 'Technology and trade: empirical evidences for the major five industrialized countries', *Weltwirstschaftliches Archiv*, 130(3), 494–520.

Nelson, R.R. (ed.) (1993), *National Innovation Systems*, New York: Oxford University Press.

Neven D. and C. Wyplosz (1996), 'Relative prices, trade and restructuring in European industry', *CEPR Discussion Paper n. 1451*.

OECD (1996), *Globalisation of Industry*, Paris.

Padoan, P.C. (1998), 'Trade knowledge accumulation and diffusion: a sectoral perspective', *Structural Change and Economic Dynamics, n 4*.

Padoan, P.C. (1999), 'Europe's industry, competitiveness and technological integration', *Journal of International Development Planning Literature*, 14(4), October–December.

Padoan, P.C. (ed.) (2000), *Employment and Growth in Monetary Union*, Cheltenham: Edward Elgar.

Pasinetti, L.L. (1981), *Structural Change and Economic Growth*, Cambridge, MA: Harvard University Press.

Pavitt, K. (1984), 'Sectoral patterns of technical change: towards a taxonomy and a theory', *Research Policy* 13, 343–75.

Perez, T. (1995), *Imprese Multinazionali e Diffusione Internazionale della Tecnologia*, unpublished PhD thesis, University of Ancona.

Rifkin, J. (1995), *The End of Work*, New York: Putnam.

Romer, P. (1990), 'Endogenous technological change', *Journal of Political Economy*, 98, pp. S71–S102.

Venables, A. (1995), 'Economic integration and the allocation of firms', *American Economic Association P&P*, 85, 296–300.

4. Mergers and acquisitions in globalizing Europe

William R. Emmons and Frank A. Schmid

European Economic and Monetary Union, ongoing financial liberalization, and a solid economic recovery have combined to create an explosion in transactions volume in the European market for corporate control. European mergers and acquisitions (both domestic and cross-border) occurred at a rate of about $500 billion per quarter during 1999–2000. The majority of the firms involved in the world's largest cross-border mergers in recent years have been European. British, German, French, Dutch and Spanish firms each carried out total cross-border takeovers of at least $25 billion during 1999. At the same time, foreign firms made total acquisitions of at least $25 billion in the UK, Sweden, Germany, France and the Netherlands during 1999. While the balance of cross-border mergers and acquisitions activity in the major European countries was positive – that is, each nation's firms made more purchases of foreign firms than foreign firms made of domestic companies – the cross-border mergers and acquisitions balance of trade for the United States was a massive negative $139 billion during 1999 alone.

The corporate control market, broadly construed, encompasses many disparate events and transactions at various stages in the life cycles of corporations. For example, bank and other debt-financing, venture capital and other private equity investments, initial public offerings and other 'going public' events, including privatizations, management buyouts and other types of ownership restructuring, are all corporate control events. However, one high-profile part of the market for corporate control has captured the lion's share of public attention. European mergers and acquisitions are headline news and, indeed, these transactions have the potential to transform the structure of many European economies and industries rapidly and radically. Repercussions for other spheres of European economic and social life are likely.

There is no consensus among participants or observers regarding the relative importance of the forces driving the current extraordinary level of takeover activity involving European firms, nor is there consensus on what the implications are likely to be. One thing is clear, however: the current takeover boom unfolding in continental Europe exists in the shadow – and under the influence – of similar booms in takeover activity in the Anglo-American markets for many decades (Gaughan, 1999). In one sense, therefore, the continental European takeover boom is merely a reflection of the 'Wall Street culture' that has been imported into mainland Europe in recent years.

In another sense, of course, the takeover boom is deeply threatening to the distinctive economic, financial and social environments of (particularly continental) European nations. Assisted by aggressive American investment banks, home-grown advocates of 'financial modernization' in Europe have used several arguments to convince sceptics to lower their resistance to the 'Americanization' of Europe's corporate-governance systems. One argument frequently employed by financiers and other self-styled reformers is that adoption of the more financial market-driven corporate culture of the Anglo-American world will bring huge benefits to continental European investors in terms of more efficient use of scarce capital, and hence higher returns on investment. Ironically, European capital appears to be flooding out of the region as the takeover boom unfolds, suggesting that there has not been a scarcity of domestically generated investment funds relative to the investment opportunities at hand.

Another argument often advanced in support of radical change in European financial systems is that formerly opaque and insider-dominated corporate-governance regimes should be made transparent and fair in order to encourage wider participation in capital ownership. Small shareholdings, for example, should be encouraged both to strengthen social cohesion and a sense of shareholder democracy, as well as to prepare an aging population to shoulder a larger part of the burden of providing for its own old age.

A somewhat different argument offered by apologists for the Anglo-American system is that resistance is useless in any case: the future of finance is the Anglo-American model, and the best approach is to embrace it quickly in order to participate in it and to exert influence on its local implementation. The alternative, according to this point of view, is to lose control over future financial decision-making and, perhaps, even of some vital parts of national economies. For example, several large European banks have undertaken an essentially defensive strategy toward financial market reform, spending large sums on British and North American specialist investment banks in hopes of 'transplanting' the financial market culture that thrives in London and New York into their larger organizations both in Europe and abroad. Similarly, many continental European stock exchanges are exploring mergers or cooperation agreements with US and UK exchanges, graphically symbolizing the 'bear hug' strategy being followed by an increasing number of important players in European financial markets.

This chapter provides background on mergers and acquisitions in both the US and Europe. We review the potential advantages and disadvantages of takeovers from the standpoint of overall economic efficiency as well as the empirical evidence that attempts to measure the actual gains and losses of takeovers in practice. We present three case-studies of recent cross-border takeover attempts in Europe and, finally, draw conclusions regarding the potential impact of the recent takeover boom in globalizing Europe.

BACKGROUND ON US MERGERS AND ACQUISITIONS

The history of mergers and acquisitions in the United States may be particularly relevant for Europe today for several reasons. First, the United States' system of corporation law is two-tiered. There is federal (that is, national) jurisdiction over some aspects of business, such as interstate commerce and banking. At the same time, individual states retain important roles in shaping the legal environment in which corporate activity takes place. Takeover legislation, for example, has differed across states and has led to distinctive patterns in the choice of legal domicile of corporations and the takeover tactics employed in particular contests. The European corporate governance environment is also two-tiered, consisting of both European Union and national competencies in particular circumstances.

Another important reason for examining the US history of mergers and acquisitions is the apparent tendency for financial and business practices to converge across major economic areas over time. If it is true that continental Europe is globalizing in an Anglo-American direction – that is, if broad and deep financial markets and shareholder rights are in the ascendance throughout Europe – then it behooves serious scholars of European corporate governance to examine the institutions, motivations and precedents that have characterized US developments.

After reviewing the theoretical and empirical literature on mergers and acquisitions in the US in the sections below, we summarize the historical record of US mergers and acquisitions. Scholars typically speak of 'waves' of merger activity, and we organize our historical discussion into five major merger waves that occurred in the US during the last 100 years.

Theoretical Considerations

Why do takeovers occur? Hirshleifer (1995) and others have suggested numerous possible advantages and disadvantages associated with takeovers. The top half of Table 4.1 provides a summary of the most commonly cited reasons for takeovers from the standpoint of overall economic efficiency. The bottom part of Table 4.1 lists possible reasons why some of the takeovers that occur may not be efficient for the economy as a whole.

Table 4.1   Potential advantages and disadvantages of takeovers

---

Potential Advantages

Economies of scale in:
Production
Information systems
Marketing
Financing

Economies of scope (synergy):
Complementary business lines
Re-usable information
Re-usable managerial resources

Replacement of weaker by stronger management teams

Potential Disadvantages

Transaction costs:
Fees paid to lawyers, accountants, bankers, consultants
Disruption for managers and employees
Disruption for customers and suppliers

Pure wealth redistribution:
Tax-driven takeovers
Expropriation of bondholders' wealth
Expropriation of minority shareholders' wealth
Wealth transfer from acquiring firm shareholders to target firm shareholders ('overpaying')
Wealth transfer from target firm shareholders to acquiring firm shareholders ('overvalued stock')
Post-merger exercise of market power in product markets

Manifestations of agency costs:
Takeovers as empire building
Management plundering of firm value (excessive compensation, excessive consumption of perquisites)
Unanticipated (or unacknowledged) diseconomies of scale or scope

---

Potential advantages

The potential advantages of takeovers are all related to increased efficiency that can be translated into greater shareholder value (top half of Table 4.1). A takeover may allow a firm to exploit greater economies of scale in production, information systems, marketing, financing of its operations, or any number of other basic business functions. This justification is nearly always cited by the managers and owners proposing a takeover. Another common justification for a takeover is that it will allow the firm to capture economies of scope – that is, synergistic benefits – by combining previously separate businesses. Scope economies may exist in the form of truly complementary business lines; as with scale economies, the payoff could come from any one of several basic business functions that can be performed more efficiently after the businesses are combined. Other sources of scope economies are information or managerial resources that can be transferred and reused in carrying out the acquired activity. A third potential efficiency-related advantage of a takeover is to replace a weak management team with a stronger one. Clearly, identification of the relative abilities of management teams is difficult and will not be made easier by both management teams' attempts to embellish their own credentials. The fact that the stock prices of some 'serial acquirers' remain high suggests that financial markets sometimes do give a large weight to a management team's track record in making acquisitions and integrating the acquired firms into the bidder's operations.

For every potential advantage of a takeover, there is a downside as well. Even if some potential advantage can be identified in advance, it may not be achievable in practice. In fact, many case studies of failed mergers cite poor execution of an otherwise reasonable plan as the source of the merger failure. As the bottom half of Table 4.1 indicates, however, there are many more things that can go wrong in a takeover than simple poor execution. Ultimately, the net benefits of takeovers can be ascertained only with empirical evidence, to which the next section turns.

Potential disadvantages
As noted, potential disadvantages of takeovers consist not only of the *failure* of the promised advantages to materialize, but also of the associated costs that takeovers incur or reveal. Drawing an analogy from the debate between advocates of active and passive investment strategies in financial markets, firms that attempt takeovers must do better than break even because, like active investment managers incurring trading costs, acquirers must 'pay to play'. That is, there are significant transaction costs in takeovers that must be covered first in order to justify doing the deal at all. These costs include the fees paid to lawyers, accountants, commercial and investment bankers, management consultants, and all the other supporting professionals and firms needed to prepare and carry out a bid. Other transaction costs that may be hidden because they do not involve explicit cash outlays, include disruptions and distractions experienced by managers, employees, customers and suppliers of both firms.

Another potential disadvantage of takeovers from the standpoint of overall economic welfare is the possibility of wealth redistribution. Although redistribution of wealth itself is not necessarily a dead-weight cost to society, transfers that are perceived to be arbitrary or unfair can create resentment and a political backlash that could reduce efficiency. For example, a takeover that is motivated by tax savings alone creates no gain for the economy as a whole because the tax saving of the firm corresponds exactly to the tax loss of the government. A perception that existing tax laws are being abused – perhaps by using 'excessive' amounts of tax-deductible debt to finance a takeover – could lead to counter-productive restrictions being inserted into the tax code. Other pure wealth redistributions that could arise include expropriation of bondholders' or of minority shareholders' wealth as a result of market repricing of securities in light of a proposed takeover. Similarly, shareholders of acquirers or targets could receive windfall gains or experience windfall losses as a result of a bid price that is far from the previous market price. Acquirers that 'overpay' inflict losses on their own shareholders, while acquirers with strong stock prices – or an 'overvalued' exchange rate if based abroad – can shift some of the risk of a crash in their own stock price (or exchange rate) to the target's owners. Finally, a takeover that results in greater market power allows a firm to extract wealth from customers and/or suppliers, although competition authorities have been alert to this possibility for many decades.

The final category of potential disadvantages of takeovers involves the dead-weight costs associated with managerial agency conflicts that may be manifested in – and abetted by – the takeover process. CEOs who overestimate their own ability to manage large firms-summarized by Roll (1986) in his 'hubris hypothesis' – or who crave the prestige and perquisites of corporate power, may be able to satisfy these selfish motives by building a corporate empire through acquisition. Shareholders and other stakeholders may suffer some of the consequences of ill-fated empire-building because they are unable to control the firm's management adequately.

Similarly, executive compensation and perquisites may escalate as firm size increases even if efficiency is not enhanced. A somewhat different version of the basic agency problem that is aggravated by the ability to carry out takeovers appears in the form of a CEO or management team that has been successful in the past, but which overextends itself. If controls are weak, a past winner may even enjoy greater latitude in making potentially large mistakes. Failure to recognize or acknowledge potentially serious diseconomies of scale or scope associated with a proposed takeover could therefore destroy a great deal of value and inflict harm on many third parties.

Empirical Evidence on US Takeovers

What are the actual results of takeovers? Hirshleifer (1992) summarizes the extensive empirical evidence, largely drawn from the US. A basic outline of the facts is as follows. Shareholders of sellers – that is, firms that are the targets of successful takeover bids – typically earn very large positive returns over the transaction period, often on the order of 20 to 30 per cent. Shareholders of buyers – firms that successfully take over other firms – typically earn much smaller returns; evidence of *negative* returns is not statistically conclusive but there are certainly not large positive stock market returns or efficiency gains available to bidders on average. Similarly, overall gains to a merger or acquisition – that is, the sum total of net economic benefits created – may be slightly negative or positive, but are certainly not large and positive on average. Interestingly, one possible exception to these generalizations is that successful hostile takeovers appear to be value-enhancing, on average.

There is evidence that wealth redistribution among financial and other stakeholders is common in takeovers. As noted already, selling shareholders are usually winners; acquiring shareholders and bondholders are often losers. Finally, the likelihood of any given firm being involved in a takeover is strongly related to the level of takeover activity occurring at the time. This is evidence of 'fads' or 'waves' of takeovers. The fact that takeover activity tends to be concentrated among certain industries at certain points in time is further evidence of 'contagious' behaviour in conducting mergers and acquisitions.

Gains to sellers, buyers and overall

Bradley, Desai and Kim (1988) reported that shareholders of firms that are acquired received large premiums relative to the pre-acquisition market price of the firm. The typical premium varied over different time periods, but was consistently positive. Bidders' returns were typically negative, but the overall returns – sellers' returns plus buyers' returns, weighted by relative market capitalizations – were positive. Franks, Harris and Mayer (1988) found that the abnormal negative returns to bidders continued for two years after the acquisition. A recent paper focusing on UK acquirers of British and overseas companies during the 1990–96 period came to the same conclusion (Chatterjee and Aw, 2000).

Wealth redistribution

Asquith and Wizman (1990) documented losses imposed on bondholders in highly leveraged takeovers. Shareholders appeared to gain, but by less than the loss incurred by bondholders. Shleifer and Summers (1988) argued that corporate stakeholders, such as workers, are often harmed in takeovers, particularly hostile ones. If workers make non-transferable investments in their jobs or enter into other types of implicit contracts with their employers, they may possess very little bargaining power after new management arrives. Simply keeping their jobs may be the best these workers can hope for, so they are willing to make concessions in order to do so. In the absence of a takeover, workers would have been better off.

Evidence of merger waves

The next section discusses five periods in the twentieth century during which an unusually large number of mergers and acquisitions took place. The clustering in time of takeover activity suggests that something besides pure value maximization is behind takeovers; otherwise, it would seem that the flow of merger activity would be more nearly constant (Matsusaka, 1993). Many theories have been proposed to rationalize takeover waves; most are related to some version of the idea that there is 'safety in numbers'.

Five Twentieth-Century Merger Waves in the United States

Gaughan (1999, Chapter 2) describes five distinct 'merger waves' in the United States, including the current one. A merger wave is defined as a clear and sustained (but temporary) pick-up in takeover activity along with – at least in hindsight – certain recurring themes, justifications or outcomes that are common to a large fraction of the takeovers that took place during the period.

The First Wave, 1897–1904

The merger wave 100 years ago was characterized by hundreds of horizontal mergers – that is, mergers between firms in the same industry – culminating in vast accumulations of market power by leading firms in several important US industries. An outstanding example of this merger wave was US Steel, which represented the amalgamation of 785 separate steel-producing firms. Hammered together by J.P. Morgan and Andrew Carnegie, US Steel accounted for as much as 75 per cent of the United States' steel-making capacity at one time. Not to be outdone, American Tobacco once commanded approximately 90 per cent of its domestic market and Standard Oil (owned by John D. Rockefeller) controlled 85 per cent of the oil market. Some of the merger activity certainly was driven by increases in the minimum efficient scale of production. Large-scale amalgamation also appears to have been driven by the desire of leading financiers and industrialists to eliminate 'ruinous competition' among separately owned and managed firms in the same industry.

In principle, the Sherman Antitrust Act of 1890 should have limited the degree of industrial concentration that occurred. The Act was obviously in-effective, although Gaughan (1999, p. 23) argues that this was due primarily to the failure of the United States Department of Justice to enforce it effectively.

It took the trust-busting fervour of the Theodore Roosevelt and William Howard Taft Administrations (1901–9, 1909–13) and the passage of the Clayton Act in 1914 to exert effective control over market power increasing horizontal mergers in the United States. Some of the combinations created around the turn of the century were eventually reversed; few others were allowed to form. Gaughan (1999, p. 26) reports that the majority of horizontal mergers ultimately failed, suggesting that greater scale alone was not sufficient justification for some of the takeovers that occurred, and that the First Wave was destined to be self-limiting.

The Second Wave, 1916–29

If the First Wave was characterized by horizontal mergers with the intent of monopolizing markets, the Second Wave was marked by vertical mergers – acquisition by a firm of its supplier or customer – and the formation of oligopolies (Gaughan, 1999, pp. 26–7). This wave produced the first group of significant conglomerate mergers (that is, takeovers of firms in different or loosely related business lines). The Sherman and Clayton Acts were largely silent on these types of business combinations, and the focus of competition policy turned to combating price-fixing rather than structural remedies.

Small groups of investors discovered during this period that they could control large firms through pyramid holding companies – a set of shell companies whose purpose was to concentrate effective control while investing only a fraction of the ultimate target firm's equity. Pyramids are present in Europe today, also, although their frequency and importance are not as great as sometimes asserted; only about 13 per cent of a sample of large German firms contained a pyramid among its ownership structure in 1992 (Gorton and Schmid, 2000, p. 16).

As in later merger waves – particularly the Fourth Wave in the 1980s – Second Wave mergers were characterized by large amounts of debt financing, a capital structure that turned out to be disastrous when the economy later fell into depression. The Second Wave ended with the stock market crash of October 1929, even before the Great Depression took hold. Household and business confidence eroded after the stock market crash, bringing to an end the expansion and merger plans of many firms.

The Third Wave, 1965–69

As in the two previous US merger waves (and the two subsequent ones, as will be seen below), the takeover boom of the late 1960s coincided with an economic boom. As in the Second Wave, conglomerate mergers were prominent; the Federal Trade Commission reported that 80 per cent of the mergers and acquisitions during the 1965–75 period were of this type. Horizontal and vertical mergers were reviewed more critically by the Justice Department throughout the 1960s, having been armed since 1950 with the stricter provisions of the Celler-Kefauver Act, the third major component of US antitrust legislation. A setback at the US Supreme Court in 1972 halted the aggressive anti-monopoly campaign of the Justice Department, however, setting the stage for later merger waves. The Supreme Court ruled at that time that the relevant market for antitrust analysis was international, rather than national, a finding that continues to reverberate in the United States and Europe today. The Williams Act of 1968, which regulated public tender offers, is another product of this merger wave that has had lasting effects.

As in earlier merger waves, the long-term performance of participating firms appears to have been no better, and may have been worse, than that of non-merging firms. Gaughan (1999, p. 38) reports that 60 per cent of the cross-industry (conglomerate) acquisitions that occurred during the 1960–82 period had been sold or divested by 1989.

The Fourth Wave, 1981–89
Gaughan (1999, p. 43) suggests that the most significant aspect of the Fourth Wave of US mergers was the frequency of hostile takeovers. The peak of activity in hostile takeovers was 1988, when 217 tender offers were launched; 46 of these were contested by the target firm. This was the year of the Kohlberg Kravis Roberts leveraged buyout of RJR Nabisco, a transaction that came to symbolize the 'decade of greed' on Wall Street. Merger terminology that entered the Wall Street vernacular during this decade included 'greenmail', 'corporate raider', 'white knight', poison pill', and many other colourful – if somewhat uncomplimentary – expressions.

Another feature of the Fourth Wave was the relatively large size of many targets. Many billion-dollar deals – some hostile – were carried out with the help of aggressive investment banks such as Drexel Burnham Lambert, which pioneered the original-issue junk-bond market. As in the Second Wave of US mergers in the 1920s, large amounts of debt became available to finance large takeovers. Two other notable features of the Fourth Wave were a resurgence of activist state law-making to protect indigenous firms, and the emergence of non-US firms as important bidders for US targets. Many European firms sought significant shares of selected US markets, as when British Petroleum acquired Standard Oil of Ohio in 1987. By the end of the decade, Japanese firms had become active buyers of US firms, real estate and other assets.

The Fifth Wave, 1992–present
Although it is still premature to write the history of a merger wave that is still under way, it appears that the Fifth Wave will be distinguished from previous waves by several features. The sheer size and number of mergers and acquisitions in the US during the 1990s dwarf anything seen before. Average deal size

more than doubled in the late 1990s relative to the early 1990s and earlier years (Gaughan, 1999). The nearly 8,000 US takeovers taking place each year beginning in 1997 are more than double the number in any previous year except 1969 and 1970, at the peak of the Third Wave.

Other differences characteristic of the Fifth Wave thus far are also of degree rather than of kind. Hostile takeovers have been less frequent in the 1990s than during the 1980s; leverage has been less prominent even though debt financing is abundantly available; and relatively more takeovers have been to strengthen existing business lines rather than to expand into new ones. As in all previous merger waves, the roles of a strong economy and high stock valuations should not be underestimated. Banking and telecommunications have been the industries most affected by merger activity so far during the Fifth Wave.

Lessons from US Merger Waves

US merger waves are of more than historical interest for those interested in European mergers and acquisitions today. As Gaughan remarks:

> various merger waves provoked major changes in the structure of American business. They were instrumental in transforming American industry from a collection of small and medium-sized businesses to the current form, which includes thousands of multi-national corporations (Gaughan, 1999, p. 21).

Clearly, mergers and acquisitions are capable of reshaping a nation's economy. Something similar appears to be under way in Europe, as Economic and Monetary Union coincides with revolutionary changes in financial markets and in corporate governance practices.

At the same time, it is sobering to recall that mergers and acquisitions appear to have achieved a very modest success rate for the US firms involved (although it is too early to pass judgement on the latest merger waves). This puzzling failure of mergers and acquisitions on average to produce the dazzling payoffs confidently predicted by managers when the deals are proposed could be related to the fact that mergers seem to happen in waves. In other words, the motivation for many mergers may be as much the fact that 'everybody is doing it', as an independent and soundly reasoned economic justification. Alternatively, there may be legitimate efficiency gains in many cases that are offset in part or entirely by some of the disadvantages of mergers described above.

A policy lesson that emerges from an examination of merger waves in US history is the fact that anti-monopoly legislation by itself is not enough to prevent industrial concentration. Sufficient political will and administrative competence to enforce the laws are also necessary. A related factor is the complexity and ambiguity created by a two-tiered system of takeover regulation – state and federal in the United States, national and at EU level in Europe.

Continuing tension between overlapping jurisdictions can be expected for the indefinite future.

The role of hostile takeovers in improving the efficiency of US industry is still hotly debated. The large number of hostile takeovers carried out or unsuccessfully attempted during the Fourth Wave in the US have yet to age sufficiently to allow definitive evaluation of their merits. In principle, involuntary changes in corporate control, if executed in a fair and transparent market, could create substantial improvements in management efficiency. This follows from the extensive documentation of pervasive agency conflicts in the management of large corporations, and some evidence of operating efficiency gains after successful hostile takeovers. On the other hand, hostile takeovers may create or be driven by distortions of their own. For example, a raider may be able to extract concessions from an incumbent workforce or may 'steal' from minority shareholders or bondholders whose property rights are inadequately protected.

MERGERS AND ACQUISITIONS IN EUROPE

How active is the takeover market in Europe today? What are some of the themes we can identify in the mergers and acquisitions that are – and are not – taking place? Should we view the current takeover boom in Europe as a harbinger of far-reaching changes in the European industrial and economic landscape? Or are other forces at work? This section turns to the recent European mergers and acquisitions experience.

Magnitude of Current European Takeover Activity

All cross-border mergers and acquisitions worldwide totalled $720 billion during 1999, compared to $151 billion during 1990 (UNCTAD, 2000a, 2000b). European Union firms were responsible for about $500 billion of the total as buyers, and for about $350 billion as sellers. Total European mergers and acquisitions – that is, including both cross-border and purely domestic transactions – amounted to $528 billion in the fourth quarter of 1999 alone, and to $414 billion in the first quarter of 2000, according to J.P. Morgan (Skorecki, 2000). Tables 4.2, 4.3 and 4.4 provide details on global cross-border merger and acquisition activity during 1999.

The prominent participation of European firms is quite striking in the figures cited above and in the tables. Table 4.2 shows that three-quarters of the firms involved in the world's ten largest cross-border mergers during 1999 were European (KPMG, 2000). Table 4.3 shows that British firms completed $246 billion of cross-border acquisitions in 1999 – and this does not include the

Table 4.2   Ten largest cross-border mergers and acquisitions in the world, 1999

(European firms in **bold** type)

Bidder	Country	Target	Country	Value ($ billion)
Vodafone Group plc	**UK**	Airtouch Communications Inc	USA	69.3
Zeneca Group plc	**UK**	**Astra AB**	**Sweden**	37.7
BP Amoco plc	**UK**	Arco Atlantic	USA	34.0
Mannesmann AG	**Germany**	**Orange plc**	**UK**	28.5
Hoechst AG	**Germany**	**Aventis/JV Rhone-Poulenc SA**	**France**	22.0
Repsol SA	**Spain**	Ypf Sa	Argentina	15.5
Deutsche Telekom AG	**Germany**	**One-2-One**	**UK**	13.6
Total SA	**France**	**Petrofina SA**	**Belgium**	11.3
ScottishPower plc	**UK**	Pacificorp	USA	10.8
Wal-Mart Stores Inc	USA	**Asda Group plc**	**UK**	10.6

Source: KPMG, 'Cross-border M&A reaches all-time high', http://www.kpmg.com/library/00/february/story3_b2_ac.asp

Table 4.3   Ten countries with largest amount of cross-border purchases and sales completed, 1999

(European countries in **bold** type)

Buying countries	Value ($ billion)	Selling countries	Value ($ billion)
UK	**245.6**	USA	293.4
USA	154.6	**UK**	**123.0**
Germany	**92.7**	**Sweden**	**59.2**
France	**92.2**	**Germany**	**42.4**
Netherlands	**43.8**	**France**	**35.6**
Spain	**25.4**	Canada	28.9
Japan	20.4	**Netherlands**	**26.9**
Belgium	**17.5**	Argentina	20.6
Canada	16.3	**Belgium**	**16.4**
Italy	**14.5**	Japan	15.8
All other countries	75.0	All other countries	136.0
World	798.0	World	798.0

Source: KPMG, 'Cross-border M&A reaches all-time high', http://www.kpmg.com/library/00/february/story3_b2_ac.asp.

largest takeover in history, that by the UK's Vodafone AirTouch of Germany's
Mannesmann, which took place during 2000. German firms made cross-border
acquisitions of $93 billion during 1999 – and this does not include the takeover
by Daimler Benz of Chrysler, which occurred in 1998. French, Dutch and
Spanish firms each carried out total cross-border takeovers of at least $25 billion
during 1999. Meanwhile, foreign firms made total acquisitions of at least $25
billion in the UK, Sweden, Germany, France and the Netherlands during 1999.
Table 4.4 shows that the net cross-border takeover balance of many European
countries was strongly positive during 1999. The largest seller of companies in
the world during 1999 was the United States, where firms worth $293 billion
were sold to non-US acquirers. US-based firms, by way of contrast, made cross-
border acquisitions of 'only' $155 billion, resulting in negative net purchases
of some $139 billion.

*Table 4.4   Net cross-border mergers and acquisitions, 1999 (selected
             countries)*
(European countries in **bold** type)

Country	Net cross-border purchases,[*] 1999 ($ billion)
UK	**122.6**
France	**56.6**
Germany	**50.4**
Netherlands	**16.9**
Japan	4.7
Belgium	**1.0**
Canada	−12.6
USA	−138.8

Note: [*] Net purchases are defined as total purchases minus total sales.

Source: KPMG, 'Cross-border M&A reaches all-time high', http://www.kpmg.com/ library/
00/february/story3_b2_ac.asp.

Case-Studies

We turn now to three case-studies of recent European mergers and acquisitions.
All three involve at least one German firm in order to maintain a thread of institutional continuity. Collectively, these cases illustrate just how rapidly the
corporate control market is evolving in continental Europe, and how profoundly
the new mergers and acquisitions environment may end up affecting Europe.
The case studies are:

- the 1997–98 takeover battle between Krupp and Thyssen;
- the 1999–2000 hostile takeover by Vodafone AirTouch of Mannesmann; and
- the failed friendly merger of Deutsche Bank and Dresdner Bank in early 2000.

We draw lessons from these cases below.

Thyssen's merger with Krupp

Friedrich Krupp GmbH, a German steel and engineering firm, acquired Hoesch AG in 1997 using 'stealth' tactics reminiscent of many hostile takeovers carried out in the US during the 1980s.[1] Krupp acquired 24.9 per cent of the equity of Hoesch, another steelmaker, in the open market before announcing its position. This was possible because German law at that time did not require any shareholder to disclose its stake if it remained below 25 per cent (the comparable threshhold in the US is 5 per cent and it has been lowered subsequently in Germany to 5 per cent, also). In addition, Krupp had worked with a Swiss bank to acquire the stake, rather than with Deutsche Bank, Krupp's *Hausbank*. Hoesch resisted Krupp's approach at first but gave in eventually.

Emboldened by its success in taking over Hoesch, Krupp then set its sights on Thyssen, the largest German steel firm. Like Krupp, Thyssen combined steelmaking with engineering operations. Thyssen rebuffed Krupp's first (friendly) advances, at which time Krupp enlisted Deutsche Bank for the purpose of mounting a hostile bid. Krupp announced an unsolicited tender offer to Thyssen's shareholders in March 1997. Thyssen's management denounced the bid; Thyssen workers demonstrated against the action; high-ranking political leaders suggested Krupp should reconsider (or withdraw) its offer; and general public opinion appeared to oppose a hostile takeover of a leading German firm. Krupp withdrew the offer as observers complained that a hostile takeover was contrary to the spirit of 'Rhineland capitalism', a consensus-oriented economic model that had served Germany well in the post-Second World War period.

Krupp continued talking with Thyssen in negotiations mediated by the Prime Minister of North Rhine-Westfalia, the domicile of both firms. Krupp suggested a limited merger that would combine only the steelmaking operations of the two firms. This proposal met with success and the formation of Thyssen Krupp Stahl AG was announced in April 1997.

Word leaked out in August 1997 that the two firms had continued to talk secretly about a complete merger. The Krupp and Thyssen management boards (*Vorstand*) announced in September that they recommended a full-scale merger. The Thyssen supervisory board (*Aufsichtsrat*) narrowly approved the proposal in January 1998, and the Krupp supervisory board followed in February. Thyssen Krupp AG thus emerged not as a direct result of Krupp's original hostile bid, but in essentially the form proposed at that time by Krupp.

The roles of banks and workers in this merger were noteworthy. Individual high-ranking bankers were found to have encountered serious conflicts of interest. In one case, a Deutsche Bank executive simultaneously served on the supervisory board of Thyssen while Deutsche Bank was advising Krupp in its hostile bid for Thyssen. Similarly, the chairman of Dresdner Bank's supervisory board served on Thyssen's supervisory board while his bank was participating in the financing of Krupp's hostile bid. Workers were key players in the protracted merger contest, in large part due to the differing types of worker codetermination (*Mitbestimmung*) in place at the two firms.[2] One aspect of the difficult negotiations was choosing which type of codetermination would apply to the merged firm. Thyssen's workers fought to retain – but ultimately lost – the larger role in corporate oversight they enjoyed while Thyssen remained independent.

Vodafone AirTouch's hostile takeover of Mannesmann

Vodafone AirTouch plc was a rapidly expanding UK-based firm focused on wireless communication when, in late 1999, it set its sights on Mannesmann AG of Germany, a diversified firm that included automotive, steel, engineering, fixed-line communications and wireless communications in its portfolio of businesses.[3] Mannesmann's shareholders were dispersed both in number and nationality relative to the concentrated domestic ownership structure of many German firms, making a tender offer viable. Vodafone believed it could efficiently extend its own wireless communication network to continental Europe by acquiring Mannesmann's network. At the same time, Vodafone believed it could add value by sharpening Mannesmann's focus – that is, by breaking up the firm and selling its disparate businesses. Vodafone's CEO presented an unsolicited takeover offer to Mannesmann's CEO in November 1999, who rejected it. At this point, Vodafone announced a tender offer directly to Mannesmann's shareholders that represented an 84 per cent premium over the price of Mannesmann's shares before rumours of the bid had begun circulating.

As in the Krupp-Thyssen case two years earlier, the reactions of the German public and of prominent politicians were predominantly negative. The German Chancellor stated that hostile takeover bids 'destroy the culture' of the target company. The Mannesmann management put up a spirited defence, which included its own plans to restructure the firm. Vodafone responded by undertaking a large-scale public relations campaign not only in Germany but in other European countries as well, where large numbers of Mannesmann's shares were held.

The public tender offer was completed successfully in February 2000. The Mannesmann CEO pledged his cooperation in merging and restructuring his firm as part of Vodafone; in return, he was compensated very generously. German and non-German observers began to wonder which German firm would be the next target – or bidder – in a hostile takeover involving the formerly closed 'Deutschland AG'.

Failed friendly merger between Deutsche Bank and Dresdner Bank

The long-awaited large-scale consolidation of the German banking sector appeared to be at hand in March 2000 when Deutsche Bank and Dresdner Bank, two of the largest universal banks in Germany, announced a full-scale merger. Presenting their grand alliance as a courageous step into the twenty-first century global financial market-place, the CEOs of both banks stressed the significant cost savings that would be available from reducing their combined retail banking networks, as well as the global reach and clout they could attain in the 'super-league' of global investment banking. Public misgivings about large-scale job losses were voiced, but investor reaction was positive. Politicians were circumspect, perhaps having accepted the notion that, like Mannesmann, many German firms faced the prospect of being taken over by foreign competitors if they did not quickly steel themselves for making cross-border acquisitions themselves. A large-scale domestic merger might be the necessary first step in this process. Dresdner Bank's leading shareholder (and a smaller investor in Deutsche Bank), the Allianz insurance group, was actively involved in the negotiations to merge the two banks.

Public self-congratulation by the three major players – Deutsche, Dresdner and Allianz – soon turned to mutual recrimination as the deal collapsed in April. Deutsche Bank's CEO had assured the investment bankers at Dresdner Bank that they would be integrated into Deutsche Bank's operations. The executives leading Deutsche Bank's investment banking operations, meanwhile, began grumbling publicly that they had not been consulted about how integration was to occur. When it became clear that Deutsche Bank's investment banking strategy would not easily accommodate Dresdner's operations, what had been a trickle turned into a flood of Dresdner Bank investment bankers leaving the firm. Dresdner Bank reacted by pulling out of the deal. The CEO of Dresdner resigned and many called for Deutsche's CEO to follow suit. Allianz managers appeared stunned by the unpredictable course that events had taken.

The industrial logic of this combination had been acknowledged by all sides. German retail banking is not profitable for most private sector banks and efforts by German banks to crack the top bracket of global investment banking had foundered. Was it really a case of botched communication and irreconcilable personality differences? Or did the German banks reveal their 'feet of clay' when it came to the new world of corporate finance that they, themselves, had trumpeted in their roles as fledgling advisors in previous takeover contests? In short, why did Deutsche not 'go hostile' when Dresdner pulled out if the economics of the deal were so compelling? In the end, the looming presence of a conservative dominant shareholder in Dresdner – the Allianz group – probably precluded a successful hostile bid, at least for the present.

Although later chapters may yet be written in this case, two of Germany's leading banks and the country's leading investor have revealed that they are at present ill-equipped to operate an Anglo-American style takeover market. Ironically, the matchmaking role of Allianz turned out to be counterproductive. Does the widespread presence of large blockholders in many European firms mean that mergers and acquisitions in Europe will evolve along a different track than the one blazed on Wall Street and in the City of London?

Lessons from the case-studies
The lessons we draw from these cases can be summarized briefly. First, the cases illustrate the presence and persistence of several formidable obstacles to the emergence of an Anglo-American-style market for corporate control in Germany particularly, and in continental Europe more generally. These include:

- powerful banks with vested interests in the existing system of corporate finance and corporate governance;
- distinctive ownership structures among European corporations, including still-significant state ownership in some countries and large private-sector blockholders of shares in many companies;
- worker codetermination in Germany and similar 'stakeholder' legal protections in other countries; and
- deeply conservative public and political attitudes regarding business practices and the role of financial markets in the economy.

Taken together, these institutional features of the continental European economic and financial environment suggest that one should not expect the unfolding European merger wave to resemble the Fourth or Fifth Waves in the US all too closely. Instead, we might expect the current European merger wave to resemble the First or Second Waves in the US. These were periods characterized by horizontal and vertical mergers which were, in part, a response to the rapidly integrating national market and rapid technological change.

The second set of lessons we draw from the case-studies relates to the potentially far-reaching transformation that appears to be under way in European finance despite the obstacles to change just identified. European corporate strategies increasingly reflect a greater emphasis on achieving global scale while sharpening product focus. Ownership structures are becoming more dispersed – that is, less concentrated among a few large shareholders – and cross-border equity ownership is increasing. Large-scale, internationally targeted privatizations of state-owned enterprises typify these trends in ownership structures. And while the general public and politicians' attitudes reflect resistance to change, competition authorities and private sector opinion leaders increasingly view product markets and the competitive environment in pan-European or even global terms.

The focal point of change – and of resistance to change – is the European financial system itself. To function properly, a takeover market requires broad and deep financial markets: broad in the sense of offering many different financial instruments, and deep in the sense of having many large and risk-tolerant investors prepared to purchase the financial instruments issued by merging or restructuring firms. At the same time, European financial institutions must cease to act as gatekeepers and begin to act as facilitators for their corporate clients.

In the end, the vitality of the European takeover market will depend on the ability and willingness of European financial institutions to transform themselves and Europe's financial markets into an integrated network for raising and distributing capital quickly and efficiently. If European financial institutions do not grasp this opportunity, American and other financial innovators are likely to step into the void created by European inaction.

DISCUSSION

European mergers and acquisitions activity may soon rival that of US firms. The types of takeovers carried out and the investment bankers assisting firms on both sides of the deal already have a US flavour. Hostile takeovers are now part of the landscape in Europe, and five of the top six advisors on European mergers and acquisitions during 1999 were American (Harris, 1999).

What is Driving the European Takeover Boom?

We noted that the Fourth and Fifth Waves of US takeovers were characterized, in part, by large and sometimes aggressive transactions and (during the Fifth Wave) by a quest for product focus and global scope. The European case-studies we considered suggest that some similar themes are emerging in Europe. As international trade volumes increase and international capital markets become more integrated, a single global market for corporate control may be taking shape.

It is important to point out, however, that the Fourth Wave's hostile takeovers did not spread to continental Europe during the 1980s when they were in vogue in the US. This might have been due to the presence of higher barriers to involuntary changes in corporate control and correspondingly greater costs in Europe, as already noted.[4] On the other hand, it is possible that hostile takeovers did not flourish in Europe because the inefficiencies caused by the separation of ownership and control were not as severe as in the United States. Concentrated ownership and tighter controls – both legal and cultural – on executive compensation in Europe might have eliminated much of the rationale for hostile takeovers in the first place.

It is certainly the case that formidable resistance to wholesale adoption of the Anglo-American takeover model exists. Public and political conservatism, entrenched workforces, and conservative banks and investors that have strong vested interests in maintaining the *status quo* cannot be ignored. In addition, different governance arrangements in continental Europe – most notably, more concentrated ownership structures and deep-rooted involvement of banks and governments in many companies – may cause merger and acquisition activity to develop in somewhat different ways. To the extent that takeovers in public markets reflect the failure of internal control structures to produce appropriate governance (Jensen, 1993), the more concentrated and potentially more effective owners of European firms may preclude the high rate of change of corporate control via financial markets that is evident in the US.

The Role of Competition Policy

Important factors shaping the European mergers and acquisition climate are the Single Market Programme and especially European competition policy. Although competition policy in the form of antitrust review and enforcement typically is done at national level, the European Commission's competition review has become the most important factor in determining which combinations will be allowed. The European Parliament also plays an important role, as its blocking in November 2000 of the long-awaited takeover directive indicates (Hargreaves, 2000). Amendments introduced by members of the European Parliament may strengthen the hand of European managements facing takeover bids to such an extent that most companies will become immune to hostile takeover. Some cases would be thrown into national courts, defeating the original purpose of EU-wide takeover standards.

European merger control is exercised under Regulation No. 4064/89 on the Control of Concentration Between Undertakings (European Merger Control Regulation, or EMCR). Originally passed in late 1989, EMCR was amended in 1998. The basic principle of EMCR is to serve as a 'one-stop shop' for significant European merger and acquisition transactions. The European Commission thus serves as the European Union's supreme antitrust authority, with transaction reviews carried out by a Merger Task Force. The European Commission has issued detailed guidelines concerning the applicability of EMCR to particular transactions (Picot, 1999, pp. 75–80).

While regional competition policy corresponds more closely to the cross-border nature of competition that actually occurs in many economic sectors, there is a risk that the boundaries drawn for competition review are still too narrow. Would it be more appropriate to have a three-tiered system of competition policy – national, regional and global (multilateral) – rather than the emerging model of regional blocs (for example, EU and NAFTA)? Such a multilateral competition body might appear to be a natural adjunct to multilateral institutions dedicated to international economic development (World Bank), international capital flows (IMF), international labour issues (ILO), international security (UN) and international trade (WTO). Yet such a cooperation regime to oversee direct investment in the form of cross-border mergers and acquisitions appears remote (Shelton, 1998). The fact that many multilateral institutions – including the IMF, the World Bank and the WTO – are engaged in a very public rethinking of their basic missions and competencies, indicates that international consensus and cooperation are fragile things, in general. The prospects of a multilateral direct investment institution are further diminished by the controversial nature of mergers and acquisitions themselves. And while the European Commission might prefer to see competition policy come under the multilateral purview of the WTO, the US Justice Department has preferred to rely on a series of bilateral information-sharing and consultation agreements.

Will Increased Mergers and Acquisitions Activity in Europe Lead to Higher Concentration and Less Competition?

Europeans concerned about the implications for competition of a vigorous cross-border market for corporate control might take some comfort from the outcome thus far of the consolidation of the US banking sector. Evidence from the recent rapid consolidation of the US banking sector suggests that a hectic pace of merger activity does not necessarily lead to anti-competitive outcomes.

The number of commercial-bank charters in existence in the US has declined by between 3 per cent and 5 per cent annually since 1988, resulting in a nine-year (1988–97) cumulative disappearance of 33 per cent of all bank charters (Berger, Demsetz and Strahan, 1999, Tables I and 2). Mergers accounted for about 84 per cent of disappearances and failures for 16 per cent during this period. Local deposit market concentration, however, actually declined slightly during this period. Average commercial bank deposit Herfindahl indexes in metropolitan statistical areas fell from 0.2020 to 0.1949, and those in non-metropolitan counties fell from 0.4316 to 0.4114 (Berger, Demsetz and Strahan, 1999, Table 1).[5]

Thus, consolidation need not imply increased concentration. One might expect something similar to happen in Europe: multinational corporations may become even larger, but competition in various product markets within a single nation may become fiercer as relatively efficient firms enter from abroad to contest local markets.

CONCLUSIONS

Unlike the US and the UK, continental European nations retain very formidable
obstacles to greater takeover activity in the form of entrenched workers, economically conservative (and interventionist) politicians, strong investors with
substantial block shareholdings, and strong domestic financial institutions that
retain significant vested interests in the *status quo*. This financial *status quo*
entails relatively underdeveloped capital markets and relatively concentrated
domestic corporate ownership. Changes in corporate control are more often
negotiated than played out in a market setting.

Despite these obstacles to greater takeover activity, the European mergers
and acquisitions market has, by some measures, become the most active in the
world. European firms are active buyers of domestic and foreign companies. As
in the current and previous merger waves in the US, key ingredients in Europe
appear to be strong economic and financial conditions, a liberal (or liberalizing) competition policy, and a perception among business leaders that significant
industrial restructuring is inevitable.

Is continental Europe being 'invaded' by the standard-bearers of Anglo-
American capitalism? If this were the case, one might expect most cross-border
acquisitions to involve non-European buyers of European companies. The 1999
data presented above show clearly that the continental European corporate
sector is a net *buyer* in cross-border deals, however, not a net seller. This implies
that, if any pattern is evident, it is that continental European firms are on a
'shopping spree' and that British and especially American firms are 'for sale'.

The recent increase in European takeover activity may represent some catch-
up with North American and UK practice. The other – less optimistic – view
is that many European takeovers are defensive: European firms may have
decided that they must 'buy or be bought', even if they would have preferred
to remain independent and isolated.

Yet another possibility is that the continental European mergers and acquisitions market will evolve on its own terms and at its own pace, borrowing
some of the techniques of Wall Street but retaining many of the defining characteristics of the continental European business and financial environment.
Under this interpretation, one might expect some aspects of the European
market-place to be retained and, possibly, to influence Anglo-American
economies sooner or later. For example, the positive role of large block shareholders in reducing agency problems – that is, minimizing the inefficiencies
arising from the separation of ownership and control – is clear. Large and
powerful owners would probably improve the functioning of many firms in the
US and the UK, which would, in turn, reduce the level of activity in the market
for corporate control.

Thus, continental European systems of corporate governance probably will be adapted rather than abandoned altogether. If this occurs, the emerging trend of European ownership of significant US and UK business assets represents a direct channel of influence running from East to West. Indeed, it is difficult to see how the twenty-first century could witness the emergence of a global Anglo-American style of capitalism when its leading proponent, the US, is selling its commercial and financial assets to the highest bidders at a pace never before seen. In fact, continental European firms may provide leadership as the global mergers and acquisitions market evolves.

NOTES

1. This discussion is drawn from Emmons and Schmid (1998).
2. Codetermination is a set of laws that guarantees worker representation on large firms' supervisory boards. See Gorton and Schmid (2000) for more details.
3. This discussion is drawn from classroom notes prepared for the course, 'Mergers and Acquisitions', by Frank A. Schmid, University of Lueneburg, Germany, June 2000.
4. For example, political opposition within the European Union has delayed the adoption of a takeover directive (a legal framework for takeovers across all 15 EU states) for nearly ten years (Lex, 2000).
5. The Herfindahl index is computed as the sum of squared market shares of all firms in the market. The index runs from zero in a perfectly competitive market to 1.0 under monopoly.

REFERENCES

Asquith, Paul and Thierry A. Wizman (1990), 'Event risk, covenants, and bondholder returns in leveraged buyouts', *Journal of Financial Economics*, 27(1), September, 195–213.

Berger, Allen N., Rebecca S. Demsetz and Philip E. Strahan (1999), 'The consolidation of the financial services industry: causes, consequences, and implications for the future', *Journal of Banking and Finance*, February, 135–94.

Bradley, Michael, Anand Desai and E. Han Kim (1988), 'Synergistic gains from corporate acquisitions and their division between the stockholders of target and acquiring firms', *Journal of Financial Economics*, 21(1), May, 3–40.

Chatterjee, Robin and Michael Aw (2000), Cambridge University working paper, May.

Emmons, William R. and Frank A. Schmid (1998), 'Universal banking, control rights, and corporate finance in Germany', *Federal Reserve Bank of St Louis Review*, 80(5), September–October, 19–42.

Franks, Julian R., Robert S. Harris and Colin Mayer (1988), 'Means of payment in takeovers: results for the United Kingdom and the United States', *Corporate Takeovers: Causes and Consequences*, edited by Alan J. Auerbach, Chicago: University of Chicago Press, pp. 221–58.

Gaughan, Patrick (1999), *Mergers, Acquisitions, and Corporate Restructurings*, New York: John Wiley and Sons.

Gorton, Gary and Frank A. Schmid (2000), 'Class struggle inside the firm? A study of German codetermination', Working paper, May.

Hargreaves, Deborah (2000), 'Euro-MPs threaten to stymie hostile takeovers', *Financial Times*, 22 November, 2.

Harris, Clay (1999), 'A New Breed of Champions', *Financial Times*, 22 September, p. III of 'International mergers and acquisitions'.

Hirshleifer, David (1992), 'Takeovers', *The New Palgrave Dictionary of Money and Finance*, ed. Peter Newman, Murray Milgate and John Eatwell, New York: Stockton Press, pp. 638–45.

Hirshleifer, David (1995), 'Mergers and acquisitions: strategic and informational issues', *Handbooks in Operations Research and Management Science: Finance*, ed. Robert A. Jarrow, Vojislav Maksimovic and William T. Ziemba, Amsterdam: Elsevier, pp. 839–85.

Jensen, Michael C. (1993), 'The modern industrial revolution, exit, and the failure of internal control systems', *Journal of Finance* 48(3), July, 831–80.

KPMG, 'Cross-border M&A reaches all-time high', http://www.kpmg.com/library/00/february/story3_b2_ac.asp

Lex Column (2000), 'Poisoning the wells', *Financial Times*, 22 November, 16.

Matsusaka, John G. (1993), 'Takeover motives during the conglomerate merger wave', *Rand Journal of Economics*, 24(3), Autumn, 357–79.

Picot, Gerhard (1999), *Mergers and Acquisitions in Germany*, New York: Juris Publishing.

Roll, Richard (1986), 'The hubris hypothesis of corporate takeovers', *Journal of Business*, 59(2), Pt 1, 197–216.

Shelton, Joanna R. (1998), 'Competition policy: what chance for international rules?', address, November, www.oecd.org.

Shleifer, Andrei and Lawrence H. Summers (1998), 'Breach of trust in hostile takeovers', *Corporate Takeovers: Causes and Consequences*, ed. Alan J. Auerbach, Chicago: University of Chicago Press, pp. 33–56.

Skorecki, Alex (2000), 'M&A bandwagon swerves on regardless', *Financial Times*, 12 May, 35.

UNCTAD (United Nations Conference on Trade and Development) (1999), 'FDI-linked cross-border mergers and acquisitions reached US$ 720 billion in 1999', press release, 15 April 2000a, http://www.unctad.org/en/press/pr2847en.htm.

UNCTAD (United Nations Conference on Trade and Development) (2000), 'World investment report 2000', 3 October 2000b, http://www.unctad.org/en/pub/ps1 wir00.en.htm.

5. Corporate restructuring, corporate strategy and European integration

Jordi Canals

Globalization has unfettered a chain of events in Europe, in combination with the creation of the European Single Market in January 1993 and the launch of the euro in January 1999. Hence, European firms have suffered from a triple shock that is increasing rivalry in Europe and speeding up corporate restructuring.

The pressure for change is particularly intense among small and medium-sized firms that used to compete in small, fragmented national markets. With the new geographical scope of competition in the European Union (EU) and the growing importance of scale in some industries, those firms are under the process of shedding off some activities, focusing on others and developing the scale and expertise they need to compete in a more open world.

Nevertheless, the fulcrum of restructuring in Europe is not happening among those small and medium-sized firms because many of them have been or are being acquired by bigger rivals that integrate them into their own operations. The real agents of restructuring in Europe are large, multi-business firms – or corporate groups – that is to say, companies that have several business units, each of them in a different industry and under a corporate umbrella – the parent company – that provides them a brand, financial resources, management, technology or distribution channels.

In this chapter we will study the impact of globalization in Europe on those multi-business firms and how they are trying to change their way of competing in an integrated world. Globalization is bringing more competition to those companies and capital markets are placing more pressure on their performance. Many of those multi-business companies are becoming more global, but not necessarily more focused. Although there is no 'one-size-fits-all' type of strategy for those firms, we argue that a successful transformation process needs a clear definition of the view that a firm has about its future and its strategic objectives, but also the implementation of a corporate strategy that explains both how each business will compete in its industry and how the parent company will add value to the different business units.

This chapter has the following structure. In the first section I will review the role of multi-business firms in Europe. The next section will outline some of the main reasons for the existence of multi-business firms in Europe. In the following section, I will present the major shocks that have been changing the European corporate landscape in the 1990s. Next, I will discuss how those changes have affected corporate performance in some industries: telecommunications, financial services, pharmaceuticals and electronics. With the help of four case-studies, I will highlight how firms in those industries have been adjusting to the new global Europe. Some conclusions will follow.

THE ROLE OF MULTI-BUSINESS COMPANIES IN EUROPE

The observation of the corporate landscape in Europe offers an intriguing view: the number of multi-business firms and their weight in the GDP of their home countries is larger than in the US, This factor can be explained by a variety of reasons. The first is that, in a fragmented Europe, as it was the case for many years before the creation of the Single Market in January 1993, national borders were important. For many large companies, growth in other businesses inside the national boundaries was quicker and more successful than international forays (Canals, 1993).

Many top managers also thought that the dominance of some large national markets was the key factor to support a reasonable international presence (Stopford and Strange, 1991). Finally, a weaker competition at home and a lack of discipline by still underdeveloped capital markets meant that corporate groups did not have a strong incentive in improving their efficiency, but in growth and survival.

The ubiquity of multi-business firms across Europe is clear. Many of those companies were, at some point, national champions whose activities were considered by governments as of national interest. They exist in every country: Germany (Siemens, Bertelsmann, Daimler Chrysler, BASF or Deustche Bank), France (Thomson CSF, Renault or BNP), Spain (BBVA, Endesa or Telefonica), and the UK (British Telecom, British Aerospace or Barclays).

Some of those companies were state-owned in their origins and original development (as in the case of BT or Endesa). Others were family-owned businesses. As we will see in this paper, irrespective of their origins, those multi-business companies are facing new challenges due to the combination of an increasing globalization in the world economy and the trend towards a more integrated Europe.

The existence of multi-business firms and the way many of them are organized – although there is no pattern that can be singled out as dominant in this respect – have some effects on corporate performance (Montgomery, 1982; Markides, 1995; Ghemawat and Khanna, 1998).

Moreover, multi-business firms face important governance problems and challenges. On the one hand, many multi-business firms have large, dominant shareholders. This factor could be considered as healthy and positive, according to some basic conclusions on corporate performance (Shleifer and Vishny, 1986). And yet, the discipline problem that large shareholders tend to resolve in corporate groups is overshadowed by another bigger problem: the management of several business units that have to compete with more focused competitors, under the control, management or supervision of a parent company with a corporate centre.

The role of capital markets in the European economy sheds light on the challenge that multi-business firms are facing. The number of listed companies in the different European stock exchange markets is still very low in comparison with the US, both in absolute numbers and according to some relative indicators, such as the weight of total market capitalization over the GDP (Canals, 1997). This factor is important for two reasons: the access to new sources of capital is more difficult than in the US and the discipline that capital markets tend to impose on top managers is less demanding than in the US.

A second factor reinforces the first: even for listed companies in the stock exchange market, the number of shares that can be traded and the percentage of those shares over total equity is very low. This means that those companies may be listed, but the weight of minority shareholders in the management and control of the firm may not be decisive.

A third factor has to be taken into account. If the stock market is not relevant for many companies, it is difficult to assess the real net worth of those firms, or the comparison of their performance with that of other competitors round the world. This is not just a problem of valuation and information, but also of benchmarking as a source of learning and improvement. In those cases, there is a risk that top managers tend to be more inward, without paying attention to the outside world.

The fourth factor is that European companies show a high concentration of ownership (Canals, 1997). Dominant shareholders are important and, in combination with some financial institutions (as has been the case in Germany, France or Spain), they have a decisive vote on the way multi-business companies are managed. Moreover, ownership in the United States and the United Kingdom is much more dispersed than in continental Europe, in part due to the fact that the pervasive presence of developed capital markets in Anglo-Saxon countries allows investors to enter and exit freely and smoothly.

Universal banks – banks with a diversified portfolio of business units – are not only a particular case of multi-business firms, but also key players in many non-financial multi-business firms. The reason is that banks are either major shareholders of some non-financial firms – as it happens in Spain or Germany – or important lenders to many European companies, because capital markets are not so developed as to be a perfect replacement for bank financing. The presence of universal banks in the boards of non-financial firms has important effects not only on banks themselves, but also on the firms in whose boards they sit.[1]

There is a long-ranging debate on whether capital markets-based financial systems are better for non-financial firms[2] than banks-based systems. In the latter, banks play the role of dominant shareholders. Nevertheless, the advantages of large shareholders controlling multi-business firms may be offset by the disadvantages of lack of focus and managerial complexities in running large, diversified business groups.

As a result of this set of factors, the traditional separation between owners and managers, with its advantages and problems, does not happen in many European companies, in which the dominant shareholder owns and manages simultaneously.

This situation, in combination with a lack of more protection for minority shareholders, means that companies have less access to external financing, which also means less possibilities for growth in the future. This may be one of the reasons why some family-owned firms that find themselves trapped in this position are reacting and considering an initial public offering.

In this corporate context, top managers have no clear independence from the board, nor decisive power to carry out their own action plans. The trade-off between delegation with supervision versus control is tilted towards the latter.

It can be argued that multi-business firms could be useful in the early stages of the development process of a country. Khanna and Palepu (1997) have shown how diversified business groups could become useful substitutes of some key institutions, like the educational system, labour markets or capital markets when a country has not been able yet to develop them. That can be also argued for Europe and its development after the Second World War.

This corporate context could be sustainable insofar as the external need for change is not very demanding and the integration of the country in the world economy is still low. Nevertheless, when foreign competition is speeding up and local companies want to compete globally, the context is changing and the factors that might have made local multi-business firms successful are fading away. Their advantages are no longer sustainable and the long-term survival of those firms becomes a thorny issue.

WHY DO MULTI-BUSINESS FIRMS EXIST?

The reasons why multi-business groups exist are numerous and diverse. A multi-business group is a collection of firms or business units bound together by a corporate centre, with common dominant shareholders, in a more or less organized way. The roots of multi-business firms could be as diverse as the national contexts in which multi-business groups emerged and developed, or as different as the motivations that entrepreneurs or shareholders may have about their undertakings.

Some authors have discussed the reasons for the existence of multi-business groups in different contexts. Ghemawat and Khanna (1998), Khanna and Palepu (1997) and Guillén (2000), for instance, have elaborated some formal propositions on the existence of multi-business groups in emerging countries. Others have presented explanations of why corporate groups grow (Montgomery and Hariharan, 1991; Williamson, 1975). Finally, a third group of scholars have pondered on the advantages or disadvantages of corporate groups using corporate efficiency as a yardstick (Shleifer and Vishny, 1996; Caves, 1982; or Collis and Montgomery, 1997; among others).

In this section I would like to highlight some theoretical reasons about the existence of multi-business groups, taking into account the European context. Some explanations may be also valid for other political and economic contexts. Nevertheless, I want to focus here on a narrower range of reasons related to European multi-business groups.

I will present four basic categories of reasons for the existence of this type of organization in Europe: imperfections in product markets, imperfections in capital markets, job creation and investment, and public policy.

Imperfections in Product Markets

The first reason for the existence of a business group is that a certain knowledge or capability that a company has been able to develop in a particular product market or industry may be more easily transferred to another firm within the group than to an external firm (Penrose, 1959; Caves, 1982; Collis and Montgomery, 1997).

This is the case of universal banks (like Deutsche Bank, ABN Amro or Banque Nationale de Paris, among many others), a very special type of diversified financial services firms that, due to a variety of reasons, became popular in continental Europe after the Second World War.

The financial skills that some retail banks possessed and the connections that they had with some corporate and individual customers boosted those banks' intentions to dominate other areas of financial services, beyond their original competitive arena and capabilities.

The second reason has to do with the creation of multi-market power. Multi-point competitors can replicate their oligopoly games and, in some cases, tacit collusion, in some markets and operate in the same way in other markets (Ghemawat and Khanna, 1998).

Before the latest wave of deregulation, this used to be the case in some industries with multi-business groups, such as transportation, oil and gas distribution, or financial services. The degree of tacit collusion was pinned on the quality of the regulators' oversight and the degree of penetration of foreign competitors in those regulated markets.

A third reason for the existence of multi-business groups is that transaction costs are lower within a corporate group than in open markets. This is a general observation that can be applied to all types of corporate groups (Williamson, 1975), although it may not be the main reason for their existence. Nevertheless, in countries in which institutional contexts slowed down innovation and new corporate ventures – as it happened in Europe for decades – multi-business groups offered a better shield for new ventures.

It is also interesting to observe that in Europe it is difficult to see firms like Microsoft, Dell or AOL, that is to say, firms in high-tech industries with an explosive growth, that were born less than 20 or 30 years ago (Canals, 2000). Whereas in the US this is the general pattern, because entrepreneurship tends to blossom outside large firms and not so much in large, established firms, in Europe we have the opposite phenomenon: it is large firms that, until very recently, have developed new ventures, especially new high-tech ventures. It is the case of companies like Philips, Daimler Chrysler (formerly Daimler Benz), Siemens or British Aerospace, all of them firms that have been at the forefront of technological innovation in Europe.

Those firms also share in common an interesting attribute: they are multi-business groups. In their case, we can see different reasons explaining their growth: lower transaction costs within the group, but also multi-point competition, or resource and capability sharing.

Imperfections in Capital Markets

For many years, fragmented national financial markets and over-regulation prevented Europe from having an integrated capital market to provide funding for new business ventures European-wide. In this context, large national universal banks grew and developed a successful corporate banking business, and banking became the main source of corporate funding in Europe.

With the lack of organized large capital markets, multi-business groups with some cash generator units became their own banks, providing liquidity and long-term financing to the other business units in the same group and offering seed capital to new business ventures. This classical explanation for multi-business groups (Williamson, 1975) has become a textbook reason for the existence and growth of European corporate groups. As we will discuss later on, this is no longer a powerful reason within Europe today, among other reasons, because of the existence of more integrated European capital markets and the financial pressures that multi-business groups are suffering. None the less, it is a very important reason when one tries to sketch the history and evolution of European business groups.

Europe also offers a good example of another explanation given to the evolution of multi-business groups: the existence of a large shareholder that can better monitor the group management and offers a better alignment between shareholders and managers' interests. Shleifer and Vishny (1986) argue that large shareholders tend to eliminate the agency costs associated with management.

Many business groups in Europe have dominant shareholders, as is the case with Allianz, Daimler Chrysler, Solvay, Azco or Vivendi. In general, a multi-business group provides a more or less sophisticated control system, which is being exercised by the corporate centre – if that body formally exists – or by the dominant shareholder himself, who gives a more disciplined approach to management's goals and policies than can be expected from a wider spread ownership.

Another reason regarding capital markets has to do with the resource allocation process. Grossman and Hart (1980) argue that the coordination of investment decisions may improve capital allocation among alternative investment projects. Since resource allocation decisions are one of the key tasks of the corporate centre in many corporate groups (Daems, 1978), the effectiveness of their decisions may be higher than in a decentralized approach. Allen (1993), in a discussion of the efficiency of capital markets-based systems *vis-à-vis* banks-based systems, argues that the efficiency of both systems in terms of resource allocation may vary according to the nature of the industry in which firms compete.

We can extend this argument to business groups. In the case of more stable industries, corporate groups may have an experience and knowledge superior to that of other investors. Experience and competence may offset the lack of flexibility that internal capital markets have. On the contrary, in fast-changing environments with high uncertainty, capital markets may be quicker in reading the tea leaves and more agile in mobilizing resources towards new business ventures. At the risk of oversimplifying a more complex phenomenon, the explosion of Internet-based and related industries in the US has to do with the availability of external funding for new ventures and the existence of more developed capital markets, with investors willing to bet on those ventures.

The resource allocation argument has a special twist in the case of European groups, the reason being the existence of strong bank–industry relationships, in particular in some countries like Spain, Germany or France. Banks have not only become the dominant lenders to many industrial firms, but were also the dominant shareholders until the early 1990s. Still today, banks such as Deutsche

Bank, Commerzbank, Banco Bilbao Vizcaya Argentaria or Banco Santander Central Hispano own significant stakes of some of the largest companies in their home countries.

In those cases, we can see a combination of both arguments: the importance of large shareholders, and the advantage of resource allocation and coordination of this type of decision.

In a nutshell, we can argue that the fragmentation of capital markets in Europe, the dominance of bank financing in corporate Europe and the historical role played by banks in financing industry made up a powerful combination of reasons – around capital markets factors – that helps explain how ubiquitous corporate groups are in Europe. At the same time, this very same factor may have sown the seed of the destruction of multi-business groups in Europe, as we will discuss later on.

Corporate Groups, Job Creation and Investment

As Khanna and Palepu (1997) or Ghemawat and Khanna (1998) have argued, multi-business groups in emerging markets play a very important role in their countries' development. They not only overcome the lack of institutions, like a proper job market or an organized capital market, but also become the main symbols of the industrial emergence in their home countries.

This is a very important factor, because the longevity of corporate groups cannot only be explained by efficiency factors. Those groups are important economic and social agents in their countries (Guillén, 2000) and unless they have some legitimacy, their survival may pose complex social and political issues.

In many cases, economic efficiency is not the only source of their social legitimacy, but two other important dimensions of the economic and political landscape in any country play a key role: job creation and new investment. For many years, multi-business groups in Europe were the driving forces behind job creation. They not only offered employees a long and safe professional career, but working with some of those companies became a symbol or a signal of a special professional status.

This is no longer true today, because those groups are under the threat of extinction or, at least, of shrinking in size, and, even more important, because entrepreneurship is blossoming in Europe.

Nevertheless, when looking at the formation of corporate groups in Europe, one cannot forget how important they were in providing their home countries with a job engine and investment in new industrial projects that could become the next step in terms of technological development, and eventually, if they were successful, of national pride.

Policy Factors

The final category of factors behind multi-business groups is related to public policy factors. It is clear that, in the context of protected national markets and regulated industries, the incumbents' advantage in the short-term can be very important, enough to stifle the chances of potential entrants.

In the case of multi-business groups, this factor is extremely important, not because it may be the driver of some corporate diversification decisions, but because it protects the corporate group from additional rivalry, and reinforces in this way certain corporate decisions that otherwise may not have led to a sustainable performance.

In this regard, a very special policy, taxation, may be a factor that induces corporate groups to grow in scale and scope (Ghemawat and Khanna, 1998). When corporate and sales taxes turn out to be lower when a firm is a group member than in the case where it enjoys full independence, an additional incentive for the creation and growth of corporate groups exists. Again, it may not be the most important reason, but might offer a good explanation that reinforces the *status quo*.

Taxation used to be a very important reason in countries like Spain or Germany for the formation and growth of corporate groups. With the reforms brought about by the European Single Market, many of those tax distortions have disappeared, and more fiscal convergence in the areas of capital gains and corporate taxation may be the final nail in their coffin. Nevertheless, their importance in explaining the strength of corporate groups in some countries for some decades cannot be downplayed.

THE EFFECTS OF THE 1990s SHOCKS: A NEW COMPETITIVE LANDSCAPE FOR EUROPEAN MULTI-BUSINESS FIRMS

The 1990s were a decade of abrupt change around the world. The end of the former Warsaw Pact and the Iron Curtain, the disintegration of the Soviet Union, the access to global markets of emerging countries like China, South Korea or Brazil, and the growing erosion of trade and investment barriers, not to mention the great impact of the new information technologies and the explosion of bandwidth in telecommunications, contributed to create a disruption in world affairs.

Multi-business groups in Europe have not been immune to the growing globalization and the new opportunities and threats coming from technology, new competitors and emerging countries. The outcome of this upheaval for multi-business groups is clear: their survival is no longer guaranteed. Moreover, some of the logical arguments behind their existence that we have presented in the previous section have lost their power, or, at least, they can not display the same conviction as they did in the past. Add to this factor a lacklustre performance over the 1990s in some cases and the warning signal of a change in paradigm is very strong.

In particular, European corporate groups have faced three consecutive competitive shocks that have European roots, plus a fourth shock that they share with other companies worldwide.[3]

The first shock was the internal Single Market of 1993.[4] This programme brought about an uproar in product markets, with the elimination of trade and investment barriers within the European Union, that increased competition and generated a larger market – at least for most products and services. This combination offered lower prices for final customers, but also put some financial pressure on companies that were not able to match lower prices with more internal efficiency and lower costs, resulting in an erosion of their profitability. Firms like Volkswagen, Philips or Thomson were on the brink of collapse, were it not for the support of their dominant shareholders, or, in other cases, the helping hand of governments.

The main problem that the Single Market brought about for multi-business groups was not only an increasing competition, but also a more focused set of competitors – that is to say, firms that were not diversified as corporate groups, and that cultivated regional or global scale in single businesses, instead of playing in local markets in a variety of different, unrelated businesses. This was the first death knell to corporate diversification in Europe.

The second shock evolved in parallel with the launch of the Single Market and, in many industries, was part of it: deregulation. Nevertheless, it is important to separate the Single Market from deregulation, although the former required the latter. Deregulation was a more global trend in many countries, from free market economies, like the US, to more state-controlled economies like Mexico or South Korea. The role of the IMF and the World Bank encouraging the liberalization of the financial sector in the early 1990s was also an additional force that pushed governments to face tough decisions in dismantling and untangling a complex set of regulatory rules.

For European corporate groups operating in regulated industries, deregulation meant the dismantling of some rights, an increasing competition and the prospect of lower revenues and profitability unless they restructured their operations with speed and flexibility.

The harsh blow that deregulation dealt to industries is very evident in the case of telecommunications, power and oil. In these industries, the old model of integrated companies that controlled the whole value chain of the industry was under pressure from new competitors that were invited to step in with the new winds of liberalization. Since they did not have the resources to compete with corporate groups head-on, they focused their initial efforts in developing some capabilities in just one of the businesses of the value chain, and, if possible, creating a competitive advantage in it.

Mobile telephony offers a great example of this strategy, and Vodafone is a paradigm of this behaviour. Instead of replicating the model of large, integrated telecoms operators like British Telecom or France Telecom, Vodafone opted to be a pure mobile player, that is to say, a specialist in wireless telephony.

In this segment of the industry, Vodafone has built indisputable technological advantages, first in the British market, and later, with a string of corporate acquisitions, at the global level. Scale has become so important in wireless telephony that it is difficult for still national and more diversified telecoms operators, like Deustche Telecom or AT&T, to be able to compete with Vodafone in technology or costs.

In a nutshell, the main effect of deregulation has been the disruption and dismantling of the old value chain, and the emergence of more focused firms that play in just one or two of the new industries that used to be the links of the former value chain. In this respect, deregulation reinforces the effect of the Single Market in creating new competitive spaces for specialists, while putting a stronger competitive pressure on the shoulders of corporate groups.

The third major shock in corporate Europe has been the creation and launch of the euro. The Single Currency in Europe has triggered the process of creating a truly integrated financial market in the euro zone, even though this is far from complete. A new European bond market has emerged, reinforcing the trend towards disintermediation and more liquid financial markets.

The euro is also forcing national stock markets to review their strategies. Some of them have reached an agreement for joint quotes and listing. This is again a process that will take time, but many obstacles have been overcome already and a major process has been unleashed.

These changes are having a big impact on the banking and insurance industries, since they are the backbone of the financial system. Nevertheless, the creation of a more liquid, transparent and open financial market is also having effects on corporate governance, because a market for corporate control is being developed.

This market may take many forms and adopt different ways to influence corporate decisions, from giving support to hostile takeovers to a less intense pressure such as the constant comparison of financial performance of companies in the same industry in different countries. This may seem obvious, but before the euro the comparison of performance was not only less immediate, but of less interest to national investors whose foreign assets were in general a low proportion of their total investments. All this has changed with the euro.

This less intense form of corporate control is having already a profound impact in the way companies act and argue their decisions in front of shareholders, financial analysts or public opinion. European companies and, in particular, European multi-business groups are feeling the pinch. Shareholders expect similar returns in the same industry across countries, and the performance of US firms is always a common benchmark. Even in countries in which blocking mechanisms make takeovers difficult, the launch of the euro, in combination with the liberalization of capital movements, means that national investors may prefer to own utilities in the US rather than in Germany or France. Since they cannot vote the board or the executive committee out yet, they choose to vote with their feet.

Since multi-business firms, in general, trade at a discount due to the conglomerate effect, the pressure to increase performance is stronger than ever among European corporate groups. And shareholders and analysts are telling them a message that reinforces the effect of the two shocks analysed earlier: corporate groups need a narrower focus, unless the parent companies are able to convince the business and financial community that some individual firms are better off inside the corporate group than outside. In other words, that the group is the best parent that any of its companies can get.

This is very difficult to prove in practice and demands a well-elaborated and well-executed corporate strategy, that is to say, a strategy that explains what business a company should be in and how the corporate centre adds value to each one of those business units.

The task is formidable, and becomes even more complex if one takes into account that new technologies, both in high-tech industries like telecommunications or Internet-based, and in traditional businesses like car engines or steel, tend to favour focus and global scale, rather than a wider scope.

The shocks that I have presented here have a different impact on each industry, depending upon a variety of factors, such as the previous exposure of each industry to competition, its potential for globalization, or the nature of ownership and the existence of publicly-owned firms.

In Table 5.1 I summarize the combination of those competitive shocks in several industries, through their most likely channels of transmission, as I have discussed above: product markets and capital markets pressure.

The main factors that affect the pressure that capital markets put on corporate groups and their performance can be split up in two groups: structural factors and performance factors. The structural factors include some dimensions such as the role of institutional shareholders in each industry; the existence of dominant, controlling or blocking shareholders; the presence of family-owned business; the role of government ownership; the structure of capital markets, and the role that banks play in the industry as lenders or shareholders; finally, the advance in the use of practices of good corporate governance, that are usually a guarantee that investors have about transparency and professionalism in the board of directors and the executive committee.

From this list of factors, one can conclude that the launch of the euro is contributing to clarify the role of shareholders in corporate governance, on the one hand, and, on the other, to press for more corporate transparency, both for firms that are already public and those that are not public yet, but may like to become so or count on debt markets to finance their future expansion. The pressure of capital markets can be observed in many countries outside the European Union, both in North America and in other emerging countries. Nevertheless, it is true that the depth and speed of change in the case of Europe are very special.

Table 5.1   European competitive shocks: a first approach to their impact on corporate groups

| | | Product markets pressure | |
		High	Low
Capital markets pressure	High	– Consumer electronics (Philips, Olivetti) – Telecommunications (KPN, Telefónica)	– Retail banking (BBVA, Deutsche Bank) – Pharmaceuticals (Glaxo, Novartis)
	Low	– Automobiles (Volkswagen, Renault) – Power (ENDESA, Electricité de France)	– Airlines (Lufthansa, KLM) – Retailing (AHOLD, El Corte Inglés)

Regarding the product markets pressure, the main factors that can be singled out here as driving and shaping competition in different industries are the number of players in each industry, the existence of a truly global rivalry, multipoint competition, and the depth of the deregulation process in industries still under the control of the government – such as telecommunications, airlines, power, gas and oil.

The evidence from the industries presented in Table 5.1 highlights the existence of a variety of competitive contexts for different industries. This means that the pace of change is not uniform across industries and depends very much on the intrinsic characteristics of the industry (scale, cost structure, types of competition, level of deregulation, or history) and the role of institutional factors (type of shareholders, ownership or government intervention in the management and control of firms).

I distinguish between four categories of industries that reflect different combinations of product markets competition and capital markets pressure. Low capital markets pressure does not mean that shareholders are not interested in corporate performance. It simply reflects the fact that, even when shareholders' interest in getting a decent return on their investment is taken into account, the structure of ownership or some institutional arrangements affecting corporate governance (for instance, the existence of a golden share, owned by national governments), in practice, mean that the pressure of capital markets is not enough and it turns out that investors may stop developing an interest in that industry in some specific countries.

It is also interesting to see how industries that share some common attributes, such as power and telecommunications (in both, network effects, regulation and important sunk costs are decisive) or retail banking and retailing (in both, the number of physical channels and closeness to the final customer are key success factors) are under different competitive pressures, not only because of different patterns of deregulation, but also because of the different level of corporate transformation that the firms in each industry have gone through.

In the next sections, I will discuss how some European corporate groups are facing these huge competitive shocks that swept through Europe in recent years by reacting to them and adjusting to the new competitive landscape that those shocks are defining.

CORPORATE STRATEGY AND EUROPEAN MULTI-BUSINESS FIRMS IN THE 1990s

European multi-business groups have reacted in different ways to the competitive shocks experienced in the 1990s. It is not easy to cover all the decisions that those companies took in order to survive and adjust to a more competitive world.

In this section, I want to offer a typology of corporate strategic decisions that helps explain the actions that some European multi-business firms have taken to reinvent themselves in this new competitive world. In this respect, it could be useful to consider that multi-business firms define their corporate strategy through those actions: the set of policies and decisions on what business the firm wants to be in, the way to enter them and the principles and actions that the corporate parent plans to use in order to add value to each one of the individual firms that belong to the group.[5]

In general, corporate strategy is not very popular among firms, nor is it understood by senior managers or analysts. For the former, finding ways to add value to the individual firms inside a corporate group is not easy, and the advantage for a firm of belonging to a group is not always clearly superior to a situation of full independence.

For this reason, analysts have a difficult time trying to see advantages and potential synergies among businesses in a corporate group. They have grown weary of diversification and tired of conglomerates, which is a reason why they trade at a discount.

Those perceptions also have some empirical support.[6] Thus, in a landmark study, Lang and Stultz (1994) point out that Tobin's q and firm diversification were negatively correlated throughout the 1980s, and this correlation holds for different diversification measures. In general, firms that choose to diversify are worse performers than firms that do not.

More recently, Amilund and Lev (1999) show that corporate diversification generally results in value loss for shareholders, while a focused strategy tends to be value enhancing. Moreover, Markides (1995), using a sample of 250 Fortune 500 firms in 1985 that had diversified, shows that moving away from diversification and refocusing are associated with a clear improvement in corporate performance.

Following a classical distinction (Rumelt, 1974), Markides and Williamson (1996) distinguish between related and unrelated diversification, and make an important distinction. In the past, related diversification used to be considered superior in terms of performance to unrelated diversification. Based on their empirical work, Markides and Williamson conclude that related diversification improves performance only when it allows a firm to obtain preferential access to some strategic assets. Those assets are rare, valuable and costly to imitate.

The scepticism towards diversification has always been around. Nevertheless, the impact of diversification on corporate performance may be more negative in times of change, when companies experience competitive shocks like those suffered in Europe in the 1990s. An external context of rapid and dramatic change was the trigger that European multi-business firms needed to reflect again on their corporate strategy.

Many companies reacted to this new context restructuring their businesses, closing plants and cutting costs. Other companies took a step further and refocused their business portfolio, reducing the number of activities they were involved in.

It is useful to distinguish between different types of restructuring, as Bowman and Singh (1993) suggest. Financial restructuring is the easiest and consists of cutting costs and reshuffling the firm's financial liabilities. A second, more sophisticated step is portfolio restructuring, by which senior managers decide to increase or decrease the shareholdings in some of the firms within a multi-business group. Finally, organizational restructuring involves new ways of configuring activities within a group, the policies to coordinate them and, eventually, how to get and profit from group synergies.

Hoskinsson and Hitt (1994) found that the main reason for downscoping – narrowing the business portfolio – is that senior managers over-diversified their firms: in part because management control systems were inadequate to monitor senior managers, in part because strategy formulation was very poor (Hoskinsson, Johnson and Moesel, 1994).

What is clear is that, in general, corporate diversification comes associated with an important cost in the long term in terms of performance; this cost can be lowered when groups tend to favour related diversification over non-related diversification; related diversification has superior effects when it provides access to certain strategic assets; in all the cases, those decisions require a good corporate strategy that provides a framework for entry and exit decisions, and a set of principles on how a group should be managed and how the corporate centre can add value to each one of the business units.

This last question – how a corporate centre can add value to each one of the business units – is debatable, but is key in any solid formulation of a corporate strategy. Campbell, Goold and Alexander (1994) define the notion of 'parenting advantage', by which they mean that the corporate centre of the group is the best parent each firm in the group can have when it creates more value for each individual firm than other parents would do.

Collis and Montgomery (1997, 1998) offer a more comprehensive answer to the question of how a corporate centre creates value. In particular, they try to explain that some corporate groups may be worth more than the sum of their parts. The reason is that corporate strategy is a system of interrelated parts made up of three main factors: resources, businesses and organization. This system should be guided by a vision on how the group can create value. In this process, groups have to define and develop three major activities: creating a competitive advantage for each business, coordinating the different business units and controlling them. In the end, if this system is coherent, a multi-business group may be sustainable, but the litmus test should be the same: the company's business units should not be worth more to another owner.

In the process of restructuring the business portfolio, downscoping activities or reformulating corporate strategies, we have observed two basic dimensions that define the orientation of European multi-business groups in the 1990s. On the one hand, the business scope, that is to say, the number and relatedness of the businesses they compete in. On the other, the geographical scope or the competitive space where those groups deploy their activities.

The reason for choosing those two dimensions is clear. The experience of the firms observed in the four industries studied – telecommunications, financial services, pharmaceuticals and electronics – signals towards this direction. From a conceptual point of view, this choice is obvious, since the competitive shocks described in the previous sections are having the greatest impact in redefining the businesses and geographical boundaries of multi-business groups.

Using those two dimensions, we can observe and distinguish four groups of companies (see Table 5.2): focused firms within a regional space and a narrow business portfolio; diversified firms within a regional space; global firms with a focused business portfolio; and global firms with a wider business portfolio. It is important to keep in mind that we refer in all cases to multi-business groups, so that the notion of narrow portfolio does not mean that they only have a business unit, but several of them.

In the four categories described, the number of changes in corporate strategy those firms went through in the 1990s is important, and the qualitative steps they had to take in order to implement change quite remarkable. Many of those companies went through the process of changing their 'dominant logic', as Prahalad and Bettis (1986) put it to explain why so many institutions find it so hard to change or, moreover, why so many institutions see change in their environment and are not able to react to it.

In the next sections I will illustrate those changes using as a reference four firms that could epitomize the challenges and the opportunities of the pathway that they chose, and the challenges ahead they still have to face.

Table 5.2   Redefining corporate strategies in European multi-business groups: the context of change

		Business scope	
		Focused	Diversified
	Regional	– British Telecom – TSB – Peugeot	– BBVA – Fortis – Fiat
Geographical scope			
	Global	– Glaxo Wellcome – Nokia – Volkswagen	– Philips – Vivendi – Reuters

British Telecom: Refocusing the Business Portfolio

The telecommunications industry went through a major upheaval in Europe in the 1990s. British Telecom (BT), a state-owned firm that was early privatized by the British government in 1985, seemed to be destined to play an important role in consolidating the industry at the European level. In 1985, about 90 per cent of its total revenues came from fixed telephony and voice transmission. Little by little, BT started a process of corporate diversification, offering new services and moving away from fixed telephony. For many years, it was one of the favourite companies in the industry among investors: its international strategy, alliances and entry into wireless telephony, and a management team that seemed knowledgeable and with a clear view about the future, were ingredients that made the company very attractive.

After several years of important internal revenue growth in the UK, in 1996 BT and MCI announced a merger to form a group with annual turnover of around £26 billion. The logic of the deal seemed compelling. Both companies had complementary geographical areas and business: MCI was very strong in long-distance telephony in the US, and BT was very strong in the local telecommunications market in the UK and some other European countries.

Table 5.3   British Telecom

Year	Revenues (£m)	Profit before taxes (£m)	Capital expenditure (£m)
1999	21,903	3,198	3,680
1998	18,223	3,474	3,269
1997	16,039	3,461	3,030
1996	14,935	3,203	2,719
1995	14,446	3,019	2,771
1994	12,600	2,662	2,671
1993	11,450	2,756	2,171

Nevertheless, another suitor for MCI came in: WorldCom. In the middle of an incredible bull market, it offered a better deal for MCI shares. On 10 November 1997, MCI recommended a merger with WorldCom to form MCI WorldCom. BT decided not to match the MCI offer and sold out the 20 per cent stake that it had in MCI. Although Concert, the alliance that BT and MCI set up to offer new innovative services to multinational customers, was still alive, nobody had a strong faith in its future.

After the failure, BT needed another master stroke. On 26 July 1998, BT and AT&T announced a new global joint venture to serve the needs of multinational firms for international calls. It was initially designed as a venture owned equally by BT and AT&T. It would combine the cross-border assets and operations of both firms. That meant that BT would transfer the majority of its international activities to the new firm.

This joint venture was meant to be for BT not only an exit to the situation created after the failure of the deal with MCI, but a much better alliance, due to the technological and marketing strengths of AT&T. This venture was launched in 1999, and it is still too early to say how strong its impact on BT will be.

The bottom line for BT at the end of 2000 was that revenues had grown from £14.4 billion in 1996 to £21.9 billion in the year ended in March 2000. The snag was that profitability did not grow at that pace. Moreover, since 1998, BT has had important problems, because net cash flow from operating activities went down from £6 billion in 1998 to £5.8 billion in 2000.

The deterioration of BT performance was a direct result of the increase in rivalry in the British market and the subsequent fall in prices. Nevertheless, BT's financial structure looked increasingly leveraged and financial expenses went up. After the failure of the merger with MCI and the slow speed at which Concert was proceeding, investors became nervous with BT.

In a reaction to what seemed to be an uncertain situation, in May 2000, BT announced a radical restructuring of its operations by creating some new international businesses units, each with different focus and priorities: Ignite – a broadband network business focused on the corporate market; BT Openworld – an international, mass market Internet business; Yell – international directories and e-commerce ventures; and BT Wireless – an international mobile business unit.

BT also announced its intention to separate the UK fixed business into a wholesale business and a retail business. The idea was to have a more focused management and boost value creation in a very demanding and competitive market. Both markets were already suffering a strong cannibalization coming from wireless services, including BT's own services.

Nevertheless, the implementation of that strategy was very slow and the financial debt was growing, due to the cost of the 3G licences and some other minor acquisitions the firm was making. In the meantime, the stock market was already anticipating that BT was going through a major restructuring process that could include a split-up of the whole group. In October 2000, BT shares were trading at a 25–30 per cent discount. Goldman Sachs, in its 23 October 2000 report on BT, estimated that the firm's sum of the parts provided a value of 955p per share and the discounted cash flow a value of 763p per share. That was a clear signal that the market was waiting for more radical action at BT.

On 9 November 2000, BT announced a restructuring that did not encompass the break-up of the group and moved along the pathway outlined in May. Nevertheless, the main suspicion among analysts was that the plan presented was good to meet the immediate need to pay down debt, by committing BT to raise £10 billion before the end of 2001 through asset sales and the partial IPO of up to 25 per cent of Yell and BT Wireless.

It is too early to say what the outcome of those more recent actions will be. What seems to emerge from the evolution of BT strategy in the past few years is that the competitive pressures discussed in a previous section seem to be in full display: product market pressure, capital market pressure and new competitors coming in.

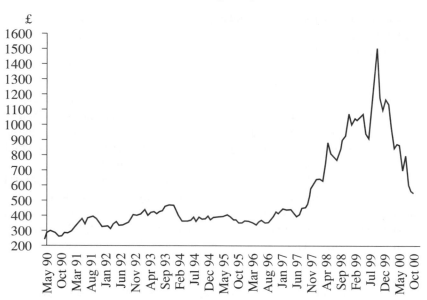

Figure 5.1   British Telecom share price

   BT has moved from unrelenting growth and global alliances and acquisitions to becoming a more modest player. Before facing new deals with other large players, BT will have to put itself in order. In many ways, BT epitomizes corporate growth in an era of expansion and deregulation which was quickly followed by a shake-out and increasing rivalry. In this context, a corporate group should have a clear focus or a well-synchronized corporate strategy. BT did not have either, or, at least, could not fully display neither of them.

Banco Bilbao Vizcaya Argentaria (BBVA): Regional Growth

This Spanish bank is the outcome of a merger between Banco Bilbao and Banco Vizcaya in 1988 – which gave birth to Banco Bilbao Vizcaya – and the subsequent merger between BBV and Argentaria in November 1999. BBVA is a successful retail bank that has grown very quickly since 1992, both organically and through a merger, and has become at the time of writing in November 2000 the second-largest bank by market capitalization in the euro zone, one of the most profitable in Europe, and together with its Spanish arch-rival Banco Santander Central Hispano, the largest financial group in Latin America, above Citigroup.

   These achievements are brighter when one considers them in the context of the slow growth in retail banking in Europe over the whole of the 1990s.

Moreover, other traditional retail banks such as Deutsche Bank or ABM Amro made an explicit decision to get more involved in capital markets and investment banking and move away from what seemed to be a declining industry: retail banking.

Table 5.4   BBVA

Year	Total assets (bn pesetas)	Profit before taxes (bn pesetas)	Financial margin/ assets (%)	ROE (%)
1999	39,628	482.8	1.57	21.9
1998	22,294	279.6	1.89	21.0
1997	21,139	234.9	1.77	18.4
1996	17,167	160.2	1.49	16.3
1995	14,110	135.5	1.18	13.8
1994	13,051	108.3	1.01	12.1
1993	9,845	97.4	0.85	12.4

BBVA presents a clear case for a reasonable corporate strategy that has been executed flawlessly for the past few years. We can distinguish several stages in its formulation and execution. First, a period of very strong internal growth, between 1994 and 1996, in which, under the leadership of a new CEO, the bank laid the foundations of lower operational costs, better marketing capabilities and very strong new product development. In an exercise of strategic thinking, the executive committee adopted the 1,000 Days Programme, which was a plan to revitalize the bank and tackle all the growth opportunities that the bank might have in different segments of the financial services industry.

The second stage, between 1996 and 1999, was one of international growth and careful diversification. BBVA consolidated its positioning in Latin American countries such as Chile, Brazil, Colombia, Mexico, Venezuela and Peru, becoming a regional banking power. The strategic model it followed was to transfer capabilities and products from Spain to those markets, adjust them to each country through some very quick market tests, and roll them out throughout the country. At the end of 2000, BBVA had about half of its assets and close to 40 per cent of its revenues coming from Latin America, while in 1994 the vast majority of both were concentrated in Spain.

In that stage, BBVA also embarked on a carefully monitored diversification programme. On the one hand, the bank reinforced and invested more resources in other areas of financial services beyond retail and corporate banking. Capital markets, asset management and insurance got a big boost, and BBVA was on the way to turning itself into a universal, diversified financial group.

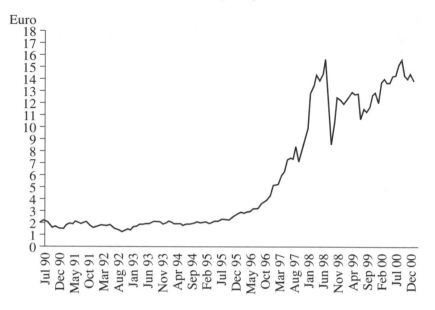

Figure 5.2   BBVA share price

On the other hand, BBVA decided to invest heavily in newly privatized Spanish companies that were leaders in their industries. The most notable cases were Repsol YPF, an oil company, and Telefónica, the largest telecoms operator in the Spanish speaking market. With these investments, BBVA aimed at several objectives: an attractive expected profitability due to the growth prospects those companies had, a special connection with some of the largest companies in Spain with which it could do business later on without getting involved in their management, and the possibilities of reaching new customers through them.

This was a thoughtful and carefully orchestrated strategy, that also took into account a basic factor in any diversification process: to grow the traditional business – retail banking and corporate banking – with dedicated and professional managers and the necessary resources, and to have a clear view of what BBVA could expect from its diversification moves. Moreover, BBVA had a strong point of view: it had to run the diversified units as stand-alone businesses, under the executive committee. In the case of investments outside financial services, the objective was the potential profitability of the investment itself, and, if possible, access to new customers.

The third stage started with the merger between BBV and Argentaria in October 1999. BBV's CEO had announced that his bank was keen on mergers, and he was able to deliver what he promised before the end of 1999. For almost a year, BBV had the pressure of the first big European bank merger after the launch of the euro, between Banco Santander and Banco Central Hispano. Its deal with Argentaria arrived later, but the merger evolved very smoothly and the performance for 2000 – apart from exceptional revenues – was outstanding, with an expected growth in net profit of 25 per cent over the combined net revenues of both banks before the merger.

BBVA illustrates some experiences in corporate strategy in times of turbulent change. Firstly, corporate strategy is not about restructuring only, but about growth. Secondly, growth should come first at home, after planting carefully the seeds of some solid and sustainable competitive advantages. Thirdly, corporate strategy requires a combination of flexibility and commitment, in particular, in the case of acquisitions or alliances. Fourthly, a corporate group should have a clear point of view about what the corporate centre can and should do, and how it plans to add value to the different businesses.

It is true that BBVA has been successful over the past few years, and that growth at some point may fade away. Caution is always good. Nevertheless, it is important not to forget that BBVA has been competing in an industry and in Europe, a competitive arena where other better established banks like Deutsche Bank, Barclays, Crédit Lyonnais or Banque Nationale de Paris, just to mention some of them, have had terrible problems of growth and profitability.

A comparison between BBVA and BT is also interesting. In some sense, BBVA is in an industry in which deregulation has been enforced and new competitors have come in. The outcome for some banks – as with BT – has been a weaker revenue base, and higher costs to attract and retain customers. BBVA has been successful in overcoming those obstacles and, according to its CEO, outstanding people and a clear corporate strategy have been decisive factors in its transformation from being a local medium-sized Spanish bank into one of the top international players in the Spanish-speaking world and one of the world's best-managed universal banks.

Glaxo Wellcome: The Power of Focus

In January 1995, Glaxo – the largest pharmaceutical firm in Europe – announced its plans to acquire Wellcome, one of the best-known pharmaceutical firms in the UK. This action was thought to be Glaxo's particular response to what had been happening in the US in previous years: some well-established pharmaceutical firms had acquired new distributors called prescription benefits management (PBM) firms. Among others, Merck had acquired Medco and Eli Lilly acquired PCS Health.

PBMs are wholesalers that purchase large volumes of prescription medicines from pharmaceutical companies and sell them to insurance companies, health maintenance organizations (HMOs) or final customers. PBMs emerged and grew out of the concern for efficiency in the US health care system. They are always looking for the lowest-cost treatment options. Through their big purchasing capacity, they can order from pharmaceutical firms at a lower price. If a PBM considers that a certain drug is too expensive, it could strike it off its list of drugs. Thus, PBMs are gaining a growing control of drug distribution in the US.

Table 5.5   Glaxo Wellcome

Year	Revenues (£m)	Profit before taxes (£m)	Research and development (£m)
1999	8,490	2,575	1,269
1998	7,983	2,671	1,163
1997	7,980	2,686	1,141
1996	8,341	2,964	1,161
1995	7,638	2,505	1,130
1994	5,656	1,835	858
1993	4,930	1,892	830

Companies like Merck and Eli Lilly decided that growth in the future could come by controlling those new distribution channels which are closer to some final customers. This decision also assumed that it was better to cannibalize some sales in-house rather than allowing other companies to snip away revenues.

On the contrary, Glaxo had other views about the future of the industry. It was a very strong R&D-driven pharmaceutical firm that believed that superior medicines based on very expensive R&D were the true foundations of survival in the long term in this industry.

The pharmaceutical industry was also under the pressure of many competitive moves. Deregulation and liberalization in the distribution of medicines still had a long way to go, but the US experience was a signal of what might happen in Europe. Well-established firms were increasing their presence in world markets. Blockbusters, new medicines with potential annual revenues over $500 million, were considered the right way to treat important diseases and to guarantee a solid stream of revenues for pharmaceutical firms. Finally, the biotechnology revolution was under way and some unknown companies with the right research capabilities needed in the new environment could potentially end up with formidable new products.

Glaxo had one of the most unique experiences in the industry in the 1980s and 1990s: the successful launch and incredible growth in the sales of Zantac, an anti-ulcerant that has become the best-selling medicine ever, until its patent expiration in 1997. Zantac showed several lessons to Glaxo, among them, the importance of R&D and the increasing role played by marketing and commercial factors in selling prescription drugs.

In this context of dramatic changes in the industry and the experience with Zantac, Glaxo's senior management decided that the future would not lie with a closer control of distribution channels, but with new blockbusters supported by strong commercial capabilities. Thus, higher investment in R&D required bigger scale and new research capabilities. This logic was clear and acquisitions became the way. It was a risky choice, because acquisitions in this industry could generate thorny problems, in particular in the labs.

Glaxo decided to start with a national merger and Wellcome was the perfect target. After announcing its offer in January 1995, Wellcome's board accepted it in a few weeks. It was a good deal for Wellcome shareholders.

All of a sudden, the R&D budget of the new firm, Glaxo Wellcome, increased by 60 per cent and scientists from both companies started to work on joint projects to combine some drugs to fight complex diseases like AIDS-HIV. Although the road was in the first years a bit bumpy, the integration was completed in less than two years.

The logic behind that merger was reinforced in subsequent years. On the one hand the performance of PBMs in the US and the benefits for their owners –

Figure 5.3   Glaxo Wellcome share price

in particular, large pharmaceutical firms – were smaller than initially expected. On the other, a consensus was emerging in the industry around the need of blockbusters to guarantee long-term survival. Only the firms with the right capabilities and the financial muscle to tackle complex research challenges could succeed in the long term.

In this context, Glaxo Wellcome confirmed its intentions to strengthen its R&D base and its marketing and sales capabilities with another merger. After a frustrated attempt in 1998, on 17 January 2000, Glaxo Wellcome and SmithKline Beecham announced their merger that would create a global company with an estimated market share of 7.3 per cent of the global pharmaceutical market – quite remarkable for a still very fragmented industry – and sales of $26 billion and a combined R&D annual budget of $3.7 billion.

The new firm, Glaxo SmithKline, was based not just on the belief that scale is necessary to develop blockbusters, but that an efficient sales force and well-developed marketing capabilities are indispensable factors. Bigger is not better here, nor in most industries. Nevertheless, scale economies seem to be very important and if cultural and personal factors do not block the way, the new firm can have a big impact in the industry.

From a corporate strategy viewpoint, Glaxo's reaction to the new competitive landscape has been very clear. It has placed emphasis on focus in terms of business portfolio – avoiding a costly diversification beyond pharmaceuticals – and with an increasing global geographical scope. Actually, the merger with SmithKline Beecham will reinforce its presence in the US and Asia.

It is interesting to consider how Glaxo would have looked like in the year 2001 if it had followed the model of some US firms in the early 1990s and had acquired a PBM. It would be much more diversified in terms of business portfolio, but narrower in terms of geographical scope, and certainly much weaker in terms of the basic capabilities in this industry: R&D and marketing.

Royal Philips Electronics: Redefining Corporate Strategy

Many European groups went through costly restructuring programmes in the 1980s and early 1990s. The pain was especially strong in industries like consumer electronics in which the cost advantage was no longer in Europe, but in Asia. For companies like Philips, that was sounding like the death knell.

Philips entered the 1990s with low expectations. In 1990 it lost £2.7 billion, almost 10 per cent of total revenues. With the implementation of several turnaround actions, the firm recovered, but in 1996 the expectations were again very poor. The firm was again in the red, and with a deteriorated morale among employees, because the restructuring efforts of the previous years had been very tough but did not seem to have been enough to put the firm back to profitability.

In 1996, a new CEO was named. He was determined to make Philips a successful company. His top management team considered that, in the past, restructuring efforts were focused on slashing costs and closing plants, but the need to think carefully about the long-term strategy was still there.

Table 5.6   Philips

Year	Revenues (€m)	Net income (€m)
1999	31,459	1,751
1998	30,459	685
1997	29,658	1,231
1996	27,100	126
1995	25,300	971

The new team set for itself the objective to regain financial credibility by the end of 1997, not just returning to the way of profitability, but also through a better management. The objective was achieved and Philips had a record year in 1997.

In the next step, the Philips management team wanted to build a platform for profitable growth, investing in new businesses, reinforcing others already existing and divesting in those that were not considered critical to the long-term success of the firm.

In this stage, the effort moved away from cost-cutting, to finding synergies among some business units, strengthening competitive advantages and managing the business portfolio more efficiently and with a short-term objective – getting a good price for the disposal, and a long-term objective – having a more balanced business portfolio.

As a result of those actions, Philips moved from having around 50 business units in 1996 to just 6 at the end of 1999: semi-conductors, components, lighting, consumer electronics, domestic appliances, and personal care and medical systems. Philips set for itself the objective of being among the top three players in each industry.

In this period, Philips acted very aggressively in buying and selling business units. It acquired the US semiconductor firm VLSI Technology, complementing Philips's strengths in fast-growing market segments for semiconductors, such as digital consumer electronics and mobile communications. It also acquired Voice Control Systems, a US firm that would reinforce Philips's positioning in speech-recognition products and its partnership with IBM in this area. It is also worth mentioning the acquisition of a 50 per cent stake in the LCD business of LG Electronics, the South Korean conglomerate. LCDs were a very strong growth area and that stake would put Philips as a world leader in active matrix displays and strengthen its consumer electronics division.

Philips not only bought but also sold businesses. The best-known was PolyGram, the music division, that was sold in 1998. It also dissolved a well-publicized joint venture with Lucent Technologies in 1998. It discontinued activities in Philips Car Systems, Philips Optoelectronics and other businesses in industrial electronics and components, after the recognition that competing in those industries required capabilities that Philips no longer had.

For the year 2000 and beyond, the Philips executive committee laid down a vision for the firm: to become an industry-shaper, or, in other words, change the structure of the industries that Philips competed in, while creating value in a sustainable way and consolidating its global reach.

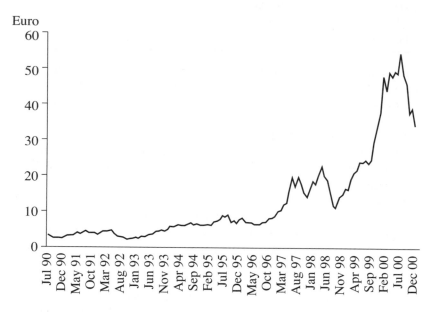

Figure 5.4   Philips share price

Philips epitomizes the strenuous effort that firms going through restructuring processes have to endure. It also shows how restructuring alone, with cost-slashing and plant closure, may not be enough, especially when the name of the game is innovation and high volume and firms need to attract and retain good people.

Moreover, a key attribute of Philips's evolution since 1996 was that it developed a point of view about the future and laid down a corporate strategy that included the leverage of resources and capabilities, better management systems, more efficient coordination efforts and a more intelligent management of its business portfolio.

The dramatic improvement in performance that Philips has shown since 1996 has to do not only with more favourable market conditions, but with a process of adjusting to a new global world and a more integrated Europe, through a clear corporate strategy that tried to confirm the firm's global reach while boosting competitive advantages in each one of its business units.

Some Lessons for Corporate Strategy

The four cases discussed in the previous sections shed some light on the question of how European multi-business firms are adjusting to an integrated single market and to a more global world economy. Those cases do not pretend to draw universal principles on how multi-business firms have changed in Europe during the 1990s, but they offer a glimpse of the strategic challenges they faced and the effectiveness of the answer they gave to those challenges.

It is important to see those cases in a wider perspective. In each one of the four industries discussed there are winners and losers, and the passing of time is the only yardstick to prove whether what seems to be a successful strategy today will also be successful tomorrow.

On the other hand, we argue that there is no 'one size fits all' corporate strategy for multi-business groups in the new competitive European landscape. There are successful firms trying to compete with a great diversity of geographical and business scopes. Nevertheless, there are some lessons which can be extracted from some of the cases analysed.

Firstly, an understanding of the forces of change, both in the product markets and capital markets, and their impact on the firm, is indispensable (see Table 5.1). This may seem obvious, but there are companies that still have big problems in coping with the nature of change in their industries. Or companies that have been good at that in the past, like British Telecom, but a sudden change in the outlook spells trouble very quickly for them.

As I highlighted above in the section on 'The effects of the 1990s shocks', the pressure for change depends very much on each industry and, within industries, on the special nature and historical evolution of each firm. In particular, when referring to capital markets, it is very important to take into account the structure of ownership, the nature of shareholders and their relative weight in the board.

Secondly, any reasonable corporate strategy needs to take into account a point of view about the future of the firm, its customers, its suppliers, its competitors and new entrants. History may prove this point of view to be wrong, but any company needs to have one. In this respect the dimensions that frame the context that multi-business groups have to define and that have been outlined in Table 5.2 seem decisive. Any multi-business firm has to make a choice about the geographical scope and the business scope it wants to have, and take into account that both in Europe and throughout the rest of the world, the new waves of rivalry that have been unleashed by deregulation and economic integration might have rendered their old approaches to those questions obsolete.

Thirdly, the choices that multi-business firms have in this respect are clear: on the business portfolio side, the choice between a wide portfolio or a narrow portfolio of different business; in the geographical dimension, to compete at a national, regional or global level.

Certainly, there is a degree of discretion that senior managers can use to choose from the different alternatives they have. Nevertheless, there are also compelling forces that are transforming previously local industries into regional or global ones. Pharmaceuticals and telecommunications are two clear examples of this category. On the other hand, there are industries in which the intensity and pressure to globalize are not that important, as with retail banking or insurance, where an efficient scale can be reached in the context of some national markets.

Another complementary issue in this respect is the growth prospects that a firm has in a small, national market, and how capital markets may read the strategy of a well-managed firm, but without great growth potential. For the past three years, capital markets have put a premium on growth companies, but the mood has changed. Nevertheless, in several industries we can observe firms like Lloyds TSB in retail banking or BMW in automobiles whose degree of geographical scope is lower in comparison with other players in their industries, but whose performance has been much superior to most of them.

This is a very important reflection in a more global world and a more integrated Europe: bigger scale does not mean better corporate performance, and there will be space for product specialists even in the more globalized industries.

Fourthly, some of the companies that have adjusted quickly and, for the time being, quite successfully to the new global world, have thought about their corporate strategy, that is to say, about their business portfolio, their geographical scope and the way to coordinate and manage the different businesses under the same corporate umbrella.

Those efforts do no mean that their senior managers have already achieved the holy grail of developing and managing synergies. Nevertheless, they are making big strides in understanding better their business portfolio, boosting the competitive advantage of each individual business unit and trying to coordinate activities among units.

For each company outlined above, we can find a company in the same industry which has products or services as good as theirs, and that face the same competitive problems, but display a bleaker outlook. Just compare Philips with

Thomson CSF or Olivetti, Banco Bilbao Vizcaya Argentaria with Banque Nationale de Paris or Commerzbank, or Glaxo SmithKline with Bayer. The difference may have to do with the quality of their senior managers and the strategic process they have gone through, which is never a guarantee of success, but a step in order to guarantee the sustainability of corporate performance in a more complex world.

Fifthly, the new forces of change in Europe have produced an upheaval in many industries, with clear losers. Nevertheless, the overall outcome is that European firms and, in particular, European multi-business groups, are healthier and stronger than ever, and better placed to innovate, create new jobs and compete in a global world.

It is true that some of today's advantages may be fleeting, and companies may see their products or services or technologies being outflanked by those of competitors. Nevertheless, this is the constant process of innovation which destroys the old to create the new.

And yet, the overall conclusion is that today in many industries Europe has multi-business firms that are global players, as competitive as their US or Asian counterparts, from retail banking to automobiles, passing through pharmaceuticals, airlines or semiconductors.

As a result, we can conclude that competition has dealt a healthy blow to many European firms and, even if the short-term effects of an increase in rivalry shake firms out of their zone of apparent comfort, it is also true that without it, Europe would be today at a clear disadvantage in many industries in relation to the US or Asia.

SOME FINAL REFLECTIONS

In this chapter I have outlined how the competitive forces unleashed by globalization, the European Single Market and the launch of the euro have affected multi-business firms, or companies with several different business units managed and controlled by the same parent company.

Those firms share a special attribute in comparison with single-business firms: they have to care not just about the competitive advantage that each business unit has and how sustainable it is, but also about the industries the group wants to be in and the relationships among the different business units, and between themselves and the parent company.

After reviewing some of the major changes affecting European multi-business groups, I have undertaken the task of explaining why multi-business firms have emerged and consolidated in Europe. This was an indispensable step in order to understand how the sweeping forces of change would affect those companies.

I have argued that many of those forces have an impact on the product markets or on capital markets, and from both there is an additional pressure on multi-business groups.

By using some real cases, I have discussed how European multi-business firms have adjusted to those pressures in the 1990s by deploying an explicit or implicit corporate strategy, and outlining their actions along two basic dimensions: their business diversification and their geographical diversification.

I would like to summarize three important conclusions from those experiences. Firstly, that there is no universal success recipe for multi-business firms, nor a strategy that fits well in any case. Each firm has to think about its history, resources and capabilities, explore threats and opportunities and decide its own future.

Secondly, some of the companies that have adjusted smoothly and more quickly to the new competitive landscape have used basic concepts of corporate strategy. They are not a substitute for actions, but may help managers figure out what businesses they should be in and why, which competitive advantage each business unit can and should develop, and how the corporate centre may add value to each one of those businesses.

Finally, even if some European industries still lag behind their US or Asian counterparts, in the 1990s European firms have made headway on many fronts and some of them have become successful global players. Competitive advantages tend to fade away and new ones have to be developed. We certainly can see that the effects of competition on multi-business firms have been positive, not only in terms of corporate performance, but in having companies able to innovate and compete in the new global context.

NOTES

1. For an overview on this topic see Canals (1997). For an analysis of the specific impact of banks on corporate governance, see Canals (1998).
2. In this respect, see Mayer (1988) for a more positive approach to the advantages of banks-based systems, and Allen (1993) and Canals (1997) for more comprehensive overviews of the advantages and problems that both systems create.
3. The notion of competitive shocks has been defined and introduced in the analysis of these problems by Ghemawat, Kennedy and Khanna (1998).
4. The volume edited by Cool, Neven and Walter (1992) offers a rich perspective of changes in the European industry through the early 1990s.
5. For more elaborated views of corporate strategy, see Campbell, Goold and Alexander (1994) and Collis and Montgomery (1997).
6. It is important to note in this respect that, as Khanna and Palepu (1997) show, focused strategies may be wrong in the case of firms operating in emerging markets. In this particular context, with an important institutional void, corporate groups can add value by creating internal capital markets, providing superior professional training and setting up standards of business behaviour.

REFERENCES

Allen, F. (1993), 'Strategic management and financial markets', *Strategic Management Journal*, Special Issue, 11–22.

Amihud, Y. and B. Lev (1999), 'Does corporate ownership structure affect its strategy towards diversification?, *Strategic Management Journal*, 20(11), November, 1063–70.

Bowman, E.H. and H. Singh, (1993), 'Corporate restructuring: reconfiguring the firm', *Strategic Management Journal*, 14, Special Issue, Summer, 5–14.

Campbell, N., M. Goold and M. Alexander (1994), *Corporate-Level Strategy*, London: John Wiley.

Canals, J. (1993), *Competitive Strategies in European Banking*, Oxford: Oxford University Press.

Canals, J. (1997), *Universal Banking*, Oxford: Oxford University Press.

Canals, J. (1998), 'Banks as shareholders: do they matter?', IESE working paper 354, January.

Canals, J. (2000), *Managing Corporate Growth*, Oxford: Oxford University Press.

Caves, R. (1982), *Multinational Enterprise and Economic Analysis*, Cambridge, MA: Harvard University Press.

Collis, D.J. and C.A. Montgomery (1997), *Corporate Strategy*, Boston, MA: Irwin.

Collis, D.J. and C.A. Montgomery (1998), 'Creating corporate advantage', *Harvard Business Review*, May–June, 71–83.

Cool, K., D. Neven and I. Walter (eds) (1992), *European Industrial Restructuring in the 1990s*, London: Macmillan.

Daems, H. (1978), *Holding Company and Corporate Control*, Boston, MA: Martinus Nijhoff.

Doz, I. (1992), 'The role of partnerships and alliances in the European industrial restructuring', in K. Cool, D.J. Neven and I. Walter (eds), *European Industrial Restructuring in the 1990s*, London: Macmillan, pp. 294–327.

Ghemawat, P., R. Kennedy and T. Khanna (1998), 'Competitive policy shocks and strategic management', in M. Hitt, J.E. Ricart and R. Nixon (eds), *Managing Strategically in an Interconnected World*, New York: John Wiley, pp. 15–38.

Ghemawat, P. and T. Khanna (1998), 'The nature of diversified business groups: A research design and two case studies', *Journal of Industrial Economics*, 46, 35–62.

Grossman, S.J. and O.D. Hart (1980), 'Takeover bids, the free-rider problem and the theory of the corporation', *Bell Journal of Economics*, 11, 42–64.

Guillén, M. (2000), 'Business groups in emerging economies: a resource-based view', *Academy of Management Journal*, 43(3), June, 362–80.

Hoskinsson, R.E., R.A. Johnson and D.D. Moesel (1994), 'Corporate divestiture intensity in restructuring firms: effects of governance, strategy and performance', *Academy of Management Journal*, 37(5), October, 1207–51.

Hoskinsson, R.E. and M.A. Hitt (1994), *Downscoping: How to Tame the Diversified Firm*, Oxford: Oxford University Press.

Khanna, T. and K. Palepu (1997), 'Why focused strategies may be wrong for emerging markets', *Harvard Business Review*, 75(4), 41–50.

Khanna, T. and K. Palepu (2000), 'The future of business groups in emerging markets: long-run evidence from Chile', *Academy of Management Journal*, 43(3), June, 268–85.

Lang, L. and R. Stultz (1994), 'Tobin's q, corporate diversification and firm performance', *Journal of Political Economy*, 102(6), 1248–80.

Mayer, C. (1988), 'New issues in corporate finance', *European Economic Review*, 32, 1.167–1.189.

Markides, C.C. (1995), 'Diversification, restructuring and economic performance', *Strategic Management Journal*, 16(2), February, 101–18.

Markides, C.C. and P.J. Williamson (1996), 'Corporate diversification and organizational structure: a resource-based view', *Academy of Management Journal*, 39(2), April, 340–67.

Montgomery, C.A. (1982), 'The measurement of firm diversification: some new empirical evidence', *Academy of Management Journal*, 25, 299–307.

Montgomery, C.A. and S. Hariharan (1991), 'Diversified expansion by large established firms', *Journal of Economic Behavior and Organization*, 15(1), 71–89.

Penrose, E. (1959), *The Theory of the Growth of the Firm*, New York: John Wiley.

Pettigrew, A.M. and R. Whipp (1993), *Managing Change for Competitive Success*, Oxford: Basil Blackwell.

Prahalad, C.K. and R.A. Bettis (1986), 'The dominant logic: a new linkage between diversity and performance', *Strategic Management Journal*, 7, 485–501.

Ramanujam, V. and V., and P. Varadarajan (1989), 'Research on corporate diversification: a synthesis', *Strategic Management Journal*, 10, 523–51.

Rumelt, R.P. (1974), *Strategy, Structure and Economic Performance*, Boston, MA: Harvard Business School Press.

Shleifer, A. and R.W. Vishny (1986), 'Large shareholders and corporate control', *Journal of Political Economy*, 94, 461–88.

Shleifer, A. and F.W. Vishny (1996), 'A survey of corporate governance', NBER working paper 5554.

Stopford, J. and S. Strange (1991), *Rival States, Rival Firms*, Cambridge: Cambridge University Press.

Williamson, O. (1975), *Markets and Hierarchies*, New York: Free Press.

6. European welfare states: regionalization, globalization, and policy change

Duane Swank

In this chapter, I extend recent work (Swank, 2000; forthcoming, a; forthcoming, b) to assess the controversial claim that global and regional economic integration produces pressures for retrenchment and market-oriented restructuring of European welfare states. As I detail below, a large contemporary literature argues that the internationalization of markets for goods, services and capital forces incumbent European governments, regardless of ideological or programmatic positions, to roll-back social insurance benefits, implement efficiency-oriented reforms of social services and otherwise move welfare policy toward a residual, market-conforming model of social protection. Institutional developments at the European level, most notably the development and expansion of the European Monetary System and the convergence criteria of the European Monetary Union, may also create significant pressures for welfare state retrenchment. On the other hand, as I argue below, some extant theory and research suggest that internationalization of markets – both at a global and a European level – is positively related to maintenance of the relatively generous and comprehensive systems of social protection that characterize the bulk of contemporary European welfare states. In addition, complementary work argues that most European welfare states are embedded in a configuration of political economic institutions that politically blunts the neo-liberal reform pressures that flow from internationalization.

I organize my analysis of these questions as follows. In the first section, I succinctly review, synthesize and extend recent theory by juxtaposing what I call the 'neo-liberalism thesis' and the alternative theory of 'contemporary embedded liberalism'. I next outline my methodological approach to assessing competing hypotheses about the welfare state consequences of internationalization and European economic integration. In the core section of the chapter, I present a brief qualitative evaluation of the relationship between internationalization and trends in European social policy and, most important, offer a systematic quantitative analysis of the welfare impacts of international capital mobility and financial integration, global and European trade openness, and European monetary integration. The final section presents a summary of my conclusions about the roles of internationalization and regionalization of markets in shaping 1980s and 1990s trajectories of European welfare states.

GLOBALIZATION, REGIONALIZATION AND EUROPEAN WELFARE STATES

Observers of contemporary European welfare states commonly cite the internationalization of markets for goods, services and capital – on both a global and a regional level – as a central challenge to the maintenance of generous and comprehensive systems of social protection (for example, Rhodes 1997a; Scharpf 2000; van Kersbergen 2000). The facts concerning the internationalization of markets are familiar. Reflecting a reduction in the transactions costs of international economic exchange – declines caused by exogenous technological and economic developments, national policy changes, and supranational agreements – trade in goods and services and (especially) capital mobility have increased dramatically in the last 30 years. For the average developed European economy, total international trade in goods and services as a share of gross domestic product (GDP) expanded from roughly 35 per cent to 60 per cent between the mid-1960s and mid-1990s; accounting for more than half of total trade in both periods, intra-European trade increased at a comparable rate.[1]

With respect to capital mobility, inward and outward flows of foreign direct investment (FDI), portfolio investments, and transnational bank lending in the typical developed democracy have risen from approximately 5 per cent to 50 per cent of GDP between the mid-1960s and mid-1990s. In 1995 alone, inward and outward flows of FDI for the OECD nations totalled $632 billion while OECD nation borrowing on international capital markets summed to $732 billion. Of these totals, approximately three-quarters was accounted for by flows among the developed democracies; for the average European political economy, most investment flows involved other European nations and North America (UN Centre for Transnational Corporations, 1996; OECD, 1996). By the mid-1990s, the *Economist* (1995) estimates that the monetary value of annual international turnover of bonds and equities was, for instance, 160 per cent of GDP in Germany and 1000 per cent of GDP in Britain. Declines in covered international rate differentials between national and international markets and (national and supranationally initiated) liberalization of controls on movements of goods, services and capital proceeded apace across Europe. While observers have noted distinct limits to internationalization (for example, Berger and Dore, 1996; Keohane and Milner, 1996), there is little question that transnational economic integration and, for the typical European country, regionalization of markets, has significantly expanded in the post-Bretton Woods era. What are the consequences of global and regional market integration for European welfare states?

The Neo-liberalism Thesis

A large contemporary literature on the domestic policy impacts of global and regional market integration predicts significant neo-liberal policy reforms in the wake of globalization and the economic integration of Europe. Specifically, numerous scholars have suggested that the internationalization of economic activity, especially expansions in capital mobility, reduce the ability of democratically elected governments to maintain generous and comprehensive social protection and the taxes needed to finance it.[2] As I have argued elsewhere (Swank, 2000; forthcoming, a; forthcoming, b), the impact of globalization on domestic social policy autonomy may be channelled through three mechanisms. First, the economic logic of internationalization posits that rises in capital mobility constrain social policy-makers through the operation of markets: in the presence of high or near perfect capital mobility, mobile asset holders pursue the most profitable rate of return on investment in international markets. In the context of high levels of international financial integration and the absence of significant international policy coordination, national policy-makers face a prisoner's dilemma: democratically elected governments, irrespective of ideological or programmatic positions, face strong incentives to engage in competition to retain and attract transnationally fluid investment through reductions in social benefits, market-oriented reforms of social services, and cuts in associated tax burdens. Increasing trade openness purportedly intensifies these forces. Rises in trade, especially between developed and developing 'low-wage' economies, may force policy-makers to cut social outlays in order to reduce welfare-related labour costs (and hence promote the price competitiveness of exports), to reduce public sector debt and interest rates (and hence bolster growth-enhancing investment), and to otherwise lessen economic inefficiencies (such as, those related to disincentives to work and invest).

The second and third mechanisms link globalization and welfare state retrenchment through politics, and together they constitute the 'political logic' of globalization. Specifically, international capital mobility may contribute to welfare state retrenchment through routine democratic politics: the credible threat of exit by mobile enterprises may augment and enhance the conventional political resources of business (for example, money, organization and access). Mobile industrial and financial businesses and their interest associations often pressure policy-makers for reductions in generous social programmes and accompanying tax burdens by arguing that the welfare state negatively affects profits, investment and employment, and by citing the advantages of foreign investment environments. Furthermore, internationalization reinforces the rationale of neo-liberal economic theories and policy proposals. As I have documented (Swank, forthcoming, a, Chapters 4–6), conservative governments and business economists and spokespersons throughout Europe commonly invoke the 'economic logic' of globalization when arguing for retrenchment and market-oriented reforms of the welfare state.

Institutional Developments in the European Union

The economic and political pressures associated with internationalization of markets are commonly regarded as a central feature of the welfare state impacts of European economic integration. However, institutional developments within the European Union may also have distinct effects on European social policy. The creation of the single market, actions by European Union institutions (most notably the European Commission and European Court of Justice), and other developments in the structure and operation of the European Union have long-term implications for national systems of social protection. Although most formal-legal initiatives in the area of European-wide social policy (such as the Social Charter) have had limited immediate consequences for national systems of social welfare provision (for example, see contributions to Liebfried and Pierson, 1995 and Marks et al., 1996), recent trajectories of European welfare states may have been affected in fundamental ways by the development of the European Monetary System.

Firstly, the (1979) initiation and (1980s and 1990s) expansion of the Exchange Rate Mechanism may have had important impacts on European social policy. On the one hand, stabilization of volatile exchange rates may have contributed to stronger economic growth and, in turn, bolstered the financial base of the welfare state; stronger economic performance also reduces unemployment and other forms of need that create fiscal pressures for welfare state retrenchment (see below). On the other hand, late 1970s and 1980s adoption of hard currency policies by formal membership (for example, a majority of extant EU members) or informal currency pegs (for example, late 1980s Norway and Sweden) were systematically linked to adoption of a neo-liberal macroeconomic paradigm and accompanied by complementary policy shifts toward domestic price stability, efficiency-oriented economic restructuring and fiscal prudence (for example, McNamara, 1998; Notermans, 2000). As such, social welfare policies were generally subject to new cost control and market-oriented reform initiatives in many European nations (for example, Swank, forthcoming, a, Chapters 4–6). Secondly, and most important, the 1992 Maastricht Treaty for European Monetary Union, and the attendant convergence criteria for EMU membership, as well as the subsequent 1996 Stability Pact, have potentially had significant impacts on social policy reforms during and since the 1990s. As is commonly known, the convergence criteria not only reinforces macroeconomic biases toward prices stability (that is, by requirements for low interest rates and stable membership in the normal bands of the ERM), but they also stipulate that potential EMU members must lower short-term deficits to 3 per cent of GDP or less and public sector debt to 60 per cent of GDP or less. As recent analyses by Teague (1998) and others have suggested, many European welfare states experienced at least modest 1990s retrenchment as national policy-makers sought to meet the convergence criteria (as well as conform to the long-term fiscal constraints mandated by the 1996 Stability Pact). Nations such as Italy, where debt and deficits significantly exceeded convergence criteria, may have been particularly affected (Swank, forthcoming, a, Chapter 5).

In addition, extensive international financial liberalization and rises in capital mobility in European nations during the 1980s and 1990s may well have interacted with monetary integration to produce substantial downward pressures on social welfare provision. This hypothesis is derived from Mundell-Flemming models of monetary policy in open economies, or the notion of an 'unholy triangle' where national policy-makers can only simultaneously achieve two of the three goals of exchange rate stability, capital mobility and domestic monetary autonomy. Beyond the social policy impacts of commitments to currency stability outlined above, the welfare state consequences of the inter-action of high levels of international capital mobility and (formal or informal) membership in the Exchange Rate Mechanism, a joint condition achieved by a significant majority of European nations by the late 1980s, are significant, albeit indirect. Specifically, as analyses by Huber and Stephens (1998), Moses (2000) and others have indicated, rises in international capital mobility and hard currency policy have stripped policy-makers in large Northern European welfare states (most notably the Nordic countries and France) of crucial policy instruments central to the maintenance of high levels of employment. These instruments include the allocation of credit through control of domestic interest rates and selective currency devaluations. The loss of these policy tools may have led, in turn, to the inability of policy-makers to effectively respond to late 1980s and (especially 1990s) rises in unemployment. Notable and sustained rises in general and long-term unemployment rates and attendant fiscal stress have certainly contributed to, if not primarily caused, the most pronounced episodes of retrenchment of the generous and comprehensive Northern European welfare states (for example, Huber and Stephens, 1998; Stephens, 1996; Swank, forthcoming a, Chapters 4–5).

The Theory of Contemporary Embedded Liberalism

In sharp contrast to the neo-liberalism thesis, several streams of theory and research argue that global and European economic integration have not produced significant movement of European welfare states toward a residual, market-conforming model in the 1980s and 1990s. This work, constituting what one might call the theory of contemporary embedded liberalism, is also grounded in an economic and political logic. With regard to economics, contemporary theory extends seminal work of the 1970s and early 1980s on the positive association between post-war (trade) liberalization, and extensive systems of government intervention and social protection. In the earlier work in this tradition, Cameron (1978), Stephens (1979) and Katzenstein (1985) demonstrated that high levels of trade openness are systematically associated with the expansion of the public economy and social protection in the developed democracies. A large public sector and welfare state enable governments in open economies to smooth business cycles, lessen insecurities and risks attendant to international market exposure, and otherwise facilitate adjustments to the competitive pressures that flow from openness. Complementing this analysis, John Ruggie (1982) argued that a multilateral international regime of 'embedded liberalism' emerged in the post-Second World War era in which a liberal international trading order was supported by significant albeit cross-nationally varied levels and forms of government interventionism and social welfare provision.

Recent scholarship by Geoffrey Garrett (1998a, 1998b), Dani Rodrik (1997, 1998) and others suggests that governments continue to provide what Garrett calls significant 'social compensation' in response to insecurities and risks attendant on internationalization. Furthermore, Rodrik (1998) presents evidence that trade openness, operationalized as the interaction between high levels of trade flows and terms-of-trade volatility, is positively associated with generous social security transfers in both developing and developed political economies in the contemporary era. Garrett (1998a, 1998b) and Garrett and Mitchell (forthcoming) also present various analyses of the relationships of trade and financial openness on the one hand, and expenditure and tax policies on the other, that are largely consistent with the 'social compensation' hypothesis.

A related and overlapping body of work by scholars such as Garrett, Boix (1998) and others suggests that a relatively generous and comprehensive welfare state may also have positive effects on economic efficiency. Most observers recognize that the social compensation of those harmed by economic restructuring and those who face new risks and insecurities in the open, post-industrial economy contributes to social stability and labour peace and, consequentially, good economic performance. Moreover, relatively large European welfare states may provide collective goods and promote general economic efficiency in other ways. As Hemerijck, Rhodes and Ferrara (forthcoming) argue, most European welfare states contribute significantly to the reduction of poverty, and hence to increases in social stability and cohesion as well as improvements in the quality of human capital. Generous and comprehensive systems of social protection also improve the functioning of labour markets where well-protected workers more readily seek better and more appropriate jobs. Active labour market programmes as well as health and other social policies contribute to a nation's human capital stock, and hence to worker productivity and growth.

In terms of politics, Cameron (1978), Stephens (1979) and Katzenstein (1985) have also emphasized that open economies are characterized by highly concentrated industrial sectors. High concentration of production, in turn, fosters strong trade union (and employer) organization, centralized collective bargaining and associated tripartite policy-making, and electorally powerful left-wing parties. The existence of these actors and institutions, or what might be identified as strong social democratic corporatism, leads to the development of generous and comprehensive welfare states in the open economies of North-Central and Northern Europe (also see Hicks and Swank, 1992; Huber and Stephens, forthcoming).

Political Institutions

Recent scholarship on the politics of welfare retrenchment suggests that contemporary European welfare states continue to enjoy strong political support as a function of the institutions in which they are embedded. First, well-known work by Paul Pierson (1994, 1996, 2000) argues that even in the face of contemporary international and domestic pressures, developed welfare states will exhibit substantial resiliency. This is so according to Pierson because of the political dynamics of welfare retrenchment: retrenchment entails cutting concentrated, politically popular benefits from organized constituencies in return for the promise of future, diffuse gains (such as, deficit reduction). Although policy-makers seeking reductions in welfare expenditures have recourse to a variety of policy approaches in the face of political resistence (for example, obfuscation or 'divide-and-conquer' strategies), institutional structures of welfare states will condition the outcome. For instance, long-lived programmes with large and unified constituencies will generally be resistant to programmatic retrenchment strategies.

In my own work (Swank, 2000; forthcoming, a; forthcoming, b), I have also argued that welfare institutions, especially the programmatic structures of universal and corporatist conservative welfare states of continental Europe in contrast to properties of liberal welfare states (see below), will foster political resiliency. Specifically, corporatist conservative welfare structures, which incorporate the social partners and constituency groups in social insurance fund administration and routine policy-making, promote the representation of pro-welfare state interests. The generous and comprehensive benefit structures of universal and corporatist conservative welfare states also cultivate the development and maintenance of large cross-class electoral coalitions of working-class and middle-class beneficiaries. In addition, in both the Nordic universal and Continental conservative welfare states, operation of the system of social protection fosters norms of social solidarity and confidence in the welfare state to reinforce social cohesion.

In addition, I have argued in this recent work that not only are the programmatic structures of most European welfare states conducive to defence of the welfare state, but that these systems of social protection are embedded in a broader set of political economic institutions that shape the degree to which welfare states are susceptible to neo-liberal reforms pressures. Specifically, the bulk of developed European welfare states are embedded in inclusive electoral institutions (that is, proportional representation, and multi-party legislatures and cabinets) and social corporatist systems of collective interest representation. These political institutions, in contrast to majoritarian electoral systems and pluralist interest group systems, promote the representation of pro-welfare state interests in national policy-making (for example, create veto points over neo-liberal reforms), enhance the political capacities of pro-welfare state groups and parties (for example, increase the votes and seats of left-wing and Christian democratic parties), and contribute to the development of norms of cooperation and consensus in the national policy process. In sum, these institutions make relatively rapid and significant neo-liberal reforms of the welfare state unlikely.

However, despite the economic and political forces that arguably support relatively large European welfare states, there is reason to temper confidence in the sustainability of embedded liberalism: recent theory and evidence that suggests the maintenance of the joint equity and efficiency gains of developed systems of embedded liberalism may indeed be tenuous in the long run. Specifically, some scholars have argued that general international financial integration and capital mobility may interact with rises in European trade and general economic integration to create additional pressures on European welfare states. That is, Rodrik (1997), Hicks (1999) and others (Pauly, 1995; Ruggie, 1994) have noted that while governments have economic and political incentives to continue to provide substantial social protection in the face of risks and economic adjustments generated by internationalization, international capital mobility will reduce the revenue-raising capacity of governments in open economies to sustain high levels of social welfare provision. In fact, Rodrik (1997) presents evidence that shows contemporary increases in capital mobility interact with high trade openness to produce moderate reductions in social security transfers in the developed OECD nations. Similarly, Hicks (1999) reports analysis that indicates internationalization produces pressures for welfare state expansion up to a point; at higher levels of international market integration, policy-makers face strong incentives to retrench the welfare state.

In sum, a substantial body of theory and research predicts that international and European market integration will produce significant neo-liberal reforms of the welfare state. The economic and political logics of internationalization may be intensified by institutional developments within the European Union, namely, European monetary integration. In sharp contrast to the neo-liberal perspective, an alternative body of work suggests that substantial economic and political forces undergird the European social welfare state. From the perspective of contemporary embedded liberalism, we should expect to see little in the way of systematic retrenchment and neo-liberal restructuring of welfare states as international and regional integration of markets takes place. I now turn to a systematic assessment of these competing sets of hypotheses.

THE METHODOLOGICAL APPROACH

In order to assess central hypotheses on the welfare impacts of globalization and European economic integration, I initially examine contemporary trends in social welfare protection across distinct clusters of European welfare states. This exercise not only provides a preliminary evaluation of central arguments, but it sets the stage for a systematic quantitative assessment of the effects of global and regional market integration on European systems of social protection. For the quantitative analysis, I examine the direct effects of international capital mobility, global and European trade, and European monetary integration on an aggregate measure of social welfare effort: total social welfare expenditures as a share of GDP. The analysis is extended by examining the welfare effects of the interaction of global and European integration as well as by assessing a subset of hypotheses with measures of both aggregate welfare effort and programmatic benefits (that is, the proportion of gross income of the average production worker replaced by social insurance and other assistance during a period of unemployment).[3]

For both the qualitative and quantitative analyses, I focus on the virtual universe of (West) European welfare states from 1979 to 1995. The nations are: Austria, Belgium, Denmark, Finland, France, Germany, Greece, Ireland, Italy, the Netherlands, Norway, Portugal, Spain, Sweden, Switzerland and the United Kingdom. Iceland and Luxembourg are excluded because of the unavailability of data for some core features of welfare states and the political economy. The time frame is limited to 1979 to 1995 because of the absence of data for some key variables (and the absence of consolidated democratic institutions in Greece, Portugal and Spain until the late 1970s). East European welfare states are excluded because of the absence of democratic institutions for much of the time frame of this study.

Empirical Models

To assess hypotheses developed above, I examine welfare effects of several
potentially relevant aspects of international capital mobility and trade openness
as well as European economic integration. I include in the analysis measures
of three features of international capital mobility. For observed capital
movements, I examine the policy effects of two dimensions highlighted in the
literature: total inflows and outflows of foreign direct investment (FDI), and a
nation's total borrowing on international capital markets. Each of these measures
is standardized by a nation's GDP and, to smooth occasionally volatile annual
movements, is operationalized as a three-year moving average (lags 1–3). To
examine the policy effects of general international financial integration, I
employ a broad measure of the liberalization of financial flows: an index of the
degree of liberalization of restrictions on capital movements plus the degree of
liberalization of controls on payments for goods and services (see Quinn and
Inclan, 1997).[4] In addition, I also explicitly and more precisely test the
hypothesis that global financial integration produces a 'run to the bottom' by
larger European welfare states. I do so by estimating the social welfare consequences of the interaction of capital mobility and past levels of welfare effort
(see below on interaction analysis).

To test hypotheses about the welfare consequences of global and European
trade openness, I employ three distinct trade measures in empirical models
estimated below: imports and exports (as percentages of GDP) between a focal
European nation and (1) other European nations, (2) developed (non-European)
political economies, and (3) developing nations. Trade with developing
countries allows assessment of a central aspect of the hypothesized linkage
between contemporary rises in trade openness and downward pressures on
welfare state costs; intra-European trade flows is a commonly-used measure
of general European economic integration (for example, Garrett, 1998c) and
allows direct tests of the welfare effects of that process.

To examine the consequences of European monetary integration for social
protection, I employ two core variables: an index of a country's participation
in the Exchange Rate Mechanism (ERM) and membership in the EU in the
post-Maastricht Treaty years. Specifically, I developed an indicator that scores
a nation 1.00 for participation in the narrow margins (+/– 2.25 per cent) of the
ERM peg, 0.75 for participation in the +/– 6.0 per cent ERM margins, 0.50 for
participation in the wide margins (+/– 15 per cent), 0.25 for an informal, non-
membership ERM peg (for example,, Norway and Sweden in the late 1980s),
and 0.00 for no formal or informal ERM peg of the country's currency. With
respect to the Maastricht Treaty, its provisions for European Monetary Union
(hereafter EMU), and the fiscal convergence criteria for EMU membership, I
initially estimated the welfare effects of a dichotomous variable coded 1.00 for

EU member country years since 1992. However, to more precisely test the welfare impact of the pending EMU and its convergence criteria, I utilize below an interaction between the dichotomous variable for the post-Maastricht Treaty era and a nation's public sector debt (as a percentage of GDP).

Finally, to assess hypotheses about the combined effect of international financial integration and European trade and monetary integration, I estimate the welfare effects of interactions between the aggregate measure of international financial liberalization on the one hand, and measures of European trade flows and participation in the ERM on the other. I detail the procedures for general statistical and interaction analysis below.

A General Model of European Welfare Provision

To evaluate hypotheses about the impacts of international and European economic integration on European welfare states, it is essential to account for a variety of significant determinants of social welfare provision. Specifically, I follow a large body of welfare state theory and research and incorporate the level of economic development (that is, per capita GDP in international prices) in a general model of social welfare effort. Rises in the level of economic development are commonly thought to increase altruism among an increasingly affluent mass public and the revenue base of the welfare state (for example, Hicks and Swank, 1992; Pampel and Williamson, 1989). Related, the objective needs and political mobilization of the elderly population are also believed to fundamentally shape social welfare effort (for example, Hicks and Swank, 1992; Huber, Ragin and Stephens, 1993; Pamel and Williamson, 1989). Thus, I incorporate the share of the population aged 65 and over in the general model. In addition, business cycle dynamics are often highlighted as central sources of variations in social welfare provision. Automatic entitlement triggers, political demands and discretionary policy actions associated with unemployment, economic growth rates and inflation are hypothesized to be important sources of variations of social welfare effort (for example, Hicks and Swank, 1992; Huber, Ragin and Stephens, 1993; Pampel and Williamson, 1989).

Political factors also play a large role in welfare state theory. Most important, scholars have devoted substantial attention to the direct welfare state effects of government control by left-wing, Christian democratic and right-wing parties. While some theoretical and empirical treatments of the welfare state have stressed left party government incumbency (for example, Cameron, 1978; Stephens, 1979) or the presence of a unified party of the right (for example, Castles, 1998), a substantial amount of work has emphasized the positive welfare state impacts of both left and Christian democratic party government control (for example, Hicks and Swank, 1992; Huber, Ragin and Stephens,

1993). Thus, I employ measures of the share of cabinet portfolios controlled by these party types in the general model of European social protection.

In sum, the empirical models estimated below incorporate core determinants of social welfare effort highlighted in extant theory and research. Unless noted, models are estimated with (one-year) lags for all control variables: economic growth, unemployment and inflation rates as well as economic development, the size of the aged population, and left and Christian democratic government incumbency. One-year lags (or, where noted, average multiple-year lags) are also used for focal international and European capital and trade variables discussed above.

Statistical Estimation

To assess the direct policy effects of dimensions of international and European economic integration on European systems of social protection, I estimate empirical models of annual 1979–95 total social spending in the 16 focal nations (previously identified) by ordinary least squares (OLS) regression with corrections for first-order autoregressive errors and panel correct standard errors (that is, heteroskedastic–consistent variance–covariance matrices for panel data) as discussed by Beck and Katz (1995). To account for a variety of potential (unmodelled) country effects (such as, the social welfare effects of political institutions), I include i-I country dichotomous variables (where i denotes the number of nations). Thus, I estimate through OLS 'fixed-effects' panel models for 1979–95 annual data from 16 nations (see, among others, Beck and Katz, 1996, on alternative panel model estimators).

Interaction Analysis

As referenced above, a subset of key hypotheses are examined through the interaction of two central variables (for example, financial liberalization and European trade integration). For example, the interaction between X_1 (such as, European trade integration) and X_2 (such as, global financial liberalization), when the dependent variable is Y (such as, social welfare effort), can be used to estimate the variation in effects of X_2 (financial liberalization) on Y (social welfare effort) across levels of X_1 (European Trade Integration). The estimated coefficient for interaction term, when multiplied by a value of X_1 (European trade integration) and added to the regression coefficient of X_2 (financial liberalization), becomes the slope for the effect of X_2 (financial liberalization) at that level of X_1 (European trade integration). Standard errors for the estimated coefficient for X_2 at some level of X_1, necessary to compute statistical significance of the effect, are easily derived. Procedures for computation of these standard errors and a thorough discussion of interactions are provided by Friedrich (1982).

EMPIRICAL ANALYSIS

Before turning to the systematic quantitative analysis, it should be useful to examine trends in social protection and the country experiences of European welfare states in light of predictions from the neo-liberalism thesis. Do trajectories of social welfare provision in the generous and comprehensive welfare states of Northern Europe reflect retrenchment, neo-liberal restructuring, and a 'run to the bottom?'; do trends in social protection in more market-oriented European welfare states (that is, Britain, Switzerland) and the developing welfare states of Southern Europe exhibit stability or evidence of additional neo-liberal reforms? The neo-liberalism thesis certainly predicts that the answer to these questions is 'yes' for the years from the late 1970s to the time of writing in 2000.

Table 6.1 reports aggregate data organized according Esping-Andersen's (1990) familiar categorization of welfare state regimes; following recent work (for example, Rhodes 1997b), the Southern European welfare states are classified as a separate category.[5] With respect to the social democratic welfare states, recent work has suggested that despite moderate retrenchments in the 1990s – reforms most pronounced in Finland and Sweden in the wake of early 1990s economic crises – the social democratic welfare state remains intact.[6] Specifically, with the exception of Denmark in the late 1970s and early 1980s, most welfare state reforms were modest before the 1990s. These primarily consisted of moderate initiatives in cost controls (such as, in response to the rise in the expense of health care), greater efficiency in the delivery of social services and planning for future reforms to address pending demographic crises (such as, population ageing). Moreover, these efforts at restraining welfare state costs were coupled with modest expansions of early retirement and active labour market programmes as well as social services. Even in the case of early 1990s reforms, policy changes have been most pronounced in the area of unemployment and social assistance and the basic features of the universal welfare states remain intact. As illustrated by data presented in Table 6.1, commitments of national resources to health and government social service programmes and the generosity of the social wage have not diminished over two decades of significant domestic and international economic pressures.

A similar story may be told for reforms of the corporatist conservative welfare states of continental Europe. In Germany, France and other corporatist conservative systems (although not Italy), moderate cost control and efficiency-oriented initiatives began in the late 1970s and continued in the early 1980s in

Table 6.1 Trajectories of European welfare states, 1980–95

Part A

	Total social protection[a]			Social wage[b]		
	1980–84	1985–89	1990–93	1980–84	1985–89	1990–95
Social democratic welfare states	25.8	26.8	31.5	0.57	0.66	0.66
Corporatist conservative welfare states	23.6	24.5	25.7	0.44	0.43	0.40
Liberal welfare states	17.3	17.9	20.2	0.32	0.42	0.43
Southern European welfare states	14.0	15.9	18.4	0.38	0.51	0.60
All	21.7	22.8	25.5	0.43	0.49	0.50

Part B

	Social services[c]			Public health[d]		
	1980–84	1985–89	1990–93	1980–84	1985–89	1990–95
Social democratic welfare states	2.7	3.0	3.8	6.7	6.8	7.1
Corporatist conservative welfare states	0.7	0.6	0.7	6.1	6.1	6.6
Liberal welfare states	0.6	0.6	0.8	5.1	5.2	6.2
Southern European welfare states	0.1	0.1	0.3	3.8	3.9	4.8
All	1.2	1.3	1.6	5.8	5.8	6.4

Notes:
a Total social welfare expenditures (OECD definition) as a percentage of gross domestic product. (See Appendix for all data sources.)
b Social wage proportion of gross income for the unemployed average production worker replaced by unemployment insurance and compensation, social assistance, and various entitled welfare schemes.
c Social services expenditure for government social services for the elderly, disabled, children and families as a percentage of gross domestic product.
d Government health care expenditures as a percentage of gross domestic product.

Welfare state types:
Social democratic: Denmark, Finland, Netherlands, Norway, Sweden
Corporatist conservative: Austria. Belgium, France, Germany, Ireland, Italy
Liberal: Britain, Switzerland
Southern: Greece, Portugal, Spain

the wake of the OPEC oil shocks and attendant economic performance problems and fiscal stress. However, while modest efforts at cost control and market-oriented reforms continued through the 1980s, these welfare states initiated limited welfare expansions and new programmes to address the problems of unemployment (including job loss linked to internationally-oriented economic restructuring), social exclusion and new dependent groups (such as, the frail elderly). In Italy, significant welfare expansion persisted deep into the 1980s with completion of the programmatic structure of the Italian welfare state and social compensation for economic restructuring. In all these welfare states, more significant welfare reforms to address demographic pressures, health care costs and the persistence of high unemployment occurred in the early and mid-1990s. As I have argued elsewhere (Swank, forthcoming, a, Chapter 5), 1990s pressures to roll-back social protection have generally been intensified by country-specific problems (for example, the costs of German unification) and Maastricht Treaty convergence criteria. However, as data presented in Table 6.1 suggest, the corporatist conservative welfare states have not been dismantled: relative and absolute levels of social welfare effort, social services and health care exhibit substantial stability during the 1980s and 1990s era of significant domestic and international pressures on developed welfare states.

With respect to liberal welfare states, programmatic features of the British and Swiss systems best represent the European counterparts to North America and Australasia. However, the aggregate data presented in Table 6.1 – data that suggest substantial stability if not modest growth in social protection in liberal welfare states – is misleading. This is so because patterns of policy reform in Switzerland largely parallel social policy change in universal and corporatist conservative welfare states in the 1980s and 1990s. On the other hand, Britain conforms to the pattern of significant welfare state retrenchment characteristic of New Zealand and the United States and, to a lesser extent, Australia and Canada. Specifically, policy reforms initiated by the Conservative governments of Prime Ministers Thatcher and Major have significantly diminished the value of public flat-rate and contributory pensions, encouraged the partial privatiza-tion of old-age security, significantly reduced unemployment supports, notably increased means-testing, and fostered significant market-oriented reforms (for example, internal markets) and privatization of health and social services. Unlike universal and corporatist conservative welfare states, these reforms are in part a direct response to internationalization (see Swank, forthcoming a, Chapter 6 and the literature cited therein).

With regard to the Southern European welfare states, the neo-liberalism thesis predicts substantial stability in social protection during the 1980s and 1990s in the context of a 'run to the bottom' or significant 'social dumping' by more developed universal and corporatist conservative welfare states. That is, the relatively underdeveloped, post-authoritarian social welfare systems of late

1970s Southern Europe serve as 'the bottom' in an regionally integrated Europe. However, as the comprehensive analysis of Guillén and Matsaganis (2000) illustrates, and as many other scholars have noted, the opposite appears to be true. That is, as the data of Table 6.1 illustrate, Southern European welfare systems have apparently 'run to the top' as national policy-makers in these systems and have pursued, in the context of substantial programmes of economic modernization, substantial increases in the levels and coverage of social insurance benefits and adopted new national programmes (for example, national health systems). However, at the same time, it is important to point out that, similar to the developed European welfare states to the north, 1990s socioeconomic pressures as well as the desire to meet Maastricht convergence criteria, have led to moderate neo-liberal reforms in the 1990s (for example, benefit roll-backs, efficiency-oriented restructuring of health and social services). Overall, the character and timing of programmatic changes, and trends in aggregate data on social protection for the Southern European welfare states as well as for universal and corporatist conservative systems, do not lend much support to the neo-liberalism thesis.

To provide a more precise assessment of hypotheses from both the neo-liberalism and contemporary embedded liberalism perspectives, I now present the results of the quantitative analysis outlined in the methodology section above. Findings from the initial estimation of models of European social welfare effort are presented in Table 6.2. I present in sequence tests of the direct welfare state effects of international financial liberalism and capital flows, European and global trade openness, and European monetary integration. With respect to capital mobility, flows of FDI and borrowing on international capital markets are unrelated to social welfare provision. However, consistent with the theory of embedded liberalism, international financial liberalization is actually positively associated with social welfare effort. Given that the mean increase in liberalization between the late 1970s and mid-1990s was roughly 4.00 (on the scale used here), results presented in Table 6.2 indicate that net of other determinants of welfare effort, liberalization was systematically associated with a rise in welfare spending equivalent to approximately 0.72 per cent of GDP.

With regard to trade openness, the second column of Table 6.2 presents the welfare effects of European trade integration, trade flows between Europe and non-European developed economies, and trade flows between Europe and developing economies. In contrast to the findings for international capital mobility, these results suggest that trade integration may have contributed to modest retrenchments in European welfare states. As the table results indicate, while European and developed nation trade integration are not significantly related to declines in welfare effort, the magnitude of trade-flows between Europe and developing economies is. However, the magnitude of this effect is modest: an increase in this category of trade of roughly five per cent of GDP

Table 6.2   The impacts of capital mobility, trade and monetary integration on European welfare states, 1979–95

	Capital mobility	EU and global trade	Monetary integration	Maastricht convergence
European and global economic integration factors				
Financial liberalization	0.1815*	0.1751*	0.1835*	0.2055*
	(0.1079)	(0.1012)	(0.0921)	(0.0967)
Foreign direct investment	0.0369	–	–	–
	(0.0764)			
International capital markcts	0.0976	–	–	–
	(0.1523)			
European trade	–	–0.0150	–	–
		(0.0296)		
Trade with other developed nations	–	–0.0311	–	–
		(0.0354)		
Trade with developing nations	–	–0.2366*	–	–
		(0.0951)		
Exchange rate mechanism	–	–	0.3930	0.1903
			(0.3680)	(0.3852)
Post-Maastricht Treaty	–	–	–0.3682	–
			(0.4048)	
Maastricht* public sector debt	–	–	–	–0.0265*
				(0.0095)
Interaction component-post Maastricht	–	–	–	1.5805*
				(0.7748)
Interaction component-public sector debt	–	–	–	–0.0143
				(0.0108)
General Model				
Old_{t-1}	0.4874*	0.3819	0.5348*	0.6166*
	(0.2700)	(0.2617)	(0.2824)	(0.2725)
$\text{Unemployment}_{t-1}$	0.2763*	0.3390*	0.2835*	0.3290*
	(0.0621)	(0.0610)	(0.0647)	(0.0606)
Inflate_{t-1}	0.0438	0.0759*	0.0410	0.0376
	(0.0345)	(0.0338)	(0.0340)	(0.0328)
Growth_{t-1}	–0.1084*	–0.1048*	–0.1128*	–0.1243*
	(0.0271)	(0.0293)	(0.0273)	(0.0283)
Affluence_{t-1}	0.5912*	0.7194*	0.6648*	0.7196*
	(0.1662)	(0.1585)	(0.1769)	(0.1697)

Table 6.2   continiued

	Capital mobility	EU and global trade	Monetary integration	Maastricht convergence
Left government $_{t-1}$	−0.0010	0.0002	−0.0007	−0.0007
	(0.0025)	(0.0026)	(0.0025)	(0.0025)
Christian democratic	0.0020	−0.0020	0.0011	−0.0021
government $_{t-1}$	(0.0171)	(0.0072)	(0.0070)	(0.0071)
intercept	1.2877	2.3964	0.1559	−1.6611
standard error of the estimate	1.2007	1.2005	1.2113	1.2212
mean of the dependent variable	23.1280	23.1280	23.1280	23.1280
Buse R^2	0.8224	0.8565	0.8307	0.8616

Notes:
Each model is estimated with 1979–95 data by Ordinary Least Squares; equations are first-order autoregressive. The table reports OLS unstandardized regression coefficients and panel correct standard errors. For discussion of this econometric technique, see Beck and Katz (1995). All models include nation-specific dichotomous variables to account for unmodelled country effects.
* significant at the 0.05 level.

(the highest increase recorded for the focal countries and time-frame) is associated with a decline in social welfare expenditures equivalent to just over one per cent of GDP. Despite contemporary arguments about the significant consequences of developed–developing nation trade, most European nations experienced stability or small increases (that is, 1 per cent to 2 per cent of GDP) in the volume of trade with developed political economies (merchandise or total trade).

With regard to European monetary integration, the third and fourth columns of Table 6.2 present core tests of the welfare state effects of the ERM and convergence criteria for EMU membership. As the findings presented in column 3 indicate, neither formal nor informal membership in the ERM or the advent of the convergence criteria are significantly associated with social welfare effort net of the effects of other determinants of social protection. However, as noted above, the principal impact of the convergence criteria has in all likelihood been felt in European welfare states with relatively high public sector debt (and deficits). This hypothesis is substantiated in the findings presented in the fourth column of Table 6.4: there is a significant interaction between the post-1992 Maastricht years (in EU members) and government debt. Recalling the procedures from computation of conditional effects discussed above, an increase in public debt equivalent to 10 per cent of GDP is – net of other forces – systematically associated with a reduction in welfare effort equivalent to approximately 0.30 per cent of GDP (that is, $-0.0143 + [-0.0265^*10]$). Given that public sector debt often increased from under 50 per cent to close to 100 per cent of GDP between the early 1980s and mid-1990s, the substantive magnitude of this 'Maastricht effect' is not trivial.

Tests of the hypotheses concerning the interaction of international financial integration and European trade and monetary integration are presented in Table 6.3. In addition, to further assess the accuracy and robustness of results of analysis based on a single aggregate measure of social protection, Table 6.3 also presents findings from analysis of data on the social wage, or the proportion of gross income replaced by unemployment insurance and related social supports for the average production worker during the first year of unemployment. As Table 6.3 suggests, there has been a significant interaction between international financial liberalization and European trade and monetary integration. In the case of all four interactions (that is, between liberalization on the one hand, and trade and monetary integration on the other, for both aggregate social welfare effort and the social wage), model estimation produces significant and negative results. That is, in European nations that had achieved high international liberalization and experienced high levels of trade with other European nations, social welfare expenditure generally, and the social wage specifically, were reduced. Similarly, nations with high levels of liberalization and full membership in the narrow bands of the ERM were also likely to experience reductions in aggregate welfare effort and the social wage.

To place these findings in concrete terms, I derived the social wage effects of rises in international financial liberalization at specific levels of European trade and monetary integration. These results are presented in Table 6.4. As indicated, at low and medium levels of trade integration (that is, European trade at 30 per cent and 60 per cent of GDP in the mid-1990s) and at low and medium levels of monetary integration (that is, no participation in the ERM or participation in the wide bands), international financial liberalization is not associated with reductions of the social wage. However, for countries that have achieved a high level of European trade integration (90 per cent of GDP) or full participation in the narrow bands of the ERM, a typical rise of 4 on the scale of liberalization of controls of international financial flows (that is, from moderate to full liberalization) is associated with a reduction in the social wage of about 0.04 ($4^*-0.0109$), or 4 per cent of gross income. Reflecting on the experiences of several European welfare states in the early 1990s, this quantitative estimate is quite consistent with the empirical record of modest retrenchment of unemployment and social assistance (see the country overviews above).

Table 6.3   The interactive impact of global financial liberalization and European trade and monetary integration on European welfare states, 1979–95

	Social welfare effort	Social welfare effort	Social wage	Social wage
Global and European economic integration interactions				
Global financial liberalization[*]	–0.0064[*]	–	–0.0002[*]	–
EU trade integration	(0.0022)		(0.0001)	
Interaction component–	0.4499[*]	–	0.0071	–
financial liberalization	(0.1324)		(0.0049)	
Interaction component–	0.0194	–	0.0037[*]	–
EU trade integration	(0.0356)		(0.0012)	
Global financial liberalization[*]	–	–0.4337[*]	–	–0.0111[*]
monetary integration (ERM)		(0.1211)		(0.0052)
Interaction component–	–	0.3549[*]	–	0.0002
financial liberalization		(0.1119)		(0.0007)
Interaction component–	–	5.7402[*]	–	0.1227[*]
monetary integration (ERM)		(1.7402)		(0.0651)

Notes:
Interactions are added to the general model of social welfare effort of Table 6.2 and an identical model for the social wage. Welfare effects of general model factors conform to those reported in Table 6.2 and are not reported here to avoid a proliferation of reported results (tables with full model results are available from the author). As with Table 6.2, the models are estimated with 1979–95 data by Ordinary Least Squares; equations are first-order autoregressive. The table reports OLS unstandardized regression coefficients for the interaction terms and their panel correct standard errors. For discussion of this econometric technique, see Beck and Katz (1995). All models include nation-specific dichotomous variables to account for unmodelled country effects.
[*] significant at the 0.05 level.

Table 6.4   The welfare impact of global financial liberalization at different levels of European trade and monetary integration, 1979–95

Level of European integration	Low	Medium	High
Social wage effects of financial liberalization across levels of European trade integration	0.0011	–0.0049	–0.0109[*]
Social wage effects of financial liberalization across levels of European monetary integration	0.0002	–0.0054	–0.0109[*]

Notes:
Effects of financial liberalization are estimated based on the interactions of Table 6.3 and the models discussed in Table 6.3's note.
[*] significant at the 0.05 level.

CONCLUSIONS

During the years from the late 1970s, all European welfare states have experienced some retrenchment of the system of social protection. Incumbent governments of the left, centre and right have, to varying degrees, rolled back social insurance benefit levels, restricted programme eligibility, and implemented cost controls and market-oriented restructuring in health and social services. The role of global and European economic integration in this process of welfare state reform is controversial. A substantial body of theory and research suggests that internationalization of markets and institutional developments within the European Union, such as the European Monetary System, have significantly pressured policy-makers to adopt relatively extensive neoliberal reforms of the welfare state. On the other hand, a distinct body of literature argues that the post-war system of embedded liberalism, or the combination of (trade) liberalization and significant government intervention and social welfare provision, has effectively been sustained in the contemporary era. In this view, contemporary globalization and Europeanization have not substantially eroded the joint efficiency and equity gains of what Polyani (1944) described as the 'great transformation'.

The analyses presented above have attempted to assess the comparative merits of the 'neo-liberalism thesis' and the theory of contemporary embedded liberalism. Several findings stand out. First, the direct effects of rises in global and European trade and capital mobility on social welfare states appear to be limited. While increases in trade between Europe and developing political economies have been associated with small declines in social welfare effort, most dimensions of internationalization and regionalization of trade and capital markets have not been systematically related to European social welfare policy change. In fact, there is some evidence that general financial liberalization has been accompanied by modest expansions of social compensation. On the other hand, analyses have suggested that European monetary integration has been relatively important for the trajectories of welfare states. First, in European polities with high levels of public sector debt, the advent of the Maastricht convergence criteria for membership in the EMU has created systematic, albeit moderate, pressures for welfare retrenchment. Statistical analysis as well as case-studies of individual countries support this conclusion. Moreover, European political economies that have experienced both high levels of international financial liberalization and full participation in the European Monetary System have faced pressures for welfare retrenchment. As theory suggests, exchange rate stability and international financial integration may well have come at a cost: a number of European welfare states have arguably lost some national macroeconomic capacity to address the problem of high unemployment and, in turn, faced increasing unemployment-related pressures to reduce welfare state costs. In the future, the fate of European systems of social protection may well hinge, at least in part, on the ability of EMU institutions and national policy-makers to generate economic growth and employment.

Finally, other developments at the EU-level have potentially significant impacts on national systems of social protection. On the one hand political, institutional and legal barriers exist to limit direct EU encroachment on national social policies. Moreover, a variety of EU policies (for example, common standards, social minimums) support generous systems of national welfare provision (Leibfried and Pierson, 1995). On the other hand, some actions by EU institutions potentially constrain national policy makers. For instance, European Court of Justice decisions typically enforce market compatibility requirements and hence, limit national policy-making autonomy and favour market-oriented reforms. The widely discussed development of EU-wide markets for private social insurance and services – itself a correlate of regional economic integration and reinforced by EU policy – has a number of negative implications for national welfare states. Perhaps most critically, greater reliance on supranational private insurance and services by increasingly mobile, upscale citizens may further fragment and weaken national pro-welfare state coalitions. While the anayses presented here underscore the resiliency of the national welfare states, these EU-wide developments in combination with continued demographic and fiscal pressures present significant challenges for the maintenance of generous public systems of social provision by European politics in the twenty-first century.

DATA SOURCES

International and Regional Market Integration Data

Total exports and imports of goods and services: OECD, *National Accounts*, Paris: OECD.

Exports and imports between European economies and between European nations and non-European developed and developing countries, *Direction of Trade*, Washington, DC: International Monetary Fund.

Participation in the European Monetary System (Exchange Rate Mechanism margins): Apel (1998).

Foreign direct investment, portfolio investment, and bank lending: IMF, *Balance of Payments Statistics*, Washington, DC: IMF; OECD, *Foreign Direct Investment in OECD Countries*, Paris: OECD.

Borrowing on International Capital Markets: OECD (1996), *International Capital Market Statistics: 1950–1995*, Paris: OECD.

Social Policy Indicators

Total social welfare outlays and expenditures for social services and public health: pre-1980 data are from OECD (1994), *New Orientations in Social Policy*, Paris: OECD. 1980s and 1990s data are from OECD (1996), *Social Expenditure Statistics of OECD Member Countries*, Labour Market and Social Policy Occasional Papers, No. 17. Paris: OECD; OECD (1999), *Social Expenditure Database, 1980–1996*. Paris: OECD.

Social wage: OECD Database on Unemployment Benefit Entitlements and Replacement Rates, Paris: OECD, forthcoming.

Political Data

Cabinet portfolios: Eric Browne and John Dreijmanis (1982), *Government Coalitions in Western Democracies*, Longman; *Keesings Contemporary Archives*.

For party classification: (1) Francis Castles and Peter Mair (1984), 'Left–Right Political Scales: Some "Expert" Judgments,' *European Journal of Political Research*, 12, 73–88; (2) Country-specific sources.

Socioeconomic Data

Per cent unemployed, population 65 and older: OECD, *Labor Force Statistics*, Paris: OECD.

Gross Domestic Product, consumer price index: OECD, *National Accounts*, Paris: OECD, various years.

Real per capita GDP in constant (1985) international prices: The Penn World Table (Mark 5.6), National Bureau of Economic Research (http://www.nber.org).

NOTES

1. Sources for all data are provided in the Appendix. Unless otherwise noted, data cited in this section pertain to (annual or period) averages for the 16 focal nations of this study: Austria, Belgium, Denmark, Finland, France, Germany, Greece, Ireland, Italy, the Netherlands, Norway, Portugal, Spain, Sweden, Switzerland and the United Kingdom. (See below on issues surrounding country selection.) On the causes of internationalization of markets see reviews and analyses of Cohen (1996) and Garrett (2000). For literature reviews and analysis of the sources of European integration (for example, adoption of the Single Europe Act and Maastricht Treaty), see, among others, contributions to Sbragia (1992) and the work of McNamara (1998).
2. On general internationalization and domestic policy autonomy, see, among others, Bates and Lien (1985), Cerny (1996), Gill and Law (1988), Greider (1997), McKenzie and Lee (1991), Mshra (1999) and Strange (1996). On the welfare state impacts of European regional economic

integration, see, among others, the analysis of Aspinwall (1996) and the synoptic reviews of theory and research as well as new analyses in contributions to Alber and Standing (2000).

3. The use of one aggregate measure of social welfare effort allows a concise analysis of welfare effects of several features of international and European integration. In addition, although expenditure-based measures of social protection have been criticized (for example, Esping-Andersen, 1990), they provide – with proper need, income and business cycle controls – useful (albeit imprecise) summary indicators of benefit generosity and eligibility standards over extended periods of time and sets of countries. With exceptions (for example, the social wage data used here), similarly extensive programmatic measures of benefit levels, eligibility criteria and other aspects of social policy are simply not yet available.

4. Comprehensive time-series data for the whole of Europe on intra-European capital flows is not available. However, as noted above, the bulk of cross-border capital movements for a typical European nation occur between it and North American, Australasian and (especially) other European economics; as such, the measures employed here capture a substantial amount of the temporal and cross-national variations in European capital mobility.

5. Following Esping-Andersen's seminal work (1990, 1996) and more recent elaborations (for example, Huber and Stephens, forthcoming; Swank, forthcoming, a), social democratic welfare states are characterized by generous, universal and relatively equal social insurance benefits as well as extensive, universally available and publicly provided social services. Corporatist conservative welfare states are characterized by relatively generous and comprehensive yet occupationally fragmented social insurance benefits and low levels of publicly provided social services. Liberal welfare states offer a mix of modest to low social insurance and flat-rate universal benefits, low levels of government social services, and high levels of means-testing and private insurance. The Southern European model reflects core elements of the corporatist conservative type, including occupationally stratified benefits and low levels of social services; it is distinguished from developed corporatist conservative systems by less generous and comprehensive insurance benefits and a prevalence of clientilism in the social welfare system (for example, Rhodes 1997b).

6. I draw on my extensive analysis of internationalization and social democratic welfare states in Swank (forthcoming, a, Chapter 4) and works by John Stephens and Evelyne Huber (Stephens 1996; Huber and Stephens 1998; forthcoming). For corporatist conservative and liberal welfare states, I draw on my analysis in Swank (forthcoming, a, Chapters 5 and 6, respectively). For the Southern European welfare states, I rely on Guillén and Matsaganis (2000) and contributions to Rhodes (1997b).

REFERENCES

Alber, Jens and Guy Standing (eds) (2000), 'Special issue: Europe in a comparative global context', *Journal of European Social Policy*, 10(2), 99–203.

Apcl, Immanuel (1998), *European Monetary Integration 1958–2002*, New York: Routledge.

Aspinwall, Mark (1996), 'The unholy social trinity: modelling social dumping under conditions of capital mobility and free trade', *West European Politics*, 19(1), 125–50.

Bates, Robert and Da-Hsiang Donald Lien (1985), 'A note on taxation, development and representative government', *Politics and Society*, 14, 53–70.

Beck, Nathaniel and Jonathan Katz (1995), 'What to do (and not to do) with time-series – cross-section data in comparative politics', *American Political Science Review*, 89(3), 634–47.

Beck, Nathaniel and Jonathan Katz (1996), 'Nuisance versus substance: specifying and estimating time-series–cross-section models', *Political Analysis*, 6, 1–36.

Berger, Suzanne and Ronald Dore (1996), *National Diversity and Global Capitalism*, Ithaca, NY: Cornell University Press.

Cameron, David (1978), 'The expansion of the public economy: a comparative analysis', *American Political Science Review*, 72, 1243–61.

Castles, Francis (1998), *Comparative Public Policy: Patterns of Post-war Transformation*, Brookfield, VT: Edward Elgar.

Cerny, Philip (1996), 'International finance and the erosion of state power', in Philip Gummett (ed.), *Globalization and Public Policy*, Brookfield, VT: Edward Elgar.

Esping-Andersen, Gøsta (1990), *Three Worlds of Welfare Capitalism*, London: Polity Press.

Esping-Andersen, Gøsta (ed.) (1996), *Welfare States in Transition: National Adaptations in Global Economies*, Thousand Oaks, CA: Sage.

Garrett, Geoffrey (1998a), *Partisan Politics in a Global Economy*, New York: Cambridge University Press.

Garrett, Geoffrey (1998b), 'Global markets and national policies: collision course or virtuous circle', *International Organization*, 52(4), 787–824.

Garrett, Geoffrey (1998c), 'The transition to Economic and Monetary Union', in Barry Eichengreen and Jeffry Freiden (eds), *Forging an Integrated Europe*, Ann Arbor: University of Michigan Press, pp. 21–48.

Garrett, Geoffrey (2000), 'The causes of globalization', *Comparative Political Studies*, 33(6/7), 941–91.

Garrett, Geoffrey and Deborah Mitchell (forthcoming), 'Globalization and the welfare state: income transfers in the advanced industrialized democracies, 1965–1990', *European Journal of Political Research*.

Gill, Stephen and David Law (1988), *The Global Political Economy*, Baltimore, MD: Johns Hopkins University Press.

Grieder, William (1997), *One World, Ready or Not*, New York: Simon and Schuster.

Guillén, Ana and Manos Matsaganis (2000), 'Testing the social dumping hypothesis in southern Europe: welfare policies in Greece and Spain during the last 20 years', *European Journal of Social Policy*, 10(2), 120–45.

Hemerijck, Anton, Martin Rhodes and Maurizio Ferrera (forthcoming), 'The future of the European social model in the global economy', *Journal of Comparative Policy Analysis*.

Hicks, Alexander (1999), *Social Democracy and Welfare Capitalism*, Ithaca, NY: Cornell University Press.

Hicks, Alexander and Duane Swank (1992), 'Politics, institutions, and social welfare spending in the industrialized democracies, 1960–1982', *American Political Science Review*, 86, September, 658–74.

Huber, Evelyne, Charles Ragin and John Stephens (1993), 'Social democracy, Christian democracy, constitutional structure and the welfare state', *American Journal of Sociology*, 99, 711–49.

Huber, Evelyne and John D. Stephens (1998), 'Internationalization and the social democratic welfare model: crises and future prospects', *Comparative Political Studies*, 33(3), June, 353–97.

Huber, Evelyne and John D. Stephens (forthcoming), *Partisan Choice in Global Markets: Development and Crisis of Advanced Welfare States*, Chicago, IL: University of Chicago Press.

Katzenstein, Peter (1985), *Small States in World Markets*, Ithaca, NY: Cornell University Press.

Keohane, Robert and Helen Milner (eds) (1996), *Internationalization and Domestic Politics*, New York: Cambridge University Press.

Leibfried, Stephan and Paul Pierson (1995), *European Social Policy: Between Fragmentation and Integration*, Washington, DC: Brookings.

Marks, Gary, Fritz Scharpf, Philippe Schmitter and Wolgang Streek (1996), *Governance in the European Union*, Thousand Oaks, CA: Sage.

McNamara, Kathleen (1998), *The Currency of Ideas: Monetary Politics in the European Union*, Ithaca, NY: Cornell University Press.

McKenzie, Richard and Dwight Lee (1991), *Quicksilver Capital: How the Rapid Movement of Wealth Has Changed the World*, New York: Free Press.

Mishra, Ramesh (1999), *Globalization and the Welfare State*, Northhampton, MA: Edward Elgar.

Moses, Jonathon (2000), 'Floating fortunes: Scandinavian full employment in the tumultuous 1970s and 1980s', in Robert Geyer, Christine Ingrebritsen and Jonathon Moses (eds), *Globalization, Europeanization, and the End of Scandinavian Social Democracy?*, pp. 62–82. New York and London: St Martin's and Macmillan.

Notermans, Ton (2000), *Money, Markets, and the State: Social Democratic Economic Policies Since 1918*, New York: Cambridge University Press.

Pampel, Fred and John Williamson (1989), *Age, Class, Politics, and the Welfare State*, New York: Cambridge University Press.

Pauly, Louis (1995), 'Capital mobility, state autonomy, and political legitimacy', *Journal of International Affairs*, 48(2), 369–88.

Pierson, Paul (1994), *Dismantling the Welfare State: Reagan, Thatcher and the Politics of Retrenchment in Britain and the United States*, New York: Cambridge University Press.

Pierson, Paul (1996), 'The new politics of welfare', *World Politics*, 48(2), 143–79.

Pierson, Paul (ed.) (2000), *The New Politics of the Welfare State*, New York: Oxford University Press.

Polanyi, Karl (1994), *The Great Transformation: The Political and Economic Origins of Our Time*, Boston, MA: Beacon Press.

Rhodes, Martin (1997a), 'The welfare state: internal challenges, external constraints', in Martin Rhodes, Paul Heywood and Vincent Wright (eds), *Developments in West European Politics*, London: Macmillan.

Rhodes, Martin (ed.) (1997b), *Southern European Welfare States: Between Crisis and Reform*, London: Frank Cass.

Rhodes, Martin (2000), 'The political economy of social pacts: "competitive corporatism" and European welfare reform', in Paul Pierson (ed.), *The New Politics of the Welfare State*, New York: Oxford University Press.

Rodrik, Dani (1997), *Has Globalization Gone too Far?* Washington, DC: Institute for International Economics.

Rodrik, Dani (1998), 'Why do more open economies have bigger governments?', *Journal of Political Economy*, 106(5), 997–1032.

Ruggie, John Gerard (1982), 'International regimes, transactions, and change: embedded liberalism in the postwar economic order', *International Organization*, 36(2), 379–415.

Ruggie, John Gerard (1994), 'Trade, protectionism, and the future of welfare capitalism', *Journal of International Affairs*, 48(1), 1–11.

Sbragia, Alberta (ed.) (1992), *Euro-politics: Institutions and Policy Making in the New European Community*, Washington, DC: Brookings.

Scharpf, Fritz (2000), 'The viability of advanced welfare states in the international economy: vulnerabilities and options', *Journal of European Public Policy*, 7(2), 190–228.

Stephens, John D. (1979), *The Transition from Capitalism to Socialism*, Atlantic Highlands, NJ: Humanities Press.

Stephens, John D. (1996), 'The Scandinavian welfare states: achievements, crises, and prospects', in Esping-Ansersen (ed.), *Welfare States in Transition: National Adaptations in Global Economies*, Thousand Oaks, CA: Sage.

Strange, Susan (1996), *The Retreat of the State. The Diffusion of Power in the World Economy*, New York: Cambridge University Press.

Swank, Duane (2000), 'Political institutions and welfare state restructuring', in Paul Pierson (ed.), *The New Politics of the Welfare State* (forthcoming), New York: Oxford University Press.

Swank, Duane (forthcoming, a), *Global Capital, Political Institutions, and Policy Change in Developed Welfare States*, New York: Cambridge University Press

Swank, Duane (forthcoming, b), 'Withering welfare? Globalization, political economic institutions, and the foundations of contemporary welfare states', in Linda Weiss (ed.), *States in the Global Economy: Bringing Domestic Institutions Back In*, Cambridge: Cambridge University Press.

Teague, Paul (1998), 'Monetary Union and social Europe', *Journal of European Social Policy*, 8(2), 117–37.

Van Kersbergen, Kees (2000), 'The declining resistance of national welfare states to change', in Stein Kuhnle (ed.), *The Survival of European Welfare States*, New York: Routledge.

7. The EU in world finance

Brian Scott-Quinn

European capital markets, although still nationally segmented because of differences in corporate law, are becoming more integrated as securities houses, operating across all countries in Europe, forge a common approach to fundraising, securities trading and merger activity. This increasing commonality of approach has been aided by the European Commission's Directive on Investment Services and, more recently, by the introduction of the Single Currency at the beginning of the year 2000.

Europe has always had close ties to the United States through trade and through direct and indirect investment flows. To date, however, there has been little portfolio investment in Europe by US investors due in part to the seeming complexity of multiple European markets compared to the set of national markets in the US. In contrast, portfolio investment in the US by European investors has been increasing over the decade. This has been in large part due to the perceived superior investment opportunities in US corporations compared with European, based both on the macro view that a higher rate of economic growth was likely in the US and the micro view that greater opportunities were available in the US to invest in new technologies. Partly in consequence of investment outflows, the euro since its launch declined substantially through the year 2000 relative to the US dollar.

Since the start of 2001, the macro environment has been somewhat different. US stock markets in fact saw a decline in 2000 against expectations that stocks would continue to advance; the euro started to rise against the dollar at the end of 2000 and has advanced substantially, while expectations of the US growth rate have declined relative to those of European economies. Even in terms of underlying dynamism, European firms in conjunction with their advisory investment banks (principally US owned) have shown a clear dynamic, leading to substantial change in perception of the 'European economy'. There has been a rapid rise in merger and acquisition activity within Europe, much of it cross-border. Indeed, there were more takeovers in 1999 in Europe than in the United States (source: Computasoft Research). What is also likely is that over the next decade continental industry will be restructured and reformed not, as in the past, by politicians and commercial banks but by the investment bankers and the industrialists breaking away from 'consensus management'. This should lead to greater growth rates in Europe relative both to the past and to the US. Examples of such a change can be found already in the French company Vivendi, the German company Bertelsmann and the British company Vodaphone amongst others.

THE CHANGE IN EUROPEAN FINANCE OVER THE 1990s

The European capital markets enter the twenty-first century looking very different indeed to the markets that existed at the beginning of the 1990s just ten years before. While there is not yet a single market in financial services in Europe, changes over this period have resulted in continental European finance taking on a shape much closer to that in the Anglo-Saxon countries – the United Kingdom and the United States. That there is not yet a single market is evidenced by the 'Financial Services Priorities and Progress – Third Report' issued in November 2000 by the Commission of the European Communities. This details progress towards the creation of a single financial market and priorities for helping to achieve such a single market over the next five years. That report is discussed towards the end of this chapter.

Indicative of the change that has taken place in Europe is the fact that at the start of the 1980s, over 80 per cent of external financing of continental European firms was provided by banks and there was no commercial paper market at all. Today, however, the raising of finance through the issuance of equity and corporate bonds has now overtaken bank loans as a source of corporate finance.

European corporate bond issuance growth has been very strong, much of it being driven by the telecoms sector. The growth in corporate bond issuance in 1999 was 58 per cent and comparable growth was expected for 2000. Equity trading volume growth has also been substantial, amounting to around 30 per cent per annum over the period 1995–2000. There has also been a substantial growth in new equity listings resulting both from privatization and from private companies coming to the market in order to allow faster expansion. The number of companies listed on the exchanges of the 15 EU member states has grown steadily from 6401 in 1995 to 8111 in 1999.[1] Increased equity financing does not, however, appear to have yet substantially changed the dominant position of concentrated holdings.

In investment markets, there has been a rapid rise in transactions volumes in equities undertaken by retail investors with, for example, the number of shareholders in Germany directly owning shares rising by 25 per cent in 1999. In the wholesale markets, investment funds have started to increase the proportion of equities held in portfolios. In 1994, only around 20 per cent of portfolio investments were equities (the balance being principally bonds) while today the figure is around 40 per cent though this is still well below the 60 per cent figure in the United States.

THE CREATION OF A SINGLE MARKET

Progress towards a single market in financial services has come about as a result of number of factors:

* changes in regulation within the European Community;
* changes in technology;
* changes in the ownership structure of the securities industry;
* changes resulting from the move towards a single currency in some EU states.

Regulation

We begin with regulation as this has probably been the most pervasive influence. If we look back to 1986, the year of 'Big Bang' in the United Kingdom, this was the year when fixed commissions in the UK equity market were abolished. At the same time, the principle under which there had been a separation of dealing houses from broking houses was abandoned allowing for the first time the creation of 'broker-dealers' in the United Kingdom parallel-ing the typical structure in the United States. In continental Europe, on the other hand, there had never been a divide between broking and dealing. More impor-tantly, in continental Europe, unlike the UK and the United States, capital market activity had always been a function of commercial banks – universal banks active in both commercial banking and securities. This was in sharp contrast to the UK and US where in the former case there had always been a *de facto* split in these activities and the US where there was a *de jure* split.

The fact that the financial intermediaries in continental Europe (the commercial banks) also controlled the securities markets has meant in practice that they had little incentive to extend disintermediation by developing the financial markets. This has resulted in continental European markets being relatively unimportant in corporate financing compared with, in particular, those in the US. In the US, investment banks have operated until recently as quite a separate category of financial firm from commercial banks and thus competition between market-based and intermediated financing has been strong since the Glass Steagall Act of the 1930s. Today, of course, US investment banks and commercial banks are once again reuniting – a good example being the takeover of J.P. Morgan by Chase Manhattan Bank. A long-run equilib-rium may see the financial structures in the US and Europe looking much more similar, particularly as the dominant players in both markets are the same firms (see below).

Differences in regulation and custom have led to differences between UK and continental European markets and also differences between markets within continental Europe itself. These differences have resulted in a drive within the institutions of the European Community to minimize such differences in order to create a 'single European capital market'. This was part of a drive to create a Single Market in goods and services within Europe. The process started with the publication in 1985 of a white paper 'Completing the Internal Market'. This identified 300 pieces of legislation that would have to be adopted by the EU and implemented in national law in each member state in order to remove restrictions that were seen to be preventing the development of a Single Market. In respect of financial services the objectives were:

- the complete liberalization of capital movements;
- the unification of national markets for financial services;
- the establishment of a common regulatory structure for financial institutions.

The timetable for their introduction required the whole programme to be in place by the end of 1992. One approach would have been to try to achieve complete harmonization of the regulatory framework across the EU. However, such an approach would have taken a very long time to implement, would probably have been inflexible and would almost certainly have stifled innovation. The approach taken by the Community has been to accept that each country has, and will continue to have, its own securities market regulation. Thus it was accepted that there would continue to be 'competition amongst rules' in the EU regulatory framework. However, in order to prevent these differences in rules creating barriers between member States, the Commission developed a principle known as 'mutual recognition' under which all member states agree to recognize the validity of each other's laws, regulations and standards and thereby facilitate free trade in goods and services without the need for prior harmonization. Once mutual recognition has been agreed as the governing principle for EU regulation there follows a need for a rule to determine which country's regulatory framework applies in particular cases. The most logical rule is 'home country control'. Under this approach, home country rules are accepted as those to be employed in the control of the activities of host state branches and in cross-border provision of services. However, in a slight weakening of this approach, it was also agreed that 'conduct of business' rules will be those of the host state.

The first major piece of EU legislation to apply the principle of mutual recognition was the Second Banking Coordination directive (2BCD) which was adopted in December 1989 and implemented on 1 January 1993. This directive has provisions to create what is commonly known as a 'single passport' under which credit institutions incorporated in an EU member state would be allowed to offer, in any member state, a range of services listed in an annex as activities subject to mutual recognition. Although the directive applies to credit institutions, the 'passported' services include securities trading, underwriting securities issues and portfolio management advice. It was not until 1992 that the Investment Services Directive (ISD), the equivalent directive in respect of 'investment firms', as distinct from credit institutions, was implemented (and indeed delayed implementation until 1995 was allowed for some member states).

The ISD, as well as implementing the 'single passport' for investment firms also introduced the concept of a 'regulated market'. This is one governed by the rules approved by a competent authority in its home state and which complies with the rules in the ISD on reporting, transparency and concentration. This has been a highly contentious area and one that we deal with below.

This new regulatory framework has formed the basis of much of the repositioning of firms within the European securities market over the 1990s. Somewhat to the surprise of those who conceived of the ideas of a unified European capital market, it has not been the European-based securities houses which have taken most, and most immediate, advantage of the single passport. It has been the US securities houses. These houses have been used to operating within a continent (the United States) with a single legal framework applying across all states. They have also not had the same domestic mentality of securities houses and banks based in a European state. They thus took advantage of opportunities well before the rather sluggish indigenous firms.

In November 2000, the European Commission issued a paper, 'Financial Services Priorities and Progress – Third Report' which noted that 'there was yet to be the quantum leap needed to achieve the 2005 deadline set by heads of state and government at the Lisbon European Council'. This refers to the fact that some of the requirements of the Investment Services Directive have not yet been implemented in some countries of the EU. In addition, some new or modified directives are required in order to establish a truly common legal framework for integrated securities and derivatives markets, to move towards a single set of financial statements for listed companies, to allow the raising of capital on an EU-wide basis, to contain systemic risk in securities settlement and to move towards a secure and transparent environment for cross-border restructuring. This paper is discussed in more detail at the end of this chapter.

Changes in Technology

Changes in technology have affected both securities houses and the markets on which they transact. Technology has been of three types. First has been the development of electronic market mechanisms that have allowed market floors to be replaced by electronics. This has also allowed some telephone (OTC) markets to move towards the substitution of screens for telephones. Second has been the development of electronic networks to link participants in these new electronic markets using private networks. Third, of course, has been the development of Internet protocol (IP) technology which, both in terms of the public internet and high-speed networks using browser technology, have allowed developments that have completely changed the face of markets in the 1990s.

The technology available in Europe is no different from that in the United States. Two points are relevant, however. Firstly, markets in Europe made the transition to electronic mechanisms within domestic marketplaces much more quickly than those in the United States – whether NASDAQ, NYSE or the Chicago derivatives exchanges which in the latter two cases are floor-based markets. Secondly, the integration of markets in Europe even prior to the euro has been hastened by the availability of networks which allow distant members of exchanges. Thirdly, the EU rules in the ISD on 'remote membership' have facilitated the Europeanization of the union markets in Europe. Fourth, the multiplicity (around 35) of equity and derivative exchanges in Europe prior to EMU as well as a large number of securities settlement systems (SSS) and central counter-parties is rapidly reducing, aided greatly by developments in technology that allow greatly increased volumes of securities transactions to be processed.

It is a combination of the ISD, the euro and new technology which is allowing the markets of Europe to move towards a configuration much closer to that in the United States and to link much more closely to US markets as part of an effort to create a global securities market. These aspects are dealt with in more detail in the section on securities markets.

Changing Ownership Structure of the European Securities Industry

The dominance of American firms in European finance is a key feature of the changes in the 1990s. Some of this dominance has arisen from changes in the corporate structure and governance structure in European industry which has resulted in indigenous banks being put at a disadvantage.

An important factor has been the change in ownership of continental European industry. Traditionally, cross-shareholdings amongst companies have been common, and in particular banks holdings of equity in companies to which they provide finance. As these holdings have been unwound (as banks have come under pressure to utilize their capital more effectively) and as ownership of relatively high proportions of European companies has shifted from domestic shareholders to global shareholders (often US- or UK-based investment managers), the requirement to reach US rates of return on investment have increased greatly. These new shareholders are simply interested in improving returns, and to achieve this requires attention to minimizing the cost of funding as well as achieving operational efficiency. Minimizing the cost of funding may require that a company move to securities market financing. Maximizing operational efficiencies may require cross-border mergers. In neither case may the traditional house bank be the appropriate supplier of these services. As a result, companies in continental Europe have increasingly been turning to non-domestic investment banks to help achieve lower operational and financial costs in the new corporate governance environment.

Traditionally the UK had a strong contingent of domestic investment banks (known in the UK as merchant banks) which provided corporate finance and merger and acquisition services to UK companies. In addition, the clearing banks (the main commercial banks) almost all had investment banking subsidiaries. Today, however, almost all the merchant banks have been absorbed into other, mainly US, groups while the clearing bank subsidiaries have mostly been closed down or now operate in a restricted part of the market. There are no UK-owned investment banks which are global.

In continental Europe the weakness of most of the commercial banks in the field of securities financing and cross-border mergers and acquisitions has resulted in two developments:

- European commercial banks have made acquisitions of UK or US investment banks in order to strengthen their European and global position;
- US investment banks have set up offices in the major European centres (in addition to their London bases) to take advantage of the gap in provision of services by EU-based banks and have been successful in selling their services to continental European corporates and governments.

Today the investment banking world in Europe is dominated by global players with head offices in New York with a smaller number of nascent global players which are European-based. In the UK the list is virtually restricted to HSBC and Barclays Capital as contenders. Among the strong continental European contenders are ABN Amro (Holland), Deutsche Bank (Germany), Dresdner Kleinwort Benson (Germany), Union Bank of Switzerland (Switzerland), Credit Suisse First Boston (Switzerland and the US) and BNP Paribas (France). Until late in 2000, ING Baring might have been included but it has now been effectively destroyed as a potential global force as a result of a management decision to scale back activities. This was done in the belief that only the top players were likely to achieve adequate returns on capital from their investment banking activities and that becoming a top player would require an excessive commitment of capital.

The main driving force for this consolidation of banks and investment banks and of the move from commercial to investment banking has been the intensification of market forces in the EU, in part consequent on the Single Market legislation. Also, while traditionally EU governments have tried to reserve the bond markets for their own financing, the limitations on debt financing by EU governments have provided greater capacity for corporate financing through debt markets. This has coincided with a massive increase in demand for finance from 'telcos' (telecommunications providers) which could, at least initially, be met less expensively from the debt markets than from bank finance. Curiously, the fact that much of this need for financing was created by the auction of third-generation (3G) mobile licences, the proceeds of which were then paid to governments, means that in fact much of the proceeds of the first of these huge corporate financings substituted for government borrowing.

Impact of the Single Currency

The Single Currency which came into effect on 1 January 2000 has had a number of effects on the European capital market. In terms of banks operating in wholesale markets, it has removed the domestic advantage of national banks in respect of financing in their own currency zone. Thus, for example, German banks had an advantage in financing German firms since they had no currency risk in lending in Deutschemark (DM), they could claim to be experts in DM financing and they knew the customers in Germany better than foreign banks. With a single currency, only the last advantage remains. Today, therefore, firms operating in goods and services markets which themselves are increasingly competitive because of the Single Currency, are now likely to choose their financing bank or investment bank on the basis of cost of funding rather than relationship. This has disadvantaged those banks which have not been able to adapt to the requirements of capital markets or to create the global links which are necessary to minimize cost of funding. In particular, global links mean access to the US investor market as a source of funds rather than being restricted to purely European investors.

A very good example of the impact of global pressures on universal banks in Europe is Deutsche Bank. It was reported in the *Financial Times* that Deutsche Bank, Germany's largest bank, was planning to shake up its organizational structure in a way that would put the investment bank business at the heart of the company. The changes in Deutsche Bank have been driven by the lack of profitability in traditional banking and the wish of Deutsche to be a major global investment bank. This process has been aided by its acquisition in 1998 of a US investment bank – Bankers Trust. These changes have been driven through by the chairman, Rolf Breuer. Interestingly, the announced changes have come just shortly after two Americans joined the bank's *Vorstand* (management board).

What is clear is that the single currency is achieving its creators' objective of increasing competition in goods and services markets across Europe in every field including financial services. On the other hand, the introduction of the euro has not achieved an objective which some of its creators had intended – making the European capital market a global alternative to that of the United States. In practice, there is one global financing market and virtually all large financings are undertaken by spreading the new issue paper over investors in all the major markets. The concept of an independent European market is not really appropriate.

The move to a Single Currency has changed the nature of bond markets in that it has allowed pricing to be clearly spread-based, that is, not simply quoted on a yield basis but as a spread over the equivalent government bond as in the United States. Credit spreads have become an important area in financial markets as a much wider range of credits is now available compared with in the early 1990s. Much of the paper now on offer is what was once (and often still is) described in the United States as 'junk bonds', that is, bonds with a credit rating below investment grade. Such a development is very positive for the European economy as until recently it lacked sources of funds (except from banks) for projects and companies that did not conform to traditional high credit norms.

The fall in the value of the single currency since its launch (around 30 per cent) has meant that international investors who are dollar-based have either suffered large losses or have simply avoided euro-denominated paper. We are unlikely to see a true integration of dollar and euro markets until the euro stabilizes and is a currency of little greater risk than the dollar. Thus we would take the view that all the efforts to create a European capital market as part of a global market are unlikely to come to fruition unless the macroeconomic and political issues within Europe are resolved in a satisfactory way. Resolution of these issues may remain difficult if, as some[2] claim, international portfolio investment offers European fund managers opportunities for tax avoidance as well as, until recently at least, higher returns.

THE EUROPEAN EQUITY MARKETS AND EXCHANGES

The European equity exchanges are trying to find a structure appropriate to the new competitive position in which each finds itself. There are two important factors:

- investors are increasingly requiring equity analysis across competitor firms in a particular industry within Europe rather than between different companies in different industries in a single European country. They also wish to transact within Europe at the same transaction cost or less than that for transacting within their 'domestic' market;

- having moved on from a domestic to a European perspective, investors are wishing to undertake share comparisons on a global industry basis rather than a purely European basis, and wish to be able to transact on a global basis as easily and cheaply as on a local country basis.

As a result, exchanges are not only looking at how to reduce costs and improve access within Europe, but are also trying to find a way of linking up with US and (potentially) Japanese and other Asian markets in a way which would create a 'global' exchange. Thus rather than talk about the creation of a European exchange as has been the tendency for the last decade, the debate since the turn of the Millennium has moved on from purely European concerns to how to create a global exchange.

To see how much the equity markets in Europe have changed it is necessary to go back to 1986 when London followed the New York example of 1975 and introduced competition into stockbroking as we noted earlier. It did this by abolishing fixed commissions on equity trades. This caused a dramatic restructuring of the industry which was known as 'Big Bang'. It allowed, for the first time, the merging of stockbroking and stockjobbing (that is, sales and trading) within single entities. One outcome was that US investment banks, who had had a long experience of being broker-dealers, were able to seize a large market share in both UK equity and bond markets.

At this time, continental European markets had not modernized and were still based in a world in which companies were often controlled by family groups with only a small free float of shares available to the public or controlled by the government or by banks. Proper investment research was very limited, liquidity was very limited and markets were generally undeveloped. This allowed the London market with its more sophisticated mechanisms to provide a service to the (relatively few) global investors who wanted to deal in some of the, relatively few, large European stocks. In the late 1980s and early 1990s, it looked as if some Continental exchanges might be wiped out by competition from London. However, the competition galvanized these exchanges which then leapfrogged London by moving to purely electronic markets (order-driven rather than quote-driven markets).

In the first half of the 1990s these exchanges took back most of their market as a result of their modernization. However, there remained in Europe some 35 exchanges (equity and derivative) – far more than was required. Pressure for merger has come from institutional user demands. Principally the demand has been for easier access to both markets and clearing and settlement facilities across Europe in order to obviate the need for a separate technology infrastructure in investment banks for each market in which they trade. Pressure for merger has also come from the ability of any exchange to offer transaction services (though not listing services) in securities not from its 'domestic' market and also from the advent of new electronic markets – electronic communication networks (ECNs) which have the capability (in theory at least) to supplant established exchanges.

The main baffle for supremacy, first in European markets and subsequently in global markets, took place in the year 2000. Some European exchanges have already formed groupings. In particular Euronext was created in early 2000. Euronext is a merger of the Amsterdam, Brussels and Paris exchanges. They now operate as a single company and intend to migrate to the same platform. The trading platform will be based on the French NSC system, there will be a central counter-party, netting and clearing for all three markets through Clearnet SA and the unified settlement and custody platform will be with Euroclear.

It is claimed the merger will give rise to savings of euro 50 million per year and the use of a single rulebook will simplify transactions. Whereas exchanges were traditionally member-owned with members buying 'seats', this exchange is a private company. However, Euronext intends to become a public company and list itself on Euronext.

Most interesting are its plans for 'globalization'. In June 2000, the exchange announced that the New York Stock Exchange, the Australian Stock Exchange and the exchanges of Tokyo, Toronto, Mexico and Sao Paulo had set about trying to create a worldwide market. It is the intention of these parties to interconnect their trading systems to make one market with a single order book. The total market capitalization of these exchanges would amount to 60 per cent of the value of all companies listed worldwide, with investors having access to the global market through their own national exchanges.

While these plans for a 'global 24-hour exchange' sound interesting, it is hard to know at this stage what they actually will mean in practice. In no sense will this be a single exchange. Each exchange will keep its own identity. It would seem to be simply that on a single screen there will be buttons for each exchange and pressing them will bring a trader to the electronic interface for that exchange. The trader would presumably still have to be registered with that exchange. Also, the New York Stock Exchange does not currently operate an electronic order book of the type that could be integrated into a 'single order book'. It is possible, however, that at some point the NYSE will move towards an electronic order book and away from its floor market and specialists just as European exchanges have.

The largest (in terms of market capitalization though not turnover) and most international exchange is the London Stock Exchange (LSE). It has been trying to forge alliances or to merge with European exchanges in order to try to become the dominant exchange in Europe with the subsequent intention of forging international (principally US) links. In early 2000 it announced, along with Deutsche Borse (the German stock exchange) that the two exchanges were joining together to create iX (as an international exchange). However, by the autumn, the proposed merger had been abandoned. In practice it was not clear what advantage there would have been to users of the exchange from the proposed merger. The problem was that in order to avoid one exchange taking over another, which could be seen as the demise of one exchange, the iX was designed on compromise principles. It was subsequently thought that the Deutsche Borse might bid outright for the LSE but that has not come to pass.

After managing to fight off a bid by OM, the Scandinavian exchange group, the LSE announced that it had decided on a strategy which involves it remaining independent but forming alliances with other exchanges. It looks most probable that the London exchange will enter some type of arrangement with the US NASDAQ market. NASDAQ has started the internationalization process by opening a market in Tokyo, but apart from that there has been little evidence of a globalization strategy. To date its ambitions have been held in check by its ownership structure and its lack of any 'currency', as a member-owned entity, with which to make acquisitions.

Our own view is that within a small number of years, there will be perhaps three major exchange groups all with pretensions to being global exchanges and incorporating exchange mechanisms from Europe, Japan and the United States. Over time even these groups may merge when a technology overhaul is required in order to keep down costs. In addition there will be a number of alternative exchange mechanisms competing for business. An example of this is Jiway – a retail exchange which opened for business in late 2000 providing retail transaction, clearing, settlement and safekeeping services in equities from all the major European markets. This venture is a European–US collaboration with the technology being provided by one partner – the OM exchange from Scandinavia – and Morgan Stanley, the other partner, providing expertise across a range of aspects as well as providing market-making services in UK equities.

What is clear about the way in which the European securities markets have developed is that the concept of a 'single European exchange', which was the 'buzz' expression through the 1980s and 1990s, is now little discussed while technology has moved on to allow links between exchanges, between clearing and settlement mechanisms and between European and US and Japanese exchanges.

SECURITIES CLEARING AND SETTLEMENT

It is estimated that at present securities clearing and settlement costs in Europe's domestic markets are around ten times those in the US. Once cross-border clearing and settlement has to be undertaken, costs again rise dramatically.

Europe has two types of clearing house. Firstly, each country has a domestic central securities depository (CSD). Secondly, there are two international central securities depositories (ICSD), Euroclear and Clearstream. These were created in the 1970s to service the needs of the newly created Eurobond international fixed income market. Euroclear was the first to be set up and was operated by Morgan Guaranty Trust Company (though owned by members). Clearstream (previously known as Cedel) was set up to provide a 'European' competitor to Euroclear. In the year 2000, there were two developments. First, Euroclear severed its connection with Morgan Guaranty in order to become more 'European' and is setting up as a bank. It also merged with the French CSD Sicovam, and the Dutch and Belgian CSDs. Clearstream also started the process of seeking economies by merging with the German domestic clearing house Deutsche Borse Clearing.

Much of the pressure for reducing clearing and settlement costs and merging existing institutions has come from the belief that if it is not achieved by European entities, the US entity – DTCC – will enter the European market offering much lower charges than domestic clearers. The DTCC which was created by merging the Depository Trust Corporation (DTC) and the National Securities Clearing Corporation (NSCC) has a monopoly in the clearing and settlement of equity transactions in the United States. Provided European organizations can merge quickly and in a manner which results in lower costs, the US challenge is unlikely to be successful.

The model which seems to be emerging in Europe as the preference of those operating in the securities market is the 'horizontal' as opposed to the 'vertical silo' model. These terms are simply industry terms for vertical or horizontal integration. The London Stock Exchange does not control clearing and settlement which is provided through Crest – a separate company. The German Stock Exchange (Deutsche Borse) on the other hand operates Deutsche Borse Clearing (part of Clearstream) and is thus vertically integrated.

As noted above, there is now a widespread belief that competition between exchange mechanisms, although it can result in the creation of a number of smaller pools of liquidity rather than a single pool, is valuable in providing a range of low-cost services to customers. To the extent that this fragments a market it is also possible, technologically, to link markets together using technology services such as those provided by Investor Technology Group (ITG) or Royal Blue's Fidessa system, so that investors can see bids and offers or orders on all mechanisms providing trading services on a single screen. But once a deal in any European market has been executed, investors and their intermediary brokers want to achieve settlement of all that investor's transactions, in whatever market, through a single settlement system. This could mean either that all executed orders could go to a single CSD which would settle all the transactions or that it would seamlessly pass on non-domestic transactions for settlement in the appropriate market mechanism. In order to ensure that costs of settlement systems are kept down, many investors would like to see competition between a small number of settlement systems rather than a monopoly utility provider.

In addition to issues of settlement, there has been extensive debate in Europe on the issue of a central counter-party (CCP) for all European equity transactions. Such an entity (for example London Clearing House) acts as the counter-party to both sides of a transaction and thus provides both anonymous trading and much lower counter-party risk in trading. Traditionally this is the approach that has been taken in derivative markets (use of margining) but not in equity or bond markets. In addition to anonymity benefits, there are substantial benefits in terms of a reduction in the amount of capital that has to be committed to covering counter-party risk. This can be further reduced if in addition the central counter-party nets off all transactions between any two counter-parties over all instruments, not just equities, in which they are trading. Thus there is considerable pressure to establish a single European central counter-party across all markets which would give intermediaries substantial savings on required capital as well as a reduction in counter-party risk.

THE MARKET FOR CORPORATE CONTROL

This market, known better in Europe simply as the merger and acquisition market, is increasingly adopting an Anglo-Saxon appearance as we enter the twenty-first century.

Traditionally there has been a vast divide between the approach to corporate governance taken in the United States (and also, but to a lesser extent, in the UK) and that taken in continental Europe and Japan. In continental Europe, governance has been through consensus, agreement, workers councils, relationships, influence of house banker, government intervention, opposition to US involvement and a dislike of market forces. In the US, in contrast, industrial structure has been determined by the actions of corporate raiders, providers of funds such as Drexel Burnham (up to 1989), shareholder activism and free market forces.

What has become clear in the late 1990s and beyond is the shift in perception of European observers from the point of view that the European way was better to the realization that US corporations, over the 20-year period of restructuring from 1980 onwards, have become dominant in so many sectors in terms of technology, productivity, market share and also return on capital. In contrast, European corporations have been falling behind in many areas of business, and also not creating employment on the scale on which it has been created in the United States.[3]

Merger and acquisition activity has involved a number of different types of transaction. These have included those between:

- companies both of which are resident in a single European country;
- companies resident in more than one European country;
- a US company acquiring a European company;
- a European company acquiring a US company.

While there have been many transactions within countries, this is much less of a new development than cross-border acquisitions. Domestic transactions have been undertaken by domestic advisors who have the knowledge of the local environment – firms, local authorities, large shareholders, government, banks and so on – through which mergers have traditionally been mediated. What has been new in the last decade has been the cross-border, and often hostile, trans-actions within Europe. Equally, what has differentiated these transactions from domestic ones has been that traditional commercial bank advisors have not been involved (or have been relegated to the sidelines) and the deals have been undertaken by the US investment banking powerhouses which have been building up a European cross-border capability over the 1990s.

Some reasons for the increase in transactions in Europe in the 1990s include:

- budgetary constraints which resulted in governments using privatization as a way of raising revenue and eliminating subsidies;
- the availability of Eastern European companies (suffering from very low productivity) which could be acquired by European acquisitors;
- the need for improved financial performance to meet the requirements of the new, non-domestic shareholders who were increasingly acquiring interests in European companies (particularly US institutional investors);
- the effects of globalization on the optimum size and geographic structure in many industries.

One of the most unexpected cross-border deals was the Vodaphone takeover of Mannesman. It was believed in Germany that such a takeover, as well as being offensive to the German public, was not possible given the protection against takeovers by foreigners offered by the German system. But in consequence of the industrial logic of the deal, the existence of many non-German shareholders in Mannesman and the pressure on institutional shareholders even in conti-nental Europe to maximize returns to their investors, Vodaphone was successful in its acquisition.

European companies have traditionally not undertaken complete takeovers but have developed 'strategic alliances' with partners either for offensive or for defensive purposes. This contrasts with the United States where full takeover has been the model, based on legal, tax and accounting advantages. Today, however, the increasingly competitive European scene has resulted in such alliances leading to frictions between the partners. The result has been an unwinding of such relationships or a bid by one party for the other.

Although merger and acquisition activity increased dramatically in Europe in the 1990s, it is still held back by a multiplicity of different rules in each European state. This problem is now being addressed by the European Commission in its Financial Services Action Plan (referred to above). It is also being addressed by the Lamfalussy committee of 'wise men' who have been asked to review Europe's securities markets with a view to making recommendations leading to the creation of a 'single securities market in Europe'.

Returning to the M&A field, however, what is quite clear is that it is the US-based investment banks which made most of the running in European M&A. The top four firms in 1999 were Morgan Stanley, Goldman Sachs, Merrill Lynch and J.P. Morgan. Numbers five and six were two Swiss firms where their US (international) investment banking arms were the drivers in their success – UBS Warburg Dillon Read and Credit Suisse First Boston.

THE EUROPEAN FINANCIAL SERVICES INDUSTRY

As in the United States, there are more banks than are needed to create a competitive banking environment or to achieve the maximum economies of scale and scope. Banks in continental Europe have traditionally been relatively inefficient and have operated in many cases like a branch of the civil service. This has resulted from the desire of the authorities in many European countries to put stability and solvency considerations before efficiency considerations. In effect, many financial institutions in Europe have been little more than public utilities run, in effect, by public servants. It was only the huge losses experienced by many continental banks in the 1980s combined with the evidence that US investment banks were starting to transact with 'their' customers, that led to a rethink by some of the major bank groups. This resulted in many mergers and acquisitions not only of small weak banks but also some substantial transactions by major groups. Notable amongst these were the acquisition of Union Bank of Switzerland (UBS) by Swiss Bank to create a new UBS. UBS had long been a stodgy, unimaginative bank with little expertise in securities markets and little international experience (or interest in international markets). Swiss Bank, by contrast, had acquired a highly successful Chicago derivatives firm, O'Connor Associates, which had, in management terms, effected a reverse takeover of the then somewhat stodgy Swiss Bank. When UBS demonstrated that it was not generating sufficient shareholder value, Swiss Bank was able to acquire it and reduce the number of major banks in Switzerland to two (the other being Credit Suisse, the owner of Credit Suisse First Boston).

In Germany, the three major commercial banks have all attempted to make some impression in investment banking. Commerzbank has been quite unsuccessful and may be relegated to a quite junior role in Europe. Dresdner Bank acquired the UK merchant bank Kleinwort Benson as its entry route into international investment banking. That transaction has been quite successful but has not yet allowed Dresdner to establish itself as a successful 'bulge bracket' house.

The most successful of the German banks in attempting to convert itself from a commercial bank to a global investment bank has been Deutsche Bank. It has gone from very tentative beginnings to having a clearly defined strategy for attempting to become a 'global powerhouse' in investment banking. Its original investment in securities was in Morgan Grenfell, a UK merchant bank, in the 1980s. Initially this was allowed to operate independently. But over time it was 'acquired', the name was dropped and it became simply a part of Deutsche.

The problem that all European universal banks have faced is that without a strong US presence, it is difficult even to be to be a major European player. The reason is that US markets comprise such a large proportion of total investment funds that without direct access to this market, a European investment bank is unlikely to be able to offer equity or debt funds to a European client as cheaply as a US house.

To overcome this problem Deutsche Bank, in 1999, acquired Bankers Trust, a US commercial bank that had transmogrified into an investment bank with particular strength in complex derivatives transactions. It is too early to say whether or not this was a financially successful transaction (the cost was approximately \$12 billion). What is clear, however, is that for any European bank to prosper in the world's largest financial market is difficult. The most successful firms are not for sale. Many of the second-tier firms have already been acquired. What remains is not necessarily the best entry into this market.

Deutsche Bank has also made changes in its commercial bank operations. It has long been held back from making an internationally acceptable return on capital in this operation by the existence of the Länder banks in Germany. These are state-supported banks which are able to borrow on the strength of a state guarantee and are therefore able to finance their books more cheaply and take risks that would not be acceptable to private sector banks. While the European Commission is trying to eliminate such public sector subsidy, Deutsche Bank is now trying to rebuild its retail bank operations around Bank 24 – a clicks and mortar 24-hour retail bank which it set up.

THE EUROPEAN COMMISSION'S PRIORITIES FOR THE FIVE-YEAR PERIOD TO 2005 IN RESPECT OF FINANCIAL SERVICES

The Lisbon meeting of the European Council in 2000, referred to earlier, recognized the central role of efficient financial markets for long-term European competitiveness and for the development of the 'New Economy' – the strategic aim over the next decade being for the Union to become:

> the most competitive and dynamic knowledge based economy in the world capable of sustainable economic growth with more and better jobs and greater social cohesion ...

One has to take this mostly as rhetoric since many other actions, or lack of action, on the part of the Commission and national governments militates against such an outcome. Such an outcome would also require Europe to move ahead of the United States in its economic dynamism, in particular in the New Economy sector, which seems an unlikely development within the five-year time horizon of the Financial Services Action Plan (FSAP). It is, however, a step in right direction to using market forces to help overcome the Eurosclerosis that was much written about in the 1990s.

The Commission's initial priorities include:

- effecting Directives that will help achieve a single EU wholesale market;
- E-commerce – policies to create open, secure retail markets;
- creating a Securities Committee concerned with prudential rules and producing Directives on prudential rules.

The Commission report is also concerned with what it describes as global issues:

> in an increasingly integrated global financial market, rules on supervision are of crucial importance. The EU must play its part in encouraging high standards of regulation world wide. The EU continues to play a full and active role in forging an international consensus and widespread implementation of best practice in financial regulation. Its support for the work of the IASC (International Accounting Standards Committee) to secure a globally accepted set of financial reporting standards that will enhance financial transparency and facilitate the task of financial supervisors, is a good example.
>
> Core elements of existing EU bank capital requirements are now being re-examined to bring them up to date with supervisory practices and banking trends. This process takes place in parallel with similar discussions in the Basel Committee on Banking Supervision in which the regulators of our main banking competitors participate. The EU is continuing its efforts to take a leading role in tackling issues to maintain a level playing field taking into account the heterogeneous structure of the EU banking sector.

CONCLUSION

While at one time, Europe was described as suffering from Eurosclerosis, today the continental European economies seem at last to be adapting to the exigencies of a much more competitive world economy. In the past, it was widely believed that government planning and micro-intervention would lead to improved industrial performance in Europe. The governance model with a small number of strong shareholders – governments, banks and industrial groups – with the banks providing a major part of the financing of companies and being actively involved in their activities, was viewed as a positive model for economic growth. Today, however, the benefits arising from a more Anglo-Saxon model of governance and financing are becoming rapidly apparent to governments, bankers and industrialists in continental Europe.

The European capital markets are in the van in this restructuring of the European economy, with the major investment banking groups being the leaders. While Europe does not yet have a Single Capital Market, this is relatively unimportant in overall terms since global financing for projects is as readily available in Europe as elsewhere. None the less, progress towards a financial markets model more on the lines of that in the US, particularly in the case of equities, would reduce further the cost of fundraising and portfolio investment. However, the concept of a 'European Capital Market' as an independent entity is an outdated one in the age of global markets. The markets located in Europe form part of a global market-place for money, equities, fixed income investments, venture capital and other forms of financing. What is perhaps lacking in such a global market is low-cost mechanisms to finance small local companies and trade their shares at a relatively low cost in the region where the company can be known by, and understood by, those who are located in the same region. Increasingly, however, 'private equity' funds are being established which can take companies through to the stage prior to becoming 'global equities'.

Overall, European financial markets are today in very good shape, having developed dramatically over the 1990s even in the absence of a Single Currency. The advent of the Single Currency should encourage further efficiency gains, market deepening and more international participation in European markets.

NOTES

1. Information and statistics on market developments from 'Initial Report of the Committee of Wise Men on the Regulation of European Securities Markets', Brussels, 9 November 2000.
2. See Julian S. Alworth (1999), 'Taxation, financial innovation and integrated financial markets: some implications for tax coordination in the European Union', in Assaf Razin and Efraim Sadka (eds), *The Economics of Globalisation*, Cambridge: Cambridge University Press, Chapter 9.
3. See, for example, Kurt W. Rothschild (2000), 'Europe and the USA: comparing what with what?', *Kyklos*, 53(3), 249–64.

8. The changing nature and determinants of EU trade policies

Paul A. Brenton

EU trade policies and the environment in which they are applied have fundamentally changed since the coming into being of the EEC in 1957. In the 1960s and 1970s external commercial policy was focused upon tariffs and other border measures and trade in goods. This was a time when the relevant political economy paradigm was one in which the interests of import-competing firms were offset against those of export-supplying firms when contemplating and negotiating international agreements to liberalize external commercial policies.

During this period the EU embraced both multilateral and bilateral liberalization. The common external tariff of the EU for industrial products has declined from an average of over 15 per cent in the early 1960s to around 3 per cent today. At the same time the EU became notorious for establishing a pyramid of trade preferences with different groups of countries in different tiers of market access. Thus, the level of formal trade protection in the EU is now generally very low. There are some exceptions, with high tariffs remaining in particular sectors, primarily agriculture and textiles and clothing.

Commercial policy nowadays is much more diverse. It is no longer just policies affecting trade in goods which are on the agenda. The policy environment affecting trade in services and conditions influencing foreign direct investment have become increasingly important. In addition, EU preferentialism in trade policy is no longer synonymous with regionalism as the recent agreements with South Africa and Mexico demonstrate. As tariffs and quantitative restrictions have declined in importance, attention has turned much more to a whole range of non-border policies, captured under the term of regulatory issues, which affect trade flows. These include technical standards and regulations and rules on intellectual property rights. The EU is addressing these issues at the multilateral level in the WTO, in regional trade agreements and in bilateral agreements on specific regulatory issues, such as the mutual recognition of testing and conformity assessment.

The last four decades have also seen the rising importance of multinational firms and the growth of intra-industry trade and substantial cross-boundary sourcing by large corporations. This has led to a substantial change in the political economy environment in which the European Union determines trade policy decisions.[1] The typical model remains relevant for sectors such as agriculture and perhaps textiles and clothing that have largely been excluded from the liberalization of border measures. However, for modem sophisticated industrial products, which now dominate EU imports and exports, the main corporate players operate large international networks and are both importers and exporters. The attention of large corporate business has become concentrated upon removing differences in national regulatory systems, such as technical regulations, which raise the costs of operating global production systems. In general most of the effort at removing the barriers to market access caused by these differences in regulatory systems has taken place at the regional and bilateral level.

The aim of this chapter is to take stock of EU trade relations and trade policies in this new environment. The paper outlines the nature of both multilateral and bilateral trade policy commitments in goods, and briefly in services. I then discuss in some detail bilateral agreements on regulatory issues and concentrate upon issues relating to technical barriers to trade and specifically the mutual recognition of conformity assessment procedures. It is contended that, if as is most likely, such agreements have a significant effect on reducing the costs of exporting between the two parties to the agreement, then they will be discriminatory. Since the EU has concentrated upon such agreements with MFN partners this suggests that the shape of the pyramid of preferences which is the standard analogy for EU trade policies is becoming distorted.

THE GEOGRAPHICAL AND COMMODITY COMPOSITION OF EU TRADE

This section begins with a quick and simple overview of the main changes in the nature of EU trade over the past 30 to 40 years. Figure 8.1 shows the geographical structure of total (internal and external) EU imports of goods in three years: 1965, 1990 and 1998. In all three years the structure of trade for the current 15 members of the EU is presented. Thus, we can look backwards from the current EU membership and see how the geographical structure of this block has changed over the past 35 years. The figure shows the share of the main continents, which in trade policy practice are fairly synonymous with regional economic groupings or identities.

It is clear that the main growth in intra-European trade (including trade between what are now EU members as well as trade with the Balkan states, Central and Eastern European countries, EFTA and EEA countries, Turkey and

CIS countries) occurred prior to 1990. The share of all European countries in the imports of the current 15 EU members increased from 59 per cent in 1965 to 72 per cent in 1990. This rise in the share of imports from other European countries occurred at the expense of falling shares for all other regions with the exception of Asia. The share of North America, for example, declined from 14 per cent of the total in 1965 to 8 per cent in 1990. The shares of both African and Central and South American countries were halved during this period. In the 1990s however, the broad geographical structure of EU imports remained relatively constant. The key feature being a slight decline in the share of EU (15) imports coming from other European countries and an increase in the importance of imports from Asia.

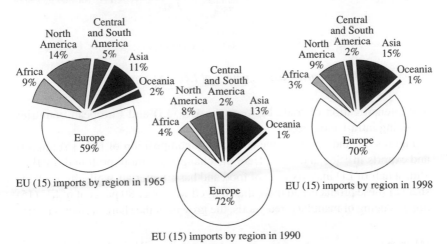

Figure 8.1   The geographical structure of EU (15) imports, 1965–98

The picture for EU (15) exports, shown in Figure 8.2, is very similar to that of imports: substantial growth in intra-European trade between 1965 and 1990 and relative stagnation of the share of such trade in the 1990s. The increase in the share of European countries in EU (15) exports in the 1970s and 1980s led to a relative substitution away from EU exports, primarily to Africa but also to North America and Central and South America. The share of Asia in EU (15) exports remained fairly constant. In the 1990s the importance of North America and Asia as a destination for EU (15) exports increased very slightly whilst the share of European countries in the exports of the EU (15) countries fell. The information on both export and import shares suggests significant growth in the importance of European countries in the period before 1990 but little subsequent change. The major integration episodes of the 1990s, the Single Market and the enlargement of the EU to 15 member countries have not led to

Globalizing Europe

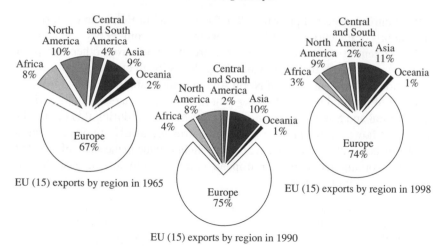

EU (15) exports by region in 1965

EU (15) exports by region in 1990

EU (15) exports by region in 1998

Figure 8.2   The geographical structure of EU (15) exports, 1965–98

any intensification of trade between the EU (15) and European countries including intra-Union trade.

Figures 8.3 and 8.4 show the commodity composition of EU (15) imports and exports in 1965 and 1998. Here the changes are more profound. In 1965 almost half of EU imports were of food and basic materials whilst by 1998 the share of these products had more than halved with over 80 per cent of EU (15) imports being of manufactured goods, the growth in the share of manufactures

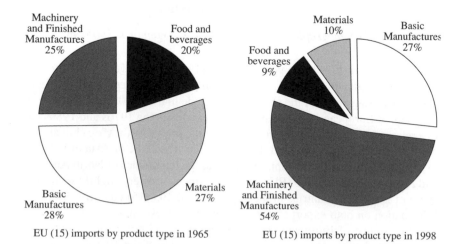

EU (15) imports by product type in 1965

EU (15) imports by product type in 1998

Figure 8.3   The commodity structure of EU (15) imports, 1965 and 1998

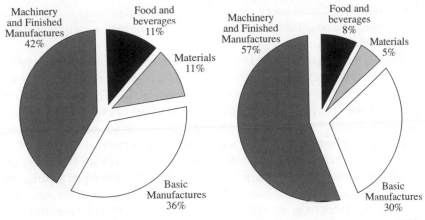

EU (15) exports by product type in 1965   EU (15) exports by product type in 1998

Figure 8.4   The commodity structure of EU (15) exports, 1965 and 1998

being entirely concentrated upon finished manufactures. With regard to exports the importance of food and basic materials declined from 22 per cent in 1965 to 13 per cent in 1998. Again the rise in the importance of manufactures is due entirely to the rising share of finished manufactures. Thus, these figures reflect the well-known fact that EU trade is increasingly of an intra-industry nature – the two-way exchange of finished manufactured products. This chapter now proceeds to look at how EU trade policy has changed over the past decades and briefly summarize the current state of multilateral and bilateral access to the EU market.

THE COMMON EXTERNAL TRADE POLICY OF THE EU: TARIFFS, QUANTITATIVE RESTRICTIONS AND ANTI-DUMPING MEASURES

Tariffs

The Common Commercial Policy of the EU has been in a constant state of flux since its inception in the 1960s. This reflects the series of trade liberalizations negotiated under the GATT, the increasing number of preferential trade agreements and more recently the implementation of a genuinely uniform policy across member states after the creation of the Single Market in 1992. The discussion of EU trade policies starts with the common external tariff and quantitative restrictions and then considers the evolving nature of EU preferentialism.

There follows a discussion of the increasing role of regulatory issues in EU trade policy and how these issues are likely to become increasingly prominent as globalization proceeds.

The EU position on trade and trade liberalization is clear (Pelkmans, 1997). The Maastricht Treaty (Art 3a) clearly defined the principle governing external trade policy as that 'of an open market economy with free competition'. More generally, the Treaty of Rome laid down the objectives of external trade policy as 'the harmonious development of world trade, the progressive abolition of restrictions on international trade and the lowering of customs barriers' (Art. 110). Thus, in general there is a bias in the treaty towards trade liberalization and liberal trade. This has in turn been reflected by the active participation of the EU in the various GATT rounds. The (weighted) average tariff for industrial products has fallen from around 17 per cent in the late 1950s (Swann, 1992) to around 3 per cent after the Uruguay Round commitments are fully implemented. Thus, since the inception of the EC the importance of tariff protection has dramatically declined. There are, however, some important sectoral exceptions to this general leaning towards open markets and trade liberalization, most notably in agriculture and also textiles and clothing.

Table 8.1 shows the current trade weighted average common external tariff for the EU for industrial products. These averages are calculated using total 1997 trade values as weights and so do not take account of preferences granted to particular suppliers. However, as shown by Sapir (1998), over 70 per cent of imports enter the EU market at the Most Favoured Nation rate. This issue is discussed below in the section on EU preferential policies. According to these data the EU average tariff for industrial products will fall to below 4 per cent in 2005.[2] The table also shows that the proportion of trade entering at a zero tariff rate will increase from around 13 per cent in 1997 to almost 30 per cent in 2005.

The table also shows the key remaining problem with regard to the EU tariff, that of tariff peaks. Although the average industrial tariff is now relatively low, a significant proportion of imports enter the EU at very high tariff rates. In 1997 almost 13 per cent of imports were subject to a tariff in excess of 10 per cent. This was only partially addressed in the Uruguay Round, as there will only be a modest reduction by 2005, to around 10 per cent, in the share of EU imports subject to high tariffs. In the main this issue is concentrated upon clothing products where more than 90 per cent of imports in 2005 will still be subject to tariffs in excess of 10 per cent. The implication of this is that developing countries, who, in general, tend to specialize in the production of labour-intensive products such as clothing products, on average face higher tariff barriers in entering the EU market than OECD countries. This is compounded by the very high trade barriers to the EU market for agricultural products.

Table 8.1 The structure of extra-EU imports of industrial products and import tariffs

	Imports	Share	Weighted average tariff 1997	Weighted average tariff 2005	Share of imports with t = 0		Share of imports with t > 10	
	ECU '000				1997	2005	1997	2005
Pharmaceuticals	7870030	1.71	0.00	0.00	0.00	100.00	0.00	0.00
Inorganic, Organic Chemicals and Fertilizers	23647614	5.13	5.41	4.44	21.95	25.77	7.82	0.02
Other Chemicals	13476458	2.93	5.80	4.66	2.30	23.17	1.88	0.11
Plastics	19214501	4.17	6.63	5.12	11.93	12.90	25.74	0.00
Raw Hides and Skins	3177045	0.69	1.83	1.69	58.10	58.14	0.00	0.00
Wood	10955426	2.38	2.14	1.41	51.06	73.28	0.00	0.00
Wood Pulp	11935585	2.59	3.18	0.00	46.34	49.44	0.00	0.00
Textiles	15839614	3.44	6.32	4.85	21.34	22.59	20.93	0.04
Clothing	39105933	8.49	12.76	11.62	0.18	0.18	94.18	92.41
Footwear etc	8299742	1.80	9.62	8.93	0.22	0.22	28.62	28.62
Stone, Cement etc	2801607	0.61	4.96	4.11	2.38	20.78	11.20	11.20
Iron and Steel	16492414	3.58	3.56	1.37	9.54	55.88	0.00	0.00
Base Metals	23273435	5.05	3.65	3.24	34.26	36.15	1.80	0.00
Non-electrical Machinery	94852731	20.59	2.61	1.51	7.12	38.79	0.01	0.00
Electrical Machinery	75789835	16.45	5.06	4.07	1.33	13.90	7.64	6.49
Motor Vehicles	30414253	6.60	8.47	7.97	0.00	2.56	8.15	3.13
Other Transport Equipment	18655524	4.05	0.59	0.43	82.24	82.87	0.01	0.00
Precision Instruments	27421251	5.95	3.90	2.60	5.34	30.27	0.00	0.00
Miscellaneous Manufactures	17489947	3.80	3.73	2.02	0.34	42.14	0.34	0.00
Total Industrial Products	460712945		5.01	3.93	12.69	29.62	12.73	9.71

The EU does offer the developing countries preferential access in the form of the Generalised System of Preferences. However, for products such as textiles and clothing, which are defined as 'very sensitive', the duty reduction from the MFN rate is only 15 per cent. In addition, administrative rules ensure that only a fraction of imports from developing countries actually benefit from GSP treatment. Sapir (1998) reports that 79 per cent of dutiable imports from GSP beneficiaries in 1994 qualified for preferential access to the EU market, yet only 38 per cent actually entered the EU market with a duty less than the MFN rate. The reasons for this difference being the effects of rules of origin which specify the requirements for products to be treated as 'originating' and therefore subject to GSP treatment, and tariff quotas for particular products, which set limits on the amount of imports which can receive beneficial access to the EU market.

Thus, even with GSP treatment, developing countries face relatively high tariff barriers compared with developed countries. Table 8.2 shows that the average tariff for industrial products for US exporters to the EU was 3.5 per cent in 1997 and this will fall to 2.5 per cent in 2005. Table 8.3, on the other hand, shows that China, a GSP beneficiary, faced an average tariff on industrial products in 1997 of 6.4 per cent, which will only fall to 5.3 per cent in 2005. Other examples are also informative. Moldova, a country in transition with average GDP per head of around $500 per annum, on average faces a considerably higher tariff on its exports to the EU than it levies on its imports from the EU. In other words EU producers, in general, face lower tariff barriers in exporting to the Moldovan market than do Moldovan exporters when seeking to sell in the EU market.[3]

The major achievement of the Uruguay Round in relation to agriculture was to increase transparency in the application of border policies and to obtain commitments on the level of domestic and export subsidies. With regard to border policies the main commitment was the tariffication of the range of non-tariff and variable levies that were previously used to protect EU agriculture, and a reduction in the average level of the tariff. Between 1995 and 1997 the simple average EU tariff for agricultural products declined by 25 per cent to reach a figure of almost 21 per cent in 1997.[4] However, these commitments appear to have done little to improve overall access to the EU market. Between 1995 and 1998 the volume of EU agricultural imports (HS 0–21) from non-member countries fell by over 6 per cent and the share of the volume of extra-EU imports in total EU imports (extra + intra) declined from 38.6 per cent to 35.1 per cent (Brenton and Nunez-Ferrer, 2000).

The EU tariff schedule for agricultural products is still dominated by tariff peaks for products such as meats, cereals and milk products. For example, in 1997 the simple average tariff (taking account of the *ad valorem* equivalents of specific duties) for fresh meat of bovine animals was 107.5 per cent with a

Table 8.2   The structure of EU imports of industrial products from the US and import tariffs

	Imports	Share	Weighted average tariff 1997	Weighted average tariff 2005	Share of imports with t = 0 1997	Share of imports with t = 0 2005	Share of imports with t > 10 1997	Share of imports with t > 10 2005
	ECU '000							
Pharmaceuticals	3261537	2.95	0.00	0.00	0.00	100.00	0.00	0.00
Inorganic, Organic Chemicals and Fertilizers	6283667	5.68	4.84	4.12	28.43	31.47	4.87	0.05
Other Chemicals	5568076	5.03	5.38	4.27	1.82	28.23	0.86	0.15
Plastics	4996221	4.52	7.01	5.28	12.11	13.80	32.14	0.00
Raw Hides and Skins	379122	0.34	2.79	2.33	39.37	43.87	2.38	0.00
Wood	1542466	1.39	2.14	1.58	56.05	69.63	0.00	0.00
Wood Pulp	3539149	3.20	2.41	0.00	55.96	60.78	0.00	0.00
Textiles	1439430	1.30	6.94	5.43	8.92	8.94	19.36	0.01
Clothing	783375	0.71	11.54	10.45	3.92	3.92	81.22	73.18
Footwear etc	152855	0.14	7.56	6.98	0.51	0.51	10.62	10.62
Stone, Cement etc	920772	0.83	4.37	3.47	1.15	19.13	2.90	2.90
Iron and Steel	1416315	1.28	3.92	1.94	4.67	38.99	0.00	0.00
Base Metals	2533101	2.29	4.61	3.98	9.28	12.72	0.40	0.00
Non-electrical Machinery	33273890	30.08	2.39	1.49	15.79	38.27	0.00	0.00
Electrical Machinery	18415024	16.65	4.28	3.20	2.67	18.74	1.21	0.76
Motor Vehicles	4694891	4.24	7.22	6.35	0.00	8.48	3.15	2.73
Other Transport Equipment	9031319	8.17	0.86	0.65	75.69	75.89	0.02	0.00
Precision Instruments	10770911	9.74	3.24	1.62	7.83	47.98	0.00	0.00
Miscellaneous Manufactures	1604603	1.45	3.44	1.88	2.88	36.68	0.06	0.00
Total Industrial Products	110606724		3.53	2.50	17.57	37.33	2.99	0.81

Table 8.3   The structure of EU Imports of industrial products from China and import tariffs

	Imports	Share	Weighted average tariff 1997	Weighted average tariff 2005	Share of imports with t = 0		Share of imports with t > 10	
	ECU '000				1997	2005	1997	2005
Pharmaceuticals	89876	0.26	0.00	0.00	0.00	100.00	0.00	0.00
Inorganic, Organic Chemicals and Fertilizers	1238287	3.55	5.44	4.66	19.42	21.30	6.00	0.00
Other Chemicals	504081	1.44	5.40	4.48	7.41	22.66	0.92	0.13
Plastics	1508003	4.32	6.91	6.09	1.56	2.05	4.08	0.00
Raw Hides and Skins	2523980	7.23	5.40	4.51	0.49	1.03	13.83	0.00
Wood	449594	1.29	3.31	1.72	0.89	53.52	0.00	0.00
Wood Pulp	281929	0.81	6.15	0.00	19.88	20.73	0.00	0.00
Textiles	1058811	3.03	6.20	4.92	20.40	29.12	22.99	0.00
Clothing	5639833	16.15	12.56	11.49	0.02	0.02	90.20	89.88
Footwear etc	2142287	6.13	10.09	9.14	0.55	0.55	34.49	34.49
Stone, Cement etc	503909	1.44	6.45	5.61	1.70	7.19	17.28	17.28
Iron and Steel	987910	2.83	4.02	2.81	0.12	9.63	0.00	0.00
Base Metals	1116828	3.20	5.00	3.84	13.03	16.05	16.75	0.00
Non-electrical Machinery	3440671	9.85	2.80	1.39	3.62	58.28	0.06	0.00
Electrical Machinery	6129641	17.55	5.43	4.36	3.86	12.88	16.48	12.90
Motor Vehicles	217889	0.62	4.87	3.81	0.00	1.32	0.57	0.51
Other Transport Equipment	148468	0.43	0.36	0.27	88.96	89.79	0.00	0.00
Precision Instruments	1872625	5.36	4.87	3.93	0.36	6.44	0.00	0.00
Miscellaneous Manufactures	5070191	14.52	4.57	2.97	0.00	24.13	0.41	0.00
Total Industrial Products	34924813		6.44	5.26	3.60	16.41	22.53	19.15

narrow range from 94 per cent to 125 per cent. For wheat the simple average tariff in 1997 was almost 77 per cent whilst for milk and cream the simple average was 59 per cent with a maximum tariff of 134 per cent (WTO, 1997). The Uruguay Agreement on Agriculture has made transparent these very high levels of border protection for certain agricultural products. Progress in making further reductions of these tariff rates is likely to be an important aspect of the next round of multilateral negotiations on agricultural trade.

Quantitative Trade Restrictions

Non-tariff border measures have substantially declined in importance in EU external trade policy. The principal non-tariff measures imposed by the EU and EU member states in the past have been quantitative import restrictions and voluntary export restraints (VERs). Anti-dumping measures are separately discussed below. The 1990s have seen a clear tendency towards the decreasing use of quantitative trade measures. Having significantly reduced tariff protection during the 1970s and 1980s the EU has now substantially alleviated the incidence of quantitative trade restrictions. In 1988 almost 11 per cent of EU imports were covered by core non-tariff measures (primarily quantitative restrictions and VERs). By 1996 this coverage ratio had fallen to just over 4 per cent.[5]

Two factors lie behind the declining use by the EU of quantitative trade restrictions: the Uruguay Round agreements and the completion of the Single Market. Under the Uruguay Round the use of voluntary export restraints was prohibited. In addition, the Agreement on Agriculture led to the tariffication of non-tariff measures. As noted above, however, this did not necessarily improve market access, since some quantitative restrictions and variable price levies were tariffed at very high and probably prohibitive levels. The Uruguay Round also addressed the other main sector where quantitative restrictions are prevalent: textiles and clothing. The industrial countries agreed to phase out the Multi-Fibre Agreement (MFA), which together with its predecessors has controlled imports from developing countries for over 40 years since the comically-titled Short-Term Agreement. The Uruguay Round agreement stipulated that bilateral quotas should be liberalized over a ten-year period from the creation of the WTO in 1995. However, under the terms of the agreement the industrial countries have been able to backload liberalization of the most binding quotas for the most sensitive products until the final date at the end of 2004.

The fact that the most sensitive items will be liberalized at the final moment has led some commentators to suggest that in the face of substantial domestic pressures quotas will be prolonged or that a raft of safeguard measures will be introduced. This seems to be a realistic concern in the US, but in Europe the clamour for continued protection has not been heard. EU industry, following substantial outsourcing, appears resigned to the death of the MFA and is devoting its efforts to opening export markets in the developing countries whose quota access to the EU will be liberalized.

The EU countries adopted a common external tariff in the 1960s, as is fundamental in a customs union. However, the individual member states maintained their battery of national quotas for textiles and clothing products. In the 1970s the product scope of these restrictions was widened under the MFA, and quantitative limits were based upon VERs negotiated at the EU level but then distributed on a national basis. Thus, for textiles and clothing the EU effectively became a free trade area with national volume protection (Pelkmans, 1997). Throughout the 1970s the scope of national volume protection increased to cover cars, footwear, bags, umbrellas, steel, televisions and a range of other products.

National volume protection requires the partitioning of national markets via border controls to prevent trade deflection (imports entering highly constrained markets via more liberal neighbours). Although this is inconsistent with the maintenance of a common commercial policy, which was required by the Treaty of Rome, and the freedom of movement of goods, national volume restrictions were never challenged by the Commission. It was not until the Single Market programme, which started in the late 1980s and necessitated the removal of border controls between member countries, that national volume restrictions were removed and a genuinely common external policy for trade in goods was finally established at the beginning of 1993. All trade restrictions maintained individually by member states were removed and were, in general, not substituted by EU-wide restrictions. The exceptions are textiles and clothing products, where quotas will be fully liberalized by 2005; certain footwear products and Japanese cars, where the restrictions have subsequently lapsed; and bananas and steel products.

EU trade policy regarding bananas is rather unique in that external trade restrictions are not driven by the consideration of protecting domestic producers,[6] but rather by developmental policy towards African and Caribbean producers. EU policy has been subject to a series of complaints at the WTO and is currently being reformed towards a tariff-only system. There has been a massive reduction in the number of quotas and VERs in the steel sector. The number of tariff lines in the steel sector subject to non-tariff measures fell from 37 per cent in 1988 to less than 1 per cent in 1996. There remain a number of restrictions on imports from Russia, the Ukraine and Kazakhstan.

Thus, although the incidence of non-tariff measures increased significantly in the 1970s, the late 1980s and 1990s saw an annihilation of national quantitative restrictions and VERs in Europe following the Uruguay Round and the completion of the Single Market. After the phase-out of the MFA and the removal of remaining steel quotas, quantitative restrictions will effectively be a trade measure of the past in Europe.

Anti-Dumping Measures

The main trade defence, or contingent protection, instrument used by the EU is anti-dumping measures. Safeguard measures and countervailing duties are not of significance. The use of anti-dumping measures by the EU increased rapidly in the 1980s but the number of measures in force has subsequently stabilized. In 1990 there were 139 anti-dumping measures, there was a slight increase to around 150 measures in 1993 and 1994, but a subsequent fall to 141 and 142 measures in force in 1997 and 1998 respectively.

The products most often involved in these anti-dumping cases are mineral products and chemicals (primarily organic chemicals), textile products and machinery and equipment, mainly electrical machinery and equipment. Other products affected range from metals and steel products to footwear, handbags and bicycles. Asian countries are most subjected to anti-dumping measures. In 1998, of the 142 measures in place, 92 (67 per cent) concerned Asian countries. There were only three cases against African countries, five against Central and South American countries and three cases involving North America. Most of the remaining 39 cases applied to Central and Eastern European countries and countries of the former Soviet Union. A very large proportion of EU cases involve countries in transition. In 1998 about one-half of the cases where definitive duties were applied involved China and the members of the former Comecon (Central and Eastern European Countries and the former Soviet Union) bloc.

Where anti-dumping measures (*ad valorem* duties, specific duties, minimum prices or price undertakings) are applied the average duty tends to be very high. Brenton (2000) calculates for a sample of cases from 1988 to 1995 an average duty (including *ad valorem* equivalents of specific duties) in excess of 25 per cent. Thus, anti-dumping measures are likely to have a major impact upon trade in the products covered. The average duty is considerably higher than the level of tariff protection affecting most products, with the exception of agricultural goods and products such as tobacco and alcoholic drinks. As noted above, the average tariff for industrial products entering the EU is now around 3 per cent. However, anti-dumping actions are by definition discriminatory. Imports from targeted countries are not only discriminated against relative to domestic producers in the EU, but also relative to non-named extra-EU countries. Brenton (2000) and Messerlin (1989) show that EU anti-dumping policies cause trade diversion and that this accrues primarily to non-EU suppliers. Prusa (1997) has found similar results for the US.

Anti-dumping policies are now very well entrenched as a part of EU external trade policy. Around 250 personnel are employed in the European Commission solely to deal with anti-dumping and anti-subsidy (of which there are very few) investigations. However, they remain subject to an extreme amount of criticism and continued suspicion that rather than a precise and careful application of well-specified rules, they are simply a protectionist device.

Finally, it is a misapprehension to expect that a free trade agreement with the EU would have a significant impact upon the use of anti-dumping measures by the EU. Specific undertakings regarding anti-dumping and safeguard measures have never formally been included in preferential agreements by the EU except for the European Economic Area (EEA). The option of precluding anti-dumping measures in the future has been included in the EU–Turkish customs union. The Europe Agreements between the EU and ten countries in Central and Eastern Europe (the CEECs) specify that before implementing anti-dumping measures the EU must provide the Association Council with all the relevant information with a view to finding a solution acceptable to both sides. However, after changing from the initial treatment of the CEECs as 'state trading' to 'market economies', the number of EU anti-dumping investigations increased despite this process of prior consultation. The Europe Agreements contain no provisions for the phasing out of anti-dumping policies or the threat of their use. The Essen Council of December 1994 gave an undertaking that 'as satisfactory implementation of competition policy and control of state aids together with the application of those parts of Community law linked to the internal market are achieved, so the Union should be ready to consider refraining from using commercial defence instruments for industrial products'. The key issue, which has not been elucidated by the Council or Commission, is what constitutes 'satisfactory implementation' and under what conditions the Community would consider refraining from using contingent protection. In practice, anti-dumping measures will only be proscribed once these countries accede to the EU.

EU PREFERENTIALISM

A key feature of EU commercial policy has been that on the one hand the EU has been a keen proponent of multilateral liberalization and the construction of an effective body of world trade law, whilst on the other hand the EU has been at the forefront of discrimination in world trade in the form of the proliferating number of preferential trade agreements that it has signed. There have been two waves to this preferentialism, with perhaps a third wave emerging at the start of this new decade.

The EU was at the heart of the first wave of post-war preferential trade agreements in the 1960s and 1970s. The formation of the European and Steel Community in 1951 and then the European Economic Community in 1957 contributed to a series of attempts to emulate customs unions among less-developed countries in the 1960s. Economic integration amongst the initial six members led directly to a response in Europe from non-participating countries in the form of the European Free Trade Association (EFTA) formed in 1960.

The EU was also pre-eminent in the subsequent spread of preferentialism, concluding association agreements with Turkey and Greece and the Yaoundé Agreements (and then the Lomé Treaties) providing non-reciprocal, often duty free, access to former colonies in the 1960s. Bilateral free trade areas in industrial goods were introduced with the six EFTA countries and a series of preferential, non-reciprocal agreements were signed with Mediterranean countries in the 1970s. These agreements together with the implementation of the EC's Generalised System of Preferences in the early 1970s started the construction of the EU's infamous pyramid of preferences. Discussion of how the pyramid has evolved will be provided in more detail below, where it will be argued that as the range of trade-related policy issues included in bilateral agreements has expanded the shape of the pyramid has become more complicated.

The second wave of EU preferentialism started to evolve in the late 1980s. As with the first wave, the preferential agreements were synonymous with regionalism. The only exceptions being the Lomé conventions and the GSP, which were primarily developmental in focus, with the former also reflecting historical legacies. This wave has been characterized both by a proliferation of new trade agreements as well as by the extension and enhancement of existing bilateral relationships. On the one hand, the deepening of integration between EU members, in the form of the programme to create the Single Market, led to a reformulation of the relationships between the EU and the EFTA countries in the form of the EEA and ultimately to the accession of three of the EFTA countries. The increasing number of agreements came first from the end of the division of Europe. The EU implemented free trade agreements with each of the ten countries in Central and Eastern Europe (CEECs) who have subsequently requested membership of the EU. EFTA quickly followed with its own agreements with these countries, and mutual trade between a group of the CEECs was liberalized under the CEFTA. In addition, the EU sought to enhance and reinvigorate existing trade agreements with Mediterranean countries. In part this reflected the perceived need to give attention to the southern borders of the EU.

This second wave of EU preferentialism in fact followed a bout of regionalism elsewhere in the world, although it is generally felt that the actions of the EU indirectly contributed to the initiation of regional schemes in the Americas. The EU's fixation on creating the Single Market in the mid- and late 1980s led to the perception that the EU was relatively uninterested in multilateralism, which in turn pushed the US to seek strategic regional deals first with Canada and then with Mexico in the NAFTA (Pelkmans and Brenton, 1999).

Figure 8.5 shows the current state of EU preferentialism in the form of the (typically referred to) pyramid. The figure shows the composition of the various

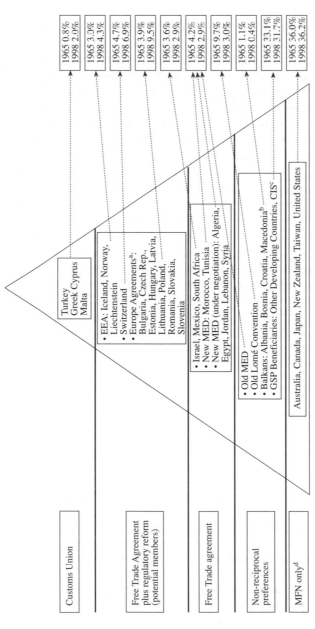

Figure 8.5 The structure of EU preferential agreements (with share of EU (15) imports in 1965 and 1998)

Notes:

a The data for 1965 do not include Estonia, Latvia and Lithuania.

b The data for the Balkans include data for Yugoslavia (Serbia and Montenegro), but all trade preferences are currently suspended.

c The data for 1965 include Estonia, Latvia and Lithuania.

d The EU has signed an MRA with the US and is negotiating similar agreements with other MFN partners. MRAs form part of the customs union with Turkey. This issue is discussed more fully in the text.

tiers which represent different degrees of preferential access to the EU market together with the share of external EU (15) imports in 1965 and 1998 accounted by the various groups of countries. At the base are those countries which have only MFN, non-preferential access to the EU market. Although the number of these countries is small, six, they account for a very large proportion of EU external imports, 36 per cent in 1998. It is interesting to note that the size of the base has remained unchanged since the 1960s. In 1965 these countries accounted for exactly 36 per cent of extra-EU imports for the 15 member countries. However, there has been some substitution between members of the MFN group. The share of the two North American countries has fallen from almost 29 per cent of the total to around 23 per cent, whilst the combined share of Australia and New Zealand has fallen from 5 per cent to less than 1.5 per cent. On the other hand the share of the two Asian MFN countries has risen from 2 per cent to almost 12 per cent.

Next in the hierarchy come non-reciprocal preference schemes. As noted above, the extent to which these agreements translate into actual preferential market access is limited by often complex origin rules, tariff quotas and quantitative restrictions. For example, in the EU agreement with Albania the EU offers exemption from customs duties and quantitative restrictions subject to a series of product specific annexes. Although the annexes in the Albania agreement cover only 5 per cent of the tariff lines they cover 62 per cent of Albanian exports to the EU (TDI, 2000). These annexes typically set quantitative ceilings after which duties are imposed.[7]

Similarly, around 60 per cent of imports from the GSP countries pay the MFN duty. Figure 8.5 shows that in 1998 imports from the GSP beneficiaries accounted for around 30 per cent of external EU imports. Hence the MFN base of the pyramid is very broad. In this tier African and Caribbean countries who are party to the Lomé Convention have also been included. This agreement has primarily entailed non-reciprocal market opening by the EU. The new Lomé Agreement negotiated in 2000 extends this for a further period of eight years. However, after September 2002 the EU will initiate negotiations on reciprocal economic partnerships, with the aim of concluding such agreements by the end of 2007.

Within the GSP group the EU has made vague commitments to consider free trade agreements with the European CIS countries (Belarus, Moldova, Russia and the Ukraine) and with MERCOSUR, the Andean Pact and the Central American Common Market. The EU has been negotiating for many years a free trade agreement with the Gulf Cooperation Council (GCC). Currently the process is blocked by the EU's insistence that the GCC members first form a customs union.

Next in the hierarchy of preferences comes a group of free trade agreements with non-European countries. With the exception of the agreement with Israel, all of these agreements are new (Mexico, South Africa, Morocco and Tunisia) or under negotiation (other MEDs) and all of these countries have climbed up from the non-reciprocal tier. Above this tier comes a group of free trade agreements with European countries, characterized by much deeper integration in terms of regulatory reform, an issue which is discussed in more detail below. The agreements with the EEA countries and Switzerland are long-standing and have been subject to substantial evolution. The Europe Agreements with the Central and Eastern European countries are more recent (negotiated in the early 1990s). All of the agreements in this group are with countries who are potential members of the EU.

The discussion suggests that a third wave of EU preferentialism has perhaps become apparent in the 1990s in the form of preferential agreements which do not have a regional identity. It should also be noted that recent agreements have been implemented with countries having substantially different levels of income and development than the EU. This trend will continue if progress is made in adopting the range of prospective agreements that have been raised by the EU. The EU has recently signed free trade agreements with South Africa and most recently Mexico. The free trade agreement with Mexico is clearly linked to the NAFTA. However, neither agreement has been driven by pressing border-related foreign policy concerns, as was the case with the Europe Agreements and the MEDs.

Potential EU membership has always been a defining characteristic of the depth and often breadth of EU agreements. Being European is a prerequisite for EU membership. However, the scope for additional trade agreements in Europe is now limited. The ten countries in Central and Eastern Europe have extensive free trade agreements and are in the process of the comprehensive adoption of all EU rules and regulations as part of the process of their accession to the EU. Turkey, too, is now seriously considered as a future EU member. That leaves the Balkans and the European CIS countries. These countries form a major challenge to EU foreign and commercial policy in the next decade, on which there will be some further discussion below.

How far will this third wave extend? Sapir (1998) and Pelkmans and Brenton (1999) discuss why countries seek free trade agreements with the EU and the reasons why the EU is interested in negotiating such agreements. Both stress the mixed motives behind the EU's approach to bilateral free trade agreements. The main factors seem to be:

- Foreign policy issues: 'trade policy has always been the principal instrument of foreign policy for the EU' (Sapir, 1998, p. 726). The pattern of preferential trade agreements of the EU reflects the differing geo-political interests of the individual member states. In addition, the EU has always used free trade agreements as an essential element towards providing regional stability on its borders.

- Commercial diplomacy: to improve market access for EU suppliers in third-country markets.
- Development policy issues: Lomé, the first generation of MED agreements and the GSP reflect development concerns. The use of trade policies to try and achieve development objectives is particularly apparent in the high-profile case of bananas.

Within each of these broad categories a range of economic and political issues are represented. An important issue is that as the EU grew in economic size and political importance it began to act as an active economic hegemony. It has combined a liberal approach to multilateral trade liberalization with a far-reaching concessionary approach to preferentialism in its expanding sphere of influence. The latter is used in a way which seeks to strengthen domestic reforms in the partner and promote multilateral liberalization. Access to the EU market, financial aid, economic cooperation and infrastructural links are used to ensure compliance and preclude free riding (which was initially tolerated from the MEDs, Turkey and the African and Caribbean signatories to the Lomé treaty). This economic hegemony can be politically sensitive when the hegemonic power refuses to make significant concessions in policy areas of high importance for partners (agriculture, for example).

This problem arises when considering the potential for the third wave of EU preferentialism, that is with countries where issues of regional stability are not paramount.

The difficulty that the EU faces in extending its network of free trade agreements to other countries is WTO rules and the CAP. Article 24 of the GATT demands that free trade agreements cover 'substantially all' trade between the partners. This is now generally accepted within the Commission as meaning that any agreement must cover at least 90 per cent to 95 per cent of trade.[8] This coupled with the absolute resistance within the EU to the liberalization of trade in sensitive agricultural products (grains, beef, milk, dairy products and sugar) makes it difficult to see how agreements could be concluded with countries in say Mercosur or in the Andean pact. Table 8.4 shows that the share of agricultural products in the exports of these countries to the EU are substantial, around 60 per cent in the case of Mercosur and almost 75 per cent for the Andean countries. The share of agriculture in EU imports from partners with recently concluded free trade agreements is much lower. Only 32 per cent of South African exports to the EU in 1998 were of agricultural products, whilst in the same year around 28 per cent of Mexican exports were of agricultural products.[9]

Table 8.4   The importance of industrial products and technical regulations in EU trade

	Share of industrial products		Share of products subject to EU technical regulations	
	EU imports	EU exports	EU imports	EU exports
INTRA-EUR (15)	85.54	86.10	70.77	71.30
EXTRA-EUR (15)	80.66	90.86	60.77	77.29
EFTA (4)	77.23	90.55	65.07	68.71
SWITZERLAND	96.86	89.93	45.84	72.71
ACP (70)	40.21	82.29	67.46	68.85
TURKEY	83.62	95.24	65.75	78.09
CEEC10	91.25	92.26	58.02	72.55
Balkans	91.16	84.77	39.50	70.63
CIS	57.19	81.62	52.98	71.10
MED	41.60	85.57	61.56	72.74
SOUTH AFRICA	68.28	94.58	33.20	77.56
UNITED STATES	92.29	93.09	71.64	79.48
CANADA	78.01	89.92	61.13	80.48
MEXICO	71.93	94.51	65.63	79.29
CACM	21.48	91.24	9.26	87.69
Andean	24.71	89.67	28.59	81.50
Mercosur	38.83	93.63	37.74	79.36
CHILE	62.60	95.44	22.13	74.86
Indian SC	88.10	96.05	54.66	82.64
New Nics	85.68	94.41	42.95	85.91
CHINA	94.88	96.18	46.92	85.12
NICS	99.02	94.05	53.64	78.75
JAPAN	99.70	87.39	75.90	69.91
ASNZ	56.29	94.78	41.84	81.16

Currently, free trade negotiations on agricultural products proceed on a detailed product-by-product basis. This ensures a minimal amount of market opening in the EU, since special interests are able to influence the negotiations at a very detailed level with little scope for trade-offs. It also reflects the hegemonic power of the EU and the way that the EU currently wields that influence.

Note that EU bilateral trade agreements are now fundamentally different from those of the 1950s and 1960s. The EU is now actively pushing for the end of non-reciprocity in its agreements with the ACP countries and the Mediterranean countries. In the past the EU tended to conclude reciprocal agreements only with potential members of the EU. This reflects the opposition at the time of the US to the expansion of preferential trade agreements. Indeed, Sapir (1998) documents that the original plan for trade preferences with the ACP countries was for reciprocal arrangements, but in the face of US objections this was abandoned and a non-reciprocal system was implemented. This has now changed, of course, by the participation of the US itself in preferential trade schemes. It is interesting to note from the data on the shares of EU (15) imports in 1965 and 1998 (in Figure 8.5) that the countries and country groupings which have been in the non-reciprocal tiers (Mexico, South Africa, MEDs, Lomé, the Balkans and GSP) have all lost market share. This non-reciprocal group of countries as a whole provided 51 per cent of EU (15) external imports in 1965 but only 40 per cent in 1998. Countries which have implemented agreements requiring mutual abolition of trade barriers have increased their share of EU imports. However, some of this increase is due to the Central and Eastern European countries whose trade with the EU prior to the 1990s was suppressed under the previous regime, but which quickly achieved the levels of trade associated with 'normal' market economies by the mid-1990s (Brenton and Gros, 1997).

In addition trade agreements are now about much more than trade policies. A key feature of recent agreements is that they go far beyond the removal of tariffs and quantitative restrictions, and cover a whole range of regulatory issues relating to technical regulations and standards, rights of establishment, competition policy and state aids, and trade in services. Attention to these issues has been termed as 'deep integration' (Lawrence, 1996), to which the discussion now turns. It is somewhat ironic that as formal trade barriers have declined, the demand for trade agreements with the EU has increased. As shown above, with the exception of agricultural products, which are in part or in the main excluded from liberalization under EU agreements, EU tariffs are generally quite low. Thus, the desire for free trade agreements with the EU is now stimulated by much more than just the removal of tariff restrictions.

The inclusion of the new issues is asserted to be non-preferential and therefore not subject to the rules of Article 24 of the GATT. However, a number of authors are now beginning to actively question this assumption (see Baldwin, 2000, for example). In a number of cases the EU, as in the mutual recognition agreement with the US, has signed agreements on regulatory issues outside of formal free trade agreements. It will be argued below that these types of agreement cover a significant proportion of trade from MFN partners and if, as there are grounds to suspect, these agreements provide preferential access for the products covered, then the structure of the pyramid of trade preferences is becoming distorted. Thus, for example, countries towards the top of the pyramid, such as Mediterranean countries and the CEECs, do not face tariff barriers on their exports of industrial products. However, domestic firms in these countries face the costs of achieving conformity assessment to technical standards in both the home market and in the EU. On the other hand, for certain products, US exporters have to pay the MFN tariff to access the EU market but may avoid some costs of exporting since testing to EU standards carried out in US laboratories can be accepted as conformity assessment in the EU. If the cost reduction from avoiding duplicity of conformity assessment exceeds the magnitude of the external tariff for a particular product, then US exporters may have the most preferred access to the EU market.

CURRENT TRENDS IN EU TRADE POLICIES: DEEP INTEGRATION

The current environment in which EU trade policies are set is considerably different from that of 40 years ago when the EU's common trade policies were being established. Today, tariffs and quantitative trade restrictions are substantially lower and less prevalent. However, it has been increasingly recognized that considerable problems still face firms wishing to trade and invest abroad. These barriers arise from differences in the regulatory regimes imposed in various countries, which act to segment markets along national lines, constraining the ability of firms to effectively compete across national boundaries. The market segmenting effects of these policies may not necessarily be intentional. For example, conformity with health, safety and technical standards requires testing and certification, which will normally be required of both domestic and imported products. But if every country maintains its own standards and testing procedures then exported products will face a multiplicity of conformity assessment and hence higher compliance costs, and this will tend to reduce international trade flows.

At the same time, and in part due to the reduction in traditional trade barriers, the world economy has become more integrated. This has been reflected in rising volumes of trade and investment flows and increasing international interdependencies between firms. The activities of multinational firms are now much more important and this is altering the political economy which envelops trade policy-making. A large proportion of trade is now intra-firm trade, that is trade which takes place within multinational enterprises. Over 40 per cent of trade between the US and the EU is intra-firm trade (Clausing, 2000). More generally, there has been an increase in the extent to which firms outsource parts of the production process to overseas suppliers, leading to a 'sequential, vertical trading chain stretching across many countries' (Hummels et al., 1999).

A number of important implications for trade policy follow from this environment, the key issues being:

- Further trade liberalization is strongly supported by large corporations, that is multinational firms and firms which both import and export. The traditional political economy model where pro-protection import-competing firms vie with pro-liberalization export firms in the political market for protection is now much less valid. As a result, political efforts become focused upon achieving liberalization with countries and within industries where firms are both exporting and import-competing, that is where intra-industry trade is dominant (Baldwin, 2000).
- The emphasis of liberalization will be upon eliminating differences in national regulations which segment markets and make internationally integrated production costly. Tariff barriers are now relatively unimportant and, where significant, can be circumvented by multinational firms through transfer pricing policies.

It is in this context that the leaders of large corporations have strongly supported recent regional and bilateral trade initiatives in Europe (the creation of the Single Market), in North America (NAFTA) and in Asia (APEC). The role of business in influencing deep integration has been increasingly institutionalized, for example, in the Transatlantic Business Dialogue (TABD) and in the Pacific Business Forum. Much of the initiative for, and the propulsion behind, the EU–US agreement on mutual recognition of conformity assessment came from the TABD, which is pushing for further liberalization of market access barriers. Business leaders are not ignoring the possibility of multilateral initiatives through the WTO. However, the gradualist approach and the perceived inability of the WTO to keep abreast of actual developments in the world market appears to be dampening business enthusiasm.

Deep integration can be defined as agreements by governments to reduce the market-segmenting effects of differences in national regulations by the coordination, harmonization or mutual recognition of national laws, regulations and enforcement mechanisms.[10] This chapter now proceeds to discuss the EU approach to regulatory barriers, looking first at internal liberalization and then at EU external policies in this area. Concentration is focused upon technical barriers to trade, which remain one of the most important causes of market segmentation and which have been particularly important in recent EU bilateral trade policy initiatives.

Technical barriers to trade (TBTs) can arise whenever a producer may have to alter their product in order to comply with differing partner country requirements, such as for health, safety, environmental and consumer protection issues. These requirements can be imposed by both governments (technical regulations) and non-governmental organizations (non-regulatory barriers, standards). The legal character of technical regulations distinguishes them from non-regulatory barriers or standards; namely, the latter are voluntary, not legally

binding and arise from the self-interest of producers or consumers involved –
for example, to improve the information in commercial transactions and ensure
compatibility between products. The former mainly relates to either technical
specifications or testing and certification requirements such that the product
actually complies with the specifications to which it is subjected (conformity
assessment).

Technical regulations strike at the heart of business operations affecting
business pre-production, production, sales and marketing policies. The need to
adapt product design, reorganize production systems, and for multiple testing
and certification, can entail a significant cost (or technical trade barrier) for
suppliers of exported goods to a particular country, the magnitude of which
differs across products. The removal of TBTs within the EU is a central tenet
of the Single Market since it is crucial for the provision of equal conditions of
market access throughout the whole of the European Economic Space. The
removal of such barriers promotes trade and efficiency and serves to strengthen
competition by undermining the fragmentation of the EU market.

Previous analysis of the completion of the Single Market in the existing EU
countries suggests that the removal of technical barriers to trade may be of great
significance. CEC (1998) calculates that over 79 per cent of intra-EU trade may
have been affected by technical regulations in 1996. Similar calculations are
shown in Table 8.4 for EU trade with a range of countries in 1997. These data
demonstrate that a large share of EU imports and exports are of products which
are subject to technical regulations in the EU.

Instruments for Removing Technical Barriers to Trade

EU policy related to standards, testing and certification requirements is currently
based upon two approaches: enforcement of the Mutual Recognition Principle
(MRP) and if this fails, the harmonization of technical standards in each member
country. Each approach will now be discussed in turn.

Mutual Recognition

The basic EU approach has been to promote the idea that products manufactured
and tested in accordance with a partner country's regulations could offer
equivalent levels of protection to those provided by corresponding domestic
rules and procedures. However, this often requires accreditation of testing and
certification bodies and a mutual recognition arrangement (MRA) between
bodies, because member states often regulate for the same product risks in
slightly different ways (or in the same way but requiring duplication of
conformity assessment). Mutual Recognition tends to apply where products are
new and specialized and it seems to be relatively effective for equipment goods

and consumer durables, but it encounters difficulties where the product risk is high and consumers or users are directly exposed.

Harmonization

Where 'equivalence' between levels of regulatory protection embodied in national regulations cannot be assumed, the only viable way to remove the TBT in question is for the member states to reach agreement on a common set of legally binding requirements. Subsequently, no further legal impediments can prevent market access of complying products anywhere in the EU market. EU legislation harmonizing technical specifications has involved two distinct approaches, the 'old approach' and the 'new approach'.

The old approach mainly applies to products by which the nature of the risk requires extensive product-by-product or even component-by-component legislation (chemicals, motor vehicles, pharmaceuticals and foodstuffs) and is carried out by means of detailed directives. In the main, achieving this type of harmonization has been slow for two reasons. First of all, the process of harmonization became highly technical since it sought to meet the individual requirements of each product category (including components). This resulted in extensive and drawn-out consultations. Secondly, the adoption of old approach directives was based on unanimity in the Council. As a result the harmonization process proceeded extremely slowly. Indeed the approach was ineffective, since new national regulations proliferated at a much faster rate than the production of EU-level directives on a limited set of products (Pelkmans, 1987).

It became increasingly recognized that there was a need to reduce the intervention of the public authorities prior to a product being placed on the market. Moreover, the decision-making procedure needed to be adapted in order to facilitate the adoption of technical harmonization directives by a qualified majority in the Council. This has been done by the adoption of the 'new approach', and applies to products which have 'similar characteristics' and where there has been widespread divergence of technical regulations in EU countries. What makes this approach 'new' is that it only indicates 'essential requirements' and leaves greater freedom to manufacturers as to how to satisfy those requirements, dispensing with the 'old' type of exhaustively detailed directives.

The new approach directives provide for more flexibility than the detailed harmonization directives of the old approach, by using the support of the established standardization bodies, CEN, CENELEC and the national standard bodies. The standardization work is achieved in a more efficient way, is easier to update and involves greater participation from industry. A further feature of the new approach is the use of market surveillance and the choice of attestation methods that are available: by self-certification against the essential requirements, by using generic standards or by using notified bodies for type approval and testing of conformity of type.

At the multilateral level, the traditional GATT approach of reciprocal concessions is not easily applied in the area of regulatory differences and deep integration. The WTO Agreement on Technical Barriers to Trade reiterates the principles of most favoured nation treatment and of national treatment as being applicable to all aspect of standards and conformity assessment. However, the agreement goes further in obliging governments to ensure that technical barriers are not more trade restricting than necessary to achieve a legitimate objective, in committing governments to harmonize national standards with international standards, in providing for acceptance of equivalent testing procedures in third countries, and in providing a framework for dispute settlement. In practice, however, the issue of reciprocity of conformity assessment procedures and acceptance of test results from other members has not received any significant attention in the multilateral context.

Bilateral Agreements on Conformity Assessment

Harmonization and mutual recognition have been actively pursued by the EU in external bilateral agreements, not always in the context of a comprehensive trade agreement. Mutual recognition is also one of the most important objectives on the agenda of APEC. Baldwin (2000) distinguishes between negotiated harmonization, hegemonic harmonization and mutual recognition. At the international level negotiated harmonization is unlikely to be feasible. Hegemonic harmonization and mutual recognition are currently being employed by the EU in bilateral agreements. Hegemonic harmonization entails small countries and less-developed countries adopting the regulations of the EU, although there are substantial differences in obligations between the various agreements that the EU has entered into. The EU has followed the mutual recognition approach with countries such as the US, Canada and Japan.

For example, Article 51 of the Partnership and Cooperation Agreement (PCA) between the Ukraine and the EU contains a general commitment on the part of the Ukraine to adopt the *acquis*, or body of law, of the Community, such that 'Ukraine shall endeavour to ensure that its legislation will be gradually made compatible with that of the Community' (Article 51(1)). A similar clause is present in the Europe Agreements with the Central and Eastern European countries although the Central and Eastern European countries must use their 'best endeavours' to ensure compatibility with Community legislation.

Elsewhere, the free trade agreement with Mexico contains little substance on regulatory issues, and in particular on technical barriers to trade, whilst the agreement with South Africa includes a commitment to develop agreements on mutual recognition of conformity assessment. The EU has no formal trade agreement with the US but it does have a mutual recognition agreement for conformity assessment of specific products. Under an MRA each country is given the authority to test and certify in its own territory, and prior to export, the conformity of products with the other country's regulatory requirements.

The EU–US MRA agreement covers the following selected sectors: telecommunications equipment, electromagnetic compatibility, electrical safety, recreation craft, pharmaceutical good medical practices, and medical devices. Table 8.5 shows the share of these products in EU imports from various countries in 1998. Thus, the MRA with the US covered almost 13 per cent of EU imports from the US. The value of this trade exceeds the value of EU imports in the top tier of the pyramid in Figure 8.5. Thus, if recognition by the EU of US conformity assessment for the sectors covered significantly reduces the costs of exporting to the EU for US firms, then the pyramid of preferences will become rather distorted.[11]

Mutual recognition agreements can be expected to bring a number of benefits. In particular, the expense, time and unpredictability of obtaining approval can be reduced if the product can be tested for conformity in the country of production. Unfortunately, at present there are no good estimates of the impact that the MRA will have on the costs of exporting. Survey evidence from OECD (2000) suggests that 'mutual recognition agreements of conformity assessment procedures have had a distinct and beneficial effect on the costs of compliance'. There is also the argument that the amount of resources and effort dedicated by business in pushing forward the agenda on mutual agreements strongly suggests that the benefits to firms of such agreements are non-negligible. Thus, in the near future a substantial proportion of trade from those countries in the bottom tier of the pyramid (all bar Taiwan have either negotiated or are negotiating an MRA with the EU) could enter the EU market more easily than goods from other countries in higher tiers.

Interestingly, a much smaller share of EU exports to the US comprises products covered by the MRA; around 7 per cent in 1998. The table also shows that these products are also an important part of the exports to the EU of a number of other countries. Over one-sixth of Taiwanese exports to the EU in 1998 were of products covered by the EU-US MRA, these products also being important in the exports of Korea and Japan to the EU. Thus, if the MRA has a significant impact on the costs of US exporters of these products it could have important implications for the exports of other suppliers of the EU market.

The EU and the US have put forward the MRA as being consistent with WTO obligations. This is true in the sense that the Agreement on Technical Barriers to Trade calls upon members 'to be willing to enter into negotiations for the conclusion of agreements for the mutual recognition of results of each other's conformity assessment procedures'. This appears to grant MRAs an exception to the most favoured nation (MFN) obligation of the WTO. Mathis

Table 8.5 Share of trade in products covered by EU–US MRA and by all new approach directives

	Products under US–EU MRA except GMP		All products under NA	
EU imports		EU exports	EU imports	EU exports
TURKEY 1.50		TURKEY 5.43	TURKEY 2.66	TURKEY 15.67
POLAND 3.38		POLAND 5.89	POLAND 5.21	POLAND 14.14
CZECH REP. 7.00		CZECH REP. 8.01	CZECH REP. 11.04	CZECH REP. 14.17
SLOVAKIA 2.73		SLOVAKIA 8.35	SLOVAKIA 5.01	SLOVAKIA 14.57
HUNGARY 6.11		HUNGARY 8.06	HUNGARY 7.72	HUNGARY 12.72
ROMANIA 0.77		ROMANIA 5.63	ROMANIA 2.04	ROMANIA 14.68
BULGARIA 1.53		BULGARIA 4.52	BULGARIA 2.86	BULGARIA 9.73
UKRAINE 0.27		UKRAINE 4.89	UKRAINE 0.69	UKRAINE 11.29
RUSSIA 0.16		RUSSIA 7.72	RUSSIA 0.36	RUSSIA 14.11
US 12.62		US 6.88	US 15.71	US 12.08
CANADA 5.68		CANADA 4.48	CANADA 8.10	CANADA 10.61
S.KOREA 14.22		S.KOREA 6.23	S.KOREA 15.37	S.KOREA 15.62
JAPAN 9.99		JAPAN 6.80	JAPAN 15.06	JAPAN 11.13
TAIWAN 17.74		TAIWAN 10.47	TAIWAN 20.76	TAIWAN 18.69
INTEU 12 5.15		INTEU12 5.62	INTEU12 7.76	INTEU12 8.53
EXTEU12 7.45		EXTEU12 6.84	EXTEU12 10.03	EXTEU12 12.80

(1998) argues that this exception could be challenged if an MRA imposes origin rules which preclude the possibility of third-country goods to be accepted in one party to the MRA after conformity assessment in the partner. However, given that MRAs reduce the costs of market access to the signatories of the agreement but not for excluded countries, they are preferential, violate the principle of non-discrimination which underlies the WTO and are potentially trade diverting. MRAs which contain rules of origin merely exacerbate the degree of discrimination.[12]

The European Council has specified a list of priority countries with whom negotiations on MRAs should be conducted. The list comprises the US, Canada, Japan, Australia, New Zealand, Hong Kong, Israel, Singapore, the Philippines, China, South Africa, Malaysia, Indonesia, Thailand and Turkey. Recently, the EU has signed Protocols on European Conformity Assessment with a number of Central and Eastern European countries as part of the process of accession to the EU. Note that all South American countries and all bar one African country are excluded from this list. In terms of the spirit of the GATT/WTO and the principle of most favoured nation treatment it would seem appropriate that the EU not preclude an MRA with any trading partner. In fact the EU should be more open in stating that any country which can demonstrate appropriate testing systems should be able the negotiate an MRA with the EU. This could encourage companies which provide testing and conformity assessment procedures in EU or other OECD countries to invest in countries which do not have strong facilities in this field.

The Commission has raised the possibility that the range of bilateral MRAs that the EU may shortly have could be made plurilateral. Indeed it has been suggested that EU bilateral MRAs could be networked with those of other countries or trading blocs (APEC has made some progress on conformity assessment) to create a plurilateral framework. However, this enhances the danger that countries in Africa, Asia and South America, which are denied the possibility of negotiating such agreements, will be increasingly marginalized.

The agenda of mutual recognition between the EU and the US is being pushed forward, under the influence of the TABD. It is expected that two further agreements will be signed on machine safety equipment and calibration. More generally, these bilateral negotiations offer the scope for mutual recognition agreements on all products covered by the 'new approach' in the EU as well as a number of 'old approach' sectors. Table 8.5 shows that if mutual recognition agreements were to be negotiated for all existing 'new approach' products then nearly 16 per cent of EU imports from, and 12 per cent of exports to, the US would in total be affected.

At present, integration between the EU and the US has been confined to the mutual recognition of conformity assessment. There has been no attempt to move towards the mutual recognition of regulations or towards harmonization of regulations. However, the MRA may be a stepping stone to more adventurous integration in the future. The forces pushing for bilateral agreements on mutual recognition are in general quite different to those which typically underlie free trade agreements negotiated by the EU, where, as argued above, a range of factors including foreign policy considerations as well as economic implications are important. A key feature of EU–US relations on this issue has been the dominant role played by business and the lack of the typical political market for protection whereby the Commission has to balance the interests of import-competing firms against those of exporters. Baldwin (2000) suggests that the main losers from the liberalization of technical barriers to trade are small firms. The removal of factors which cause market fragmentation has a pro-competitive effect that leads to the taking over, merging or exit from the market of the least efficient, usually small, firms. The result is a market structure with fewer, larger, more efficient firms.

It is unlikely that large business will be content to stop at mutual recognition agreements. As certain cost-raising barriers are removed, such as the duplication of conformity assessment, the impact of remaining technical barriers to trade will become even more apparent. As was mentioned above the increasing importance of international production networks will lead to ever greater demands for the removal of cost-raising differences in national regulatory regimes, Indeed, the Seville Declaration, which launched the TABD, states that the goal is to 'ensure that laws and regulations converge wherever possible to allow market forces to accelerate economic growth'. In. addition, the increasing importance of multinational firms and the greater role of business in influencing regulatory decisions suggest that there will be forces pushing towards the informal international harmonization of standards and regulatory barriers. For example, the main industry players often make an important contribution to the setting of standards. If these main players are the same on both sides of the Atlantic then there will be a tendency towards common standards.

TRADE IN SERVICES

Trade in services has increased in importance in recent years. The key services which are now traded are travel and tourism, transportation services, financial services including banking and insurance, and professional services such as accountancy and business consultancy. In the EU around 50 per cent of total trade between members comprises services (Barth, 1999). However, there remain severe restrictions on services trade. Internally, the EU has been much less successful in removing barriers to trade in services than it has in creating a Single Market for industrial goods. This is suggested by the fact that whilst the share of internal goods trade increased from 28.4 per cent to 31.5 per cent of Union GDP between 1992 and 1997, the share of traded services increased little over this period. Nevertheless, there are signs of increasing integration from the amount of foreign direct investment in services activities within the Union which has increased more rapidly than overseas investment in other activities (CEC, 1999).

International service transactions can often be distinguished by the direct contact between providers and consumers that needs to take place, although some services, such as international telephone services, can be traded across borders in the same manner as trade in goods. In many cases either the consumer must move to the place of production, as in tourism, or the factors used to produce the service must be located in the country of consumption. The latter can be undertaken through foreign investment to create an overseas commercial presence, as is usually the case in the provision of financial services, or through the temporary movement of workers, for example, in the provision of business services. Thus, liberalization of services requires not just the removal of barriers to cross-border flows of service products, but also the effective elimination of obstacles to foreign direct investment and the movement of workers.

Current EU external trade policy with regard to services reflects both multilateral commitments made under the General Agreement of Trade in Services (GATS) and provisions in bilateral trade agreements. The EU is, however, far from establishing a common commercial trade policy for services.[13] This reflects in part the desires of member states to maintain a degree of national discretion in setting policy for certain services, for example, in providing access to national airports for foreign airlines. It also encapsulates a continuing evolution in the EU as to the extent of the Union's competence to conclude international agreements in services. The Union's competence to conclude international agreements can come from two sources:[14] express provisions in the treaty – for example, Article 133 provides for the Union to negotiate tariff agreements; and the jurisprudence of the European Court of Justice. With regard to the latter the court has ruled that other provisions of the treaty and measures adopted within those provisions may confer external competence. The existence of 'internal rules' bestows external competence to the Union. Hence there is a relationship between the exercise of internal competence and that of external competence.

Although it is not disputed that the EU has exclusive competence for the Common Commercial Policy, there is contention over the exact scope of the policy. For trade in goods it is now clear, after the creation of the Single Market and the removal of the national quantitative restrictions, that the EU has exclusive competence to conclude international agreements and that because of the primacy of Union laws over domestic law there is little scope for national policy discretion.[15] For trade in services the situation is less clear. In the face of the increase in the number and range of issues on the negotiating table under the Uruguay Round, the Court of Justice was asked to decide the extent of the

Common Commercial Policy. In the meantime a compromise was reached between the Commission and the member states on defining common positions. In effect the Commission negotiated on behalf of all member states, who then entered country-specific reservations on particular services and market access issues. With regard to services, the court, consistent with the GATS, identified four modes of supply – cross-border supply, consumption, commercial presence and movement of persons – and concluded that the Common Commercial Policy applies only to the first method.

The court did rule that existing 'internal rules' with regard to transport and intellectual property did convey limited external competence in these areas. For example, counterfeit goods fall under external EU competence but other aspects of intellectual property rights are subject to concurrent competence. However, the Amsterdam Treaty inserted a new provision (Article 133 (5)) that exclusive EU competence could be extended to services and intellectual property, subject to consultation with the European Parliament and a unanimous decision in the Council. In the absence of such an agreement it is likely that Union competence will increase as more 'internal rules' are adopted in these areas (sometimes by qualified majority voting).

The GATS was the first multilateral agreement on trade in services. However, whilst bringing some extra discipline to the area of trade in services it is generally accepted that this first step towards multilateral liberalization did not generate substantial market opening (Hoekman, 1995). The agreement did, however, start a process by which effective liberalization may be provided in future negotiations. The contracting parties accepted two key sets of obligations under the GATS. Firstly, a set of general concepts and rules, of which unconditional MFN treatment is the principal obligation, which apply to measures affecting trade in all service sectors, except those explicitly mentioned in the Annex to the agreement (the 'negative list'). In principle, the exemptions may not last longer than ten years, and will be subject to negotiation in future rounds. Secondly, there are specific commitments on market access and national treatment regarding listed sectors and sub-sectors (the 'positive list'), although particular qualifications, limitations and conditions can be maintained for each of the itemized sectors and sub-sectors. It is obstacles to market access which are prohibited, with the following six measures being explicitly identified: limitations on the number of suppliers; ceilings on the value of transactions or assets; restrictions on output; limitations on employment or on the number of persons supplying a service; constraints on the type of legal entity via which a service is provided; and ceilings on foreign shareholdings or on the value of foreign investment.

It is very difficult to ascertain the extent and magnitude of trade barriers in services and the extent to which these will be alleviated by the GATS. There is, however, little doubt that for many service products constraints on trade remain considerable. Analysis of the commitments made under the GATS suggests that in many service sectors substantial violations of national treatment and significant restrictions on market access remain. Hoekman and Primo Braga (1997) calculate that commitments made by high-income countries represent just under half of the total commitments that could have been made. Of these commitments only one-quarter entail the removal of all restrictions on market access and national treatment. The degree of liberalization by low-income countries is substantially less. One important feature of the GATS is the commitment to progressive liberalization in the form of 'successive rounds of negotiations' to reduce barriers to trade in services and provide effective market access.

The first set of mandated negotiations commenced in 2000. There are a number of reasons why the EU will be keen to achieve a successful outcome from these negotiations. The continued presence of substantial barriers to trade in services, together with low tariffs and non-tariff barriers on industrial products, leads to the possibility that effective rates of protection for these industrial goods may be negative if the prices of intermediate service inputs are substantially higher than world market prices. Thus, pressure from manufacturing industries for low-cost service inputs to enhance ability to compete on international markets, is likely to keep the issue of services trade liberalization high on the EU agenda. In addition, the EU perceives that in certain service sectors, such as financial services and telecommunications services, EU countries have a comparative advantage, which has been enhanced by the liberalization of internal EU trade. Thus, standard mercantilist concerns will generate pressures for increasing access to overseas markets.

The issue of services also arises in EU bilateral free trade agreements, although coverage and the extent of liberalization vary greatly across the different agreements. Similar to the rules governing preferential trade in goods, the GATS (Art. V) requires that bilateral trade agreements have 'substantial sectoral coverage' and that they eliminate 'substantially all discrimination'. The GATS also requires that overall barriers to services trade of countries not included in the preferential agreement should not rise for each sector and sub-sector.

Liberalization tends to be much deeper in agreements with countries who are prospective members of the EU, such as the Central and Eastern European countries, although the recent agreement with Mexico offers the prospect of far-reaching liberalization. Within three years of this agreement entering into force a joint council 'shall adopt a decision providing for the elimination of substantially all remaining discrimination in the sectors and modes of supply covered'. Nevertheless, this decision can be delayed until after the mandated negotiations at the WTO for further multilateral liberalization under the GATS. In contrast, the agreements with Tunisia and South Africa, for example, contain little substance on services and rights of establishment beyond a restatement of existing commitments under the GATS.

CONCLUSIONS: THE FUTURE OF EU EXTERNAL COMMERCIAL POLICIES

EU trade policies will continue to be determined by different and sometimes conflicting factors. The final part of this chapter attempts to identify the key issues and influences and how they vary according to relations with different regions of the world. Thus, in relations with North America and Asia the strong influence of large corporate interests will push forward an agenda on removing regulatory barriers to trade. However, this will take place within the context of the broad foreign policy importance attached to these regions.

In Europe strategic and foreign policy concerns are paramount. The key remaining commercial policy dilemmas facing the EU are in its relations with countries in the Balkans and with the European CIS countries. Their location, and the similarities of their industrial and trade structures with the acceding countries in Central and Eastern Europe, mean that these countries are likely to be economically affected by the next enlargement of the EU.[16] Given their political instability and geopolitical importance, they will be priority cases in terms of EU foreign policy. However, the implementation of the standard EU foreign policy response of a free trade area is complicated in these countries by problems of judicial and administrative capacity to implement the increasingly onerous obligations that the EU seeks in such agreements. The EU will also have to offer unprecedented access in agricultural products if FTAs with these countries are to be consistent with the accepted requirements of the WTO and substantial trade diversion for certain agricultural products from the next enlargement is to be avoided.

In North Africa and the Mediterranean region trade relations will be determined by the extent to which free trade agreements, such as those with Tunisia and Morocco, can be implemented with other countries in the region. Again, this area is important in the foreign policy context of the EU. Trade relations with African and Caribbean countries will continue to be determined in a development context, with energies over the next ten years being concentrated upon implementing a system of reciprocal bilateral free trade agreements as envisaged under the new Lomé agreement. In both of these cases the hegemonic role of the EU is a dominant factor.

The sphere of influence of the EU is weaker in Latin America and there is little possibility of the EU negotiating free trade agreements that exclude sensitive agricultural products from tariff liberalization. Thus, the extension of EU preferential treatment into Central and South America will be constrained by the extent to which the CAP is further reformed. Reform of the CAP is also a crucial issue with regard to further multilateral trade negotiations. Without genuine market opening by the EU for key agricultural products, such as beef, milk products and cereals, there is little prospect of success in the ongoing negotiations in Geneva on agricultural trade liberalization or in a wider trade round if that were to be launched.

Trade relations with North America and Asia will reflect the growing importance of large corporate interests in pushing forward their agenda on trade facilitation. The process with the US and Canada is much more advanced, as reflected by the mutual recognition agreements. In addition, formal relations are clearly defined on a bilateral basis with these countries and the TABD has proved to be effective in influencing policy priorities. With regard to Asia the principal forum with the EU is the Asia–Europe Meeting (ASEM) in which dialogue takes place between the EU and seven members of ASEAN (Brunei, Indonesia, Malaysia, the Philippines, Singapore, Thailand and Vietnam) together with China, South Korea and Japan. Again, corporate interests are involved via the Asia–Europe Business Forum, but progress on addressing technical and other regulatory barriers to trade is likely to be much slower than in transatlantic relations.

Thus, EU trade policy is becoming increasingly diverse whilst covering a broader range of issues and a wider set of bilateral relations. The forces framing trade policies are varied and different frameworks are evolving for different issues and for trade with different regions and countries. Given the absolute magnitude of the trade flows involved, increasing importance is being given to transatlantic relations and the removal of technical barriers to trade, which are of particular interest to large multinational corporations seeking to most efficiently operate global networks of production facilities.

The trend towards ever increasing flows of foreign direct investment suggests that the role of multinationals in influencing trade policy developments will continue to be enhanced. This is leading to a trade policy process which is necessarily bilateral and often discriminatory and one which is selective in terms of product and sector coverage. These are issues which have typically been of concern to the WTO in assessing the impact of preferential trade agreements on third countries. Given the current lack of clear WTO disciplines in preferential trade facilitation it is important that the EU consider carefully the impact of this trend in bilateral trade policies on trade in general. This requires an assessment not just of the implications for current trade flows but whether such agreements may affect the ability of developing countries to enter the markets for particular goods as they climb the ladder of technical sophistication in the array of goods that they produce.

NOTES

1. Since the European Union does not have a legal personality, responsibility for external trade policy for goods (the issue of services will be discussed later) remains with the European

Communities. However, for simplicity and to avoid confusion we will refer throughout to the European Union.

2. These averages do not include the effect of the Information Technology Agreement which will abolish tariffs on IT products.
3. In 1997 the average tariff on Moldovan exports to the EU was around 9 per cent (around 7 per cent with full GSP benefits but in 1997 only one-third of Moldovan exports to the EU which were entitled to preferences actually received them) whilst the average tariff on EU exports to Moldova was just over 4 per cent (Brenton, 1999).
4. WTO (1997)
5. These figures and subsequent data in this section are taken from Auboin and Laird (1999).
6. Apart from small-scale production in the Canary Islands there is no domestic output of bananas in the EU.
7. The EU has recently (COM, 2000, 351) revised its commercial policy approach to the Balkans and reduced the number of tariff ceilings. Nevertheless, only limited duty free access remains for textile and clothing products and for agricultural products.
8. Note that this does not mean that 95 per cent of all tariff lines must be covered. It is 95 per cent of tariff distorted trade which is measured. Thus, products subject to prohibitive tariffs tend not to be liberalized.
9. This did not prevent some bitter haggling in the South African case over the use specific names for certain alcoholic beverages.
10. From Hoekman, Schiff and Winters (1998).
11. The extent to which any cost reductions are actually realized will depend upon the way that the MRA is implemented. Initial suggestions are that the amount of effort being devoted to implementation is considerably less than the amount of energy devoted to negotiation.
12. Origin rules are present in the EU–Switzerland MRA. Baldwin (2000) quotes sources suggesting that the EU sought to have rules of origin in the MRA with the US. The US, however, resisted not on the grounds of discrimination against other trading countries but on the grounds of the practicality of identifying the country of origin for sophisticated industrial products.
13. If ratified, the Treaty of Nice, agreed at the European Council meeting of December 2000, will allow for qualified majority voting, rather than unanimity, for trade in a range of services with exceptions in the areas of culture and audio-visual services. This will facilitate the role of the Commission in defining external trade policies in this area.
14. See House of Lords (2000) Appendix 4.
15. There is one area, export credit agencies, where national competence has not been relinquished.
16. For example, a very large proportion of Moldovan exports to the EU comprises apple juice. Poland is also a major producer of apple juice. After accession Polish producers will enjoy a more than 20 per cent margin of preference in the EU market relative to Moldovan producers. It is most likely that the accession of Poland will lead to trade diversion away from Moldovan producers.

REFERENCES

Auboin, M. and S. Laird (1999), 'How important are trade defence measures and non-tariff barriers for LDCs – with particular emphasis on those of the EU?', in O. Memdovic, A. Kuyvenhoven and W. Molle (eds) *Multilateralism and Regionalism in the Post-Uruguay Round Era: What Role for the EU?*, Boston, MA: Kluwer.

Baldwin, R. (2000), 'Regulatory protectionism, developing nations and a two-tier world trade system', mimeo, Graduate School of International Studies, Geneva.

Barth, D. (1999), 'The prospects of international trade in services', study for the European Commission, Brussels, http://europa.eu.int/comm/trade/pdf/study_m1.pdf

Brenton, P. (1999), 'Trade policies in Moldova and the EU: implications for a free trade agreement', study prepared under the TACIS programme of the European Commission, mimeo, Centre for European Policy Studies, Brussels.

Brenton, P.A. (2001) Anti-dumping policies in the EU and trade diversion, *European Journal of Political Economy*, 17, 593–607.

Brenton, P.A. and D. Gros (1997), 'Trade reorientation and recovery in transition economies', *Oxford Review of Economic Policy*, 13, 65–76.

Brenton, P. and J. Nunez-Ferrer (forthcoming), 'EU agriculture, enlargement and the WTO', in S. Bilal and P. Pezaros (eds), *Agricultural Trade and the 'Millennium' WTO Round*, London: Kluwer.

CEC (1998), 'Technical barriers to trade', Volume 1 of Subseries III Dismantling of Barriers of *The Single Market Review*, Luxembourg: CEC.

CEC (1999), 'Economic reform: report on the functioning of community product and capital markets', Communication from the Commission to the Council, 20 January. http://europa.eu.int/comm/internal_market/en/update/econ/cardiffen.htm

Clausing, K. (2000), 'The international trade of multinational firms: the empirical behaviour of intrafirm trade in a gravity equation model', Working Document 147, Centre for European Policy Studies, Brussels, June.

Hoekman, B. (1995), 'Tentative first steps: an assessment of the Uruguay Round Agreement on services', Discussion Paper 1150, CEPR, London.

Hoekman, B. and C.A. Primo Braga (1997), 'Protection and trade in services', Policy Research Paper 1747, World Bank, Washington.

Hoekman, B., M. Schiff and L.A. Winters (1998), 'Regionalism and development: main messages from recent World Bank research', World Bank, Washington.

House of Lords (2000), Select Committee on European Communities: Tenth Report, www.parliament.the-stationery-office.co.uk/pa/ld199900/ldselect/ldeucom/76/7613.htm

Hummels, D., J. Ishii and K. Yi (1999), 'The nature and growth of vertical specialization in world trade', Staff Report 72, Federal Reserve Bank of New York.

Mathis, J.H. (1998), 'Mutual recognition agreements – transatlantic parties and the limits to non-tariff barrier regionalism in the WTO', *Journal of World Trade*, 32, 5–32.

Messerlin, P. (1989), 'The EC antidumping regulations: a first economic appraisal, 1980–1985', *Weltwirtschaftliches Archiv*, 125, 563–87.

Pelkmans, J. (1987), 'The new approach to technical harmonization and standardization', *Journal of Common Market Studies*, 25, 249–69.

Pelkmans, J. (1997), *European Integration: Methods and Economic Analysis*, Harlow: Longman.

Pelkmans, J. and P. Brenton (1999), 'Bilateral trade agreements with the EU: driving forces and effects', in O. Memdovic, A. Kuyvenhoven and W. Molle (eds), *Multilateralism and Regionalism in the Post-Uruguay Round Era: What Role for the EU?*, Boston, MA: Kluwer.

Prusa, T. (1997), 'The trade effects of US anti-dumping actions', in R. Feenstra (ed.), *The Effects of US Trade Protection and Trade Promotion Policies*, Cambridge, MA: National Bureau of Economic Research.

Sapir, A. (1998), 'The political economy of EC regionalism', *European Economic Review*, 42, 717–32.

Swann, D. (1992), *The Economics of the Common Market*, London: Penguin.

TDI (1999), 'Study on trade policy in south east Europe', prepared for Department for International Development, London.

WTO (1997), *Trade Policy Review of the European Communities*, Geneva: WTO.

9. Macroeconomic management in the European Union

Ray Barrell and Nigel Pain[*]

Over the 1990s there were significant changes in the structure of governance and the framework for macroeconomic management in the European Union. The Single Market Programme has significantly fostered economic integration by reducing barriers to product market access and capital market constraints. The euro has been successfully introduced and a new institution, the European Central Bank, has been established with a clear mandate to pursue a stability-oriented monetary policy. Preparations for Monetary Union led to the establishment of a comprehensive framework for the coordination of economic policies and encouraged national governments to undertake significant fiscal consolidation in order to establish and maintain sound public finances in the medium term. All these developments affect both the policies available to undertake macroeconomic management and the impact of macroeconomic policies on the European economy.

The EU member states now face some important policy challenges. Those countries inside the euro area have to adjust to the loss of sovereign monetary policies and a new framework that also places limits on their freedom to vary fiscal policies. Countries outside Monetary Union have to evaluate carefully the costs and benefits of retaining their national currencies. Greater mobility of capital also impacts on policy choices, and some forms of taxes may now face *de facto* harmonization, even though there remains *de jure* independence. New institutions have to become established and in many cases their ability to respond effectively to potential problems has yet to be tested. The new policy framework raises issues about the coordination of fiscal and monetary policies and the effectiveness of the surveillance procedures in place to monitor developments. In an environment with increasing constraints on national macroeconomic policies, microeconomic reforms can also be an important

[*] We are grateful to Gavin Boyd, Paul Brenton, Thomas Brewer, Bill Emmons and Pier Carlo Padoan for helpful comments and suggestions and to the UK Economic and Social Research Council for financial support (grant number L138251022). We would also like to acknowledge the contribution of Karen Dury to the joint work on which some of the material in this paper is based.

means of pursuing macroeconomic objectives such as reducing economic volatility and improving welfare. Reforms to national labour markets may have a particularly important role to play.

We attempt to discuss all of these issues in this chapter. We begin by comparing the macroeconomic performance of the European Union with that of the United States over the 1970s, 1980s and 1990s. This section emphasizes that the process of convergence in living standards between the two regions appears to have come to an end in recent years. Economic growth has been slower in Europe than in the US, and labour market impediments appear to have held back productive potential. We then go on to discuss the evolution of monetary and fiscal frameworks, the new structures that are in place and the challenges they face. These frameworks have to be evaluated within the context discussed in the next section which looks at EU institutional structure and sur-veillance procedures, and in particular at the coordination of policies within the new 'constitutional' structure. Given the constraints on macroeconomic policy, some of which have been in places in some countries since the early 1980s, other policies have to be used to address the medium-term evolution of unemployment and employment. We turn to these in the following section which discusses labour markets policies and the new employment-related National Action Plans. In a world of declining barriers and increasing integra-tion it is also important to take account of these factors in assessing the macroeconomic framework, as we do in the next section which discusses capital mobility, location and their implications for policy in Europe.

MACROECONOMIC PERFORMANCE IN THE EU AND THE US

The macroeconomic performance of the European Union in the 1990s was dis-appointing, both in comparison with the past and with the United States. Perhaps the clearest indication of this is provided by per capita incomes in the United States and the EU, measured using purchasing power parities. Per capita incomes in the EU are presently around 70 per cent of those in the US, much as they were at the start of the 1990s. The figures shown in Figure 9.1 indicate that the long-standing process of gradual convergence in living standards appears to have come to an end. A key question for policy-makers in the EU is to understand why this has happened. Some potential explanations are revealed by the other two series in Figure 9.1. These show comparative figures for output per employee in the EU and output per employee hour. There is much less evidence that convergence has ended using either of these measures.

——— Per capita ········· Per employed person ----- Per working hour

Figure 9.1   European Union GDP at current prices and current PPPs (USA = 100)

To understand the differences in these series, it is useful to decompose output per capita as follows. Letting Y denote GDP (at constant prices), and P population:

$$\frac{Y}{P} = \frac{L}{P} * \frac{E}{L} * \frac{Y}{EH} * H \tag{1}$$

where L represents the labour force, E denotes the number of employees and H hours worked per employee. In terms of output per employee hour (Y/EH) there is now little difference between the EU as a whole and the US, whereas back in 1970 the EU level was only about 60 per cent of that in the US. The gap between the EU and the US begins to widen once measured in terms of output per employee ($[Y/EH]^*H$), reflecting the fact that the average employee in the United States works for more hours a year than the average European. Of course this may not be of any concern if it just reflects a conscious choice to consume more leisure in Europe.

Comparing output per capita with output per employee it is clear that other differences in labour markets matter a great deal. Labour-force participation is lower in Europe than it is in the United States, as is the employment rate. In 1998 73.8 per cent of the working-age population (ages 15–64) were in work in the US, compared to 61.5 per cent in the EU (OECD Employment Outlook, 2000). Indeed it is possible that the high level of output per employee hour in Europe can in part be explained by the lower employment rate and the corresponding likelihood that those members of the labour-force with comparatively few skills, and hence lower productivity, are not in work.

The differences in labour market outcomes in Europe and the US are also shown clearly in Table 9.1. The average annual rate of labour productivity growth in the EU has been consistently higher than in the US, at least until the recent past, but employment growth has been consistently stronger in the US. The unemployment rate rose significantly in both regions in the late 1970s, but whereas it has subsequently fallen back in the United States towards the levels seen in the 1960s, it averaged over 10 per cent in the EU during the 1990s. Inflation, as measured by the GDP deflator, has clearly moderated in the EU since the early 1990s, but economic growth has been disappointing in this period, with little sign in Europe of the favourable economic conditions in the United States spurred by the wave of investment in information and communication technologies (Commerce Department, 2000).

Table 9.1   *European Union macroeconomic performance (annual average growth rates, %, except unemployment, % pts)*

	1961–73	1974–85	1986–90	1991–95	1996–99
Real GDP					
EU (15)	4.8	2.0	3.2	1.5	2.3
Euro area	5.2	2.1	3.3	1.5	2.3
USA	4.4	2.8	3.3	2.4	4.2
GDP deflator					
EU (15)	5.2	10.6	5.0	3.8	1.9
Euro area	5.2	10.0	4.4	3.6	1.7
USA	3.3	6.7	3.3	2.5	1.5
Labour productivity					
EU (15)	4.4	2.0	1.8	1.9	1.3
Euro area	4.8	2.2	1.9	1.8	1.3
USA	2.3	1.0	1.0	1.3	2.2
Employment					
EU (15)	0.4	0.0	1.4	–0.4	1.0
Euro area	0.4	0.0	1.4	–0.3	0.9
USA	2.0	1.8	2.2	1.1	1.9
Unemployment rate					
EU (15)	2.4	6.4	8.9	10.0	10.2
Euro area	2.5	6.6	9.3	10.2	11.0
USA	4.6	7.5	5.9	6.6	4.8

Source: European Commission Economic Forecasts, Spring 2000.

Convergence across Countries and Sub-National Regions

There were several reasons why catching up was particularly rapid in the early post-war period in Europe. Liberalization of intra-European trade was particularly beneficial (Ben-David, 1993) and particularly rapid. The transfer and adaptation of American technologies to European conditions was aided both by the rapid spread of US multinationals in the area and also by conscious attempts to ensure that diffusion of best-practice US technology took place as part of the reconstruction of post-war Europe (Crafts and Toniolo, 1996). There were also abundant human resources, with education levels and human capital being well in advance of the level of available physical capital in most European economies in 1950. The post-war phase of European growth, at least until the 1970s, was rapid by historical standards, and there was a relatively clear tendency for countries with lower initial incomes to grow more rapidly than richer ones (beta convergence), as is documented by UNECE (2000). However it is clear that initial conditions explain much less of the cross-sectional cross-country variation in economic growth after 1973. There is also evidence that the dispersion of per capita incomes has declined in the post-war period (sigma convergence). In 1950 only two countries in Western Europe had a per capita income within 10 per cent of the median, and the maximum per capita income was 5½ times the minimum. By 1998 there were ten countries within 10 per cent of the median and the range was only fourfold (UNECE, 2000, Table 5.3.9).

However, the relative successes and failures of this period make it clear that initial conditions mattered a lot and there were aspects of 'social capability' (Abramovitz, 1986) and national institutional structures that had a significant influence on the success of countries. This can be seen from Figure 9.2, which shows national GDP per capita relative to the EU for 14 EU member states in 1973 and 1998. In 1973 four of the peripheral economies – Ireland, Greece, Spain and Portugal – had per capita incomes well below the average in the EU as a whole.[1] Two other countries, Italy and Finland, had incomes 5 per cent or so below the average. Progress in convergence has been very uneven since 1973. Spain and Portugal have made modest gains, Ireland has experienced rapid improvements, whilst Greece has stagnated. These differences suggest that there is more to the growth process than simply lags in the diffusion of technology. In the case of Ireland, the rapid growth seen over the 1980s and 1990s reflects the favourable impact of a wide range of factors, notably the growth of inward investment and the expansion in the supply and quality of labour as a result of in-migration and long-term reforms to improve educational standards.

A further aspect of convergence is related to developments in individual regions of the EU. The available evidence suggests that economic activity is much less dispersed in the EU than it is in the United States, possibly reflecting

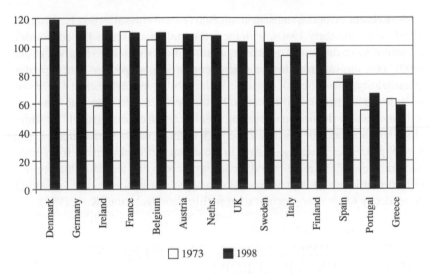

Figure 9.2   Real GDP per capita (EU = 100)

the extent to which national borders and barriers to market access have prevented industries producing tradeable goods and services from concentrating in single locations. Table 9.2 reports coefficients of variation for GDP and GDP per capita across 49 US states and 50 EU NUTS1 regions. GDP is clearly more concentrated across the US states, as shown by the higher coefficient of variation, but despite this, regional GDP is less concentrated than in the EU, reflecting a much higher level of labour mobility in the US. The data indicate that regional dispersions widened in Europe in the first half of the 1990s, helping to explain why industrial policies to reduce regional disparities have recently been given greater emphasis in many countries.

Table 9.2   Dispersion of GDP and GDP per capita in US states and 50 EU regions (coefficient of variation)

| | GDP | | GDP per capita | |
	US	EU	US	EU
1978	1.136	0.850	0.175	0.327
1990	1.220	0.801	0.185	0.229
1995	1.136	0.849	0.158	0.302

Source: CEPR (2000, Table 1.1)

More recent evidence suggests that geographical specialization has risen in the EU since the early 1980s, with the industrial structures of EU economies becoming more dissimilar over time, albeit slowly (Midelfart-Knarvik et al., 2000). This has implications for macroeconomic management, since greater specialization raises the risk of greater vulnerability in sub-national regions or countries to industry-specific shocks. However it is fair to point out that most of the available evidence on increasing specialization concerns manufacturing, which now accounts for less than 25 per cent of total GDP in most countries. The general process of structural change in the composition of demand from manufacturing towards location-bound service sector activities tends to make regions with similar levels of income have similar levels of concentration, offsetting the tendency for greater specialization within manufacturing (Kim, 1997).

THE EVOLUTION OF MONETARY AND FISCAL ARRANGEMENTS IN EUROPE.

The Transition to Monetary Union

The formation of the EMU in January 1999 was the end point of a process of convergence of inflation, fiscal consolidation and exchange realignment. The process started with the formation of the Exchange Rate Mechanism (ERM) in 1978. The initial participants in the ERM set themselves the objective of minimizing currency realignments and hence coordinating monetary policy. Initially realignments were common, but as policies converged and barriers to the movement of capital were removed they became less necessary and less productive. From 1987 the ERM became 'hard' and realignments less common, and inflation rates began to converge in Europe. However, a union of different countries with a common exchange rate and a common inflation rate may not be sustainable if real exchange rates are not sustainable, or if the system is hit by external shocks that it cannot absorb.

Problems with the ERM began to emerge in the early 1990s just after it looked as if the system would succeed in its objective of delivering a smooth transition to Monetary Union in Europe. Monetary policy in the ERM was led by the Bundesbank which had the clear objective of targeting and controlling inflation in Germany. It had been successful in doing this, and convergence in the ERM was designed to copy this success. However, in 1990 two unrelated events built in strong internal pressure. The UK joined the ERM at a level which was widely felt to be 20–25 per cent above the long-run sustainable level (Wren-Lewis et al., 1991). This could have course have been removed at a fixed nominal exchange rate if UK inflation had been below that of its partners for some years. However, this outcome seemed unlikely given the slow speed of reaction in labour markets, and the required deflation would have produced a significant recession. The systemic problems of the ERM were worsened by the expansionary effects of German unification and the Bundesbank's tightening of monetary policy in response.[2] The increase in interest rates that was needed to control German inflation along with the consequent rise in the exchange rate put deflationary pressures on a number of ERM members, and by the summer of 1992 pressure on the system became intense. A large-scale realignment took place in September 1992, with the UK dropping out of the system and Italy and Spain eventually devaluing significantly.

This crisis made the formation of a Monetary Union look problematic, but the Treaty on European Union (commonly termed the Maastricht Treaty), agreed in 1991 and signed in 1992 laid sound foundations. The commitment to the goal of Monetary Union remained high in much of Europe, helping to enforce macroeconomic discipline. The treaty set targets for government budget deficits and debt stocks in the run-up to a potential EMU, with deficits required to fall below 3 per cent of GDP, and debt stocks to be on a path that would ultimately bring them below 60 per cent of GDP. In addition inflation had to converge so that with potential members it would be at a rate no more than 1.5 percentage points of the three 'best' performers. There were also clear rules on interest rate convergence, and membership of ERM was essential. At first it looked as if the treaty targets would be hard to meet, particularly for countries such as Spain, Italy, Portugal, Finland and the UK who had histories of comparatively high inflation. Between 1985 and 1995 interest rates in the 'core' ERM countries (Germany, France, Belgium, the Netherlands and Austria) were around 4–4.5 percentage points below those in other ERM members. But monetary policy convergence was rapid after 1995, as can be seen from Figure 9.3, helped in part by the endogenous adjustments of long-term interest rates as financial markets reached a collective judgement that the political impetus was such that monetary union would begin irrespective of whether all the economic criteria for membership were fully met.

Improved macroeconomic management, in particular fiscal consolidation, along with reforms to labour and product markets also helped to ease inflationary pressures in countries such as Italy and Spain by the mid-1990s. Fiscal deficits and debts have dropped, but much more remains to be done. As can be seen from Table 9.3, general government debt continued to rise in what would ultimately be the euro area after the Maastricht Treaty was signed, and fiscal consolidation was relatively slow even after that date. However, by 1998 the putative members of EMU had all achieved the deficit target, albeit sometimes quite narrowly, as in the case of Germany and France. The out-turn for the deficit in 1996–99 was better than it had been, but definitely worse than had been expected at the time the treaty had been drawn up. As a result, the

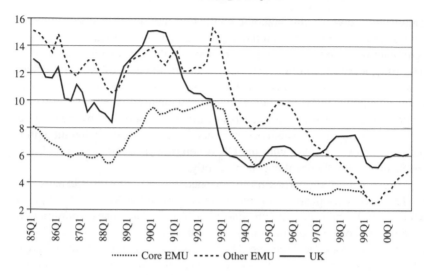

Figure 9.3　Three-month interbank rates 1985Q1–2000Q4 (%)

Table 9.3　Fiscal trends in Europe (% of GDP, annual averages)

	1970–73	1974–85	1986–90	1991–95	1996–99
General government expenditure					
EU (15)	37.1	45.6	47.7	50.2	48.5
Euro area	36.8	45.5	48.6	50.7	49.4
USA	30.6	32.9	34.9	35.4	33.2
General government receipts					
EU (15)	36.9	41.9	44.5	45.0	46.3
Euro area	36.1	41.6	44.5	45.8	46.8
USA	29.0	29.7	30.7	30.8	32.5
General government fiscal balance					
EU (15)	–0.3	–3.7	–3.3	–5.1	–2.2
Euro area	–0.7	–3.9	–4.1	–4.9	–2.6
USA	–1.6	–3.3	–4.2	–4.5	–0.6
General government gross debt (end year)					
EU (15)	36.5	52.9	54.4	69.5	67.6
Euro area	30.2	51.8	58.0	71.4	72.3
USA	39.2	53.5	60.9	68.3	59.3

Source:　European Economy Supplement A, No 1/2, April 2000.

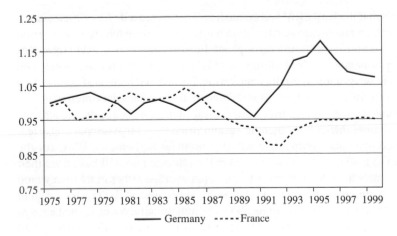

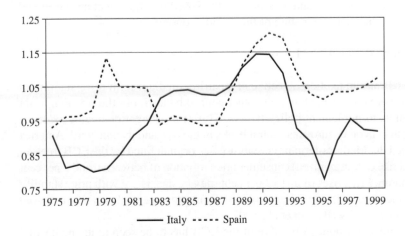

Figure 9.4   Real effective exchange rates vs euro area (1980–89 = 1.0, whole economy unit labour costs)

Amsterdam Treaty of 1998 introduced a new set of guidelines embedded in the Stability and Growth Pact. These were designed to eliminate deficits, and ensure that budgets were balanced over the cycle. As a result of this treaty both the monetary and fiscal frameworks in the euro area were new at the formation of the EMU in January 1999.

The euro area was established after a period of real exchange rate convergence and stabilization, as can be seen from Figure 9.4. This resulted in part from the realignments of 1992 and 1993, which removed many of the deeper problems that the hard ERM had created, and generated a *de facto* appreciation in the German real exchange rate. These realignments were followed by a period of low and similar inflation throughout Europe, and hence exchange rates remained sustainable. In addition, new labour market reforms, along with increasing integration in product markets in Europe and increased competitive pressures from globalization, all acted to constrain inflationary pressures.

If countries with strong trade and capital market links fix their exchange rates it is more difficult for them to sustain price levels that are not consistent in a more open and competitive world. Countries that entered EMU (or the build up to EMU) with an overvalued real exchange rate will have seen their inflation rates held down below the euro area average rather more than would have been anticipated from past relationships, because of the greater freedom of capital to move to lower-cost locations. Symmetrically, countries that entered undervalued would find that the pressure to remove this discrepancy had increased. The process of adjustment of price levels in Europe was relatively rapid in the late 1990s and in 2000, and the speed of adjustment has depended in part on the changing nature of the world economy.

Monetary Policy in the Euro Area

The ECB has an explicit objective of ensuring medium-term price stability in the euro area. In contrast to most other central banks it has the freedom to set as well as to implement policy targets. This is a stronger degree of independence than in other euro area central banks in the past and than in North America and the UK. Medium-term price stability has been defined by the ECB to be an annual rate of (harmonized) consumer price inflation of between 0 and 2 per cent per annum. Price rises of up to 2 per cent may be consistent with price stability given the expected, but difficult to measure, improvements that can be achieved in product quality (Boskin et al., 1997).

The monetary policy objective of the ECB has to be seen in its intellectual and institutional context. The ECB is the intentional heir to the Bundesbank, which was the most successful major central bank in the post-Bretton Woods era, keeping inflation lower and less variable than either the Bank of England or the Federal Reserve. The Bundesbank was one of the core institutions in the post-war German constitution, and its objective was set as maintaining price stability. The importance of price stability was stressed by German Ordoliberals in the construction of the post-war consensus (Barrell and Duty, 2000) and price-level stability has for many years been a central part of the contract between state and society in Germany. The ECB has inherited this remit, with the goal of enabling long-term contracts in the private sector to be written in nominal terms without significant real risks to one party or the other. The ECB is a new institution which has to build its reputation, unlike the Bundesbank, and hence it has felt a need to be clearer about its strategy than its predecessor had been.

The monetary policy strategy followed by the ECB has two broad pillars – a reference value for broad money growth and a broadly-based assessment of the outlook for price developments. The reference value for annual monetary growth has been 4.5 per cent per annum since the inception of the euro, reflecting the medium-term target for inflation, plus an estimated long-term trend decline in the velocity of circulation of 0.5–1 per cent per annum and trend GDP growth of 2–2.5 per cent per annum. The two-pillar strategy has sometimes been criticized for a lack of clarity (Allsopp and Vines, 1998), with confusion over the weights given to the different pillars and confusion over whether the ECB is targeting inflation, prices or monetary growth.

Some of this criticism is misplaced. The ECB has a completely new targeting structure, and a different set of tasks from its predecessors. For almost two decades the members of EMU had been increasingly linked to the Deutschemark (both in number and firmness), but the core central bank, the Bundesbank, had a remit only to maintain price stability in Germany. This created tensions within the fixed, but adjustable, system of exchange rates maintained in the ERM, particularly when Germany was subject to asymmetric shocks, such as unification in 1990. The ECB has a similar remit for the euro area, but it has not built up the understandings with financial markets and labour markets that ensured the Bundesbank could operate effectively (Soskice, 1990). Given that the ultimate objective is one of maintaining price stability in the medium term, the monetary aggregate must not be seen as an end in itself, but rather as an intermediate indicator that gives information of the ultimate target, the trajectory for the price level (Niehans, 1980).

The ECB can be described as taking account of two broad issues: the evolution of nominal aggregates in the medium term and the emergence of inflationary and deflationary pressures in the short term. The evolution of short-term interest rates and the workings of different policy regimes may be usefully evaluated using a simple feedback rule of the form:

$$r = \gamma_1 \lfloor (p_t y_t) - (p_t y_t)^* \rfloor + \gamma_2 [\pi_{t+i} - \pi_{t+i}^*] \tag{2}$$

where r denotes the nominal interest rate, p_t and y_t are the (log) price level and output level at time t, π denotes the inflation rate and an * denotes a target variable. We use nominal GDP in (2) since a detrended nominal broad monetary aggregate can be expected to move in line with it in the medium term. In the short term the feedback is more likely to be on the deviation of inflation from target, as represented by the second term and the second pillar of the ECB strategy. Policy can feed back on the deviation of current inflation ($i=0$) or expected inflation from target. In a regime of pure inflation targeting such as that presently followed in Canada, Sweden and the UK, $\gamma_1=0$.

An alternative formulation of (2) helps to clarify what role the output gap might play in monetary policy decisions:

$$r = \gamma_{11}\lfloor p_t - p_t^* \rfloor + \gamma_{12}\lfloor y_t - y_t^* \rfloor + \gamma_2\lfloor \pi_{t+i} - \pi_{t+i}^* \rfloor \tag{3}$$

The first term in (2) can be split into a feedback on the difference between output and target and a feedback on the difference between the price level and the target price level. If the two feedback coefficients are the same, then in almost all circumstances the response of the authorities would be the same as in (2). However, writing the feedback in the alternative form highlights the potential importance of the accommodation of changes in equilibrium output and provides a clearer focus on the role of price level stability in the medium term.

Policies that raise potential output, such as labour market reforms that raise employability, or supply-side measures that encourage innovation and entrepreneurship should, other things being equal, be reflected in lower interest rates for any given level of current activity. This simply reflects the fact that the economy can for a period grow more rapidly than it previously could without generating significant inflationary pressures. In the United States in the late 1990s the Federal Reserve has clearly acted to accommodate the higher level of output made possible by the gradual development of ICTs, by holding short-term interest rates at a level lower than they might otherwise have been expected to be at when unemployment had fallen to its lowest level for 30 years. Of course monetary policy cannot indefinitely prevent a higher level of potential output from being achieved, but a failure on the part of the monetary authorities to recognize that a higher level of potential output is now possible will not be without significant short-term costs.

There are important distinctions between a regime with a pure inflation target and one with the medium-term objective of price stability. Inflation targeting can build in long-run price-level drift in response to a shock such as an increase in the oil price, and hence breaks the long-term contract between state and society. A price-level target puts mean reversion into the long-run price determination process. Nominal or price-level targeting is a very useful position in periods of low inflation (Gaspar and Smets, 2000) as inflationary shocks can be negative and can lead to liquidity traps and deflationary spirals where output stays below capacity. Price-level targeting supports inflation expectations and holds up demand in a world with forward-looking, rational agents. The economies of Europe are more inertial than the US, and hence the choice of policy framework becomes a more significant factor in determining the outcome to shocks (Barrell and Dury, 2000a). The stronger the degree of nominal inertia the more price-level targeting stabilizes output and inflation.

Given that the remit of the ECB is to maintain price stability in the medium term and it plans to keep inflation within a specified range whilst doing so, it has to pay specific attention to exchange rate developments. If the exchange rate falls, even in a relatively closed economy, then there could be inflationary consequences unless there are good structural reasons for the fall. If the monetary authority sticks to a long-term target for the price level then this will be reversed in the longer term, but perhaps only with a large downward swing in inflation. Hence the ECB cannot ignore the exchange rate even when it is concerned only with domestic issues.

However, it has no constitutional right to a unilateral exchange rate policy (even if that could be separated fully from monetary policy) as powers over the exchange rate have been allocated to the Council of Finance Ministers, as we discuss below. There is no clear evidence that intervention has much impact unless accompanied by strong changes in monetary policy. The ECB has had a difficult path to follow in the first two years of monetary union, with the euro depreciating sharply and inflationary pressures building up during 2000. It is, however, clear that the ECB will and should eschew competitive devaluation as a policy, even if this might bring substantial and perhaps permanent gains through the relocation of FDI toward a temporarily over-competitive euro area economy.

There are many other difficult issues that the ECB needs to address. Structural changes in money markets can affect monetary developments. The size of the euro area means that the euro has automatically become an important international reserve currency. Increasing capital market integration in Europe resulting from the Single Market Programme might also be expected to affect the demand for money, much as financial innovation did in the UK and the US in the 1980s. Both these factors make it difficult to interpret short-term monetary developments, and have made it necessary for the ECB to rely more heavily on the evaluation of medium-term prospects from current inflationary developments and on projections of inflation and growth in the euro area.

The increasing integration of capital markets across the EU as a whole also means that euro area monetary policy cannot be separated entirely from national banking developments, including those outside the euro area, even though the ECB does not have any general responsibility for the stability of the financial system. Financial supervision has been separated off from the System of European Central Banks and is largely in the hands of the financial regulators in each individual country. However, monetary stability and the prospects for inflation and deflation cannot be separated, as the example of the US recession between 1929 and 1933 makes clear. At some point the ECB may be compelled to intervene in financial regulation in order to ensure price stability is maintained. This is a potential tension within the new macroeconomic arrangements which has yet to be tested at the time of writing.

In a Monetary Union persistent inflation differentials could easily undermine the competitiveness of high-inflation countries, weaken growth and push up their unemployment. Hence in some circumstances the Single Monetary Policy may be too tight for some countries and too loose for others. Policy-makers in high inflation countries may have to deal with this problem through a tighter fiscal policy and/or structural reforms designed to increase labour market flexibility and improve productivity. At the end of 2000 the euro area economies had inflation rates that varied between 1 and 5 per cent. This might be seen as worrying for the ECB, as countries could be seen as diverging in a way that cannot be contained because of the lack of national monetary policy instruments. But there are situations in which inflation differentials may not be only sustainable but, to a given extent, even desirable and so may not be a concern for the policy-makers. Differences in price levels and inflation rates are not necessarily a problem within an integrated area if, for instance, higher inflation rates are experienced by countries with lower initial price levels. Inflation differentials may reflect not only different cyclical positions but also structural differences among countries that will take longer to be reduced.

Economic convergence is not yet complete in the euro area, as is clear from the discussion above in section on 'Macroeconomic Performance in the EU and the US'. Some countries, such as Italy and Ireland, appear to have entered Monetary Union with comparatively lower real exchange rates compared to past experience, whilst others with lower initial per capita incomes, such as Spain and Portugal, can be expected to have stronger rates of medium-term growth. In both cases divergence of their national inflation rates from the average for the euro area as a whole can be compatible with long-term convergence.

Price levels and output per person hour are related, with lower-productivity countries having lower wages and hence lower costs in service provision and a lower overall price level. There is no fundamental reason why productivity levels in countries with lower per capita incomes should not ultimately converge to the EU average, and hence their price levels can be expected to converge also. The so-called Balassa–Samuelson effect means that some real exchange rate appreciation, measured using relative consumer prices, should be expected to occur in countries with faster rates of productivity growth in their traded goods sectors. Higher productivity growth will mean higher wage growth. As productivity tends to be low in non-tradeable sectors (typically services), any spillover of these wage increases from tradeable to non-tradeable sectors results in a relatively high average rate of consumer price inflation in the lower-income countries. This does not affect the competitiveness of producers in tradeable sectors because they are able to enjoy the benefits of higher productivity.

The ECB has to weigh up developments of this kind in formulating its monetary policy judgements. A medium-term target of, say 1.5 per cent for euro area inflation means that some countries will have inflation of 2–2.5 per cent, and others, including those such as Germany and France that account for a relatively large share of the euro area, will have inflation of 1–1.25 per cent. There is no reason at all to conclude that for the next few years it would be optimal for all member states to have the same inflation rate. However, we would gauge the allowance for Balassa–Samuelson effects should not be larger than about half a percentage point on aggregate consumer price inflation in the euro area.

The new system does appear to be relatively successful, and it has clearly developed some credibility, at least amongst financial market participants. Although inflation in the euro area rose above the medium-term target ceiling of 2 per cent during the course of 2000, the evidence suggests that financial markets continue to have confidence in the ability of the ECB to achieve medium-term price stability. One means of estimating long-term inflationary expectations in the euro area is to examine the difference between the yield on the ten-year nominal government bonds and inflation-indexed bonds issued by the French government. The break-even inflation rate over 1999 and 2000 is shown in Figure 9.5. Inflation expectations remain below 2 per cent, even though they have risen since the start of monetary union.

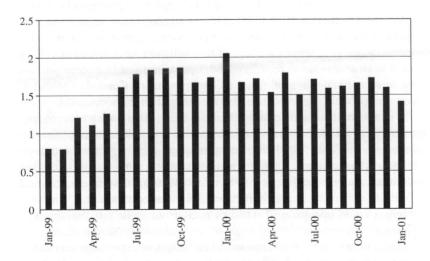

Figure 9.5   Break-even inflation rates on French 10-Year Index-Linked Bonds (per cent)

Fiscal Policy

Although monetary union has been established in Europe without a full fiscal or political union, there are important constraints on budgetary behaviour arising from the Stability and Growth Pact (SGP). The SGP extends the fiscal rules previously embodied in the Maastricht Treaty by requiring all the members of the euro area to adopt a medium-term objective of achieving budgets close to balance or in surplus. The pact is underpinned by an 'excessive deficit procedure' involving surveillance and possible penalties. A general government budget deficit above 3 per cent of GDP is considered excessive unless the European Commission judges it to be temporary, and likely to last for only a year, and there are special circumstances. Exemption is granted automatically if there is an annual fall in output of more than 2 per cent, an event experienced only by Finland and two non-participants – the UK and Sweden – in the last 40 years. Exemption may also be granted if there is a fall in output between 0.75 per cent and 2 per cent. A failure to take corrective action to deal with a deficit judged to be excessive will lead to the imposition of financial sanctions.[3]

To date all the euro area countries have succeeded in holding their budget deficits under 3 per cent of GDP and so it remains an open question whether the pact will prove to be an effective and sensible means of preventing excessive fiscal deficits. Its operation is discussed in Dury and Pina (2000) who suggest that if the medium-term guidelines for budget deficits are actually achieved, breaches of the pact will be extremely rare. At present the problems facing the pact and policy-makers in Europe is that it puts no constraints on countries such as Ireland who are running significant public sector surpluses whilst operating their economies at or above capacity. In this situation a cut in taxes might be deemed to be as unwise as breaching the 3 per cent floor in a recession, but under current arrangements all that the Commission and Council of Ministers can do is to publicly suggest to the Irish that they should not cut taxes.

One of the most common criticisms of the SGP is that it may prevent governments from making full use of fiscal stabilization policies in an economic downturn, as the 3 per cent ceiling may curtail the workings of the automatic stabilizers in the economy. There are a number of ways in which this criticism can be evaluated. Buti and Sapir (1998) undertake some descriptive statistical analyses based on historical evidence. They suggest that the European economies could operate well within the SGP guidelines if they broadly followed a balanced budget, although some, such as the Nordic economics, should aim for a surplus. Estimates based on historical experience may not be the best guide to the future, however. The Nordic economies exhibited volatile business cycles through the 1970s and 1980s and into the early 1990s because they went through a sequence of booms and downturns induced by currency devaluations. This is much less likely in the future given current monetary policy commitments in Finland, Denmark and Sweden.

Barrell and Dury (2000a) present extensive results on fiscal issues and summarize recent analyses in a number of papers using stochastic simulations on the Global Econometric Model NiGEM maintained by the National Institute of Economic and Social Research.[4] These papers calculate the probabilities of breaching the SGP in differing ways, but all conclude that the targets for budget deficits announced in the latest Stability and Convergence Programmes presented by member states are compatible with the automatic stabilizers continuing to work freely and that they could cope well in stabilizing the economy given a variety of shocks. Clearly the closer to zero the target deficit is, the easier it would be for the fiscal stabilizers to work. Barrell and Dury (2001) calculate the target deficit required for there to be only a 1 per cent chance of exceeding the 3 per cent ceiling, under the dual assumptions that the euro area economies face economic shocks similar to those experienced in the recent past and that monetary policy is operated successfully. In this particular set of circumstances it would be possible for most countries to have a target deficit greater than 1 per cent of GDP.[5] Other estimates imply that policy would have to be tighter than this (Buti and Martinot, 2000).

The results based on stochastic simulations have the advantage of being based on a model of the European economies that is designed to reflect the current and expected future structure of these economies with a policy environment that is a reasonable idealized description of the current framework. Estimates based solely on historical experience are open to the criticism of not taking account of structural changes in the economy and in policy regimes.

The SGP rules were introduced to prevent excessive deficits in a single state generating costs for all via their effects on interest rates, and clearly will act as an effective discipline on governments that need to undertake measures to improve their budgetary position. But the targets are arbitrary, much tighter than the objectives previously embodied in the Maastricht Treaty, and take little account of the particular needs of national economies. One of the key policy changes recommended in the BEPGs issued in 2000 was for member states to shift the structure of their public finances from consumption to investment expenditures. In the recent past public investment in infrastructure has been a prime target for budgetary cuts, despite the wider evidence that such a policy might reduce the potential for medium-term economic growth (Kneller et al., 1999). In some countries, such as the UK, the BEPGs also called for an expanded level of public investment, particularly in areas such as transport infrastructure.

Consideration needs to be given as to whether the requirements of the Stability and Growth Pact pose a constraint when there is an urgent need for higher public investment after years of underinvestment. The targets set out in the SGP have been useful in establishing a medium-term framework for public finances in Europe. The decision to put further constraints on the potential for public borrowing was clearly wise in the early period of construction of Monetary Union in Europe. However, in the medium term it may be necessary to discuss alternatives to the SGP, looking in particular at the sustainability of public finances in the European Union and at the role of the public sector in strengthening the prospects for output growth. It is not clear that the SGP is necessarily the best framework for these objectives.

Public sector infrastructure investment can be an important source of productivity growth, and there may be periods when it would be wise to raise public investment well above its current levels, for instance in a period of rapid technical change. At these times, it could be optimal to raise borrowing, rather than taxes, so that the costs of the increased investment could be shared by the generations who would benefit from it. The SGP as it stands could prevent this if the extra level of investment pushed national budgets into deficit, and hence it is possible that the SGP and the associated surveillance procedures may inadvertently reduce the level of public investment in Europe if they are implemented to the letter. The policy debate in Europe should consider whether the fiscal framework should evolve towards a position where public borrowing could, over the cycle, be justified in relation to public investment. This is currently the position in the UK, and in the past has been the case in countries such as Germany and the Netherlands (Barrell and Hubert, 1999).

However, there are good reasons for continuing to keep a close eye on the evolution of fiscal policy even if the targeting framework is changed to allow scope for more public investment. An effective, coordinated, monitoring process is required in order to ensure prudent fiscal policies in good times as well as bad times (Buti and Martinot, 2000). The 'close to balance' rule can also be seen as being designed to offset some of potential biases introduced into the budgetary system from politicians who find it difficult to ascertain the difference between a cyclical improvement in the public finances and a permanent one that results from the implementation of their policies. The target balance that is embedded in any European fiscal policy guidelines has to be set to take account of the asymmetric nature of the out-turns for the deficit. Experience suggests that governments find it difficult to run budgetary surpluses for a long time even when they are appropriate to the cyclical position. On this view a target tighter than strictly necessary would be appropriate as it would allow automatic stabilizers to work fully in recessions and allow some offset for bureaucratic laxity in upturns.

There are thus many issues to be considered in the surveillance of national countries' fiscal policies. We now turn to consider the design and influence of the mechanisms set up to undertake surveillance and coordinate economic policies.

POLICY COORDINATION AND SURVEILLANCE

The European Union has an unusual governance structure by the standards of other advanced economies, with responsibilities delegated to a wide range of bodies. Whilst the broad frameworks for monetary and fiscal policy are becoming clearer, there are a number of institutions that have responsibility for surveillance and coordination of the macroeconomic policy mix. In this section we review the respective roles of the Council of the European Union and the European Commission and highlight some of the potential difficulties that could arise from the complex decision-making process now in place. It is of course the case that the replication of established patterns of institutions from other regions, such as the United States, is not necessary for the conduct of successful policies. However, particular thought has to be given to the construction of a completely new structure, and it is not always clear that sufficient consideration has been given to this in Europe.

The Council of the European Union

The Council of the European Union is the Community's legislative body. It coordinates the general economic policies of the member states and concludes, on behalf of the Community, international agreements between the latter and one or more states or international organizations. The Council is composed of one representative at ministerial level from each member state, who is empowered to commit his government. Council members are politically accountable to their national parliaments. Meetings of the finance and economics ministers are known as ECOFIN.

ECOFIN plays a central role in macroeconomic management within the EU. It has issued annual Broad Economic Policy Guidelines for Member States since 1993 and is the main forum for undertaking surveillance decisions of national economic policies. Responsibility for exchange rate policy in the euro area is divided between the ECB and the Council, even though the ECB has sole responsibility for implementing monetary policy. (Exchange rate policy is solely a matter for national governments in the non-euro area members of the EU.) The Council has the right to enter into formal exchange rate arrangements after consultation with the Commission and the ECB and can, in exceptional circumstances, unilaterally provide general orientations for exchange rate policy. These powers have yet to be exercised, and so the extent to which there could be a clear conflict between the instructions issued by ECOFIN and the constitutional objective of the ECB to ensure price stability remains unknown. The ECB did participate in coordinated intervention to support the euro during the course of 2000, but this appears to have reflected a common judgement by the ECB and other central banks and finance ministers that the euro was in danger of becoming misaligned.

Where the Council acts as legislator, the right of initiative lies with the European Commission, which submits a proposal to the Council. The proposal is examined within the Council, which may amend it before adoption. In the acts which it adopts, the Council may confer implementing powers on the Commission. In many cases, including the internal market, Community legislation is adopted jointly by the Parliament and the Council under a 'co-decision' procedure. The European Community's budget is also approved by the European Parliament and by the Council.[6] Voting procedures vary. Depending on the case, the Council acts by a simple majority of its members, by a qualified majority, in which case at least eight countries have to agree, or unanimously. Matters of taxation and exchange rate arrangements require unanimity. Ministers of countries outside the euro area do not vote on matters relating to exchange rate policy or the application of sanctions under the Stability and Growth Pact.

Policy coordination in the euro area is also discussed at informal meetings of ministers of the euro area member states. Whilst it continues to be agreed that the ECOFIN Council should remain at the centre of the economic policy coordination and decision-making process, there are issues such as euro exchange rate developments, current account positions and capital market developments that are of more direct concern to participating member states. It is useful if the euro area governments can formulate common positions for discussions in international fora, but equally, there is obviously a danger that the views of the *de facto* Euro-12 Group over matters such as monetary and fiscal developments may differ from the judgements arrived at by the complete ECOFIN Council. Uncertainty about prospective macroeconomic policies is unlikely to enhance the prospects for sustained growth, and greater clarity about the role and influence of the informal euro area grouping is likely to be needed in the future.

The European Commission

This is the executive body of the EU and also has an important role in forming the overall macroeconomic environment. In most instances the Council of Ministers is unable to legislate unless there is a proposal from the Commission. The Commission has a central role in the preparation of surveillance decisions regarding the economic policies of member states, and has primary responsibility for operating competition policy, regulating the internal market and undertaking external trade negotiations. International openness and product market competition are both known to be important factors that can stimulate productivity growth and hence the macroeconomic prospects for the EU as a whole (Nickell, 1996; Hoeller et al., 1998).

The Commission has little role to play in stabilization policy at present. There is a small EU budget of just over 1 per cent of GDP, which is primarily spent on assistance to agriculture via the Common Agricultural Policy, and to less developed regions via the use of structural funds. Deficit financing is prohibited. It remains an open question whether the absence of fiscal federalism of the kind seen in the United States raises the costs from abolishing internal exchange rates within the euro area (OECD, 1999).

The Broad Economic Policy Guidelines

The Broad Economic Policy Guidelines (BEPGs) have a key role in the policy-making process, covering both macroeconomic and structural policies. Article 98 of the Treaty of the European Union requires member states to conduct their economic policies with a view to contributing to the achievement of the objectives of the Union and in the context of the Broad Economic Policy Guidelines. Article 99 of the treaty requires member states to regard their economic policies as a matter of common concern and to coordinate them within the Council of the European Union. It is important to note that this applies to all members of the EU, so that non-euro area governments still have to produce annual Stability and Convergence Programmes and face surveillance of their macroeconomic policies. Since the start of Stage 2 of Economic and Monetary Union, the Council of Finance Ministers has adopted new BEPGs each year, acting on a recommendation by the Commission and in the light of the priorities established by the European Council.

Member states face broadly the same challenges and policy needs and hence there are typically a number of general recommendations that apply to all of them. However, differences in economic performance and prospects as well as structures and institutions mean that, within the overall strategy, policy priorities differ somewhat across member states. Hence there are also country-specific economic guidelines.[7] The Broad Economic Policy Guidelines adopted in 2000 focused on the medium- and long-term implications of structural policies and on reforms aimed at promoting economic growth, employment and social cohesion, as well as on the transition towards a knowledge-driven economy.

There are important synergies between macroeconomic management and the BEPGs. Measures to facilitate the introduction of new technologies and employ-ability can obviously enhance the prospects for economic growth. But the nature of macroeconomic policy can itself affect the prospects for growth, as it can facilitate new developments and also provide an environment to enhance investment. A policy that is too restrictive may reduce the level of investment at just the stage in the cycle of innovation and product development when increasing the capital stock is central to medium-term growth. A more stable macroeconomic framework should reduce the degree of perceived uncertainty about the future, which will also encourage investment and innovation.

The process of institution-building in Europe is still under way, and there are clear gaps to be filled. The recognition that short-term, interventionist macro-economic policies were often unproductive has influenced the construction of the new institutions. In particular, the decision to eschew the existence of a powerful central fiscal authority reflects in part this view. However, it also reflects the need to construct compromises between individual sovereign states. If fiscal policy is needed to deal with a serious problem that affects all member states, such as a major recession, then it remains available. It would be in the interests of all to use it, and the institutions described above could ensure rapid and effective reactions to problems, although they may not do so, and they are not required to act. Problems that hit individual countries should be able to be dealt with within the confines of the SGP, but this may need reform and clarification so that countries do have the ability to deal quickly with their own temporary problems. The European Constitution is not yet written, and it may never be so, but the process of constructing it is under way. Significant improvements within the constraints of multiple sovereignty remain possible. In particular, issues of location and growth within such a confederation need to be considered carefully.

EMPLOYMENT STRATEGIES AND MACROECONOMIC POLICIES

The need to implement policy reforms to improve the workings of national labour markets has been recognized in Europe. Following the Treaty of Amsterdam in 1997, EU member states are now obliged to produce annual National Action Plans (NAPs) explaining the measures being taken to achieve a high level of employment. The Lisbon European Council in March 2000 led to agreed objectives of raising the aggregate employment rate in the EU to 70 per cent (that is, approaching US levels) by 2010, and raising the female employment rate to 60 per cent.

The agreed European Employment Strategy is built on four pillars:

- Improving employability. This includes measures to reduce youth and long-term unemployment, changes to tax and benefit systems, and reforms to enhance workforce skills and ensure 'lifelong learning'.
- Developing entrepreneurship and job creation. This includes measures to encourage business start-ups, and reductions in taxes on labour.
- Encouraging adaptability of businesses and their employees. This includes measures such as flexible contracting to improve organizational efficiency.
- Strengthening equal opportunities for men and women. This includes measures to tackle gender pay-gaps and reforms in areas such as childcare arrangements which affect the ability to work.

Every year a set of guidelines are adopted for each of the pillars which generate a number of targets for member states to achieve in their employment policies. These are transposed into concrete measures in the NAPs. The measures must be consistent with the Broad Economic Policy Guidelines and are evaluated in a Joint Employment Report produced annually by the European Commission and the Council of the European Union.

Each NAP has to offer discussion of the effects of public expenditure and taxes on employment and suggest details for the implementation of specific employment-oriented initiatives. These features have to be backed up by a sound coverage of relevant labour market statistics. The first three pillars are backed by clear quantitative guidelines from the European Commission. If specific guidelines are achieved, then the Commission will adjust the guidelines and targets it sets for individual countries to achieve.

If successful, reforms to labour markets will offer a number of important macroeconomic benefits. If employment rises and productivity improves then productive potential and hence future living standards will be higher than they would otherwise be, even if European workers do not choose to work the same hours as those in the US. Greater flexibility in labour markets may also help minimize the costs of any asymmetric shocks that affect national economies.

Many of the policies put forward in the European Employment Strategy echo those emphasized by the OECD Jobs Strategy, but they do not emphasize so strongly the role of wage flexibility and wage dispersion in job creation. There is also much less emphasis on reforms to employment protection. This reflects both emerging evidence and political realities within Europe. It is not as clear as the OECD work suggests that increased flexibility enhances job creation, at least in simple ways, and the evidence on the reduction of employment protection on the level of employment is also mixed. The focus of the European employment creation process is more clearly on the development of the skills of the potential workforce to enhance their flexibility in response to labour market conditions.

The agreed employment guidelines recommend that incentives to work are improved and that tax and benefit reforms are encouraged in order to increase employment. In particular, stress is placed on measures to ensure that the unemployed find jobs more easily. All the guidelines have some common targets. In particular every unemployed person should be offered a new start before 6 months (for youths) or 12 months (for adults) unemployment by the year 2002. At least 20 per cent of the unemployed should be in training schemes by the same time in all countries in the Union. There is also a strong emphasis on the reduction of the regulatory and administrative burdens placed on businesses, and especially on new firms. The need for this latter emphasis has been strengthened by the focus of the Lisbon 2000 Summit on the need to ensure that the information society develops in Europe as well as in the USA. The NAPs are designed individually and hence it is difficult to assess the process.

However, even where there were common targets, success has been rather variable. Policies to give the unemployed a new start within a year have been implemented in a number of countries, but compliance has been slow in Italy, Greece and Belgium. The desire to ensure that the unemployed were placed into training schemes appears to have largely been met, although it is not clear that this has yet been achieved in France, Austria, Portugal and Ireland. The existence of minimum wages means that all EU countries have to have conscious policies to support the unskilled. In order to reduce unemployment they have either to ensure that the unemployed and the inactive have sufficient skills that they become employable at wages that the market can pay, or face the prospects of permanent distortionary employment subsidies to produce an acceptable level of employment amongst these groups.

Reductions in the sustainable level of unemployment are not the only objective of labour market policies. As the guidelines emphasise, there are a number of countries in the euro area where the participation of the population in the workforce remains low as compared to the US.

Recent trends in the labour markets of the EU economies are summarized in Table 9.4. Total employment rose in all of the member states over the period considered and the standardized unemployment rate declined in ten of them. Employment has grown particularly rapidly in Finland, Ireland, the Netherlands, Portugal, Spain, the UK and Denmark. It is clear that favourable macroeconomic conditions are likely to be associated with improved labour market outcomes, in that the four countries with the fastest rate of annual employment growth – Ireland, Spain, the Netherlands and Finland – are also the four with the fastest rates of output growth. Thus policies that help to raise the future growth rate of the European economy are likely to raise the chances that the European Employment Strategy will be successful. However, other factors may have been at work in improving employment performance.

The successes and problems of different strategies are very variable. There are similarities between the approaches adopted by the UK and Denmark, for instance, and between Denmark and the Netherlands, but these countries also have features that are distinctive. Other, distinct reforms have worked well in countries such as France and Italy. All have adapted the employment guidelines to their own circumstances and there are signs that they have begun to have some significant successes. The forecasts published by the OECD in December 2000 suggest that total employment in the EU rose by 1.9 per cent in 2000. Of course economic growth was unusually strong in 2000 as well, so we need to assess whether the employment strategies themselves are the cause of the improved performance.

Table 9.4   Recent labour market trends

	Average annual GDP growth 1995–99 (%)	Average annual employment growth 1995–99(%)	Change in unemployment rate 1994–99 (% pts)	Unemployment rate 1994 (% pts)
Euro area	2.2	1.0	−1.6	11.6
Austria	2.0	0.4	0.0	3.8
Belgium	2.5	0.8	−0.9	10.0
Finland	4.7	2.3	−6.5	16.7
France	2.2	0.9	−1.0	12.3
Germany	1.5	0.3	0.3	8.5
Ireland	9.3	5.8	−8.7	14.4
Italy	1.7	0.5	0.1	11.2
Netherlands	3.4	2.8	−3.8	7.1
Portugal	3.3	1.7	−2.5	7.0
Spain	3.5	2.8	−8.2	24.1
Denmark	2.5	1.2	−3.0	8.2
Greece	2.9	0.7	2.4	10.0
Sweden	2.7	0.7	−2.2	9.4
UK	2.7	1.4	−3.5	9.6
European Union	2.3	1.1	−1.9	11.1

Note: Standardized unemployment rates for all countries apart from Greece, where the national definition is used.

Source: OECD Economic Outlook, December 2000.

The more successful countries have in general been undertaking reforms for some time. The UK started to restructure its labour market in the 1980s. In the early and mid-1980s, employment protection was reduced and the power of trade unions significantly curtailed. These reforms were accompanied by a significant reduction in the replacement ratio for many of those who were unemployed. These changes had little impact initially, and any gains they may have been producing were overwhelmed by the strong macroeconomic upturn of the late 1980s and the subsequent sharp downturn in the 1990s.[8] The effects of the reforms were significantly delayed by this period of extreme turbulence. The 1990s saw a new set of reforms in the UK along the lines of those pioneered by Denmark. In both countries the unemployed and those on benefits were activated,[9] and both introduced schemes that would both reskill and encourage the unemployed and those on benefits with low skills. The UK introduced the Job Seekers' Allowance in 1995, restricting unemployment benefit to active job seekers, and from 1994 the Danes introduced a programme giving all unemployed people 'the right and the duty to be activated'. Periods of benefit availability were reduced in both countries, albeit from very generous levels in Denmark, at least, and job seekers were given significant encouragement and assistance in finding jobs. The New Deal for the Unemployed in the UK, introduced in 1998, has also had an impact on unemployment through similar means.

The Dutch have also had a distinctive approach to labour market reforms over the last 20 years.[10] In 1982 the social partners (unions, employers, and the government in an observer role) met to discuss the 'wage round' in a period of extreme dissatisfaction with the performance of the Dutch economy. They were acting in response to the effects of strong energy-related revenues and to the slowdown in the world economy. Unemployment had risen sharply, and non-participation was an increasing problem. In particular the economy was becoming uncompetitive as gas revenues in a period of high energy prices had forced the exchange rate up. The so-called 'Wassener Agreement' set the scene for wage moderation over the next two decades. This policy had a great deal of success in moderating the growth of real wages in the Netherlands and hence in producing a 'competitive devaluation through wage moderation'. As a result employment has grown significantly in the Netherlands since the early 1980s. This policy was accompanied by continual attempts along Danish lines to reform benefits and raise participation, but these met with much less success. However, the policies were also accompanied by significant public sector job creation and widespread adoption of part-time working. Employment growth in the Netherlands in the late 1990s was particularly strong, and unemployment has fallen to very low levels whilst participation rates have risen from one of the lowest in Europe to one of the highest.

The Italian and French examples also provide clear lessons of other ways to reform the labour market. Developments in Italy have built up slowly over time. The indexation system in wage contracting was a major factor behind the acceleration of inflation in past expansionary periods, and had been gradually reformed in the 1980s, but final restructuring took place in 1992–93. The degree of price indexation of wage contracts was reduced significantly in this process, reducing the short-term nominal wage sensitivity to prices. It also appears to have reduced both real wage rigidity and the level of sustainable unemployment, reducing the short-term growth–inflation trade-off. There have also been reforms to legislation on temporary employment that have helped improve labour market performance, and more recently, reforms to an overly generous pensions system that have begun to give a significant disincentive to those planning early retirement. The French labour market has only recently begun to change, in part because legislation governing working hours introduced from 1998 has increased flexibility, albeit perhaps unintentionally. The legislation reduced average hours but increased the flexibility with which employers could utilize labour. It is too soon to be certain about the consequences, but there does seem to have been a significant and positive impact on employment.

These reforms make it clear that different countries will have to focus on different problems. For instance, targets in relation to youth unemployment are important in the UK, and matter a great deal more in Italy and Spain, where youth unemployment is a relatively serious problem. However, in countries such as Germany the structure of benefits and the nature of the intermediate skills training programmes have militated against youth unemployment. Hence there is no need to emphasize this problem in any evaluation of successes and failure in such countries, whereas it must be a central plank in the design and evaluation of strategies elsewhere. However, in general, active policies are designed to increase employment and reduce unemployment more rapidly than would otherwise have been the case. It is useful to assess how successful countries have been in doing this.

In order to evaluate the reform process we can investigate the importance of output growth and wage evolution on employment and then ask which countries have performed better than might have been anticipated. In Table 9.5 we confirm the importance of good macroeconomic performance by presenting two simple cross-sectional regressions of the factors influencing the change in employment and unemployment for the 14 economies shown in Table 9.4. In the first column we find that some 88 per cent of the cross-country variation in employment growth over 1995–99 can be explained by GDP growth and the rate of growth of real producer wages (compensation per employee deflated by the GDP deflator). Raising the rate of GDP growth by 1 percentage point raises the rate of employment growth by 0.62 per cent. Reducing the growth rate of real wages by 1 percentage point raises employment growth by 0.28 percentage points for a given rate of output growth. In the second column we find that two-thirds of the cross-sectional variation in the change in the unemployment rate over 1994–99 can be explained by the initial level of unemployment and the rate of output growth. Countries with a higher initial level of unemployment tended to experience the greatest falls in subsequent years, and countries with a higher rate of output growth also saw greater falls in unemployment.

These regressions summarize collective developments in European labour markets in recent years. It is possible to see whether some countries have differed markedly from the average by looking at the residuals from the cross-section regressions. These are shown in standardized form in Figure 9.6, with the national country residuals from the employment and unemployment regressions divided by the standard error of the regression. It is clear from these residuals that there have been particularly unusual developments in Denmark, the Netherlands and the UK. Denmark and the Netherlands have large positive residuals for employment growth, implying that employment growth has been

Table 9.5   Cross-sectional regressions 1995–99, 14 EU countries

	Employment (ΔE_i)	Unemployment rate (ΔU_i)
ΔY_i	0.6219 (3.8)	–0.9583 (5.6)
ΔRW_i	–0.2794 (2.5)	
$U_{i,\,1994}$		–0.2951 (3.4)
Constant	0.0407 (0.1)	3.6052 (3.4)
$\bar{R}^2$	0.878	0.665
Standard error	0.51	1.89

Note:
Variable definitions:
ΔE_i = average annual growth rate of employment 1995–99
ΔY_i = average annual GDP growth 1995–99
ΔU_i = change in unemployment rate between 1994 and 1999
ΔRW_i = average annual growth of real producer wages 1995–99
$U_{i,1994}$ = unemployment rate in 1994

considerably higher than in Europe as a whole given output and real wage
growth. Equally, they have large negative residuals for the change in unemployment, indicating that the comparatively strong growth of employment has
been associated with a comparatively large fall in the unemployment rate. The
UK has also experienced a comparatively large reduction in unemployment,
but this does not appear to have been associated with unusually strong
employment growth.

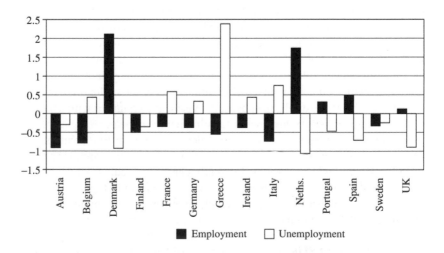

Figure 9.6   Standardized residuals table X regressions

These results are consonant with our discussions of the reform process in Europe, and they would suggest that sustained policies to increase employment and reduce unemployment can be successful. The Dutch and the Danes have had policies in place to activate and reskill the unemployed and non-participant benefit recipients, and the Dutch have had successful programmes of public sector job creation for some time. However, much of the employment growth in both countries has been in the private sector as reskilled individuals are absorbed. The UK has only recently turned to reducing the number of non-participant benefit recipients by enabling them to find work. As a result the successes show up mainly in the additional reduction of unemployment, although as similar policies to those in Denmark are now being followed, success in raising employment may also become apparent.

Not all countries have been particularly successful given developments in the macro-economy. Austria, Belgium and Italy are shown to have had unusually low rates of employment growth given output and real wage growth, whilst Greece has experienced a particularly rapid rise in unemployment. Austria and Belgium have made rather limited attempts to change the labour market, although Austria already has a low unemployment rate and relatively high participation. Italian reforms have been designed to improve the public finances (changes in retirement rules) and to increase flexibility in response to shocks, and hence have not had a major impact on short term developments. However, the sluggish response of the Italian economy remains somewhat of a puzzle, and it may reflect the problems of dealing with a dual labour market arising from regional disparities, with very low unemployment in the north and very high unemployment in the south, and these problems may have as much to do with location as with labour market policies.

LOCATION AND MACROECONOMIC POLICIES

International transfers of technology and knowledge by multinational companies are widely believed to affect the performance of host economies. This belief is reflected in the extent to which many national and sub-national governments now compete in 'locational tournaments' to try and attract mobile investors. Many new theoretical models with endogenous growth view the creation and exploitation of knowledge as two of the key factors driving the growth process (Romer, 1993), and empirical evidence suggests that there are indeed important spillovers from foreign-owned firms in the major European economies (Barrell and Pain, 1997, 1999; Pain, 2000). The location of economic activity could thus be an important endogenous influence on the size of host economies. Foreign investments by multinational companies can provide a channel through which new ideas, working practices and technologies can arrive in host economies, as well as a means by which indigenous companies are exposed to greater competitive pressures. An important macroeconomic policy objective is to design appropriate national policies and institutions to maximize the potential size of those benefits.

Western Europe, which covers the European Economic Area plus Switzerland, has become the dominant host region for inward foreign direct investment amongst the developed countries. The amount and share of investment in Western Europe has risen particularly rapidly since 1985, as can be seen from Table 9.6. This period has coincided with moves towards greater integration. The implementation of the measures to remove capital controls and non-tariff barriers to trade in the Single Market Programme, together with widespread privatization and deregulation of service industries, has clearly stimulated the mobility of capital and generated a significant change in investment patterns and levels of foreign involvement in production in both services and manufacturing (Barrell and Pain, 1997, 1998; de Menil, 1999).

Table 9.6   The global stock of foreign direct investment by recipient area ($ billion)

	1960	1985	1999
Developed countries	36.9	545.2	3230.8
	(67.7)	(71.4)	(67.7)
North America	20.5	249.2	1253.6
	(37.6)	(32.6)	(26.3)
Western Europe	12.5	236.4	1757.2
	(22.9)	(31.0)	(36.8)
Developing countries	17.6	218.2	1541.2
	(32.3)	(28.6)	(32.3)
World	54.5	763.4	4772.0

Note: Figures in parentheses are FDI in host as a share of the world total. Developed countries include otherwise unallocated stocks (0.4 per cent of the world total) in 1960.

Sources: Dunning (1988, Table 3.2) and UNCTAD (2000, Annex Table B3).

Although the Single Market Programme has pushed the process of European integration forward substantially over the past decade, national markets remain differentiated by factor endowments, consumer tastes and regulations in areas such as health and safety and environmental standards. The removal of barriers to market entry has simply made it easier for foreign competitors to enter national markets. At the same time, the external barriers to trading with the European Union faced by producers located outside Europe have encouraged additional flows of investment into the EU, with production bases now having guaranteed access to a European-wide market. This has been particularly important for many Asian companies (Barrell and Pain, 1999a; Belderbos and Sleuwaegen, 1998). The detailed statistics available on the activities of US multinational companies confirm the long-term improvement in the locational attractiveness of the EU, with the share of the gross product of all foreign subsidiaries of US parent companies produced by those affiliates in Europe rising from 40.6 per cent in 1977 to 53.1 per cent in 1989 and 55.2 per cent by 1998.

The trends in the pattern of direct investment inflows in the individual EU members are reported in Table 9.7. Some care is needed before making strong cross-country comparisons with this data as the treatment of reinvested earnings in the FDI statistics can vary across countries and over time. However, three points stand out. Firstly, the rise in the level of new investments does not appear to solely consist of new investments into the largest national markets. The UK and France have enjoyed a rising share of investment, but Germany and Italy have not. Equally, the geographical distribution of new investments suggests that foreign direct investment cannot simply be characterized as the movement of production from low return, capital-abundant countries at the core of Europe to low wage economies on the periphery. Aside from France, two of the smaller centrally-located economies, the Netherlands and Belgium, have also experienced strong growth in inward investments over time. Both countries receive a level of inward investment well above the relative size of their economies in the European Union. Finally, there is a clear suggestion from Table 9.7 that membership of the EU (or the EEA) matters. The level of inward investment in Spain and Portugal accelerated sharply following their entry into the EU in 1986, and the proportion of new investments located in Austria, Finland and Sweden rose in the early 1990s, once it became apparent that they were set to enter the EU. However it is interesting to note that Greece is an exception, suggesting that national institutions and policies may still matter.

Recent developments in theories of economic geography under imperfect competition emphasize the endogeneity of locational advantages, and the extent to which trade and capital market liberalization can change the spatial distribution of industrial activity (Fujita et al., 1999). Whether liberalization leads to the dispersion of economic activities depends upon the balance of centripetal forces, such as the agglomeration economies generated by large markets, relative to forces such as lower labour costs in less-developed locations. Small open economies may still prove good locations for investment if they are proximate to large markets of consumers or industrial complexes. Competing on factor prices alone may not suffice to attract and retain investments as integration occurs and the balance of the various influences on location begins to shift, unless clusters and networks with local firms have become firmly embedded. The possibility of cumulative causation, with agglomerations

Globalizing Europe

attracting new investments which then influence the growth process, suggests
that the size of national economies is determined in the process of integration,
rather than fixed by current factor endowments and common blueprints.

Table 9.7   EU FDI inflows (% of GDP, period average)

	1981–85	1986–90	1991–95	1996–98
France	0.40	0.82	1.46	1.66
Germany	0.12	0.23	0.23	0.53
UK	0.89	2.65	1.50	3.20
Italy	0.26	0.43	0.33	0.27
Belgium	1.70	2.84	4.44	5.06
Denmark	0.14	0.52	1.74	1.96
Ireland	0.98	0.41	2.40	3.88
Netherlands	1.15	2.66	2.52	5.35
Greece	1.08	1.19	1.08	0.84
Portugal	0.87	2.15	1.81	1.80
Spain	1.05	2.03	1.88	1.40
Austria	0.31	0.35	0.70	2.00
Finland	0.17	0.47	0.70	3.76
Sweden	0.29	0.79	2.85	5.10

Source: Calculations using data from IMF *International Financial Statistics Yearbook*, various
issues.

The available empirical evidence on the factors influencing the location of
multinational activity in Europe is presented and summarized in Barrell and
Pain (1999a, b), Hubert and Pain (2000) and CEPR (2000). Both centripetal
and centrifugal forces are found to be important. Agglomeration economics
from large markets and the size of the national research base relative to that in
other potential hosts appear to matter, increasing the scale of inward investment,
but so do the relative costs of different locations, particularly the relative cost
of labour. The results for the determinants of US investment reported by Barrell
and Pain suggest that a reduction of 6.5 per cent in relative unit labour costs in
an EU host country will have a similar effect to a 1 percentage point rise in that
country's share of either EU GDP or the total EU R&D stock. Broadly
comparable findings are reported in CEPR (2000).

Hubert and Pain (2000) investigate the scope for national governments to
affect location choice through the use of fiscal incentives, investment in infrastructure and other promotional policies. With many countries having now
entered Monetary Union, proactive fiscal policies have become one of the main

remaining policy channels through which to influence location choice. They evaluate the impact of expenditure on subsidies and fixed investment, the effective rate of corporation tax, and grants from the European Regional Development Fund using a industry-level panel data set on the location of FDI by German companies in the EEA since 1980.

The findings with regard to the different investment incentives examined are mixed. Some are insignificant and others, such as corporate tax competitiveness, appear sensitive to the specification of the model. But the level of government fixed investment expenditure relative to that in other economies is found to have a significant positive impact, particularly in more developed locations, although its direct impact is small. Location is about choice and so the impact of a change in fiscal policy depends upon what is being undertaken elsewhere.

The endogeneity of location in an integrated Europe has important implications for the design of national macroeconomic policies because of the existence of significant agglomeration forces. In such a world temporary policy changes can easily have a permanent influence on the location of economic activities. A temporary fiscal expansion that generates inflationary pressure, and hence a rise in the real exchange rate, can lead to investment being foregone, with consequential effects on the prospects for growth. Equally, temporary investment incentives, such as more generous corporate tax allowances, can have long-lasting effects if they serve to attract new investments which in turn serve to make the location more attractive for others. Even if incentives make little difference for the country as whole, it does not necessarily follow that they should be abandoned. Offering incentives may not in itself produce many gains, but foregoing them could prove costly and difficult to reverse if there are self-reinforcing agglomeration effects, providing an explanation for the increasing degree of corporate tax competition seen in Europe in recent years.

CONCLUSIONS

The European economies, and especially the countries within the euro area, face new challenges in the design and implementation of macroeconomic policies. The approaches that are available to influence both short-term stability and to encourage longer-term growth are irrevocably altered by the new structures in Europe. The construction of the new economic space in Europe has involved the removal of many pre-existing barriers to the mobility of capital and the location of production. This has also affected the prospects for effective macroeconomic policies, as has the increasingly globalized nature of the world economy.

The euro area now has a single monetary policy run by a fully independent Central Bank for its (currently) 12 members, and fiscal policy is somewhat constrained by the Stability and Growth Pact. Hence, the macroeconomic policies available to stabilize the economy in response to shocks are restricted. As a result, there is increasing relative emphasis on more micro policies to ensure that the macroeconomy displays some stability and that growth prospects are enhanced. In particular, increasing emphasis is being placed on labour market strategies at both national and European levels, and locational competition is becoming increasingly important at a regional and national level. We show that the medium-term growth of employment depends on the growth of the economy and on the policies adopted to reform the labour market, with the Netherlands and Denmark enjoying a particularly favourable performance in recent years. In addition, capital has become much more mobile within Europe, and fiscal policies to enhance the attractiveness of a country or a region to FDI are becoming more important.

Monetary policy, at least in the euro area, is directed to produce price-level stability in the medium term and to ensure that inflation stays within relatively tight limits in that process. Although it may be possible that this approach will help stabilize output, that is not its intention. Hence it is wise to adopt labour market policies that allow a much more flexible response to shocks. In the medium and long term, price stability should encourage long-term contracting and decision-making and hence enhance growth. It should hence help European output per capita catch up with that of the US, especially as the barriers to the movement of ideas and technologies between the two regions are lower now than they were in the past.

Individual countries can use fiscal policy to stabilize their economies in response to idiosyncratic shocks, and concerted fiscal policies might help cope with common shocks that were likely to cause recessions or unneeded booms. Fiscal policy that was expansionary in a country with an independent monetary authority would normally induce a response that would be designed to limit the inflationary consequences of the expansion. Interest rates would rise, the exchange rate would appreciate, and the increase in demand, costs and prices would be kept in check. This stabilizing mechanism has been lost for single countries within EMU. A fiscal expansion would force up demand, raise prices and costs, and lead to a deterioration in competitiveness that could be sustained for some time. This in turn might lead the individual member of the Union to become an unattractive and high-cost location within the Union. As a result mobile capital, and particularly investments by multinational firms, would begin to seek other locations. Such a process might have permanent effects on the level of sustainable output in an economy, and hence should put some constraints on the abuse of fiscal independence within the Union, irrespective of the requirements of the Stability and Growth Pact.

NOTES

1. The EU figures reflect the current membership of the EU. Ireland joined only in 1973, Greece in 1981 and Spain and Portugal in 1986.
2. A tightening which was entirely appropriate given the remit of the Bundesbank.
3. These will initially have a fixed component of 0.2 per cent of GDP and a variable component reflecting the size of the excessive deficit, with a ceiling of 0.5 per cent of GDP on the total annual amount. The fines will accumulate each year until the excessive deficit is eliminated. If the deficit is corrected within two years, the fines are refunded.
4. See Barrell and Dury (2001), Barrell and Pina (2000) and Dury and Pina (2000).
5. Only Sweden and Austria are found to need to run near balanced budgets to allow the automatic stabilizers to operate without breaching the 3 per cent of GDP deficit limit.
6. Representatives of civil society and local and regional authorities are also formally consulted through the Economic and Social Committee and the Committee of the Regions.
7. All country-specific guidelines on labour market issues have to be consistent with the annual guidelines issued on the National Action Plans for employment as part of the European Employment Strategy. We discuss this in the next section.
8. The papers in Barrell (1994) suggest that the reforms of the 1980s had little impact by the early 1990s.
9. The details of the programmes are discussed in Bartell and Genre (1999).
10. Some of the successes and problems in the Netherlands and the UK are discussed in Nickell and van Ours (2000).

REFERENCES

Abramowitz, M. (1986), 'Catching up, forging ahead and falling behind', *Journal of Economic History*, 46, 385–406.

Allsopp, C. and D. Vines (1998), 'Macroeconomic policy after EMU', *Oxford Review of Economic Policy*, 14(3), 1–23.

Barrell, R. (ed.) (1994), *The UK Labour Market*, Cambridge: Cambridge University Press.

Barrell, R. and K. Dury (2000), 'Choosing the regime: macroeconomic effects of UK entry into EMU', *Journal of Common Market Studies*, 38, 625–44.

Barrell, R. and K. Dury (2000a), 'An evaluation of monetary targeting regimes', *National Institute Economic Review*, 174, 105–13.

Barrell, R. and K. Dury (2001), 'The Stability and Growth Pact, will it ever be breached? An analysis using stochastic simulations', in A. Brunila, M. Buti and D. Franco (eds), *The Stability and Growth Pact: The Architecture of Fiscal Policy in EMU*, Basingstoke: Palgrave Press.

Barrell, R. and V. Genre (1999), 'Employment Strategies for Europe: Lessons from Denmark and the Netherlands', *National Institute Economic Review*, April.

Barrell, R. and F. Hubert (1999), *Modern Budgeting in the Public Sector: Treasury Rules in a Comparative Context*, NIESR Occasional Paper No. 53.

Barrell, R. and N. Pain (1997), 'Foreign direct investment, technological change, and economic growth within Europe', *Economic Journal*, 107, 1770–6.

Barrell, R. and N. Pain (1998), 'Real exchange rates, agglomerations and irreversibilities: macroeconomic policy and FDI in EMU', *Oxford Review of Economic Policy*, 14(3), 152–67.

Barrell, R. and N. Pain (1999a), 'Trade restraints and Japanese direct investment flows', *European Economic Review*, 43, 29–45.

Barrell, R. and N. Pain (1999b), 'Domestic institutions, agglomerations and foreign direct investment in Europe', *European Economic Review*, 43, 925–34.

Barrell, R. and A. Pina (2000), 'How important are automatic stabilisers in Europe?', EUI Working Paper ECO. No. 2000/2.

Belderbos, R. and L. Sleuwaegen (1998), 'Tariff jumping DFI and export substitution: Japanese electronics firms in Europe', *International Journal of Industrial Organisation*, 16, 601–38.

Ben-David, D. (1993), 'Equalizing exchange: trade liberalisation and income convergence', *Quarterly Journal of Economics*, 108, 653–79.

Boskin, M. et al. (1997), *Towards A More Accurate Measure Of The Cost Of Living*, Final Report of the Advisory Commission to Study the Consumer Price Index to the Committee of Finance of the US Senate.

Buti, M. and B. Martinot (2000), 'Open issues in the Implementation of the Stability and Growth Pact', *National Institute Economic Review*, 174, 92–104.

Buti, M. and A. Sapir (eds) (1998), *Economic Policy in EMU – A Study by the European Commission Services*, Oxford: Oxford University Press.

CEPR (2000), *Integration And The Regions of Europe: How the Right Policies Can Prevent Polarization*, Centre for Economic Policy Research.

Commerce Department (2000), *Digital Economy 2000*, US Department of Commerce, Economics and Statistics Administration.

Crafts, N. and G. Toniolo (1996), 'Postwar growth: an overview', in N. Crafts and G. Toniolo (eds), *Economic Growth In Europe Since 1945*, Cambridge: Cambridge University Press.

de Menil, G. (1999), 'Real capital market integration in the EU: How far has it gone? What will the effect of the euro be?', *Economic Policy*, 28, 167–89.

Dunning, J.H. (1988), *Explaining International Production*, New York: HarperCollins.

Dury, K. and A. Pina (2000), 'European fiscal policy after EMU: simulating the operation of the Stability Pact', EUI Working Paper ECO. No. 2000/3.

Fujita, M., P. Krugman and A. Venables (1999), *The Spatial Economy: Cities, Regions and International Trade*, Cambridge, MA: MIT Press.

Gaspar, V. and F. Smets (2000), 'Price level stability: some issues', *National Institute Economic Review*, 174, 68–79.

Grossman, G.M. and E. Helpman (1991), *Innovation and Growth in the Global Economy*, Cambridge, MA: MIT Press.

Hoeller, P., N. Girouard and A. Colecchia (1998), 'The European Union's trade policies and their economic effects', OECD Economics Department Working Paper No. 194.

Hubert, F. and N. Pain (2000), 'Fiscal incentives, European integration and the location of foreign direct investment', presented to NIESR Macro Users Group, October 2000.

Kim, S. (1997), 'Economic integration and convergence: US regions 1840–1987', NBER Working Paper No. 6335.

Kneller, R., M. Bleaney and N. Gemmell (1999), 'Public policy and the government budget constraint: evidence from the OECD', *Journal of Public Economics*, 74, 171–90.

Midelfart-Knarvik, K., H. Overman, S. Redding and A. Venables (2000), 'The location of European industry', European Commission Economic Paper No. 142.

Nickell, S. (1996), 'Competition and corporate performance', *Journal of Political Economy*, 104, 724–46.

Nickell, S. and J. van Ours (2000) 'The Netherlands and the UK: a European Employment Miracle?' *Economic Policy*, 30, April, 135–80.

Niehans, J. (1980), *The Theory of Money*, Princeton, NJ: Princeton University Press.

Pain, N. (2000) (ed.), *Inward Investment, Technological Change And Growth: The Impact Of Multinational Corporations On The UK Economy*, Basingstoke: Palgrave Press.

Romer, P. (1993), 'Idea gaps and object gaps in economic development', *Journal of Monetary Economics*, 32, 543–73.

Soskice, D. (1990), 'Wage determination: the changing role of institutions in advanced industrialised countries', *Oxford Review of Economic Policy*, 6(4).

UNCTAD (2000), *World Investment Report*, Geneva: United Nations.

UNECE (2000), 'Catching up and falling behind: economic convergence in Europe', *United Nations Economic Survey of Europe*, Vol. 20, Ch. 5.

Wren-Lewis, S., P. Westaway, S. Soteri and R.J. Barrell (1991), 'Choosing the Rate', *Manchester School*, June.

10. European macroeconomic policy interdependencies

William Thorbecke and
Christian Eigen-Zucchi

Although the US and Europe agree in many areas, they often disagree about the design of international macroeconomic policies. In terms of beliefs about democracy, human rights and the rule of law the two regions concur. In terms of the formulation of appropriate monetary, fiscal and exchange rate policies, however, the two often clash.

One reason for these conflicts is that macroeconomic policies in a large country can exert major spillover effects on trading partners. For instance, under the Bretton Woods system of fixed exchange rates, expansionary monetary policies in the US forced Germany and other trading partners to import inflation. Similarly, under the flexible exchange rate system that began in 1973, expansionary fiscal policy by the US sometimes caused European currencies to depreciate relative to the dollar, increasing prices and wages in Europe. When monetary or fiscal policies on one side of the Atlantic can affect target variables on the other side positively or negatively, disagreements become likely.

The high degree of macroeconomic interdependence between the US and Europe has spawned a large literature on the gains available from policy coordination. For instance, if a US fiscal expansion is matched by a European fiscal expansion, both sides could increase output without affecting the exchange rate or the trade balance.

Despite the potential for gains from coordination, several failed attempts have placed all but modest cooperation out of reach. As discussed below, in 1978 Germany agreed to match a fiscal expansion by the US. When inflation rose in Germany the next year, Bonn concluded that the agreement had been a mistake. Similarly, in 1987 the US agreed to reduce its budget deficit in return for a more stimulative policy by Germany. Within eight months, US Treasury Secretary James Baker began twisting the arms of German officials to force them to cut interest rates more. German officials rebuffed these attempts. The next day, 19 October 1987, stock markets in the US and Europe crashed. Following this experience, coordination has been mainly limited to intervention in the foreign exchange market when there is agreement that European currencies or the euro are overvalued or undervalued relative to the dollar.

In both the 1978 and 1987 coordination attempts and in others discussed in this chapter certain patterns emerge. Firstly, the US initially pursues more expansionary (and potentially inflationary) policies than its European trading partners. Secondly, the US urges the EU countries to adopt more expansionary policies to lower the US current account deficits that result from the unilateral expansions. Thirdly, Germany and other European countries conclude that US policies and/or their responses caused unwanted inflation, and regret acceding to US demands for domestic stimulus.

Part of the reason for this pattern is that the macroeconomic priorities of Germany and the rest of Europe probably differ from those of the United States. Germany, as Henning (1994) discusses, is averse to inflation. The disastrous hyperinflation in the 1920s led to the inclusion of a requirement in the German Constitution that the government pursue low inflation. In fighting inflation first the Bundesbank and now the European Central Bank (ECB) follow a lexico-graphic ordering of goals. As Gros et al. (2000) discuss, price stability is pursued first, and only when there is no danger on this front are other goals pursued. US policy-makers, on the other hand, also dislike inflation but are probably more willing to risk expansionary macroeconomic policies (and the concomitant dangers of inflation) than their European counterparts. The Employment Act of 1946 requires US policymakers to pursue 'conditions under which there will be afforded useful employment opportunities ... for those able, willing, and seeking to work and to promote maximum employment, production, and purchasing power'. The Full Employment and Balanced Growth Act of 1978 requires the federal government to 'promote full employment ... and reasonable price stability'. Thus macroeconomic policy in the US is mandated to focus on both full employment and price stability, while policy in Europe is mandated to pursue price stability first and other objectives second.

In addition, as Henning (1994) discusses, Germany (and other European countries) are more likely to consider the effect of the exchange rate on inter-national competitiveness while US policy-makers often ignore the international repercussions of their policies. Part of the reason for this is that Europe is more open than the United States, and thus more vulnerable to foreign shocks. This was true in the past for the individual countries making up the euro zone. However, even for Euroland as a whole, the sum of exports plus imports divided by GDP is much higher than for the US. As Gros et al. (2000) discuss, imports plus exports divided by two equals 21 per cent of GDP for Euroland when one considers all current account transactions versus 15.5 per cent of GDP for the US. For Germany this quantity equals 32.6 per cent. Thus historically the effect of exchange rate changes on output and inflation in individual European countries and even now the effect on Euroland as a whole is larger than for the US. Europe has thus had a greater incentive to focus on external factors than the US.

If Europe pursues less expansionary macroeconomic policies than the US and if Europe is more concerned about the effect of the exchange rate on international competitiveness than the US, one would expect Europe to run current account surpluses with the US. The current account balance equals the difference between national saving (NS) and investment (I). National saving in turn equals private saving plus government saving. When NS is greater than I the current account is in surplus and when NS is less than I it is in deficit. If European fiscal policy is more contractionary than US fiscal policy, government saving and NS will tend to be higher in Europe than the US. If aversion to inflation causes German policy-makers to raise interest rates more often than US policy-makers do, then I may be lower in Europe than the US. On both counts one would expect to see a more favourable trade balance in Europe than in the US. These effects would be reinforced if European policy-makers are more likely than American policy-makers to adjust the exchange rate to improve the current account balance.

The US has in fact run large trade deficits with Europe. In the 1950s and 1960s Germany, Italy, the Netherlands and France followed a strategy of export-led growth that produced a US balance of payments deficit and a dollar glut. In the early 1970s the Smithsonian Agreement failed partly because of speculative pressure on the dollar arising from US current account deficits. Later in the 1970s large US current account deficits led the US to negotiate the Bonn Agreement. In the 1980s the appreciation of the dollar from 1980 to 1985 produced US trade deficits exceeding $100 billion. In recent years the US current account deficit has increased from $248 billion in 1998 to almost $400 billion in 2000.

This chapter considers the large trade deficits and other results of macroeconomic policy interactions between Europe and the US during the post-war period. It first looks at macroeconomic interdependencies and policy coordination in theory. It then examines evidence on macroeconomic policy interactions over the post-war period.

The next section briefly considers the macroeconomic transmission channels between the US and Europe, and notes the potential gains from cooperation, especially in the context of rapid globalization. We then use a narrative history to highlight patterns of macroeconomic policy interactions between the US and Europe. The following section presents econometric evidence of the decline in monetary policy integration between Europe and the US in the 1990s.

MACROECONOMIC INTERDEPENDENCE AND POLICY COORDINATION

As far back as Adam Smith, economists have observed that economic developments and policies in one country can have profound effects on other countries. The recognition of these spillovers leads to the supposition that there may be gains from coordinating policy and from taking account of the external impacts in the initial formulation of policy.

Macroeconomic Transmission Channels

International economic interdependence flows from the external sector, including both the current and capital accounts. The exchange rate determines not only the prices of imports and exports, but also strongly influences the domestic prices of tradeable goods and the inflation rate. Net exports of goods and services affect domestic demand and employment. Capital flows affect investment, while foreign direct investment usually also brings technology transfers. A vast literature in international economics considers these interactions, and has identified several causal chains or transmission mechanisms. These depend crucially on the context, especially whether exchange rates are fixed or floating and whether capital is mobile or not. The possible combinations of features are too numerous to detail here, and we consider only a few salient examples of spillovers under fixed and flexible exchange rates.

Between the end of the Second World War and the early 1970s, much of the world followed the Bretton Woods gold exchange standard. Under this system the US fixed the value of the dollar relative to gold, and other countries fixed the value of their currencies relative to the dollar. In this arrangement the US exerted an asymmetric influence on the inflation rates of other countries because it issued the reserve currency. Other countries were required to keep their exchange rates fixed relative to the dollar, thereby forfeiting the use of monetary policy for domestic stabilization. The US was not required to fix its exchange rate relative to other currencies, allowing it to use monetary policy to stabilize the domestic economy. For example, the US could fight a recession with expansionary monetary policy. This would cause interest rates to fall and put downward pressure on the dollar. The other countries in the system would then have to purchase dollars to keep their exchange rate fixed, forcing them to expand their money supplies irrespective of domestic economic conditions. This process often caused European trading partners to passively import inflation from the US. As discussed below, displeasure with imported inflation contributed to the demise of the Bretton Woods System.[1]

Under a flexible exchange rate regime, which replaced Bretton Woods in 1973, macroeconomic spillovers between Europe, the US, and other trading partners remain significant. For example, standard open economy models indicate that with high capital mobility, a fiscal expansion in the US will raise domestic interest rates and trigger an incipient capital inflow. This in turn would appreciate the currency and lead to a current account deficit. A monetary contraction would have the same effect. A mix of expansionary fiscal policy and contractionary monetary policy, as prevailed in the United States during the early 1980s, would magnify these effects. This policy mix should increase both output and inflation in Europe. Output would rise as the depreciation of the European currencies increased net exports. Inflation would rise for two reasons. Firstly, the depreciation increases import prices, pushing up the cost of living in Europe and contributing to wage increases and a wage–price spiral. Secondly, several important commodities, such as oil, are priced in dollars. If European currencies depreciate relative to the dollar, the price of commodities in Europe will increase, raising the price of goods produced using these inputs. The existence of macroeconomic policy spillovers across countries has spawned a large literature on the role that policy coordination can play in improving outcomes.

Policy Coordination

If a particular policy stance in one country impacts on other economies, either favourably or unfavourably, then the question arises as to whether welfare in both regions can be improved through some kind of coordination, Policy-makers might attempt to take account of these external effects as part of the policy formulation process. Some of these spillovers also stem from the public goods component of policy, such as financial stability. Given that the significance of these externalities and public goods grows with macroeconomic interdependence and globalization, the potential gains from coordination are likely to have increased in recent decades, as the world's economies have become more closely interlinked.

There is some confusion in the literature surrounding the definition of 'cooperation' and 'coordination'. Part of the problem is that the term 'cooperation' in game theory is used to suggest binding commitments; in discussions of policy interactions, however, cooperation is considered the less ambitious form, and the notion of coordination is used to indicate a higher degree of consultation or joint policy formation. In this vein, it is useful to note different levels of coordination as distinguished by Currie, Holtham and Hughes Hallett (1989).[2] The spectrum moves from the weakest to the strongest form of coordination:

1. Exchanging information. Policy-makers may cooperate merely by exchanging information on their own activities, targets, models and views of how the world works.
2. Responding to crises. Policy-makers might take joint action to respond to crises, such as the financial crisis in Asia of 1998.
3. Cooperating on jointly controlled intermediate targets. Cooperation might take the form of agreeing on specific targets to avoid mutually exclusive policy initiatives, such as pursuing a specific bilateral exchange rate. In

addition to shared targets, this form of coordination also comprises the joint control over spillover targets that are intermediate to the policy-maker's more important objectives.

4. Assignment coordination. Policy-makers could agree on coordinating, say, monetary policy to achieve external balance, while leaving fiscal policy uncoordinated to achieve internal objectives specific to different countries.
5. Coordination. In this most ambitious case, policy-makers consult each other on all targets and initiatives, adjusting their own implementation to maximize gains from coordination.

Most of the examples of policy coordination fit into these categories, although the lines of distinction are sometimes blurred.

In analysing policy coordination, the literature has relied heavily on advances made in game theory. National governments are modelled as being 'unitary decision-makers', with clearly defined preferences (loss functions), who pursue their interests strategically in games with other national governments.[3] Typically, the game involves trading unemployment or inflation, based on some of the channels of transmission outlined above.

Canzoneri and Henderson (1991) focus mainly on monetary policy interactions that transmit inflationary pressure to other countries via the exchange rate. For example, if the US pursues contractionary monetary policy to fight domestic inflation, the effect is to appreciate the US dollar, depreciate the euro and increase inflationary pressure in Europe. With European policy initiatives generating a symmetrical impact on the US, the non-cooperative outcome is that both regions implement overly contractionary policy.

Others have focused on fiscal policy spillovers that transmit unemployment through the channel of exchange rates and net exports. In a context of a recession due to insufficient demand, the US might pursue expansionary fiscal policy, only to find that Europe is not expanding by as much, leading to an appreciation in the dollar and a fall in US net exports. By restricting government expenditures, Europe is able to boost domestic employment at the expense of the US. The non-cooperative outcome is that fiscal policies in both regions are not expansionary enough, with recessions lingering unnecessarily.

Modelling these sorts of games starts by specifying a loss function for the national government, stemming from some combination of unwanted inflation and unemployment. Policy-makers then maximize domestic welfare, assuming the behaviour of the other government is given. This allows the derivation of reaction functions tracing out a continuum of optimal policy responses. The intersection of these reaction functions represents the non-cooperative Nash equilibrium, where each player is pursuing its best strategy, assuming the behaviour of the other government is given. The Stackelberg variant departs from perfect symmetry and allows one national government to be the first mover.

The first mover gains an advantage from being able to choose the most favourable policy, knowing in advance how the other player will react. This framework is frequently employed in a context of unequal interaction, such as between a hegemony like the US, and smaller nations, with an outcome somewhere between the non-cooperative Nash solution and the cooperative outcome. Since the Stackelberg leader internalizes more of the joint gains from considerate behaviour, the leader sets policy at a level closer to the joint optimum.

Can the US and Europe Gain from Policy Cooperation?

Efforts to estimate the gains from cooperation empirically start by assessing the combined losses (in terms of unemployment and inflation, for example) of the players at the non-cooperative Nash equilibrium, and comparing these with the smaller losses at the cooperative solution. Oudiz and Sachs (1984) estimate that cooperation among the G3 countries would have been worth about 0.5 per cent of GDP for each country in the mid-1970s. Looking at the EU, the US and Japan, Hughes Hallet (1986) concludes that cooperation might yield benefits of between 0.5 per cent and 1.5 per cent of GDP. There are several difficulties with these estimates, including their sensitivity to different weightings of policy objectives, unclear causality and estimated gains small enough to be explained by statistical error. Another issue is that the benefits of cooperation are not evenly distributed, with the aforementioned studies finding that a disproportionate share of the gains accrues to the EU, compared to the US, when the two interact. Most of these studies seek to assess the potential gains from cooperation between the US, the EU and Japan in the 1970s and 1980s. However, with increased globalization and strengthened transmission channels, the potential gains are likely to have risen during the 1990s.

Obstacles to Cooperation

Efforts to cooperate more closely are beset by problems. For example, Rogoff (1985) suggests that the impact of cooperation on third parties may render co-operation counter-productive, because the ability to engage in policy cooperation worsens the time consistency problem between national policy-makers and the private sector. Canzoneri and Henderson (1991) also emphasize the importance of 'commitment technology', and suggest that full coordination requires some mechanism to avoid cheating, such as deferring some policy-making sovereignty to supranational organizations.[4] For most national governments, this degree of commitment is difficult.

Even assuming that coordination yields tangible benefits, other problems remain. As noted by Frankel and Rockett (1988), among others, substantial uncertainty about the true model may give rise to policy agreements that lower welfare. Not only do national governments have differing objectives, which may to some extent be internationally mutually exclusive, but they are also using different models to reach conclusions about cause and effect. In this vein, forums that allow policy-makers to exchange views on a regular basis become very important.

Model uncertainty also complicates commitment, because when a target diverges from its agreed value, it may be difficult to discern the source of the divergence. If the US trade deficit increases with the euro countries, is it due to a US monetary tightening beyond what was agreed, or have EU fiscal policies been overly restrictive? Discussions of optimal regimes have therefore emphasized agreement on rules and targets that are easy to monitor, typically exchange rates.[5] Simulations then reveal which regimes respond best to various shocks. While the welfare characteristics depend on the type of shocks, facilitating commitment is central to a good rule, since all policy-makers have an incentive to defect.

Finally, the notion that national governments can act like unitary policy-makers and engage in higher levels of cooperation may also be undermined by existing institutional structures. For example, starting in 1999, monetary policy within the euro countries has been formulated in a single, relatively independent, central bank. Yet, fiscal policy is decentralized within the parameters set by the Stability and Growth Pact.

The US also has an independent central bank in the Federal Reserve System, while fiscal policy is formulated separately. To what extent can these players engage in binding agreements towards full coordination? It may be the case that the US Treasury is interested in cooperating with the euro countries, while the Fed is intent on a different course.

MACROECONOMIC POLICY INTERACTIONS BETWEEN THE US AND EUROPE OVER THE POST-WAR ERA

To better understand transatlantic macroeconomic interdependence and co-operation, it is useful to look more closely at events over the post-war period. Several clear patterns emerge. Firstly, the US has often pursued more expansionary (and inflationary) policies than its major trading partners. Secondly, the US has urged the EU countries and others to adopt more expansionary policies, to increase demand and to appreciate their currencies to lower US current account deficits. Thirdly, several major trading partners of the US, especially Germany and Japan, have felt that they were importing unwanted inflation, and have at times regretted acceding to US demands to stimulate their economies. Fourthly, following several disappointing experiences, macroeconomic coordination is now limited to occasional interventions in the foreign exchange markets, and proposals for deeper coordination are not seriously entertained.

The post-war financial system, crafted in 1944 in Bretton Woods, New Hampshire, was strongly influenced by the difficulties of the 1930s. At that time trade wars and competitive depreciations caused international trade to dry up (see Kindleberger, 1986). To prevent a recurrence, the delegates decided on a system of fixed exchange rates and outlawed devaluations intended to promote competitive advantages over trading partners. Participating countries agreed to keep their exchange rates fixed against the dollar, and the US agreed to fix the dollar price of gold. The dollar would function as the principal reserve currency, and nations could adjust their currency's value only in the event of 'fundamental disequilibria'.

While endorsing this system, participants had arrived at Bretton Woods with differing priorities. The US, for example, was concerned about full employment, having recently recovered from unemployment rates exceeding 25 per cent. The US passed the Employment Act of 1946, stipulating that policy-makers seek maximum employment. With the addition of a statement concerning 'reasonable price stability', the Act was later reaffirmed by the Full Employment and Balanced Growth Act of 1978. In contrast, Germany was more concerned about inflation. Stung by hyperinflation after the First World War, the German polity made the Bundesbank independent, forbade it to hold government debt, and provided a constitutional mandate for the pursuit of low inflation. Thus US macroeconomic policy over the post-war period has probably been more expansionary and more willing to risk inflation than Germany's stance. Germany in turn has frequently complained about domestic inflation arising from US macroeconomic policy initiatives.

Another pattern discernable throughout the post-war period involves the US pursuing expansionary policies that lead to current account deficits and then demanding that trading partners adjust their policies in response. For example, immediately after the Second World War, US aggregate demand was strong (spurred in part by Korean War expenditures), and promoted a revival in Europe and Japan. In this environment, recovering countries followed a strategy of export-led growth. As Neal and Barbezat (1998) discuss, the export-oriented strategy was followed successfully by Germany and Italy in the 1950s and imitated by France and the Netherlands in the 1960s. The influx of goods into the US led to growing US current account deficits and a worldwide dollar glut in the 1960s. As Germany and other countries became satiated with holding dollars, the US advocated revaluing the mark while European policy-makers urged the US to implement contractionary policies to reduce its trade deficit.

US monetary and fiscal policy remained expansionary and inflationary in the late 1960s. Deficit financing of the Vietnam War and expansionary monetary policy led to inflation of over 5 per cent by 1969. As discussed above, if the reserve-issuing country pursues inflationary policies, other countries that keep their currency's value fixed relative to the reserve currency will passively import the associated inflation. Germany and other inflation-averse countries in Europe thus faced the unpleasant prospect of importing high inflation due to expansionary US policies.

As Buiter et al. (1998) discuss, European leaders decided to pursue monetary union partly as a means of resisting the inward-oriented and inflationary policies of the US. Meeting in The Hague in 1969, European leaders authorized a committee headed by Pierre Werner to develop plans for centralizing Europe's monetary policy. The resulting Werner Report proposed creating a central bank like the Federal Reserve to implement European monetary policy. European policy-makers hoped that a single central bank for Europe would be better positioned to sterilize unwanted influences from abroad and to implement policies suitable for Europe.

These plans for a European central bank were delayed by the instability surrounding the breakdown of the Bretton Woods System.[6] Speculators, perceiving the inflationary bias in US policies, launched massive attacks against the dollar. In August 1971 the US stopped exchanging dollars for gold and in December 1971 the G10 countries reached the Smithsonian agreement. This agreement held that exchange rates would remain fixed but that the dollar would be devalued about 8 per cent against other currencies. Persistently large US current account deficits, however, led to continued speculation against the dollar and the Smithsonian Agreement collapsed. In March 1973 fixed exchange rates were abandoned in favour of floating rates. If policies in Europe had been more expansionary, and the stance in the US more contractionary, then the demise of the Bretton Woods system might have been averted, but differing priorities undermined consensus on appropriate policy.

Initially, the floating exchange rate regime was to be temporary, but the OPEC oil shock in 1973–74 precluded a return to fixed exchange rates. To some extent, the flexible exchange rate system allowed each country to pursue its own inflation targets, rather than importing America's inflation rate. Higher oil prices and disinflationary policies triggered major slowdowns in the industrialized economies, and as discussed by Kreinen (1991), no country acting alone could extricate itself by expansionary policies because of balance of payments constraints. With trade balances already under pressure from the higher price of oil imports, any country engaging in stimulative policies that raised growth rates would experience a deteriorating current account.

The US attempted to use such expansionary monetary and fiscal policies in 1976 and 1977, causing US output growth and inflation to be twice as high as in Japan and Germany. The faster growth led to large US trade deficits. These deficits together with the high inflation caused the dollar to depreciate. McCallum (1996) notes that, in a familiar pattern, the US wanted to address the burgeoning trade deficit and depreciating dollar without reducing domestic demand. Consequently it pushed Germany and Japan to pursue expansionary monetary and fiscal policies. The US in turn agreed to decontrol oil prices and reduce tariffs in the future. This agreement was reached in Bonn in July 1978. The joint expansion together with the second oil shock led to higher inflation in Germany and the US. The German government then concluded that the Bonn Agreement had been a mistake.

From October 1979 to October 1982 Fed Chairman Paul Volcker implemented disinflationary monetary policy and beginning in 1981 President Reagan and Congress set in train large budget deficits 'as far as the eye can see'. As discussed above, both contractionary monetary policy and expansionary fiscal policy in the US tends to appreciate the dollar and thus export inflation to other countries. The trade-weighted real exchange rate of the dollar against the other G10 countries increased 56 per cent between 1980 and 1985. Germany and other European countries responded by implementing contractionary monetary policy to limit the dollar appreciation and to fight off inflation.

The appreciation of the dollar that did occur caused problems on both sides of the Atlantic. In the US, it led to trade deficits exceeding $100 billion beginning in 1984 and serious dislocations in trade-sensitive industries. This in turn prompted the introduction of hundreds of protectionist bills in the US Congress (see Destler, 1986). In Europe, there were complaints that the dollar appreciation was damaging the economy by driving up inflation and wages.

In September 1985 the G5 countries reached the Plaza Accord. They declared that the dollar was overvalued and that they intended to lower it through concerted action. The dollar had begun falling in February, and following the Accord it fell further. In another instance of cooperation, European and Japanese central banks lowered interest rates together with the Fed in 1986, helping the Fed to lower interest rates without eliciting a capital outflow and dollar depreciation. The goal was to help the dollar achieve a soft landing. By the end of 1986, however, the dollar had fallen about 50 per cent against the mark and yen, while US trade deficits remained large. Again, US policy-makers did not want to shrink the trade deficit by reducing domestic demand, pushing instead for a further dollar depreciation coupled with expansionary policy in Germany and Japan. The latter resisted both demands and called instead for the US to reduce its budget deficit. As Krugman and Obstfeld (2000) discuss, Germany and Japan were concerned that the depreciating dollar was making their tradeables industries less competitive while stoking domestic inflation.

The two sides made peace in the Louvre Accord of February 1987, agreeing that the value of the dollar was about right. The US promised to reduce its budget deficit while Germany and Japan agreed to stimulate their economies. The Louvre Accord also established secret target zones for exchange rates that the G5 countries and Canada agreed to defend.

By October 1987 friction had returned. US Treasury Secretary James Baker was upset that the Bundesbank had been raising interest rates. He wanted lower rates to stimulate European aggregate demand and thus increase US exports. In contrast, the Bundesbank was concerned about incipient inflation. Baker resorted to arm-twisting, threatening to push down the dollar unless Germany refrained from raising interest rates.[7] Baker's threats triggered anger in Bonn, and on the next day stock markets in the US and throughout the world crashed.[8] The fault lines were the same as before, with the US demanding expansionary policies from a trading partner and the partner resisting out of concern about inflation.

Enthusiasm for international coordination ebbed following this experience. The Fed lowered interest rates in response to the crash, allowing the dollar to fall below the range set in the Louvre Accord (see Krugman and Obtsfeld, 2000). New zones for exchange rates were established, but they were abandoned by the G7 in the 1990s. The expansionary policies implemented by Japan as part of the Louvre Accord contributed to a 'bubble economy', characterized by large increases in Japanese stock and land prices. The popping of this bubble by the Bank of Japan in 1990 has produced a protracted recession and banking crisis in Japan that persisted throughout the 1990s and weakens the drive to seek policy coordination. Moreover, in 1991 and 1992, the Bundesbank pursued contractionary monetary policy to offset the inflationary effects of German reunification while other countries of the European Monetary System (EMS) were not threatened by inflation but by recession. In order to keep their currencies within narrow bands relative to the Deutschemark, these countries had to forgo interest rate decreases, until the crisis in 1992. While the Bundesbank was tightening monetary policy, the Federal Reserve and the Bank of Japan lowered interest rates, pushing the mark to record highs, and prompting Buiter et al. (1998) to comment that the central banks of the G3 could not even achieve the mildest form of policy coordination.

In August 1995 the central banks of the G3 successfully intervened to lift the dollar, which had fallen 60 per cent against the mark and 70 per cent against the yen since 1985. The dollar continued to rise over the next few years, lifting the value of currencies such as the Indonesian rupiah and the Thai baht that were pegged to the dollar, and contributing to the Asian economic crisis of 1997–98. As the dollar appreciated 45 per cent against the Japanese yen between 1995 and the first quarter of 1997, the Indonesian and Thai currencies also appreciated, undermining the competitiveness of their exports to Japan. The ensuing fall in exports contributed to current account deficits ranging from 3.5 per cent of GDP in Indonesia to 8 per cent of GDP in Thailand. Investor concerns about the sustainability of these trends were compounded by other problems, including the fragile state of the banking systems, sparking massive speculative attacks against South-East Asian currencies. These countries soon abandoned their pegs to the dollar, and severe recessions followed.

Again, the US prodded Europe and Japan to deal with the crisis in Asia by increasing domestic demand. As Vice-President Al Gore said, 'We hope the EU sees the advent of EMU as an opportunity to press ahead with long-needed structural reforms ... to ensure that their policies support strong growth in domestic demand so that Europe, too, can assist in the Asian recovery.'[9] Similarly, US Treasury officials complained about the persistent low levels of domestic European investment and 'Europe's reliance on export-led growth'.[10] The Treasury advocated greater flexibility in labour, goods and capital markets to increase investment and thus shift the national saving–investment balance towards lower current account surpluses in Europe. Hence, US policy-makers pushed for increased demand in Europe, undoubtedly not only to help Asian economies but also to reduce the US trade deficit. Since the Stability and Growth Pact limits the ability of European countries to run budget deficits, US leaders pushed for structural changes designed to increase European investment demand and thereby reduce American trade deficits.

Disillusionment with policy coordination grew during the 1990s. As McCallum (1996) discusses, many came to view international coordination as 'thinly disguised attempts by national governments – chiefly the United States, thus far – to get other nations to take actions that might rescue them from the consequences of their own unwise but politically advantageous domestic policies'.[11] Germany in 1991 raised interest rates to fight domestic inflation even though matching interest rate increases were not in the interest of the other EMS countries, forcing many EMS countries to devalue or abandon the fixed exchange rate band to the mark. The US was also in the midst of a recession, and similarly did not welcome the German increase in interest rates. When the Fed lowered interest rates, the dollar depreciated sharply.

The post-war interactions between the industrialized countries demonstrate that although globalization is increasing macroeconomic interdependence and the potential for policy coordination, substantial obstacles remain. The recurring pattern is that the US frequently adopts a more expansionary policy stance, pre-cipitating dollar depreciations and external imbalances. The US reacts by urging the countries of the EU and others to adopt more expansionary policies, that would increase demand, appreciate their currencies and help reduce current account imbalances. Several major trading partners of the US, especially Germany and Japan, are also very concerned about importing unwanted inflation, and have at times felt pushed into pursuing inappropriately expan-sionary policies to increase domestic demand. As the perceived costs and benefits of policy coordination change, so might the prospects for closer har-monization of policies.

ECONOMETRIC EVIDENCE ON MONETARY POLICY INTERACTIONS BETWEEN THE US AND GERMANY

The discussion above indicates that German monetary policy became much more independent in the 1990s. Figure 10.1, which represents US and German monetary policy by short-term interest rates, tells the same story. Before 1990, German and US monetary policy moved more closely together than after 1990, In contrast, Canadian and US short-term interest rates continued to move together throughout the 1990s, as shown in Figure 10.2.

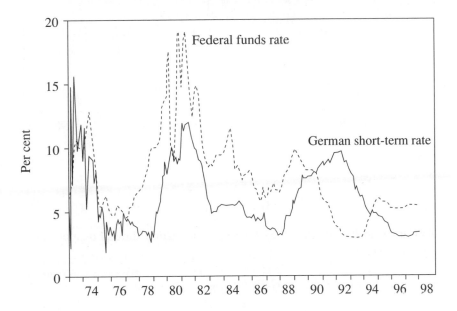

Figure 10.1   German and US short-term interest rates

More formal evidence on policy interactions can be obtained from a vector autoregression (VAR). Several authors (such as, Bernanke and Blinder, 1992; and Christiano, Eichenbaum and Evans, 1996) have used VAR techniques to infer how changes in Federal Reserve policy affect other variables. A VAR is a regression of an n by 1 vector of endogenous variables, y_t, on lagged values of itself

$$y_t = A_1 y_{t-1} + \ldots + A_p y_{t-p} + \varepsilon_t, \; E(\varepsilon_t \varepsilon_t') = \Omega. \tag{1}$$

Provided that stability conditions are satisfied, Equation (1) can be inverted and represented as an infinite vector moving average process:

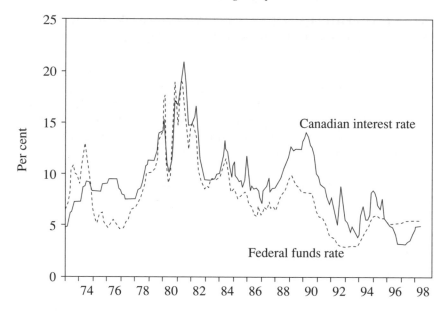

Figure 10.2   Canadian and US short-term interest rates

$$y_t = \varepsilon_t + C_1\varepsilon_{t-1} + C_2\varepsilon_{t-2} + C_3\varepsilon_{t-3} + ... \qquad (2)$$

As Christiano et al. discuss, the Cholesky factorization allows Equation (2) to be rewritten as:

$$y_t = PP^{-1}\varepsilon_t + C_1PP^{-1}\varepsilon_{t-1} + C_2PP^{-1}\varepsilon_{t-2} + ... \ \Gamma_0\upsilon_t + \Gamma_1\upsilon_{t-1} + \Gamma_2\upsilon_{t-2} + ... \ (3)$$

where $\Gamma_i = C_iP$, $\upsilon_t = P^{-1}\varepsilon_t$, and $E[\upsilon_t\upsilon_{ti}'] = I$. The variable υ_{t-1} now represents unexpected (orthogonalized) shocks to the elements of y_t. If one component of y_t represents US monetary policy and another component represents German monetary policy, Equation (3) indicates that the dynamic response of German monetary policy to US monetary policy can be traced out.

Following Christiano, Eichenbaum and Evans (1996) we measure US monetary policy using unexpected changes in the funds rate and include variables similar to those they used. They work with a system that includes the log of real GDP, the log of the GDP deflator, the log of an index of sensitive commodity prices, the federal funds rate, the log of non-borrowed reserves, the log of total reserves and sometimes another variable. We use industrial production growth, the CPI inflation rate, the CRB-Bridge index of sensitive commodity prices, the federal funds rate, the ratio of the log of non-borrowed reserves to the log of total reserves, and a foreign short-term interest rate. The system is estimated over both the January 1973 to December 1989 and January 1973 to December 1995 periods.

The results are presented in Table 10.1. The table confirms that short-term interest rates in Germany were much more responsive to US monetary policy changes before the 1990s. This suggests that the Bundesbank has become less interested in coordinating policies with the Fed, and more focused on domestic considerations such as price stability. With the decline in openness following the advent of the euro and the ECB, the weight given to US monetary policy and other external factors in the formulation of European monetary policy should continue to decline.

Table 10.1   Response of German short-term interest rates to unexpected increase in US federal funds rate[a]

	1973:1–1989:12		1973:1–1995:12	
Months in future	Coefficient	Standard error	Coefficient	Standard error
1	0.058	0.068	0.011	0.052
2	0.083	0.075	0.012	0.060
3	0.228	0.076	0.123	0.060
4	0.311	0.087	0.179	0.071
5	0.305	0.096	0.156	0.078
6	0.362	0.100	0.201	0.081
7	0.379	0.100	0.206	0.077
8	0.334	0.101	0.152	0.071
9	0.338	0.102	0.157	0.073
10	0.357	0.105	0.180	0.074

Note: [a] The table shows the response of German short-term interest rates to a one standard deviation unexpected increase in the federal funds rate. The vector autoregression system includes industrial production, the inflation rate, the CRB-Bridge index of sensitive commodity prices, the federal funds rate, the ratio of the log of non-borrowed reserves to the log of total reserves, and the German call money rate.

CONCLUSION

This chapter has considered macroeconomic interactions between Europe and the US. It has documented the long history of conflict between Europe and the US over monetary, fiscal and exchange rate policy. These clashes have arisen partly because macroeconomic policies on one side of the Atlantic can exert spillover effects on the other side. For example, under a flexible exchange rate system expansionary fiscal policy by the US can cause European currencies to depreciate relative to the dollar, increasing prices and wages in Europe. With monetary or fiscal policies on one side of the Atlantic and worsening target variables on the other side, disagreements become inevitable.

In theory, there should be gains from policy coordination between the US and Europe. For instance, if a US fiscal expansion is matched by a European fiscal expansion, both sides could increase output without affecting the exchange rate or the trade balance.

In practice, experience with coordination has been disappointing. In the 1978 Bonn Agreement, Germany agreed to match a fiscal expansion by the US. When inflation rose in Germany the next year, Bonn concluded that the agreement had been a mistake, Similarly, in the 1987 Louvre Accord the US agreed to reduce its budget deficit in return for a more stimulative policy by Germany. Within eight months, US and German officials were in open conflict, contributing to the October 1987 stock market crash. Following these experiences, coordination has been mainly limited to intervention in the foreign exchange market when European currencies or the euro are overvalued or undervalued relative to the dollar.

In the macroeconomic policy interactions discussed here certain patterns emerge. Firstly, the US tends to pursue more expansionary and inflationary policies than its European trading partners. Secondly, the US urges the EU countries to adopt more expansionary policies or stronger domestic currencies to lower the US current account deficits that result from the unilateral expansion. Thirdly, Germany and other European countries conclude that US policies and/or their responses caused unwanted inflation, and regret accepting US demands.

Part of the reason for this pattern is that the macroeconomic priorities of Germany and the rest of Europe probably differ from those of the United States. Germany, as Henning (1994) discusses, is averse to inflation. The disastrous hyperinflation of the 1920s has made the German government risk-averse towards inflation. In fighting inflation first the Bundesbank and now the European Central Bank (ECB) follow a lexicographic ordering of goals. As Gros et al. (2000) discuss, price stability is pursued first, and only when there is no danger on this front are other goals pursued. US policy-makers, on the other hand, dislike inflation but are probably more willing to engage in expansionary and potentially inflationary policies than their European counterparts. US law requires policy-makers to pursue both full employment and price stability. Thus European macroeconomic policy pursues price stability first and other objectives second, while US policy-makers attach large weight to both full employment and price stability.

In addition Germany, and other European countries, are more open than the US and more concerned with international competitiveness and similar issues. The US has often given short shrift to international considerations when designing macroeconomic policies.

As discussed above, if the US pursues more expansionary macroeconomic policies than Europe and if the US is more concerned about the effect of the exchange rate on international competitiveness then one would expect the US to run current account deficits with Europe. This is so since the trade deficit equals the excess of saving over investment. A country like the US that implements more expansionary policies will tend to have less saving relative to investment and run trade deficits. These effects would be reinforced if European policy-makers are more likely than American policy-makers to adjust the exchange rate to improve the trade balance.

In reality we have seen the US run large trade deficits with Europe, implying that large amounts of US assets have flowed into Europe. The US current account deficit in recent years has increased from $248 billion in 1998 to almost $400 billion in 2000. As US citizens have thus acquired goods from Europe, European citizens have acquired dollar-denominated assets from the US. In recent years European portfolio holders have been willing to hold US assets because prospects for growth and profits in America were favourable. If European growth accelerates relative to the US, this might change. European wealth holders might then unload US assets, causing the dollar to fall relative to the euro, US interest rates to rise, and US stock prices to fall. If these adjustments happen in an orderly manner policy-makers on both sides of the Atlantic will probably not be alarmed. If these adjustments are accompanied by overshooting and a *sauve qui peut* mentality, however, the Fed and the ECB would probably intervene to help restore stability.

Absent such a crisis, or a clearly misvalued exchange rate, macroeconomic cooperation between Europe and the US is likely to remain limited. Negative experiences with coordination have left a bad taste in European policy-makers' mouths. As envisioned in the Werner Commission report, Europe now has a central bank and an economic union strong enough to resist unwanted influences from the US and to focus on policies suitable for Europe. The ECB and the Federal Reserve will likely interact in the future like two large ships passing at sea, each aware of the other but focusing on the wind, waves and obstacles in front of them.

NOTES

1. See Krugman and Obstfeld (2000) for a detailed discussion of the theory behind the gold exchange standard.
2. As noted in Mooslechner and Schuerz (1999), 176.

3. Mooslechner and Schuerz (1999), 176.
4. Canzoneri and Henderson (1991), p. 6.
5. Mooslechner and Schuerz (1999), 177.
6. Krugman and Obstfeld (2000).
7. *New York Times*, 16 October 1987.
8. *New York Times*, 17 October 1987.
9. Henning (2000), 16.
10. Henning (2000), 16.
11. McCallum (1996), 257.

REFERENCES

Bernanke, Ben and Alan Blinder (1992), 'The federal funds rate and the channels of monetary transmission', *American Economic Review*, 82, 901–21.

Buiter, Willem, Giancarlo Corsetti and Paolo Pesenti (1998), *Financial Markets and European Monetary Cooperation*, Cambridge: Cambridge University Press.

Canzoneri, Matthew and Dale Henderson (1991), *Monetary Policy in Interdependent Economies: A Game Theoretic Approach*, Cambridge, MA: MIT Press.

Caves, Richard, Jeffrey Frankel and Ronald Jones (1999), *World Trade and Payments*, New York: HarperCollins.

Christiano, Larry, Martin Eichenbaum and Charles Evans (1996), 'The effects of monetary policy shocks: some evidence from the flow of funds', *Review of Economics and Statistics*, 78, 16–34.

Currie, David A., Gerald Holtham and Andrew Hughes Hallett (1989), 'The theory and practice of international policy coordination: does coordination pay?', Centre for Economic Policy Research Discussion Paper: 325.

Destler, I.M. (1986), *American Trade Politics: System Under Stress*, Washington DC: Institute for International Economics.

Eichengreen, Barry (1992), *Golden Fetters: The Gold Standard and the Great Depression*, New York: Oxford University Press.

Frankel, Jeffrey and Katherine Rocket (1988), 'International macroeconomic policy coordination when policymakers do not agree on the true model', *American Economic Review*, 78, 318–40.

Gros, Daniel, Olivier Davanne, Michael Emerson, Thomas Mayer, Guido Tabellini and Niels Thygesen (2000), '*Quo vadis* euro? The cost of muddling through', Brussels: Center for European Policy Studies.

Henning, C. Randall (1994), *Currencies and Politics in the United States, Germany, And Japan*, Washington DC: Institute for International Economics.

Henning, C. Randall (2000), 'US–EU relations after the inception of the Monetary Union: cooperation or rivalry?', in C. Randall Henning and Pier Carlo Padoan (eds), *Transatlantic Perspectives on the Euro*, Washington DC: Brookings Institution Press.

Hughes-Hallet, A.J. (1986), 'International policy design and the sustainability of policy bargains', *Journal of Economic Dynamics and Control*, 10, 467–94.

Kindleberger, Charles (1986), *The World in Depression*, 1929–39, Berkeley, CA: University of California Press.

Kreinen, Mordechai (1991), *International Economics, A Policy Approach*, San Diego, CA: Harcourt Brace Jovanovich.

Krugman, Paul and Maurice Obstfeld (2000), *International Economics*, Reading, MA: Addison-Wesley.

McCallum, Bennett (1996), *International Monetary Economics*, New York: Oxford University Press.

Mooslechner, Peter and Martin Schuerz (1999), 'International macroeconomic policy coordination: any lessons for EMU? A selective survey of the literature', *Empirica*, 26, 170–80.

Neal, Larry and Daniel Barbezat (1998), *The Economics of the European Union and the Economies of Europe*, New York: Oxford University Press.

Oudiz, G. and Jeffrey Sachs (1984), 'Macroeconomic policy coordination among the industrial economies', *Brookings Papers on Economic Activity*, 1, 1–76.

Rogoff, Kenneth (1985), 'Can international monetary policy coordination be counter-productive?', *Journal of International Economics*, 18, 199–217.

Salvatore, Dominick (1993), *International Economics*, New York: Macmillan.

Temin, Peter (1989), *Lessons from the Great Depression*, Cambridge, MA: MIT Press.

Tobin, James (1998), 'Currency unions, American v. European', unpublished manuscript, Yale University.

11. European Union planning for international economic cooperation

Gavin Boyd

In the international political economy the European Union is the only large advanced system of substantially institutionalized regional collective management. Its attributes and the dimensions of its structural and policy interdependencies have special significance for the development of cooperation in the rest of the world that will serve the common good, reducing the costs and enhancing the benefits of globalization. The integration of its internal market, although not complete, has growth effects which have been increased by the formation of its Monetary Union, and its system of governance, despite strains, is gradually responding to the functional logic of establishing decision processes for effective harmonization of the policies of its member states, and for the implementation of common external trade, investment and competition policies.

The most significant structural and policy interdependencies are with the USA, and they have evolved with numerous asymmetries. The USA has long been established as a large economic and political union, with an internal market that has provided scope for the development of major technologically advanced enterprises, with superior capacities for the penetration of markets in less industrialized countries. The foreign economic policies of successive US governments have promoted increasing openness in the world economy. The European Union, because of slow progress toward the integration of its internal market, and in the development of its system of governance, has not provided comparable scope for the emergence of large internationally competitive firms in medium and higher technological sectors. Growth has been slower than in the USA, causing flows of investment to that country. The size of the European Union, however, has attracted much US investment, most of which has come with a stronger entrepreneurial thrust than the European investment in the USA. Meanwhile the European system of collective management has failed to introduce a substantial common structural policy that could promise attainment of a more balanced interdependence. Interactions with the USA on trade, investment and macroeconomic issues have been affected by relative weaknesses in bargaining strengths related to the asymmetries at the structural level.

In the development of economic and political ties with the rest of the world the Union is less active than the USA. The contrasts have become more significant since the late 1990s because of Japan's financial difficulties: the USA has in effect been advantaged by enhanced opportunities for wider involvement in the international political economy, while the Union's growth prospects have become more dependent on commerce with the United States. European trade and other links with Japan have been much smaller than the USA's, although for decades it has been evident that the development of such links could contribute to higher growth in the Union and to improved bargaining strength in its Atlantic relations.

The Union's collective management processes, affected by decisional problems, have an inward-looking quality; hence there are questions about its capacity to plan for and devote energies to innovative statecraft focusing on structural issues of basic significance in its foreign economic relations. The intra-Union spread of gains from regional and external commerce is uneven, because of differences in levels of industrialization, related to contrasts in scales of involvement in global trade and transnational production. This diversity affects potentials for interest aggregation and for consensual policy-making. The challenges that demand attention in the Union's external economic relations, however, are urgent.

The high level of structural interdependence with the USA entails vulnerabilities. There is a very serious danger that a financial crisis, resulting from losses of investor confidence in speculative appreciations of US stock, could have severe repercussions in Europe, especially because the Union's expanding securities markets are being linked more and more closely with those in the USA. The linkages are facilitating flows of relatively passive investment to the United States. This affects the funding of European industries whose development is essential for the attainment of more balanced Atlantic structural interdependencies.

ASYMMETRIC GLOBALIZATION

In the deepening integration which is linking the industrialized states, and, to a lesser extent, the rest of the world, the European Union, while absorbing new members in its immediate environment, is becoming more closely associated with the USA, rather than with Japan, and is not expanding its commercial bonds with developing states as extensively as the USA. The international operations of American firms are on a larger scale, and the main concentration of direct investment by these firms is in Europe; globally they are securing greater shares of world markets, in competition against European and other competitors.[1] Relative bargaining strengths in Atlantic relations are being altered because of the market and structural changes, but possibilities for building trust and goodwill, from which the European Union especially could benefit, are being negatively affected by frictions over trade disputes with the USA.[2] Within the Union decisional problems persist because of diverging national perspectives and preferences.[3] Consensus-building and collaborative policy learning is difficult, and can be made more difficult by US policies that have divisive effects, for example in the application of selective pressures during trade disputes.[4] Problems in Union decision-making, moreover, are also in danger of becoming more intractable because of rivalries to attract investment by large US and other international firms.[5]

Since the formation of its Single Market the European Union has assumed greater importance as the principal destination of US direct investment. The American corporate presence has been expanding, mainly through mergers and acquisitions, seizing opportunities provided by the weaker competitiveness of many European enterprises and the availability of higher-volume financing at home – due especially to upward valuations in US stock markets, a process attracting much passive investment from Europe. The most prominent structural consequences of the incoming US direct investment tend to affect the automobile sector, where there is excess European capacity and no spontaneous drive for rationalization. In the financial sector, where the US presence is far greater than the European counterpart in the USA, US credit institutions have superior capacities to fund profitable ventures, regionally and globally.

The gross product of US non-bank majority-owned foreign affiliates in Europe was $297,604 million in 1997, that is about three-fifths of the global total for such affiliates, and more than three times greater than their total in Asia and the Pacific. In Europe the gross products of the affiliates as percentages of host country GDPs were 6.8 per cent in Britain, 5.5 per cent in Belgium and the Netherlands, and 2.7 per cent in both Germany and France, but 16.5 per cent in Ireland. Sales by these affiliates in Europe were $1331,199 million in 1998,[6] that is several times larger than Germany's exports to its partners in the European Union. US holdings of European stocks in 1998 totalled $959.8 billion.[7]

The European direct investment position in the USA totalled $539,906 million on a historical cost basis in 1998, and roughly half of this was in manufacturing. The US direct investment position in Europe on a historical cost basis in the same year was $489,539 million – a figure to be interpreted with reference to differences in historical costs since the post-war reconstruction in Europe. The degree of balance in Atlantic direct investment positions – depending on assessments of the historical cost figures – accounted for large rises in European direct investment during the late 1990s that seem to have been responses to higher growth in the USA and the emergence of social democratic governments in Britain, France and Germany. The largest stock of European investment in the

USA is British, and much of it appears to be relatively passive. Britain is the main destination of US direct investment in Europe.[8]

Mergers and acquisitions by British firms are mainly with US enterprises, while mergers and acquisitions by continental European firms are usually among themselves, mostly in sectors with declining competitiveness.[9] The contrasts reflect differences in corporate governance, the influence of cultural affinities and long-established commercial links.[10] The trends in mergers and acquisitions reflect intensifying competition. In this rivalry US companies, especially in higher-technology sectors, are well positioned, because of generally larger resources, greater entrepreneurial dynamism and their strengths in their home economy, as well as because they have been advantaged, in recent years, by Japan's economic difficulties.[11] A proliferation of joint research ventures in the USA's information, communication and automobile sectors during the 1990s has contributed to the maintenance of technological leads over European firms.[12]

In the world trading system the Union has considerably larger commerce than the USA with developing countries, especially in Africa and the Middle East, but trades on a smaller scale than the USA with Latin America, and lags behind the USA in commerce with East Asia. In all this external trade the most active Union members are Germany, France and Britain. Their commerce is linked increasingly with transnational production, but in proportions smaller than those in the USA's foreign economic relations. Germany, the largest Union exporter, has a solidarity-based business culture which sustains preferences for operations in the home economy. Much of the outward direct investment thus far has been going to East European countries in line for Union membership.[13]

The uneven Union pattern of international economic involvement reflects not only the restrictive effects of market separation within the Union that have been operating for several decades but also the pressures on, and the consequences of, fiscal policies, related especially to high welfare costs. These fiscal policies are now having to cope with reductions in tax revenues associated with high unemployment and slack growth, and also with outward direct and portfolio investment. With continuing population declines, slow regional growth tends to be perpetuated. Levels of government debt in the Union are high, but the regional current account is in rough balance, and asset appreciations in the gradually integrating Union financial markets are moderate: vulnerabilities to sharp changes in investor confidence result mainly from links with the USA.[14]

While the USA has been experiencing higher growth and thus drawing Union as well as Japanese investment[15] this growth is at unsustainable levels that cannot be lowered sufficiently without politically unacceptable monetary tightening. The large and expanding securities sector operates with superior capacities to draw investment from the rest of the world, and any monetary tightening adds to upward pressures on the currency generated by that sector's operations, thus negatively affecting exports and worsening the balance of payments deficits.[16] These deficits would cause currency depreciation, were it not for the investment inflows, but large volumes of these could be reversed during a financial crisis.[17]

All this means that the Union has a vital interest in managing its structural and policy interdependencies with the USA in ways that will entail reduced vulnerabilities and ensure transition to more balanced and more stable Atlantic production and trade linkages. It is also imperative for the Union to promote more regionally-based growth in its own area, and to build more extensive links with countries outside the Atlantic relationship – a task that will require efforts to assist economic development in many of those countries.

INTERNATIONAL ENGAGEMENT

The European Union has evolved with slow and conflicted policy learning about the functional logic of complete market integration and the formation of Monetary Union. Meanwhile institutional development and consensus-building for management of the Union's structural and policy interdependencies with the USA, and with other states, has become difficult. Political processes in the member states have remained distinctly national, while adjusting to multiple requirements for intra-Union cooperation, and with the intensification of corporate rivalries for market shares in Europe, competition between their governments has tended to become more active. This has been especially evident in aids to industry. Union and non-European enterprises, however, have been operating with gradually increasing autonomy in quests for market shares, and in shaping structural interdependencies, thus complicating industrial policy rivalries in the Union. Absorption in these, and in issues concerning the deepening and enlargement of the Union, has limited attention to interdependencies with the USA and the rest of the world.

European foreign economic policy has accordingly evolved reactively and slowly to external challenges, despite the asymmetries in structural interdependence with the USA, including the outflows of investment to that country, which hinder attainment of higher growth. Rational adaptation to the external challenges, in the common interest, while tending to become even more difficult because of intra-Union rivalries, has also become a more demanding task because of problems affecting the role of the European Commission as a common institution for regional interest aggregation and policy activation. Ambivalence toward the Commission, reflecting awareness of organizational deficiencies associated with its multinational staffing, has limited its scope for initiative, including its ability to promote policy learning through sponsorship of independent studies for enhancement of the Union system of collective management.[18]

Potentials for productive collaboration have depended very much on the Franco-German relationship which dominates Union policy-making. The German political economy, with well-institutionalized processes of deliberative consensual policy-making, has a superior capacity for leadership in the collective management system, and this accords with the size and dynamism of the German economy. A strong German role in Union collective management, however, is not altogether acceptable to French elites, and coherent expression of their preferences is difficult because of personality conflicts and ideological cleavages, as well as institutional weaknesses attributable to strong individualism in the political culture. With all this there is an element of frustration because of French sensitivities to contrasts in structural competitiveness between the two countries. Yet on each side there is considerable political will to maintain cooperation while responding to the interests of other member states.[19] Britain's reluctance to align with the regional integration process tends to sustain mutual awareness of interdependence in the Franco-German relationship.

The challenges of structural asymmetries in Atlantic relations are partly obscured by affirmations of confidence in the efficiencies of market forces.[20] Economic policy guidelines adopted by Union governments and the European Commission express reliance on the growth effects of free markets.[21] The main purpose has been to oblige European firms to enhance their performance in response to competitive pressures, with reduced dependence on government subsidies. Optimism about this has been encouraged by the formation of the Monetary Union, but not sufficiently to reduce substantially the large flows of investment to the USA, which have had negative effects on the funding of European industries and on the confidence of European investors. The emphasis on free market forces has limited consideration of the potential benefits of a common structural policy, the feasibility of which would depend very much on German support. There are tacit German concerns to avoid having to subsidize any major scheme for industrial development in other member states.

The engrossing effects of Atlantic trade issues have also limited Union attention to basic problems of structural interdependence, although resolution of these problems has been made more imperative by those trade issues. Within the Union the Atlantic trade issues have had divisive effects, and member governments have sought to increase their influence on the European Commission's responsibility for external trade.[22] The diverging interests of these governments, while complicating issues in the Union's foreign commerce, including those relating to items outstanding since the end of the Uruguay Round,[23] have affected potentials for effective engagement with all areas of foreign economic relations, while in effect increasing incentives for European firms to concentrate on their own strategies for regional and global expansion. At the policy level Germany's interests have assumed special prominence, as Germany is the leading European exporter to the USA and to the developing countries, and its trade and investment links with East European states are much larger than those of other Union members. The possibilities for increased Union access to the US market under future global or Atlantic trade agreements have greater significance for Germany than for France and Britain, and for these two countries the competitive pressures to be anticipated have more serious implications than they would have for Germany. French interests in maintaining a high level of agricultural protection for the Union are major sources of difficulties in trade policy interactions with the USA.[24]

The European Commission, despite its organizational problems, is a source of pressure for reductions in aids to industry by member governments.[25] In part this pressure is directed against Germany, in recognition that its subsidies are quite advantageous for its firms, and that they raise questions about its official affirmations of commitment to free market principles. There is uneven progress in the efforts to lower state aids to industry, and the hoped-for improvements in the efficiencies and competitiveness of Union firms appear to be developing slowly. The problem of lagging European structural competitiveness thus remains serious and, it must be stressed, will tend to become more serious while large outflows of investment to the USA continue.

Difficulties in interest aggregation within the Franco-German relationship limit potentials for providing constructive inputs into Union policy processes. The solidarity-based German political economy generates coordinated policy-level and corporate responses to issues in the nation's structural interdependencies, but the fragmented pattern of business representation and the institutionally weak French governance system do not offer substantial collaborative capabilities.[26] Because of the incompatibilities cooperation is a very high level process, managed instrumentally, with strains; the balance of bargaining strengths is changing, as Germany leads in the development of economic ties with other Union members. Stronger German influence in shaping the Union's foreign economic policies thus seems probable, and may be more evident after the admission of prospective East European members, but is unlikely to be exerted for the activation of a design to enhance the structural competitiveness of the entire Union.

EUROPEAN COMMISSION FUNCTIONS

The Franco-German collaboration is managed with some tendencies to assert leadership in ways that can restrict the European Commission's scope for initiative. The Commission, however, depending on the quality of its leadership, does have important advocacy potential, on the basis of formal responsibility for proposing broad economic policy guidelines for member states and the Union. These guidelines have been formulated with sensitivities to the preferences of member governments, but the Commission has status as an independent source of economic advice for the promotion of efficiencies in the Union market, with emphasis on the growth effects of sound macroeconomic management.[27] The guidelines are in effect supplemented by Commission studies which build on independent academic research; those for 1999 were preceded by a Commission volume, *Economic Policy in EMU*, edited by Marco Buti and Andre Sapir.[28] This volume stressed the likely effects of EMU on Union growth, but rather ignored the significance of investment flows for such growth, although work on this subject was being done by Portes and Rey.[29]

Since the establishment of the Monetary Union increases in European and Atlantic mergers and acquisitions, accelerating concentration trends, have made the structural significance of investment flows more evident, but the Commission's scope for promoting policy learning on this subject through studies directed at Union decision-makers appears to have been restricted by the attitudes of member governments, in part because of their investment bidding rivalries. The Commission's advocacy role however has been given some encouragement by indications that there was considerable political will behind the establishment of the European Monetary Union – unrecognized by many economists[30] – and that this has since been tested by depreciations of the euro attributable mainly to the outflows of investment to the USA. Some of this investment has gone into large-scale highly leveraged operations in international financial markets, in association with US institutions working, it appears, outside their national regulatory framework.[31]

European Central Bank studies of investment flows affecting the euro are in effect widening opportunities for the Commission to review the policy implications of the structural consequences of those flows. The Commission's scope for initiative may also be widened by growing awareness of losses of tax revenues associated with the investment flows.[32] Because of the importance of fiscal discipline in member governments for the operation of the Monetary Union, moreover, the European Central Bank may be expected to direct attention to the revenue issues, as well as to the implications of the investment flows for the funding of European industries – that is while member governments are under pressure from the Commission to reduce industrial subsidies.

The Commission's competition policy responsibilities also provide scope for initiatives to promote policy learning in member states. Judgements that have to be made about market power changes resulting from large mergers and acquisitions inevitably open up structural issues, within the Union but also in Atlantic relations. Member governments have been unwilling to increase the Commission's authority on competition issues, but this does cover questions about the use of high degrees of market power, regionally and internationally, which, with ongoing concentration trends, have increasing structural significance. Structural policy rivalries between member governments are sensitive matters of concern to the Commission, and its staff and advisors are associated informally with academic research communities within which studies of the Union's investment and trade links can be sponsored.[33]

Linkages between competition policy issues and the industrial subsidies policies of member governments are tending to become more significant in interactions between those governments and the Commission. More assertiveness by member governments seems probable, because of the political importance of hoped-for increases in the spread of gains within the Single Market. Yet the intra-Union rivalries could open the way for Commission endeavours to promote wide-ranging dialogue on the growth effects of current trends in investment flows and structural change. In this context the Union's various technology enhancement programmes would deserve close study: their benefits have been limited by the entrepreneurial deficiencies of Union firms that were intended to be aided by those programmes.[34] To the extent that technological lags have persisted, Union enterprises have incentives to seek collaboration with US companies.

MACROMANAGEMENT IMPERATIVES

The European Union, as the main destination of US foreign direct investment, benefits from resulting technology transfers, rises in levels of technological competence, social capital development, employment increases, tax revenues and infusions of entrepreneurial vigour, as well as a concerted representation of corporate interests in Brussels. The structural asymmetries in Atlantic relations, however, are challenging. The technological lags and weaker competitiveness of Union firms, their generally smaller resources, the high levels of taxation in their economies, the uncertain growth prospects of their region, and the substantial drifts of investment to the USA, obligate very active responses to achieve more balanced and more dynamic interdependencies. In the absence of a spontaneous concerting of corporate strategies aligned with that requirement, the European Commission and the European Central Bank assume special significance as institutions capable of promoting cooperation by member governments and sectoral associations in a constructive design. This could evoke positive policy-level responses by the USA and collaborative initiatives by US firms.

A primary requirement is to reduce the outflows of investment and increase the funding of Union firms from regional sources, while focusing Union elite concerns on the vulnerabilities associated with high levels of speculation in the USA, and on the fundamental need for reform in world financial markets, to ensure their service of real economies, including especially those disadvantaged by the attractions of debt-led growth areas. The structural and competition policy issues posed as Union firms are displaced or acquired by incoming US enterprises demand attention in this context, that is in the perspective of concerns to work for equitable partnering, rather than accept reliance on efficiencies generated in Darwinian competition.

The development of Union financial markets, influenced by changes in systems of corporate governance, and facilitated by the establishment of Monetary Union, is contributing to larger-scale financing of Union firms, but is also expanding opportunities for investment in the USA as a higher growth area.[35] Meanwhile the Union as a whole is becoming more exposed to disruption in the event of a US financial crisis, and there may well be increasing uncertainties about the capacities of Union financial institutions to provide emergency funding for enterprises that would be affected by the contagion resulting from such a crisis. The operations of the very large US presence in the Union financial sectors could be sharply contracted.

The formation of a strong integrated European banking system, oriented toward priority financing of Union firms, will have to be a major objective of the European Central Bank. For this, the European Commission can assist by sponsoring studies to build a firm consensus in Union elite networks – that is in conjunction with advocacy by the European Central Bank. For its responsibilities, relating to price stability, exchange rates and overall growth, a strong integrated regional banking system will be essential to limit weakening of its monetary transmission mechanism. This is being threatened by the expansion of the securities sector as it becomes more closely linked with that in the USA.[36]

Shifts toward adoption of the US agency-type system of corporate governance are driving expansion of the securities sector. The most efficient use of capital which this promotes, however, it must be stressed, is evident in the flow of investment to the USA, where there is much diversion into rent-seeking in financial markets, rather than productive activity in the real economy, and the scale of the speculative rent-seeking risks precipitating a crisis. The development of a strong integrated European banking system, then, will have to be accompanied by firm regulation of the securities sector, with orientation of its operations in line with the funding requirements of Union firms, and efforts to cope with the tax avoidance problems associated with the functioning of international financial markets, especially in the Atlantic context. The necessary policy consensus, which will have to be promoted under the leadership of the European Central Bank, will have to engage with issues in the evolution of European corporate governance systems. A guiding principle, in line with the Union's need for higher, more stable, and more regionally-based growth, will have to be that the efficiencies of relational contracting, in systems of corporate governance and intercorporate governance, are on the whole superior to those of totally competitive capitalism, with its strong con-centration tendencies, priority funding of short-term corporate achievers and high-volume rent-seeking.[37]

A notable concentration trend in the European banking sector since the mid-1980s has enhanced prospects for guided development of a strong integrated Union banking system that could offer improved service of the funding needs of regional firms. The larger banks which have been emerging, however, are moving more into profitable activities in world financial markets that are dominated by US institutions. Imperatives for effective regulation have become stronger because of the increased importance of stability in the more concen-trated sector, and its growing involvement in international financial markets with competitive pressures that motivate risk-taking. Current supervisory arrangements in Europe are inadequate, especially because of limitations on the regulatory authority of member governments, and the weaknesses of co-ordinating mechanisms that would have to deal with stresses in the sector. Regionally centralized banking supervision has become essential.[38]

The rationale for vigorous engagement with the tasks of building a well-integrated European banking system is becoming stronger as the region's vicious circle of low growth and capital flight continues. Planning for com-prehensive resolution of the Union's problems, however, will clearly require highly constructive macromanagement. It has been argued that a phase of fiscal expansion, with changes in labour and welfare policies, and with monetary loosening that would be terminated after an interval, would have substantial growth effects,[39] but this could contribute to larger outflows of investment, because of lack of confidence in the overall effects of the stimulus, and the prospect of higher tax burdens in the future to cover the costs of the expansion.

The constructive macromanagement that can be advocated would emphasize promotion of relational contracting, to build a solidarity-based system of European capitalism. Such a system has been operating in Germany, but has been weakened by strains in management–labour relations, under the pressures of high welfare costs.[40] A doctrine of solidarity-based European capitalism could be introduced into Union policy guidelines through Commission-sponsored conferences focusing on the efficiencies of relational contracting, its potentials for risk-sharing and for stable long-term planning, and its benefits for the development of institutions for the representation of aggregated corporate interests, as well as for employee security and the building of social capital. In the emphasis on efficiencies stress could be placed on the practical logic of concerting entrepreneurial initiatives in the light of ongoing advances in frontier technology and, thus, on the importance of trustful sharing of the tacit as well as codified knowledge that can generate such initiatives, with long-term per-spectives.[41] The entire promotional endeavour would have to be undertaken with awareness that delays would be costly, because of the low levels of investor confidence reflected in the capital outflows to the USA, and also because all areas of collaboration in the Union system of collective management are tending to be affected by disparities in the spread of gains from intra-Union commerce.

Without progress toward the development of a form of solidarity-based European capitalism investment, bidding rivalries between Union governments are likely to provide widening opportunities for US and, to a lesser extent, Japanese firms to take advantage, selectively, of locational factors and prospective subsidies throughout the region, and engage in more active merger and acquisition strategies. The effects on European business confidence will thus no doubt contribute to further outflows of investment to the USA. Meanwhile the US and also the Japanese companies expanding in Europe will tend to incorporate their Union operations more and more into global production strategies, so as to enhance the benefits of multinationality. The technology transfers and other advantages hoped for by host governments will thus probably assume narrower dimensions, for example of the kind associated with extensive patterns of vertical specialization. As these patterns become larger, through geographic dispersals of stages in production processes, associated technology transfers tend to become more restricted and, in the management of the dispersed production processes, there is more scope for locational changes to exploit alternative options, notably through shifts to lower-cost areas. Union firms are active in dispersed extra-regional production, but in general their capacities for this are weaker than those of US and Japanese multinationals.[42]

The structural policies of member states, especially the less industrialized ones, while tending to rely increasingly on investment bidding, are influenced by expectations of agglomeration trends, in which the attractions of German centres of innovation are major factors. Agglomerations of research-intensive production can be expected to increase in size but shrink in numbers, thus altering the regional pattern, in line with the USA's experience. The strategies of European firms and of globally more significant US and Japanese companies are likely to be increasingly significant in this trend, and it will no doubt intensify structural policy rivalries within the Union, to the advantage of large externally-based multinationals. The anticipated divisive effects and increases in structural asymmetries could be given prominence in Commission efforts to promote the development of a system of solidarity-based European capitalism.

ATLANTIC FINANCIAL POLICY COOPERATION

The funding requirements of European industries, which demand attention because of the Union's outward investment flows, indicate imperatives for collaboration with the USA, and to a lesser extent with Japan, to engage with fundamental problems in global financial markets. The very high-volume speculative operations in these markets, and their virtual priority funding of potentially high-yield US firms, obligate vigorous Union efforts to secure international support for change, in line with the basic interests of the major interdependent real economies. The speculative operations have to be recognized as the principal challenges, because of the dangers that the false optimism which they tend to generate often results in risk-taking that can be very destabilizing, that is in a context in which the probabilities of herd behaviour and contagion become greater as financial markets become more internationalized. Speculation, moreover, is the main force driving the appreciation of US stocks that attracts European investment.

A primary task in Union policy planning, then, will be to work for more effective regulation of the securities sector in the USA, and to induce the adoption of US monetary restraints that will dampen the speculation.[43] This is a task which could enlist Japanese support, as the Japanese economy is also affected by investment outflows to the USA. Union efforts in the bilateral relationship with the USA, meanwhile, could be made more effective through persuasion and leverage within the International Monetary Fund: its periodic assessments of capital markets have emphasized the potentially destabilizing effects of US stock appreciations. The Union advocacy in the IMF, it should be noted, would be more potent if linked with efforts to secure representation as a single unit in that organization, with weighted voting based on the size of the Union economy.

Speculative asset appreciation in the USA, because of its dangers for the global economy, has become an international public goods problem of vast proportions, affecting prospects for the European Monetary Union and for the regional growth which it is intended to activate. Firm representation of Union concerns will be necessary, and it must be reiterated that delays will entail increasing risks. The larger the accumulation of Union investment in the USA, the more extensive will be the European effects of a US financial crisis. Moreover the longer the management of US financial sectors remains internationally nonaccountable, and is influenced by American political interests benefiting from investor optimism, the greater will be the danger that asset appreciations will reach high levels before falling sharply, in conditions of multiple information uncertainties. The European Commission and the European Central Bank clearly have obligations to focus the attention of member governments on these problems through policy planning conferences and through the sponsorship of studies directed at US as well as European decision-makers.

Resistance from Union financial institutions and US financial enterprises in Europe could discourage the necessary initiatives. The Commission and the European Central Bank clearly have to confront member governments not only with the magnitude of the investment diversion problem but also with the related revenue effects and the growth implications of the higher rewards of trade in financial assets, compared with trade in goods. Quests for Britain's cooperation will require intense efforts, because of the size and openness of its financial sector, and because it hosts the main European US financial presence. The decline of manufacturing in Britain is a topic on which initial discussions could focus, as the funding of British industry is affected more seriously than that of Continental sectors by the flows of investment to the USA. British membership of the European Monetary Union could set the context for very productive inter-actions on fundamentals with other member states which could be prepared for by Commission and European Central Bank initiatives. The politics of intra-Union relations have necessitated nominal Commission acceptance of integration differentials within the Union, resulting from the decisions of groups of members to link their economies more closely without waiting to be joined by all members. The Commission's responsibilities to the Union as a whole, however, provide a firm basis for initiatives to engage comprehensively with all the problems of funding regional growth.[44]

A special concern which could be made evident in the proposed initiatives is that European financial institutions need a more favourable context for their operations in the USA, where their presence is much smaller than that of the US financial sector in the Union. The European presence, whose scope for expansion could be enhanced through Atlantic dialogue, could become a source of advocacy in support of European Commission and European Central Bank endeavours to secure US cooperation for the necessary reforms in financial markets. If under strong Union regulation the European financial enterprises in the USA could demonstrate superior prudential management, which could be helpful for the financing of Union growth, even while flows of investment from Europe to the USA were being facilitated.

A basic consideration in a European rationale for financial market reform is that, in the imbalanced Atlantic interdependence, the health and operational orientation of US financial institutions have vital implications for Europe and the rest of the world, and that accordingly there must be active external account-ability, in constructive Atlantic interactions. Without such interactions the activities of US financial enterprises will retain much scope for independent operations under supervisory and regulatory structures susceptible to domestic pressures and lagging behind the sophisticated innovations of financial instru-ments within the sector. The risk-taking psychology which develops in such a system during times of speculative asset appreciation, encouraged to a degree by expectations of bailouts for distressed enterprises in the event of a crisis, has to be a vital European concern: in prospect is an increasing export of that psychology.[45] Also in prospect is stronger pressure from US financial enter-prises to secure greater discretion in risk management.[46]

The scope for Union reform advocacy through the International Monetary Fund has been limited by the focus of current policy literature on the Fund's responsibilities for surveillance of Third World financial markets and the provision of aid to distressed developing states. IMF publications have warned of dangers in US financial markets, but the fund has not assumed an active role in this regard: its operations are influenced by the strong voting power of the United States. The European Union, especially if asserting its right to single membership, with appropriate voting strength, could work to expand the fund's surveillance functions in a way that would focus on international interest in potentially destabilizing trends in US financial markets, and on the potential of the Federal Reserve to provide funding for emergency stabilization, as in the case of the failed high-risk Long Term Capital Management enterprise.[47]

MONETARY POLICY ISSUES

Price stability in the Union is the European Central Bank's primary responsibility, in the interests of stable regional growth, and accordingly there is an imperative to overcome trends that could lead to a financial crisis. The provision of funds to endangered institutions could be difficult, and cleavages in the governing structure of the bank would probably be aggravated.[48] The promotion of price stability (attempted with interest rates below those in the USA) is difficult because of the increasing availability of credit through the expanding securities sector, in which, it must be stressed, US institutions have a strong presence. A further problem is that mergers and acquisitions in the Union are opening the way for oligopolistic exploitation of market strengths, which indeed are already strong in the retailing sectors.[49]

The significance of international financial flows for price stability is an increasingly important aspect of exchange rate management. A necessary concern of the European Central Bank is to ensure a steady rate to the US dollar that will be conducive to relatively balanced Atlantic trade and to adequate regional financing of Union firms. This tends to become difficult because of the changing fundamentals associated with the Union's investment flows, and the differing degrees of entrepreneurial thrust behind those flows. There is also the element of danger, it must be stressed, because of the USA's large balance of payments deficits, as well as the uncertainties about investor confidence in US stock appreciations.

The depreciation of the euro against the US dollar, which has affected confidence in the European Monetary Union since its inception, has been largely attributable to the effects of European investment outflows on financial markets, although these have been overshadowed by the unsustainability of US stock appreciations and current account deficits. European exports benefit, but motivations for the investment outflows tend to be strengthened, and European investor confidence in the Union's growth prospects is discouraged. European central banks hold large reserves in US dollars, however, and the amount in excess of prudential requirements for the euro area (possibly as much as $300 billion) could be sold and used for government reduction. The European Central Bank would then still have funds larger than those available for currency interventions by the US monetary authorities, and the euro would be less undervalued.[50] Meanwhile the attractions of the US economy for European investors could be decreased, to allow the development of a more balanced financial interdependence.

The European option of disposing of excess dollar reserves clearly requires careful consideration, in view of the sensitivities and vulnerabilities of Atlantic financial interdependence. There are imperatives for intensive planning, in dialogue on fundamentals with the USA, and on the European side there is a potential for bargaining leverage to induce the adoption of measures that would dampen speculation in US financial sectors and secure cooperation for effective taxation of trade in financial assets, as well as tighter regulation of such trade. The growth effects of European Monetary Union would be enhanced, although the area's problems of incomplete market integration, weaker entrepreneurial energies, technology lags and high unemployment would tend to persist.

The development of a solidarity-based system of European capitalism would have potentially very productive effects in Atlantic monetary policy interactions as these extended into financial market reform. The Union would begin to acquire the status and strength of a more integrated system of collective management with a stable and highly constructive approach to international economic cooperation. Interactive Atlantic policy learning would be in prospect, with participation by corporate representatives that could make possible productive exchanges between them and the policy-makers. A solidarity-based system of capitalism could thus begin to evolve in the USA, with stabilizing and energizing effects in its system of governance. For this to happen, however, the rationale for solidarity-based capitalism would have to be presented very persuasively, with reference to its demonstration effects in Europe, and their relevance for the management of monetary policy cooperation.

The intensely competitive American system of capitalism, operating with high-volume trading in shares, gives much impetus to international expansion of its securities sector. The availability of credit from this sector, to a considerable extent on the basis of funds secured internationally, reduces the significance of efforts by the Federal Reserve to resort to any monetary tightening, and tends to amplify the effects of any monetary loosening. Shifts to a solidarity-based system of capitalism would entail reductions in the trading of shares, insofar as stable cross-holdings would link firms relationally, especially in industry groups, and employee interests in corporate stability would be asserted through formal or informal systems of codetermination.[51] Such changes in the USA my seem very unlikely, because of the very strong individualism and the traditional liberalism of the culture, but studies of industrial relations in the USA have drawn attention to serious problems of efficiency and equity that have been aggravated as US firms restructure in the course of mergers and acquisitions and move increasingly into foreign operations.[52]

European forms of solidarity-based capitalism in effect restrict the growth of securities markets and the erosion of monetary policy capabilities. Commonly identified deficiencies are less active entrepreneurship (compared with the USA), weaker competitive pressures, lower levels of funding, risk aversion under pressure from employees, and a business environment that hinders the emergence of new firms.[53] Overall evaluation with reference to monetary policy objectives can take into account similarities and contrasts with the Japanese system, however, noting its higher level of solidarity, but recognizing also the greater stability of the German system. This is an advantage which deserves great emphasis in the context of structural interdependencies threatened by unsustainable speculation across the Atlantic.

European initiatives for dialogue on fundamentals will have to stress that a large advanced political economy prone to high levels of speculation will tend to have balance of payments deficits because of the import propensities of speculation-led growth, if international investment drawn by this growth sustains the speculation and aids strong corporate emphasis on transnational production for the penetration of foreign markets. The danger of financial crises generated by speculation will also have to be stressed, and on this comprehensive basis imperatives for Atlantic monetary cooperation, extending into financial market reform, will have to be set out, in long-term perspectives. With these perspectives, full exploration of the consequences of failures in financial markets will be necessary, noting that the proliferation of financial innovations is making these markets more opaque, and thus more susceptible to manipulation.[54] An important option, which could be made evident in pressure to induce acceptance of the necessary dialogue, would be to restrain the expansion of US financial enterprises in Europe, not only for more symmetry in the liberalized treatment of trade in financial services, but also for reduced vulnerability to shocks in world financial markets.

The constructive intent of European initiatives will have to be made quite clear through proposals for cooperation that would reduce the dangers of sudden declines in international investor confidence regarding the US dollar. The significance of the proposals could be made more evident through demands for full information about the creditworthiness of US financial institutions operating in Europe. Such demands could be accompanied by assurances that measures by the Federal Reserve to cope with a financial crisis in the USA would be aided by the European Central Bank.[55]

The initiatives for dialogue on fundamentals would be significant for Japan. This country's greater dependence on the US market entails vulnerabilities and lower status (especially because of the problems in its financial sector); cultural differences and a thinner network of transregional communities of experts moreover also limit the Japanese potential to initiate productive interactions on problems of structural interdependence with the USA. Japan can be less articulate than the Europeans about the exploitation of its low interest rates by US financial institutions.

Japan's vulnerability to the effects of a financial crisis in the USA is exceptional and, because of its relatively weak bargaining strength, its potential for contributing to reform in international financial markets and the development of a stronger international monetary system depends very much on cooperation with the European Union. The Union has neglected opportunities to develop ties with Japan, but the evolution of Atlantic interdependencies has made strengthening of those links very important for the Union's monetary policy, and for Japan's own interests. Japanese investors hold large volumes of US government debt.[56] European planning for monetary and financial policy collaboration with the USA will have to encourage active Japanese participation, with intensive discussion of shared interests in promoting the development of more balanced and more dynamic interdependencies with the USA.

TRADE POLICY ISSUES

The European Union's management of its involvement in the international monetary system and in world financial markets is a matter for elite expertise, but the Union's external trade policy is responsive to innumerable pressures from member governments and their interest groups. Many of these pressures tend to be protectionist, because of pervasive awareness of the lagging competitiveness of European firms, but that awareness does not generate demands for restraints on direct investment from the USA, although service of the Union market by US firms producing in Europe is at a volume much higher than imports from the USA. The intra-Union pressures on trade policy are active in relations between member governments and the European Commission, which have been tending to limit that institution's relative autonomy in this area, but the Commission's status as the Union's trade negotiating authority has been maintained because Atlantic trade issues have virtually obligated unified responses.

Management of Atlantic trade issues has involved recourse to the World Trade Organization by both the Union and the USA over questions of economic openness and fairness, and on the European side there has been increasing concern with competition policy issues assuming prominence as international markets have become more closely linked.[57] Giving the World Trade Organization responsibility in this area has been proposed, but has not been favoured by the USA. A high-priority US objective is to promote higher levels of openness in the world economy, especially to facilitate export expansion that will reduce the USA's large current account deficits. European cooperation is needed, as the Atlantic relationship dominates the global trading system, and must be expected to continue to do so because of the absence of effective regional economic cooperation systems in the rest of the world.

Union decision-makers are being challenged to plan external trade policy on the basis of projections regarding the structural basis for commerce, and with assessments of alternative futures for the World Trade Organization. Problems of structural competitiveness are immediate concerns. There is a basis for optimism concerning the impetus given to regional growth by the European Monetary Union, and by the enlargement of the internal market with the admission of new members,[58] but these effects will be slower than those in continuity with the trends in Atlantic investment flows. The structural effects of those flows are more significant, for the present, than those resulting from the increased competitiveness of European exports that has been due to the undervaluation of the euro. If there is a depreciation of the US dollar, moreover, European price competitiveness will be reduced.[59]

Policy-level attention to fundamentals in Atlantic trade relations has been restricted by concentration on diverse disputes over questions of market access and the subsidization of exports. Distrust and antagonism have tended to cause an adversarial trade policy orientation, reciprocated on the American side, and this in effect contributed to the increases in cross-investment which are gradually altering economic structures, especially in Europe. The large US corporate presence in the Union has an interest in supporting proposals for freer Atlantic trade, but has an apparently more active interest in working within the patterns of Union business representation.

Divisive issues must be expected to continue arising in Atlantic trade relations, because of the adversarial attitudes, and because interests on each side will undoubtedly react to perceived imbalances in the spread of gains from commerce. Planning to promote greater trust and goodwill in the relationship must therefore be a Union objective, so that there can be progress toward integrative engagement with the tasks of harmonizing the structural foundations of this commerce, for more dynamic and balanced interdependent growth. Initiatives for dialogue to achieve this will require a strong political will, and the generation of this, it must be stressed, will no doubt have to begin with assertions of Commission leadership, in part through the sponsorship of studies focusing on potentials for structural partnering. Conferences to bring corporate elites into frequent exchanges for entrepreneurial collaboration could be arranged for spontaneous ventures in such partnering. The Commission has technocratic expertise to support, and indeed provide some guidance for, the corporate conferences, using projections from sectoral trends.

The principal rationale for sponsoring corporate conferences is that, with constructive participation by Commission experts and representatives from the US administration, corporate strategies could be oriented more toward collegial entrepreneurship, with increasingly productive complementarities. This would tend to reduce Atlantic trade conflicts, while assisting the development of a solidarity-based Atlantic business culture. In-depth presentations of this rationale could emphasize that in such a culture competition, while moderated, would drive efficiencies, within a context of shared commitments to the public good of order and equity in the management of structural interdependencies. The theoretical basis for the general reorientation toward complementary entrepreneurship would draw on lessons from the Japanese experience of curbing destructive competition while generating productive rivalries within a cooperative entrepreneurial culture. Insights into the dynamics of this blending could be made more persuasive through references to the multiplication of advances in frontier technology. These strengthen the logic of forming business cultures oriented toward collegial entrepreneurship based on intensive intercorporate sharing of technologically sophisticated tacit knowledge.[60]

Transnational policy networks dealing with trade and investment issues could be formed with inputs from the Atlantic corporate conferences. The European Commission is well placed to sponsor the development of such networks, in which legislators and officials from Europe and the USA would meet for frequent exchanges. Corporate contributions to the activities of these networks, influenced by the orientation toward complementary entrepreneurship, could aid the growth of a spirit of cooperation among the legislators and officials. Atlantic microeconomic policy interdependencies would then be managed with more attention to ways of aligning trade, finance and infrastructure measures with evolving patterns of intercorporate cooperation.

The Atlantic corporate conferences and policy networks would assume wider significance in the world trading system if they became open to Japanese participation. Failures to develop strong economic and political links have been disadvantageous for the European Union and Japan, not only because of the consequences for relative bargaining strengths but also because of losses of opportunities for policy learning and entrepreneurial learning. Japanese participation would help to form a Triad pattern of corporate and policy-level cooperation, in which pressures of external accountability could have wider effects than those possible in an Atlantic collaborative system that did not include Japan. Involvement in such a system would help to draw Japanese firms into extensive international corporate alliances and bring Japanese policy processes into productive interaction with European and American policy communities. At the same time the sponsoring role assumed by the European Union would cause its policy-making to become less inward-looking, and more responsive to the requirements for institutional development that are evident in the challenges of structural and policy interdependence.[61]

Triad solidarity could be a potent force for sound institutional development of the World Trade Organization. Such a prospect would deserve prominence in European Union planning, as there is a potential for European leadership to promote the establishment of the WTO as an institution that could work for more orderly and more harmonious international trade arrangements. The Union and the USA dominate the WTO, on the basis of their size and the links between their economies, but in terms of bargaining leverage the Union, it must be reiterated, is disadvantaged by its failure to develop strong ties with Japan. Such ties can be planned for, but, if the logic of Triad structural partnering through corporate conferencing is accepted, the Union will have to consider whether the WTO should continue to function simply as a bargaining forum for trade liberalization, with a weak mechanism for the settlement of disputes.

A structural partnering policy, if vigorously implemented, would reduce trade disputes in Atlantic relations and in the Union's interactions with Japan, and over time could lead to the formation of a Triad trade regime, apart from the WTO, with an evolving investment regime, covering rights of establishment and matters of national treatment. Triad bargaining strength meanwhile would overshadow the WTO, in which it would continue to be effective because of the absence of strong coalitions and regional integration systems in the rest of the world.

While promoting Triad structural partnering, however, the Union could seek to transform the WTO into an institution more aligned with international public goods requirements. Whether European energies could be mobilized for this would depend to a considerable extent on degrees of absorption in the expansion of the Union's preferential trade agreements, including especially those in its immediate environment. These have increasing significance for its growth prospects and the development of its potential bargaining leverage in Atlantic relations. The attraction exerted by the Single Market, moreover, enables the Union to negotiate quite advantageous extensions of its preferential trade arrangements, and to cultivate the goodwill of the preferential partners in ways that may be useful at the WTO.[62]

The Union's slow and complex decision processes, and the pressures of member governments on the Commission's management of its trade policy responsibilities, hinder the development of a highly constructive role in the WTO. The USA has greater scope for initiative, because of decisional advantages and more extensive involvement in the world economy, and accordingly the Union has incentives to implement supportive strategies, conditioned on consideration of its interests. A shift to an active promotional strategy for the development of a stronger WTO could be discouraged by indications of US preferences for avoiding any change in the WTO's functions as a bargaining forum. Union planning for Triad structural partnering could accordingly proceed without exploration of options relating to the development of the WTO, even if Atlantic trade disputes were still being brought to that organization.

Nevertheless, for the longer term it would be appropriate for the Union to plan for more constructive engagement, as an extension of its structural partnering policy, so that the bargaining processes in the WTO could give way to more productive functions, especially with respect to competition policy issues. Such issues assume more importance for the world economy as international concentration trends continue: they become stronger as more competitive firms displace, absorb or merge with weaker rivals while expanding international operations. General increases in economic openness negotiated in the WTO facilitate intensifications of the rivalries that drive the concentration trends. The Union favours the development of a WTO responsibility in this area because discretionary competition policy cooperation with the USA has had limited benefits, and because US transnational enterprises are very prominent in the concentration trends. The USA, however, does not support proposals for such an extension of WTO functions.[63]

The Union's efforts to promote solidarity-based capitalism for structural partnering could be exploited by the anticompetitive activities of cooperating firms. Surveillance functions would have to be assumed, in collaboration with the USA and Japan, to ensure that the patterns of coordinated complementary entrepreneurship did not become oligopolistic. Longer-term planning for the evolution of the WTO would have to be in line with this requirement. US interest groups and policy-makers could well oppose the structural partnering because of the risks of collusive behaviour, and because of concerns that this and more acceptable forms of collaboration would reduce the efficiency effects of competition. The rationale for structural partnering would thus have to be formulated with care to meet the concerns about competition and efficiency as well as to indicate how appropriate institutional arrangements could be devised.

On this basis the Union's longer-term planning for a WTO more oriented toward sound development of the world trading system could proceed with the elaboration of principles of cooperation and competition, in functional and equitable balance. The purpose would be to promote consensus, in Atlantic and then Triad policy communities, on a doctrine of trade policy harmonization for the development of balanced structural complementarities identified through intensive conferencing. This, it could be stressed, would be presented with emphasis on imperatives to prevent adversarial trends in Triad trade relations. Such trends have been threatening because of increases in pressures within the USA for protectionist solutions to the nation's current account deficits, and for firm assertions of US demands in direct dealings with trading partners.[64]

Union trade policy planning with a structural partnering thrust will be difficult if there are increases in economic nationalism within member states that make collective decision-making more conflicted and more awkward for the European Commission. Germany, gaining status as the largest, most industrialized and most integrated member, may tend to place hegemonic ambitions ahead of commitments to regional collective management. This may be encouraged, to a degree, by continued fragmentation in the overall Union pattern of interest representation. For the common good, then, the European Commission can advocate very forcefully the approval of trade policy planning guidelines aiming at balances in structural interdependencies, with wide-ranging corporate cooperation. The costs of delays in this innovative enterprise could be made evident in projections regarding capital flight, Union growth and strains in external trade relations. Linked with this inwardly directed message a prime external objective will have to be winning the confidence of major US corporate groups for an Atlantic structural design.

GOVERNING GLOBALIZATION

The European Union, as it enlarges and becomes economically more integrated – although with dangers of political strains – must plan for more active involvement in the governance and structuring of globalization. Priority will have to be given to international financial market reform, and endeavours for this will have to be supported by an integrative orientation in external trade policy, to promote structural complementarities through concerted entrepreneurial strategies. Progress in this structural endeavour will assist efforts to make financial markets serve real economies more effectively. Such efforts, inspired by concepts of solidarity-based capitalism, will have to overcome the problem of capital flight from Europe, and secure a strong voice for the Union in the International Monetary Fund.

The speculative and potentially destabilizing misallocations of investment in world financial markets, in which the operations of US financial institutions are very prominent, demand high-priority engagement by the European Union, because of its increasing vulnerabilities and the adverse implications of capital flight from its area. A drive to promote solidarity-based capitalism in the Union will have slow results, and may be ineffectual because of the opportunism of European investors. A diplomacy dealing directly with US decision-makers and working very actively through the International Monetary Fund will clearly be necessary, and for that representation in the Fund as a single unit, with adequate weighted voting strength, will be vital.[65] Union consensus to work for this could build on the political will which supported the drive to establish the European Monetary Union. Emphasis could be placed on the need for an

IMF governance structure that would reduce the impact of political changes in the USA on that institution, and impose substantial external accountability on the management of US monetary policy, while enabling the IMF to assume a more effective role for regulatory reform in world financial markets.

Strong political will to promote solidarity-based European capitalism, if it can be generated, would give impetus to the development of the euro as an international currency, and thus could assist the evolution of a more stable international monetary system, in which global investor choices would tend to force the adoption of US restraints on speculative operations driving risky asset appreciation. The more equal and more challenging Atlantic relationship would be a source of pressures for constructive responsiveness on each side. There could be an intensification of consultative exchanges through which strong Atlantic policy communities could be formed. Opportunities for involvement meanwhile would draw Japanese participation, which the Union could encourage, it must be reiterated, for enhanced Triad policy learning.

In line with the efforts to promote structural partnering with the USA the Union could endeavour to negotiate an Atlantic Stability Pact, as an extension of the stability pact associated with the European Monetary Union, so as to strengthen the consultative system that would sustain Atlantic monetary cooperation and Atlantic efforts to reform global financial markets. Japan's association with an Atlantic Stability Pact could be planned for, and it could be made clear that this would have the further purpose of opening the way for Union encouragement of the formation of a Pacific Monetary System, that would operate in close cooperation with the European Monetary Union. The Pacific Monetary System, centred on Japan, would ensure the development of a large zone on financial stability in East Asia. This high-growth area, as it recovers from the stresses of the financial crises in the late 1990s, will have great significance for the development of Europe's international trade. European cooperation in the formation of the Pacific Monetary System could help to strengthen East Asian regulatory institutions whose failures entailed vulnerabilities to international financial predators in the 1990s.

All the planning endeavours that can be envisaged for the European Commission and the European Central Bank would have to draw inspiration from perspectives focusing on fundamentals. The pressures under which both institutions operate however tend to cause concentration on the negotiation of solutions to immediate problems. Immersion in the difficulties of pluralistic decision-making, with changing political alignments, has engrossing effects, to the detriment of policy learning. The Union would therefore be advantaged by the establishment of a European Council of Economic Advisers, an independent institution entrusted with setting directions for policy planning and reviewing the performance of the Commission, the European Central Bank and the Council of Ministers, as well as the member governments. The European

Council of Economic Advisers could thus contribute to stronger community formation and consensus-building, while giving thrust to the structural statecraft which the European Commission is being challenged to undertake. In the Atlantic context the European Council of Economic Advisers could perform a vital function through frequent interaction with the US Council of Economic Advisers, which is often expected to operate in the service of the administration's political interests.[66]

PROSPECTS

The European Union has to deal with issues of institutional development and macromanagement that are becoming more demanding in the setting of asymmetric globalization. While there is capital flight, there is increasing corporate scope for independent development of transnational production and trade, and for the acquisition of oligopolistic market strengths, with the exploitation of labour immobility. Balances of political power meanwhile tilt because of the effects of globalization on domestic alignments. The funding priorities of international financial markets also shift, and as these markets expand there are losses of tax revenue, as well as a weakening of regulatory controls. The divisive political effects of the structural issues thus become more serious, increasing the dangers of pluralistic stagnation in Union decision processes, with negative consequences for the advocacy, administrative, regulatory, surveillance and – in effect – agency roles assigned to the European Commission.

For the Union, policy orientations based on the expected efficiencies of free market forces have become more open to question. Transnational corporate control of markets is increasing, with concentration trends in which US firms operate with greater competitiveness. The concentration in financial sectors, associated with unfavourable shifts in priority funding, poses very sharply issues regarding the service of real economies.[67] Discussions of institutional economics, although framed mainly in national contexts, can thus be seen to have new relevance, but thus far without effects on formal Union affirmations of confidence in the working of market forces. The new relevance of institutions may become evident for European policy communities as the utility of technocratic advising and coordinating functions receives wider recognition by governments and corporate groups. Such recognition may increase, at policy levels, while structural concerns become more active with the expansion of transnational production, and with awareness of the value of entrepreneurial cooperation in response to technological advances.[68] Such cooperation is clearly needed to reduce the technological gaps between member countries, while raising the technological levels of the more industrialized states.

European Commission initiatives for the sponsorship of policy studies and corporate-technocratic conferences, which may be encouraged by research communities with which it interacts, may be complemented by European Central Bank studies exploring investment and growth issues related to monetary management. Linkages between macroeconomic and microeconomic tasks and problems, assuming more prominence for policy learning, could thus be more widely understood, in ways that would assist endeavours to promote solidarity-based European capitalism.

If the policy studies and conferences focus sufficiently on fundamentals the need for a doctrine of solidarity based European capitalism will become evident. This could be a source of policy orientations related to the costs and benefits of asymmetric globalization, in which the internationalization of market failures and efficiencies is occurring more and more as a consequence of uncoordinated and unregulated transnational corporate operations, in which US firms play the most important roles. The doctrine will have to emphasise the basic public goods requirement for highly dedicated corporate leaders and policy makers. To be faithful to Europe's most profound traditions, in line with needs for such motivations at elite levels, the doctrine will have to have a humanistic spirit, of the kind that can draw inspiration from the work of the French Jewish philosopher Jacques Maritain. The major opportunity will be to build on the political will which provided the integrative drive for completion of the single market and the establishment of monetary union.

To reduce the costs and enhance the benefits of globalization, the treatment of fundamentals for the development of the new European political economy will have to express comprehensive concerns with human capital. The professional interests of workers, as they become more significant with advances in technology, will have to be recognized in conjunction with their related interests in corporate and intercorporate stability and, therefore, in reliance on bank funding rather than the offering of tradeable securities. The professional interests of managements in productive use of their entrepreneurial expertise will have to be given complementary expression, and in this way the doctrine will accord with imperatives for organizational continuity in the intricate patterns of sectoral and intersectoral interdependence. At the same time the erosion of central bank authority will be checked, and greater regional funding for Union growth will be possible.

The danger of stagnation in solidarity-based capitalism could be seen as a hindrance to its acceptance. The German form of such capitalism has been considered suitable only for incremental progress in medium-technology sectors, due to the conservative influence of unions and banks. A new development has been the emergence of entrepreneurial dynamism in a risk-taking high-technology sector, financed by offerings of securities and by large government subsidies.[69] The vitality of this sector may well spread into

Germany's medium-technology industries. These, however, will no doubt continue to provide a large area of industrial stability in which the high-technology firms will enjoy security, especially because that stable area will generate the revenues supporting the substantial government funding of the new industries. The German government's commitment to that financing challenges the European Commission's policy of reducing state aid, so that greater efficiences will be generated by market forces, but the political will to continue this structural endeavour is likely to remain strong.

Germany's central importance in the Union will merit special attention in the formulation of a doctrine of corporate cooperation for higher regional growth and, thus, for more equal but also more dynamic structural partnering in Atlantic and Pacific relations. All other members of the Union will benefit from the development of larger and more active linkages with Germany if its form of solidarity-based capitalism generates new dynamism in high-technology sectors, with restrained expansion in its securities industry. The large-scale official funding of high-technology firms involves expanding technocratic advisory services which may well have demonstration effects across the region. Germany and the entire Union political economy, meanwhile, will learn more from Japan's high-technology achievements if solidarity-based capitalism becomes a strong force in the European political economy and in its deepening integration into the world economy.

If leadership for vigorous engagement with fundamental issues is not forthcoming, the regional integration process may falter, and the costs of delays in coping with the costs of asymmetric globalization will continue to increase. The style of incrementally bargained collective decision-making will tend to be under increasing strain because of imbalances in the spread of gains from regional and international commerce, and intensifications of the Union's external vulnerabilities, especially in Atlantic relations. Exposure to the risk of a financial crisis in the USA will become more serious while the outward investment flow hinders European growth, imposes downward pressure on the euro, and discourages business confidence. Meanwhile it may well be necessary to adapt to protectionist shifts in US trade policy, activated by frustrations with high current account deficits and with European aids to exporting industries.

Altogether, the rationale for strong policy learning and planning initiatives is very challenging. European elite recognition of the gravity of the fundamental issues is hindered by pressures to focus on the immediate specifics of reducing welfare burdens, increasing labour market flexibility, lowering the high levels of taxation and providing market-friendly environments for firms. Applications to these tasks have very limited effects, and overall the problems of enhancing growth and structural competitiveness are likely to increase. A higher level of integration in the regional political economy has to be sought, with the generation of a political will to promote wide-ranging and highly innovative entrepreneurial cooperation. This will have to be done in a spirit of solidarity, with very dedicated commitments to the regional common good, and that of the international political economy, in line with manifest potentials for Atlantic and Pacific structural partnering. There is a trend toward adversarial legalism in world trade and investment relations,[70] diverting policy orientations away from understanding of the potentials for alliance capitalism. Europe can affirm those potentials, and initiate planning for their realization.

NOTES

1. See Sylvia E. Bargas and Rosario Troia (1999),'Direct investment positions for 1998', *Survey of Current Business*, 79(7), July, 48–55. See also Subramanian Rangan and Robert Z. Lawrence (1999), *A Prism on Globalization: Corporate Responses to the Dollar*, Washington DC: Brookings Institution.
2. See Brian Hindley (1999), 'New institutions for Atlantic trade?', *International Affairs*, 75(1), January, 45–60.
3. See Sophie Meunier (2000), 'What single voice? European institutions and EU–US trade negotiations', *International Organization*, 54(1), Winter, 103–36, and William Wallace (1999), 'The sharing of sovereignty: the European paradox', *Political Studies*, 47(3), Special Issue, 503–21.
4. See Meunier, op. cit.
5. See Justin Greenwood, Londa Strangward and Lara Stancich (1999), 'The capacities of euro groups in the integration process', *Political Studies*, 47(1), March, 127–38.
6. Raymond J. Mataloni Jr (2000), 'US multinational companies: operations in 1998', *Survey of Current Business*, 80(7), July, 26–45.
7. Russel B. Scholl (1999), 'The international investment position of the United States at yearend 1998', *Survey of Current Business*, 79(7), July, 36–45.
8. See Bargas and Troia, op. cit.
9. See *World Investment Report, 1999*, ch. IIIB, Geneva, United Nations Conference on Trade and Development.
10. See discussions of corporate governance in Stephen Cohen and Gavin Boyd (eds) (2000), *Corporate Governance and Globalization*, Cheltenham: Edward Elgar.
11. See symposium on Japan (2000), *Oxford Review of Economic Policy*, 16(2), Summer.
12. See Parimal Patel and Keith Pavitt (1998), 'Uneven (and divergent) technological accumulation among advanced countries: evidence and a framework of explanation', in Giovanni Dosi, David J. Teece, and Josef Chytry (eds), *Technology, Organization and Competitiveness*, Oxford: Oxford University Press, pp. 289–318.
13. See John Zysman and Andrew Schwartz (1998), 'Reunifying Europe in an emerging world economy: economic heterogeneity, new industrial options and political choices', *Journal of Common Market Studies*, 36(3), September, 405–30.
14. See *International Capital Markets*, Washington DC International Monetary Fund, September 2000, Chs 2 and 4, and *World Economic Outlook*, International Monetary Fund, May 2000, Chs 1, 3, and 4.
15. See John Plender (2000), 'How Europe could gain a stronger euro', *Financial Times*, 29 March.
16. See Gerard Baker (2000), 'Greenspan's growing dilemma', *Financial Times*, 10 April.
17. See *Financial Market Trends*, 73, 74 and 75, Paris, Organization for Economic Cooperation and Development, 1999 and 2000.
18. See Meunier, op. cit., and Alasdair R. Young (2000), 'The adaptation of European foreign economic policy', *Journal of Common Market Studies*, 38(1), March, 93–116.
19. On the importance of this political will see David Cobham and George Zis (eds) (1999), *From EMS to EMU: 1979 to 1999 and Beyond*, London: Macmillan.

20. See (1999), *Broad Economic Policy Guidelines, 68, 1999*, Brussels: European Commission.
21. Ibid.
22. Meunier, op. cit.
23. See symposium (1999), *The World Economy*, 22(9), December.
24. See discussions of agricultural trade in ibid.
25. Mitchell P. Smith (1996), 'Integration in small steps: the European Commission and member state aid to industry', *West European Politics*, 19(3), July, 563–82, and Kostas A. Lavdas and Maria M. Mendrinou (1999), *Politics, Subsidies and Competition*, Cheltenham: Edward Elgar.
26. See symposium on France (1999), *West European Politics*, 22(4), October, and William D. Coleman (1990), 'State traditions and comprehensive business associations', *Political Studies*, 38(2), June, 231–52.
27. See Broad Economic Policy Guidelines, op. cit., and Marco Buti and Andre Sapir (1998), *Economic Policy in EMU*, Oxford: Oxford University Press.
28. Ibid.
29. See Richard Portes and Helene Rey (1998), 'The euro and international equity flows', *Journal of the Japanese and International Economies*, 12(4), December, 406–23. See also Julian S. Alworth (1999), 'Taxation, financial innovation and integrated financial markets: some implications for tax coordination in the European Union', in Assaf Razin and Efraim Sadka (eds), *The Economics of Globalization*, Cambridge: Cambridge University Press, Ch. 9.
30. See Cobham and Vis, op. cit.
31. See Financial Market Trends 75, op. cit.
32. See Alworth, op. cit.
33. See symposium on competition policy (1998), *The World Economy*, 21(8), November.
34. Jonathan Eaton, Eva Gutierrez and Samuel Kortum (1998), 'European technology policy', *Economic Policy* 27, October, 403–38.
35. See Robert A. Mundell (1999), in Mario I. Bleger and Marko Skreb (eds), *Central Banking Monetary Policies and the Implications for Transition Economies*, Norwell: Kluwer, Ch. 15; on differences in European financial systems see Stephen G. Cecchetti (1999), 'Legal structure, financial structure, and the Monetary Policy transmission mechanism', Federal Reserve Bank of New York *Economic Policy Review*, 5(2), July, 9–28; and references to US markets in Andrei Shleifer (2000), *Inefficient Markets*, Oxford: Oxford University Press.
36. See Portes and Rey, op. cit.
37. On the importance of human capital development, managing knowledge assets, and corporate entrepreneurial capabilities, see Raghuram G. Rajan and Luigi Zingales (2000), *The Governance of the New Enterprise*, National Bureau of Economic Research Working Paper 7958, October; Frederic E. Sautet (2000), *An Entrepreneurial Theory of the Firm*, London: Routledge, and David J. Teece (2000), 'Strategies for managing knowledge assets: the role of firm structure and industrial context', *Long Range Planning*, 33(1), February, 35–54.
38. See Roy C. Smith (1999), 'The European securities industry under a Single Currency', in Jean Dermine and Pierre Hillion (eds), *European Capital Markets with a Single Currency*, Oxford: Oxford University Press, Ch. 10.
39. See Rudiger Dornhasch and Pierre Jacquet (2000), 'Making EMU a success', *International Affairs*, 76(1), January, 89–110.
40. See Pepper D. Culpepper (1999), 'The future of the high skill equilibrium in Germany', *Oxford Review of Economic Policy*, 15(1), Spring, 43–59, and Stephen J. Silvia (1997), 'German unification and emerging divisions within German employers' associations: cause or catalyst?', *Comparative Politics*, 29(2), January.
41. See Sautet, op. cit., Teece, op. cit., and Mark Casson (1999), 'A cultural theory of industrial policy', in James Foreman-Peck and Giovanni Federico (eds), *European Industrial Policy*, Oxford: Oxford University Press, Ch. 14.
42. See *World Investment Report* 2000, 1999, 1998 and 1997, Geneva: United Nations Conference on Trade and Development.
43. See discussions in symposium on financial instability (1999), *Oxford Review of Economic Policy*, 15(3), Autumn.
44. These responsibilities are made evident in *Broad Economic Policy Guidelines*, op. cit.
45. See symposium on financial instability, op. cit.

46. See Gary Silverman (2000), 'Fed rule on bank's capital under fire', *Financial Times*, 10 April, and Daniel Bolger and Gary Silverman (2000), 'Risky debt may cause trouble for US banks', *Financial Times*, 22 February.
47. See symposium on financial instability, op. cit., and observations on governance issues in Frederic S. Mishkin and Philip E. Strahan (1999), *What will Technology do to Financial Structure?*, National Bureau of Economic Research working paper 6892, January.
48 See Mark Hallerberg and Jurgen von Hagen (1999), 'Electoral institutions, cabinet negotiations and budget deficits in the European Union', in James Poterba and Jurgen von Hagen (eds), *Fiscal Institutions and Fiscal Performance*, University of Chicago Press, Ch. 9; and symposium on macroeconomic policy (1998), *Oxford Review of Economic Policy*, 14(3), Autumn.
49. Paul Dobson and Michael Waterson (1999), 'Retailer power: recent developments and policy implications', *Economic Policy*, 28, April, 135–50.
50. See Daniel Gros (2000), 'The correct way to support the euro', *Financial Times*, 2 November.
51. On the interests of employees see Margaret M. Blair and Mark J. Roe (eds) (1999), *Employees and Corporate Governance*, Washington, DC: Brookings Institution.
52. The basic issues were examined in Dani Rodrik (1997), *Has Globalization Gone too Far?*, Washington, DC: Institute for International Economics. On the foreign operations of US firms see Rangan and Lawrence, op. cit. On US corporate governance see Blair and Roe, op. cit.
53. Blair and Roe, op. cit.
54. See symposium on financial instability, op. cit., and Andrei Shleifer (2000), *Inefficient Markets*, New York: Oxford University Press.
55. Gros, cited, has indicated that European central banks have adequate reserves.
56. See Russel B. Scholl (2000), The international investment position of the United States at yearend 1999', *Survey of Current Business*, July, op. cit., 46–56.
57. See symposium on competition policy, op. cit.
58. See Mundell, op. cit.
59 On the danger of dollar depreciation see Catherine L. Mann (1999), Is the US trade deficit sustainable? , Washington, DC: Institute for International Economics.
60. See Sautet, op. cit.
61. See observations on inward-looking tendencies in Union decision-making in Gareth A. Richards and Colin Kirkpatrick (1999), 'Reorienting interregional cooperation in the global political economy: Europe's East Asia policy', *Journal of Common Market Studies*, 37(4), December, 683–710.
62. See list of preferential trading arrangements in Simon Hix (1999), *The Political System of the European Union*, New York: St Martin's Press, p. 339.
63. On the complexities of antitrust policy in the USA see Lawrence J. White (1993),'Competition policy in the United States: an overview', *Oxford Review of Economic Policy*, 9(2), Summer, 133–51.
64. See Alan V. Deardorff and Robert M. Stern (eds) (1998) *Constituent Interests and US Trade Policies*, Ann Arbor MI: University of Michigan Press, and I.M. Destler (1999), 'US trade governance in the new global economy', *Brookings Trade Forum 1999*, Washington, DC: Brookings Institution, 141–55.
65. For a discussion of Union interests in the IMF see C. Randall Henning and Pier Carlo Padoan (2000), *Transatlantic Perspectives on the Euro*, Pittsburgh, PA: European Community Studies Association.
66. See Joseph Stiglitz (1998), 'The private uses of public interests: incentives and institutions', *Journal of Economic Perspectives*, 12(2), Spring, 3–22.
67. See Shleifer, op. cit., on investor behaviour.
68. See Oliver E. Williamson (2000), 'The new institutional economics: taking stock, looking ahead', *Journal of Economic Literature*, 38(3), September, 595–613.
69. See Mark Leher (2000), 'Has Germany finally fixed its high-tech problem? The recent boom in German technology based entrepreneurship', *California Management Review*, 42(4), Summer, 89–107.
70. See symposium on legalism (2000), *International Organization*, 54(3), Summer.

Index

ABN Amro 192
Andean Pact 221
anti-dumping measures 217
Atlantic Stability Pact 323
Atlantic trade issues 305
Austria 7, 10

banana trade 216
Banco Bilbao Vizcaya Argentaria 144
bank-industry relations 131
Bankers Trust 202
bargaining strengths 301
Belgium 7, 113
BNP Paribas 392
Britain 7, 10, 76, 113, 267, 313
British Telecom 141
Broad Economic Policy Guidelines 263

capital markets 127, 130, 194
CEECs 218
Central American Common Market 221
Chase Manhattan Bank 188
China 217
Clearstream 198
Commerzbank 202
Common Agricultural Policy 238
competition 133
competition policy 120, 307
concentration trends 121
continental European finance 187
cooperation, EU and USA 286
corporate financing in Europe 188, 193
corporate strategy 138, 153
corporations and trade policy 227
Credit Suisse First Boston 192

Denmark 7
deregulation 135
Deutsch Bank 117, 193
DTCC (US clearing and settlement) 198

economic geography 273
electrical machinery and equipment 217
electronic market mechanisms 191
electronic networks 191
embedded liberalism 163
employment by sectors 64, 132
Euroclear 198
Euronext 196
European Central Bank 252
European corporate bonds 194
European foreign. direct investment 302
European inward FDI 302
European Monetary Union 193, 248
European Union
    capital markets 186, 309
    competition policy 307
    corporate governance 309
    Council 261
    decisional problems 304
    dollar reserves 315
    economies of members 5
    European Central Bank 252
    European Cammission 261, 304
    financial market regulation 188
    fiscal policies 303
    foreign economic policy 304
    foreign relations 25
    Franco–German cooperation 305
    imports of industrial products 211, 224
    industrial specializations 62
    institutions 17, 21, 23, 26, 162
    interactions between members 20
    investment flows 11, 14, 32, 43–59, 186, 274, 309
    monetary policy 252
    multibusiness firms 126
    national markets 272
    outward direct investment 43–59
    political diversity 9, 15